PSYCHOLINGUISTICS

A Survey of Theory and Research Problems

WITH

A Survey of Psycholinguistic Research, 1954-1964

PSYCHOLINGUISTICS

A Survey of Theory and Research Problems

Edited by

Charles E. Osgood and Thomas A. Sebeok

WITH

A Survey of Psycholinguistic Research, 1954-1964

by A. Richard Diebold

AND

THE PSYCHOLINGUISTS by George A. Miller

GREENWOOD PRESS, PUBLISHERS
WESTPORT, CONNECTICUT

Library of Congress Cataloging in Publication Data

Osgood, Charles Egerton, ed.
  Psycholinguistics : a survey of theory and
research problems.

  Reprint of the ed. published by Indiana University
Press, Bloomington, in series: Indiana University
studies in the history and theory of linguistics.
  Bibliography: p.
  1. Languages--Psychology. 2. Communication--
Psychological aspects. 3. Information measurement.
I. Sebeok, Thomas Albert, 1920-   joint ed.
II. Diebold, A. Richard. A survey of psycholinguistic
research, 1954-1964. 1976. III. Title. IV. Series:
Indiana. University. Indiana University studies in
the history and theory of linguistics.
 ₍DNLM: 1. Communication. 2. Language. 3. Psych-
ology. P121 P974 1965a₎
 ₍P37.075 1976₎   401'.9   76-2579
 ISBN 0-8371-8730-3

Originally published in 1965 by Indiana University Press,
Bloomington

Reprinted with the permission of Indiana University Press

Reprinted in 1976 by Greenwood Press,
a division of Williamhouse-Regency Inc.

Library of Congress Catalog Card Number 76-2579

ISBN 0-8371-8730-3

Printed in the United States of America

PREFACE TO THIS EDITION

By Thomas A. Sebeok

"Mixing Memory and desire," in T. S. Eliot's haunting phrase, this edition of *Psycholinguistics* recalls a period of ferment, records a decade of solid accomplishment, and forecasts an exciting future. The idea of reuniting linguistics and psychology in the middle of the twentieth century was conceived and sparked by the Carnegie Corporation's John W. Gardner, a psychologist deeply concerned with the possible implications of such a rapprochement for educational problems at all levels, and was first articulated by John B. Carroll, a psychologist attuned to linguistics from boyhood under the tutelage of Benjamin Lee Whorf. In a seminar on psycholinguistics, held at Cornell University in the summer of 1951 under the sponsorship of the Social Science Research Council, six of us attempted to clarify, in a preliminary way, the relations between the two disciplines. Three of the participants—Carroll, Osgood, and I— continued the search, with three other senior workers and five graduate students, in a second seminar, held at Indiana University two summers afterwards and under the same auspices, resulting in the monograph published in 1954.

Psycholinguistics was aimed at an unusually large potential readership and was therefore published in two simultaneously issued but essentially identical formats: one for linguists, through the network reached by the *International Journal of American Linguistics*, and another for psychologists, through that of *The Journal of Abnormal and Social Psychology*. Both editions were rapidly exhausted. Their effects, however, continued to reverberate in many directions, punctuated by further concentrated group efforts, notably the Southwest Project in Comparative Psycholinguistics, and a series of more or less productive work conferences on selected research topics inspired by the book. Seven subjects thus considered were: bilingualism (Columbia University, May 10-11, 1954); techniques of content analysis (Allerton House, University of Illinois, February 9-11, 1955); associative processes in verbal behavior (University of Minnesota, April 25-26, 1955); dimensions of meaning— analytic and experimental approaches (Yale University, May 17-18, 1956); style (Indiana University, April 17-19, 1958); aphasia (Boston, June 16-July 25, 1958); and language universals (Gould House, Dobbs Ferry, April 13-15, 1961). Several of these conferences resulted in major collective works enmeshing an ever widening circle of scholars from a variety of disciplines beside linguistics and psychology; these foci of diffusion include books edited by I. de Sola Pool, *Trends in Content Analysis* (1959), Thomas A. Sebeok, *Style in Language* (1960, 1964), Charles E. Osgood and Murray S. Miron, *Approaches to the Study of*

Aphasia (1963), and Joseph H. Greenberg, *Universals of Language* (1963).

Sol Saporta's reader was, of course, yet another summative "attempt at shaping a large body of available information about language" in what its editor sensed was, in 1961, still an inchoate academic pursuit. His readings, in turn, provided Diebold with a frame of reference for an admirably erudite history of ideas, stimulating him to trace the many, but only seemingly separate, threads woven through the conglomeration of solitary efforts and highly organized research attacks of the past ten years, which seem at last to have crystallized into the discipline that he—as many others—prefers to continue to identify under the unifying label of psycholinguistics.

The practitioners of this discipline—which is apparently destined to continue to function under this descriptive title—are the new breed of young men and women whom Miller, in his disarming and elegant article appended to this 1965 edition, dignifies, and gives fresh character to, as "The Psycholinguists." If the 1954 monograph stirs memories, and Diebold's account links the past with the present, Miller's essay envisions the frontiers of a new science facing a range of fundamental human problems the solutions to some of which are already palpable; others—of understanding and belief—may never be tractable, at least within its scope. I envy those who will have the opportunity to review the progress of psycholinguistics from the vantage point of 1975.

January 15, 1965

CONTENTS

PREFACE by Thomas A. Sebeok

Psycholinguistics: A Survey of Theory and Research Problems

A Survey of Psycholinguistic Research, 1954-1964

FOREWORD

By John W. Gardner

The revolution in modern physics has forced us to re-examine fundamental assumptions both in science and in our everyday thinking. No man can predict the ultimate consequences of this re-examination, but nothing seems more certain than that it will lead to a more intensive study of the psychology of perception and the psychology of language. For one of the most significant yields of the recent developments in physics has been a renewed awareness of the role of the observer.

The intimate relationship between the observer and the observed is, of course, a very, very old story. Parmenides and Democritus were aware of it. Philosophers through the centuries have commented on it and some have built their philosophies upon it. The recent work in physics has simply pointed up explicitly and with considerable poignancy certain possible limitations on man's capacity to perceive and conceptualize.

Any concern with intrinsic limitations upon man's capacity to conceptualize, or limitations inherent in his mold of thought, must lead inevitably to a concern for the psychology of language. P. W. Bridgman* made the point vigorously in a recent paper: "We cast the world into the mold of our perceptions. The fact that the world I construct is so much like the world you construct is evidence of the similarity of our nervous systems, something which any physiologist could demonstrate for you more directly. We all of us perceive the world in terms of space and time. An interesting question is how inevitably we are forced to this perception by the common properties of our nervous systems, or to what extent it is adventitious, depending on universal features in early experience and in particular on necessities incident to the use of language. This question is possibly capable of some sort of experimental attack, but I think in any event we are here perilously close to the verge of meaning, itself. Some answer may eventually be found to the meaningful aspects of the question."

The renewed interest in language growing out of the perplexities of modern science is only one—and by no means the most important—of the influences which have produced intensified work on the psychology of language. Descriptive linguists came out of the war immensely stimulated by the heavy demand which had been placed on their skills during the emergency. Starting from a wholly different vantage point, communications engineers have carried through an enormously productive series of studies in acoustics, auditory perception, and the intelligibility of speech sounds. Out of these studies has developed a theory of communication which has proved of great interest to psychologists and philosophers as well as to mathematicians and physical scientists.

Through these and other developments, psychologists, anthropologists, philosophers and others who had always exhibited some interest in language developed a renewed concern for the field. But their various lines of approach to the problem of language were in some respects remarkably disparate. The descriptive linguists discussing phonemes, the communications engineers discussing binary digits, and the psychologists discussing linguistic responses seemed most of the time to be engaged in wholly separate conversations. Here and there one could find individuals whose training was sufficiently broad to participate in all three conversations, but the overlap was tenuous.

It was in this context that the Social Science Research Council set up a Committee on Linguistics and Psychology in October, 1952. The purpose of the Committee was to bring together men trained in the various fields relating to the study of language with a view to planning and developing research on language behavior.

The initial membership of the Committee was as follows: Charles E. Osgood (psy-

* P. W. Bridgman, The task before us. *Proceedings of the American Academy of Arts and Sciences,* 83: 3. 104.

chologist, University of Illinois), chairman; John B. Carroll (psychologist, Harvard) ; Floyd G. Lounsbury (linguist, Yale) ; George A. Miller (psychologist, Massachusetts Institute of Technology); and Thomas A. Sebeok (linguist, Indiana University). Joseph B. Casagrande (anthropologist) of the Social Science Research Council served as staff for the Committee. Mr. Miller resigned after serving on the Committee for one year, while Joseph H. Greenberg (linguist, Columbia) and James J. Jenkins (psychologist, University of Minnesota) were added to the Committee in the autumn of 1953.

One of the early steps taken by the Committee was to plan and sponsor a research seminar in psycholinguistics. This seminar was held in conjuction with the Linguistic Institute at Indiana University during the 1953 summer session. The seminar first set itself to the task of examining three differing approaches to the language process: (1) the linguist's conception of language as a structure of systematically interrelated units, (2) the learning theorist's conception of language as a system of habits relating signs to behavior, and (3) the information theorist's conception of language as a means of transmitting information. These various points of view were explored in order to appraise their utility for handling different problems and to discover in what respects they could be brought into a common conceptual framework. The second task which the seminar set itself was to examine a variety of research problems in psycholinguistics with a view to developing possible experimental approaches to them.

This monograph is one result of the seminar. It is a collaborative product of the entire group of seminar participants, each of whom is author of one or more sections.

The authors of the monograph, and particularly the two editors, Charles E. Osgood and Thomas A. Sebeok, are to be congratulated upon having carried through an exceedingly arduous assignment. Those who have been familiar with one or another of these fields (and the monograph is written precisely for them) will recognize how difficult it was to bring into a common framework theoretical models of the language process which had evolved independently out of differing kinds of data and differing approaches to these data. The authors would be the first to recognize the extent to which they have fallen short of their goal. Yet it seemed important to them—and this feeling must surely be widely shared—that someone undertake the difficult pioneering task of bringing together these vital lines of research.

Research workers in the special fields involved have reason to be grateful to the authors of this monograph who took time out from their own active research interests to undertake this difficult exploratory task.

May 12,1954

PREFACE

The Summer Seminar on Psycholinguistics was sponsored by the Social Science Research Council with funds provided by the Carnegie Corporation of New York and held at Indiana University in 1953. It was part of the program of study being developed by the Council's Committee on Linguistics and Psychology, most of whose members were participants. It was also in part a continuation of the interuniversity summer research seminar in psychology and linguistics held at Cornell University, June 18 —August 10, 1951. The general purpose of this Committee is to stimulate research in the field of language behavior, by conducting a survey of on-going and contemplated research, by organizing where feasible small-scale work-conferences on special problems, by serving as a communication channel among people working in this area, and by discussing and evaluating the present status of the field. It was felt that a summer seminar would provide an unusual opportunity for the members of this Committee to work together intensively over an eight-week period and thereby develop a more intimate understanding of their mutual problems in the language area, as well as placing them in a better position to organize effective work-conferences and study programs.

In the course of the seminar's activities, it was planned to examine three of the theoretical models of the language process which have been developing rather independently; the membership in the seminar included persons with training in each of these areas. Another purpose of the seminar was to study intensively a number of basic research problems, combining the training and research experiences of the participants in analysing the theoretical backgrounds of these problems and in formulating possible experimental approaches to them. In rough accord with these plans, approximately the first half of the eight-week period of the seminar was spent in the presentation and discussion of the various psycholinguistic problems as approached from these theoretical positions; during the second half of the seminar, the participants worked informally in over-lapping groups on particular problems in psycholinguistics that were felt to be of major significance.

Participants in the Summer Seminar on Psycholinguistics, and hence joint authors of this report, included, in addition to the senior staff members, Greenberg, Jenkins, Lounsbury, Osgood, and Sebeok, the following graduate student members: Susan Ervin (psychologist, Bureau of Social Science Research, Washington, D.C.), Leonard D. Newmark (linguist, Indiana University), Sol Saporta (linguist, University of Illinois), Donald E. Walker (psychologist, The Rice Institute), and Kellogg Wilson (psychologist, University of Illinois). It is fair to say that our graduate students contributed on equal terms with the senior staff both in discussion of psycholinguistic problems and in the writing of this report; it also can be fairly said that they profited greatly from the summer's experience. The development of any new interdisciplinary field must ultimately depend on young scholars who maintain in a single nervous system the habits of both sciences. Three others were able to participate only through two-week periods of the seminar—John B. Carroll (psychologist, Harvard University), Eric Lenneberg (linguist, Massachusetts Institute of Technology), and Joseph B. Casagrande (staff representative for the Social Science Research Council)—but they also joined significantly in the work of the seminar and have contributed to the content of this report. In addition, the seminar enjoyed visits from a number of scholars interested in the same general area: Grant Fairbanks (psychologist, University of Illinois) demonstrated his speech compression and expansion techniques and also discussed delayed auditory feedback phenomena and the theoretical and practical implications of this work; E. M. Uhlenbeck (linguist, University of Leyden) sat in on our discussion of entropy profiles in sequential speech and played tape recordings made of conversational Javanese; John Lotz (linguist, Columbia University) participated in discussions on the problem of meaning and Werner F. Leopold (linguist, Northwestern University) in discussions on the development of language behavior in children.

We decided to hold our seminar on the campus of Indiana University in conjunction with the Linguistic Institute. The members of the seminar were welcomed at the daily luncheons of the Institute and were thus able, informally, to meet and discuss many matters with the staff of the Linguistic Institute. Our graduate student participants typically carried two courses offered by the Institute and usually sat in on others. Most of the senior staff also took advantage of this opportunity and sat in on one or more of the courses being offered. While these "extra-curricular" activities certainly reduced the time we could devote to the seminar, they contributed to our understanding of psycholinguistic problems. The members of the Summer Seminar on Psycholinguistics thank both the Linguistic Institute, particularly its Director, C. F. Voegelin, and the administration of Indiana University, particularly Vice-President John W. Ashton, for making our summer visit both enjoyable and profitable. We also wish to express our gratitude here to the Social Science Research Council and to the Carnegie Corporation of New York for their continued support of this and other interdisciplinary studies in the area of language behavior.

A final word is in order concerning the preparation of this report and its nature. During the latter portion of the seminar, each of the informal work-groups had a chairman whose responsibility it was to organize study of a particular problem and its presentation to the seminar as a whole. When it was later decided to prepare a report for possible publication, it became each chairman's responsibility to collate materials from the members of his group and write an initial draft. Although specific sections of this report were thus written by individuals (as indicated by footnotes throughout), the actual thought and discussion of each topic was so thoroughly shared within the seminar that it would be difficult if not impossible to properly assign either credit or responsibility as the case might be. Therefore, we wish the reader to view this report as truly a joint product. We also hope the reader will keep in mind that this represents the result of only eight weeks' work. It is an exploratory survey of an interdisciplinary area, not a scholarly exposition of well-mapped territory; it formulates many problems and suggests possible attacks on them, but it does not present the results of research. So, it is with some trepidation that we offer this rather crude map of what is becoming an important research area—psycholinguistics.

Charles E. Osgood, Editor
University of Illinois

Thomas A. Sebeok, Associate Editor
Indiana University

December 1, 1953

Psycholinguistics: A Survey of Theory and Research Problems

1. INTRODUCTION

1.1. *Models of the Communication Process*

In the most general sense, we have communication whenever one system, a *source*, influences another system, a *destination*, by manipulation of the alternative signals which can be carried in the *channel* connecting them. The information source is conceived as producing one or more messages which must be transformed by a *transmitter* into signals which the channel can carry; these signals must then be transformed by a *receiver* back into messages which can be accepted at the destination. This minimal system, borrowed from Shannon's discussion of the theory of information[1] and diagrammed in Figure 1, has been applied, with

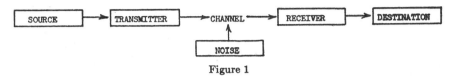

Figure 1

great generality, to information transmission in electrical, biological, psychological and social systems as well as language communication in the strict sense. In a telephone communication system, for example, the messages produced by a speaker are in the form of variable sound pressures and frequencies which must be transformed into proportional electrical signals by the transmitter; these signals are carried over wire (channel) to a receiver which transforms them back into the variable sound pressures and frequencies which constitute the message to be utilized by the listener. The activity of the transmitter is usually referred to as *encoding* and that of the receiver as *decoding*. Anything that produces variability at the destination which is unpredictable from variability introduced at the source is called *noise*.

This model of the communication process, developed in connection with engineering problems, was not intended to provide a satisfactory picture of human communication. For one thing, it implies a necessary separation of source and destination, of transmitter and receiver, which is usually true of mechanical communication systems but not of human ones. The individual human functions more or less simultaneously as a source and destination and as a transmitter and receiver of messages—indeed, he is regularly a decoder of the messages he himself encodes through various feedback mechanisms. Each individual in a speech community may be conceived as a more or less self-contained communicating system, encompassing in his nervous apparatus, from receptors to effectors, all of the components shown in Figure 1. If we rearrange the components in Shannon's model in the fashion shown in Figure 2, what might be called a *communication unit* is described, equipped to both receive and send messages. In the process of

[1] Shannon and Weaver, *The mathematical theory of communication* (University of Illinois Press, 1949). Mathematical aspects of Shannon's theory of signal transmission are discussed in section 2.3. of this report.

1

human decoding, input of some form of physical energy, linguistically or otherwise coded, is first recoded into sensory neural impulses, operated upon by receiving apparatus, and finally 'interpreted' at the destination (presumably as some pattern of activity in the higher centers). In the process of human encoding, an 'intention' of the source (presumably some pattern of activity in the same centers) is operated upon by transmitting apparatus in the motor areas, is recoded into

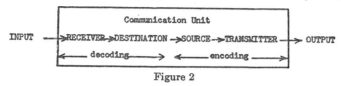

Figure 2

physical movements, and becomes the output of this unit. Translating into traditional psychological language, *input* becomes equivalent to 'stimulus,' *receiver* becomes 'reception' and 'perception,' *destination* and *source* become 'cognition' (meaning, attitude, and the like), *transmitter* becomes 'motor organization and sequencing,' and *output* becomes 'response.'

Another insufficiency of engineering models for human communication purposes is that they are not designed to take into account the *meaning* of signals, e.g., their significance when viewed from the decoding side and their intention when viewed from the encoding side. The research generated by such models has dealt almost exclusively with relations between transmitter and receiver, or with the individual as a single system intervening between input and output signals. This has not been because of lack of awareness of the problem of meaning or its importance, but rather because it is admittedly difficult to be rigorous, objective, and quantitative at this level. Nevertheless, one of the central problems in psycholinguistics is to make as explicit as possible relations between message events and cognitive events, both on decoding and encoding sides of the equation.

Human communication is chiefly a social affair. Any adequate model must therefore include at least two communicating units, a *source unit* (speaker) and a *destination unit* (hearer). Between any two such units, connecting them into a single system, is what we may call the *message*. For purposes of this report, we will define message as that part of the total output (responses) of a source unit which simultaneously may be a part of the total input (stimuli) to a destination unit. When individual A talks to individual B, for example, his postures, gestures, facial expressions and even manipulations with objects (e.g., laying down a playing card, pushing a bowl of food within reach) may all be part of the message, as of course are events in the sound wave channel. But other parts of A's total behavior (e.g., breathing, toe-wiggling, thinking) may not affect B at all and other parts of the total stimulation to B (e.g., sensations from B's own posture, cues from the remainder of the environment) do not derive from A's behavior—these events are not part of the message as we use the term. These R–S message events (reactions of one individual that produce stimuli for another) may be either *immediate* or *mediate*—ordinary face-to-face conversation illustrates the

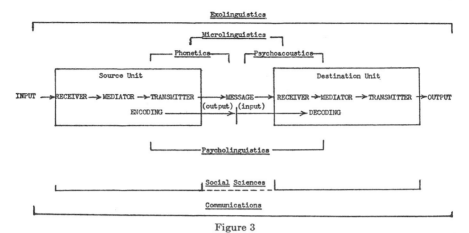

Figure 3

former and written communication (along with musical recordings, art objects, and so forth) illustrates the latter.

Figure 3 presents a model of the essential communication act, encoding of a message by a source unit and decoding of that message by a destination unit. Since the distinction between source and destination within the same communicator (as shown in Figure 2) seems relevant only with respect to the direction of information exchange (e.g., whether the communicator is decoding or encoding), we substitute the single term *mediator* for that system which intervenes between receiving and transmitting operations. The ways in which the various sciences concerned with human communication impinge upon and divide up the total process can be shown in relation to this figure.

1.2. *Disciplines Concerned with Human Communication*

Microlinguistics (or linguistics proper) deals with the structure of messages, the signals in the channel connecting communicators, as events independent of the characteristics of either speakers or hearers. Once messages have been encoded and are "on the air," so to speak, they can be described as objective, natural science events in their own right. In an even stricter sense, the linguist is concerned with determining the *code* of a given signal system, the sets of distinctions which are significant in differentiating alternative messages. The term *exolinguistics* (sometimes called metalinguistics) has been used rather loosely by linguists to cover all those other aspects of language study which concern relations between the characteristics of messages and the characteristics of individuals who produce and receive them, including both their behavior and culture. Whether or not the grammatical structure of a language influences the thinking of those who speak it is thus an exolinguistic problem. The *social sciences* in general, and psychology, sociology, and anthropology in particular, are concerned with the characteristics of human organisms and societies which influence the selection and interpretation of messages—attitudes, meanings, social roles, values, and so forth. The rather new discipline coming to be known as *psycholinguistics* (paralleling the closely related discipline termed *ethnolinguistics*) is concerned in the broadest sense with relations between messages and the characteristics of human individuals who select and interpret them. In a narrower sense, psycholinguistics studies those processes whereby the intentions of speakers are transformed into signals in the culturally accepted code and whereby these signals are transformed into the interpretations of hearers. In other words, *psycholinguistics deals directly with the processes of encoding and decoding as they relate states of messages to states of communicators.* The terminal aspect of human speech encoding, production of speech sounds, is the special province of *phonetics*. Similarly, the initial aspect of human speech decoding, whereby sound pressures and frequencies are transformed into impulses in auditory nerve fibers and relayed to the cortex, is a special field of *psychoacoustics*. Finally, the science of *human communication* would be concerned with relations between sources who select messages and destinations who interpret and are affected by them. In the broadest sense, therefore, human communications as a science includes the other disciplines that have been mentioned; in a narrower sense—and one more in keeping with contemporary activities—students of communications research have usually worked at grosser levels of analysis, concerning themselves with sources such as radio and the newspaper and destinations such as the mass audience, members of another culture, and so on.

1.3. *Plan of This Report*

Psycholinguistics is that one of the disciplines studying human communication which is most directly concerned with the processes of decoding and encoding. What are the major divisions *within* psycholinguistics itself? Mapping of this area was one of the tasks of the seminar, but it was done in a casual manner and appears as a spontaneous clustering of the research problems the participants found significant. In other words, the organization of the field of psycholinguistics followed here is one that the members of this seminar found fruitful.

Section 2 of this report provides brief and non-technical orientations to the *three approaches to language study*, linguistics, learning theory, and information theory, in which we were particularly interested. The members of the seminar spent the first few weeks in such orientation as a means of providing themselves with a more homogeneous background, and most readers of this report are probably in the same position we were in, e.g., perhaps trained in linguistics but not psychology and only remotely conversant with information theory, or possibly familiar with both learning and information theory but entirely vague about linguistics. During the course of this orientational work, discussion by the seminar repeatedly devolved upon the problem of *psycholinguistic units*—the need for clearly defined units in quantitative research, the relevance of available linguistic units, and so on. Although we have been able to do no more than set up the problem and suggest possible ways of attacking it, the prior importance of this issue justifies a separate treatment, given in section 3.

The body of this report presents theoretical analyses and suggested research within specific areas. At the time of presentation of these research problems for preliminary discussion by the seminar, it became clear that we could not organize this field in terms of the three methodological approaches, linguistics, information theory, and learning theory, since each problem seemed to require combinations of techniques drawn from all three aproaches. Rather, the various problems suggested by members of the seminar seemed to fall quite naturally into clusters based on similarity of content and underlying theory. During roughly the last half of the seminar period, its members worked in overlapping groups of about three or four people on such clusters of related problems, reporting back to the seminar as a whole for general discussion. These work-group reports, as written up by the chairman of each group, form the basis for the remainder of this published report.

The organization of content in psycholinguistics developed by the seminar can perhaps best be seen by reference to Figure 4. The temporal dimension runs, as usual, from left to right. Brief sequences of time are indicated by the banded arrows. Periods A and B may refer to either two different stages within the development of an individual speaker or two different stages in the development of a language within a speech community. The upper half of the figure represents diagrammatically the interacting levels of behavioral organization within the individual; this is the special province of psychology and, more remotely, of the other social sciences. The lower half of the figure represents the various levels or bands of the message; this is the special province of linguistics and, programmatically, kinesics (study of facial and bodily gestures) and, more remotely, all disciplines concerned with media (content analysis, aesthetics, etc.).

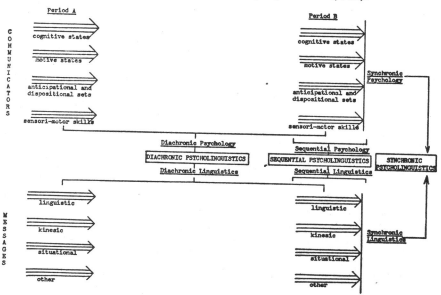

Figure 4

The levels within the communicator are here labeled cognitive states, motive states, anticipational and dispositional states (or sets), and sensory and motor skills—these labels are intended to be suggestive, not limiting. *Synchronic Psychology* would deal with organization both within these levels and between them in decoding and encoding. The various synchronous bands which comprise messages are here labelled linguistic, kinesic, situational (e.g., manipulation of significant objects, arrangement of the social or physical situation in which communication takes place) and 'other' (e.g., odor, warmth, touch, and other modalities which may contribute to communication)—signals in any of these bands may be either naturally or arbitrarily coded. *Synchronic Linguistics* in the broad sense would deal with both organization within these bands (e.g., descriptive linguistics deals specifically with the structure of linguistically coded stimuli) and between these bands (e.g., relations between linguistic, kinesic codes and the like). *Synchronic Psycholinguistics* deals with relations between momentary psychological states of communicators and momentary states of messages. Since a large number of problems fall in this area, the seminar divided them into two groups: *Synchronic Psycholinguistics I.: Microstructure* (relations of phonemic units of messages to perceptual and motor discrimination in communicators, for example) is discussed in section 4; *Synchronic Psycholinguistics II.: Macrostructure* (problems of meaning, of relations of language to thought and culture, for example) is discussed in section 7. This distinction between microstructure and macrostructure is probably not a happy one, but it seemed to serve our purposes.

Over short periods of time, at least, events at any psychological level are to some degree predictable from antecedent events at either the same level or other levels. Principles of association, for example, are concerned with the dependence of one cognitive state upon another. Similarly, enforced regularities in either input or output events (e.g., grammatical regularities) may give rise to sequential neural organization. Study of problems of this order could be called *Sequential Psychology*. On the message side, likewise, events at one point in time can be shown to be dependent to varying degrees upon antecedent message events— presumably such phenomena could be studied within kinesic or other bands as well as the linguistic. Such study could be called *Sequential Linguistics*. The relations between transitional sequences in messages and transitional sequencing mechanisms in the communicator is the field of *Sequential Psycholinguistics*, and problems in this area are discussed in section 5.

When the psychologist deals with changes in organization, either through maturation or through learning, he makes comparisons between two stages of performance in time (e.g., pre-training and post-training) and this might well be termed *Diachronic Psychology*. The same term could be applied to differences in organization between two stages in culture, e.g., comparison of the habits or associations between S and R for two sets of individuals at two discrete times. When the linguist compares the structures of messages produced by members of the same speech community at two discrete periods in time, this is called *Dia-*

.chronic Linguistics. In this report, we are extending the same term to cover the linguist's comparisons between the structures of messages produced by the same individual at two discrete periods in time—that is, to the study of first language learning, second language learning and bilingualism. *Diachronic Psycholinguistics* would be concerned with relations between the changing behavioral organizations of either the individual or the group and the changing structures of messages they produce, particularly the application of learning principles to these problems. This area is discussed in section 6.

2. THREE APPROACHES TO LANGUAGE BEHAVIOR

By way of orientation to the theoretical analyses and research proposals which form the body of the report, this section provides a brief summary of each of the three major approaches to language study under investigation, linguistics, learning theory, and information theory. These introductions are aimed, as it were, at those in other disciplines—the linguistics summary is written for non-linguists, the learning theory summary for non-psychologists, and so forth. This means that the specialist in each area may find much to take exception to, much that he would present differently, and this is to be expected. These summaries are also intended to be non-controversial, but our need for conceptions adequate to handle psycholinguistic problems has undoubtedly influenced the emphases given, particularly in learning theory and linguistics sections. For the reader who wishes to go further into the details of each field, a limited annotated bibliography accompanies each summary.

2.1. *The Linguistic Approach*[2]

As distinct from psychology, which is concerned with verbal behavior in the context of events occurring within the organism, and from the other social sciences, which analyze the contents of verbal behavior insofar as it consists of shared cultural beliefs and actions (e.g., religion, philosophy, economic and political norms), linguistic science has as its traditional subject matter the signal system as such. Its orientation tends to be social rather than individual, since the use of speech in communication presupposes a group of intercommunicating people, a speech community. In general, therefore, it has dealt with the speech of individuals merely as representative of the speech of a community. The interest in an individual's speech as such, his *idiolect*, in relation to his personality structure constitutes a relatively new, marginal, and little explored area. The distinction between language as a system and its actual employment has been variously phrased as *langue* vs. *parole* (de Saussure), syntactic vs. pragmatic (Morris) or code vs. message (information theory). However stated, it marks in general the boundary between what has traditionally been considered the province of linguistic science and what lies outside it.

2.1.1. *The Field of Linguistics*

The primary subject matter of the linguist is spoken language. Writing and other systems partly or wholly isomorphic with speech are viewed by most linguists as secondary systems. Speech has both ontogenetic and phylogenetic priority. There are even now peoples with spoken but not written languages (so-called primitives), but the reverse situation has never been obtained. Moreover, written systems are relatively stable while spoken language, by and large, changes more rapidly. It is always the written language which must make the readaptation, when it is made, by way of a new orthography. The effect of, say, alphabetic

---

[2] Joseph H. Greenberg.

writing on speech, in the form of spelling pronunciations, is a real but quite minor factor in the change of spoken language. The linguist views writing, then, as a derivative system whose symbols stand for units of the spoken language.

Linguistic science is divided into two main branches, the *descriptive* and the *historical*. Historical interests presided at the inception of modern linguistic science (ca. 1800) and have predominated until fairly recently. Within the last few decades the focal point of linguistics has shifted to problems of description. These two chief areas of study complement each other. The degree of success of historical inquiry is largely dependent on the adequacy of descriptive data. On the other hand any particular stage of a language, while it can be completely described without reference to its past, can be more fully understood if the time axis is also taken into account. A cardinal and generally accepted methodological principle, however, is the clear distinction between synchronic and diachronic investigations. In particular, descriptive grammars were, and sometimes are, so replete with historical interpretations, that the locus in time of individual linguistic facts is obscured and observed phenomena are not distinguished from inferences, so that no clear picture of the structure of the language at any one time emerges.

The aim of a scientific language description is to state as accurately, exhaustively, concisely, and elegantly as possible, the facts concerning a particular language at a particular time. It is assumed that the changes which are inevitably proceeding during the period in which the linguistic informant's speech is being studied are negligible and can be safely disregarded. It is also assumed that the speech of the informant is an adequate sample of some speech community. This concept is applied rather vaguely to any group within which linguistic communication takes place regularly. Minor cleavages within a group of mutually intelligible speech forms are called *dialects*. The maximal mutually intelligible group is a *language community*, as defined by scientific linguistics, but the term is often loosely applied on a political basis. Thus Norwegian is usually called a language although it is mutually intelligible with Danish, while Low German is considered a form of German, although objectively the difference between Low and High German is greater than that between Danish and Norwegian. The phrase 'mutually intelligible' is itself vague.

The speech of an informant is normally characteristic of that of a dialect community along with some idiosyncrasies. Language is so standardized an aspect of culture, particularly in regard to those structural aspects which are of chief concern to the linguist, that a very small number of informants usually proves to be adequate. If necessary, the linguist will even be satisfied with a single informant in the belief that systematic divergence from the shared habits of the community as a whole are likely to be of minimal significance. However, the sampling problem must eventually be faced in a less makeshift manner. The systematic mapping of speech differences on a geographic basis, through sampling at selected points, is known as *linguistic geography* and is a well-established subdiscipline of linguistics. Far more remains to be done with non-geographic factors of cleavage within the language community, on sex, occupational and class lines. Such study is a prerequisite for adequate sampling.

2.1.2. *Units of Linguistic Analysis*

' Linguistic description is carried out in terms of certain fundamental units which can be isolated by analytic procedures. The two key units are the *phoneme* and the *morpheme*, of which the phoneme has a somewhat more assured status. The phoneme is the unit of description of the sound system (phonology) of a language. Many widely differing definitions have been offered, some of which are objects of doctrinal differences between various linguistic 'schools.' Fortunately, the actual results in practice of the applications of these divergent approaches are surprisingly similar.

The *phoneme* was foreshadowed by the pre-scientific invention of alphabetic writing. An adequate orthography of this kind disregards differences in sound which have no potential for the discrimination of meaning. Moreover, unlike syllabic writing, alphabetic writing selects the minimal unit capable of such differential contrast. The naive speaker is generally unaware of sound variations which do not carry this function of distinguishing different forms. For example, speakers of English have usually never noticed that the sound spelled *t* in 'stop' is unaspirated as contrasted with the aspirated *t* of 'top.' Yet this difference is sufficient to differentiate forms in Chinese, Hindustani, and many other languages. Phonemic theory is necessary because if we approach other languages naively we will only respond to those cues as different which are significant in our own language. On the other hand, we will attribute significance, and consider as indicative of separate elements, those differences which have a function in our own language, although they may not have such a function in the language we are describing.

For example, in Algonquian languages distinctions of voicing are not significant. A naive observer with an English linguistic background will carefully mark all *p*'s as different from *b*'s. The reaction of an Algonquian would be similar to that of an English speaker if he were presented with an orthography devised by a Hindu in which the *t* of 'top' was represented by a different symbol from the *t* of 'stop.' The arbitrariness of such a procedure comes out when we realize that an untrained Frenchman would describe the sound system of a particular language in different terms than a naive Englishman or German. As a matter of fact, this has often occurred. Equally unsatisfactory results are obtained by a phonetically trained observer, unaware of the phonemic principle, who indicates all kinds of non-essential variants because his training permits him to distinguish them. Here also there is a certain arbitrariness based on the particular phonetic training of the observer. The logical outcome of such a phonetic approach would be to carry discriminations even further by instrumental means, and the result would be that every utterance of a language would be completely unique, for no two utterances of the 'same' sequence of phonemes is ever acoustically identical with any other.

The procedure of the descriptive linguist, then, is a process of discovering the basic contrasts which are significant in a language. Since he cannot know *a priori* which particular features of an utterance will prove to be significant, he must be prepared to indicate them all at the beginning by a phonetic transcription. Instrumental aids, though useful, are not essential to the preliminary research. The linguist gradually eliminates those sound differences from his transcription which prove to be non-significant so that the phonetic transcription becomes a phonemic one. In doing this, he makes use of the two principles of *conditioned* and *non-conditioned variation*. If the occurrence of one or another of a set of sounds may be predicted in terms of other sounds in the environment, this variation is said to be conditioned. If either of two sounds may be used for the other and still produce a meaningful utterance, the variation is called free, or non-conditioned. Such variant sounds grouped within the same phoneme are called allophones. In English, ḳ, a front velar sound is found before *i, I, e, E* and other front vowels (e.g., the initial sound of 'key'). A sound different enough to be a separate phoneme in many languages, ḳ, a back velar sound, is found before *u, v, o, ɔ* and other back vowels (e.g., the initial sound of 'coat'). Since the particular variant can be predicted by reference to the following vowel sound, ḳ and ḳ are in conditioned allophonic variation and are members of the same English /k/ phoneme.

The number of potential phones (sounds) in a language approaches infinity. The great virtue of the phonemic principle is that it enables the linguist to effect a powerful reduction from this complexity to a limited number of signals that constitute the code, and this represents a great economy in description. For languages so far investigated, the number of phonemes runs about 25 to 30 (the English system tending toward the higher figure). It is possible to effect a still greater economy in description. This is achieved by the analysis of phonemes into concurrent sets of *distinctive features*. Since the features which distinguish certain pairs of phonemes are found to be identical with the features which distinguish certain other pairs, the number of entities necessary to describe the significant aspects of the sound matter is thus further reduced. For example, in English /p/ is distinguished from /b/, /t/ from /d/, /k/ from /g/, and /s/ from /z/ on the basis of the same feature, the former being unvoiced and the latter voiced. Other distinctive features, such as tongue position or nasalization, produce other sets of contrasts. By contrasting every phoneme in the language with every other phoneme, each phoneme comes to be uniquely identified in terms of the set of contrasts into which it enters, this 'bundle of distinctive features' being the definition of that phoneme. The distinctive oppositions that occur in languages studied so far run about 6 to 8. These are perhaps the minimal discriminanda in language codes.

Analysis into distinctive features is a development within the past two decades, associated with the Prague School but not universally accepted. Jakobson and his associates (cf., 9, 11) go one step further still, by imposing upon the entire phonemic material *binary opposition* as a consistent patterning principle, but this needs much further exploration. Whereas American linguists usually say that sounds must be phonetically similar to be classed as members of the same phoneme, members of the Prague School state that members of the same phoneme class must share the same set of distinctive features. These criteria will generally lead to the same classificatory structure.

For example, ʞ and ʞ would be said by members of the Prague School to share the following features in common: velar articulation, non-nasality and lack of voicing. These would be the relevant features shared by all varieties of the /k/ phoneme while, in this instance, back or forward articulation is irrelevant. The /g/ phoneme shares velarity and non-nasality with /k/ but not lack of voicing. The /ŋ/phoneme (as in 'sing') shares velar articulation but not non-nasality or lack of voicing. The /t/ phoneme shares non-nasality and lack of voicing with /k/ but not velar articulation. Thus /k/ is uniquely determined by these three relevant features. Certain recent American analyses employ a methodology nearly identical with that just described.

Phonemes are sometimes distinguished as being either *segmental* or *prosodic*. The former proceed in one dimensional time succession without gap. The latter are intermittent and necessarily simultaneous with segmental phonemes or successions of segmental phonemes. Examples of prosodic phonemes are phonemes of tone (sometimes called tonemes), stress, etc. In principle, we should sharply distinguish prosodic phonemes simultaneous with a single segmental phoneme from those which are distributed over a grammatically defined unit such as a phrase or sentence. The former can always be dispensed with in analysis, though they often prove convenient. For example, in a language with three vowel phonemes /a, i, u/ and two tone levels high /´/ and low /`/ we might analyze /à/, /á/, /ì/, /í/, /ù/ and /ú/ as six separate segmental phonemes or we might make /a/, /i/ and /u/ segmental and /´/ and /`/ prosodic. This particular analysis has no doubt been largely determined by our traditional orthography which uses separate marks for pitch. The carrying through of this procedure to its logical conclusion is called *componential analysis* and results in the resolution of each phoneme into a set of simultaneous elements equivalent to the distinctive features mentioned above. The other type of prosodic element is illustrated by question or statement intonation in English. Unlike the elements just discussed, it cannot be dispensed with.

Still another type of phoneme is the juncture or significant boundary, whose status is much disputed in contemporary linguistics. The conditioning factor for phonemic variation is sometimes found to be the initial or final position in some grammatical unit such as a word, rather than a neighboring sound. For example, unreleased stops p, t, k are found in English in final morpheme or word position. Unless we indicate the boundary in some fashion we must nearly double the number of phonemes in English. Spaces, hyphens and other devices are employed to indicate the presence of these modifications. For example, the n of 'syntax' is shorter than the n is 'sin-tax.' Either we posit two different n phonemes or we describe the longer n as n plus juncture, transcribing /sintaks/ and /sin-taks/ respectively (or we deny the existence of the phenomenon altogether).[3] The agreement as to the boundaries of grammatical elements is almost never perfect, and some linguists assume that if such boundary modifications exist in some cases they must exist in all, even though they have not actually been observed to occur.

In addition to the enumeration of phonemes and their allophonic variants, the phonological section of a description usually contains a set of statements regard-

---

[3] Actually there is also a louder stress on the second syllable of 'sin-tax' and some would maintain that it is merely the stress difference which is phonemic. Even if this is true for English, the question arises in other languages.

ing permitted and non-permitted sequences of phonemes, frequently in terms of the structure of the syllable. In this as in other aspects of linguistic description it is not usual to give text or lexicon frequencies. Statements are limited to those of simple occurrence or non-occurrence. Only such quantifiers as some, none and all occur in most linguistic description.

Corresponding to the minimal unit of phonology, the phoneme, we have a unit of somewhat less certain status, the *morpheme*, which is basic for grammatical description. Bloomfield (2) states as the fundamental assumption of linguistic science that in a given speech community some utterances show partial formal-semantic similarity. For example, in the English-speaking community the utterances 'the dog is eating meat' and 'the dog is eating biscuits' are partially similar in their sequence of phonemes and refer to partially similar situations. The linguist, through the analysis of these partial similarities, arrives at the division of utterances into meaningful parts. The analytical procedure as applied to individual utterances must eventually reach a point beyond which analysis becomes arbitrary and futile. The minimum sequence of phonemes thus isolated, which has a meaning, is called a morpheme. The morpheme is a smaller unit than the word. Some words are monomorphemic, e.g., 'house.' Others are multi-morphemic, e.g., 'un-child-like.' There is some uncertainty as to the point up to which such divisions are justified and the rules of procedure may be stated in several alternate ways. Thus all would concur in analyzing 'singing' as having two morphemes 'sing-' and '-ing' and there would likewise be general agreement that to analyze 'chair' as containing two morphemes, say 'ch-' meaning 'wooden object' and '-air' meaning 'something to sit on' is not acceptable. But there is an intermediate area in which opinions differ. For example, 'deceive' contains two morphemes 'de' and 'ceive' according to some but not according to others. In such borderline cases it becomes impossible to specify the meaning of each morpheme without some arbitrariness.

2.1.3. Morphology and Syntax

The work of the descriptive linguists in this area is not exhausted by the analytic task just described. Having arrived at his units he must describe the rules according to which they are synthesized into words, phrases, and sentences. In somewhat parallel fashion to the situation in phonology, having isolated minimal units, he must describe their variation and their rules of combination.

In regard to the first of these problems, it is not sufficient to consider each sequence of phonemes which differs either in form or meaning as a different unit from every other. For example, the sequence 'leaf' /lijf/ is different in form from 'leav-' of the plural 'leaves' /lijv-z/ but we cannot consider them as units without relation to each other. We call /lijf/ and /lijv-/ morphs rather than morphemes and consider them allomorphs of the same morpheme because: (1) they are in complementary distribution /lijv-/ occurring only with /-z/ of the plural and /lijf/ under all other conditions; (2) they have the same meaning; (3) there are other sequences which do not vary in form and which have the same type of distribution, e.g., 'cliff' for which we have /klif/ and /klif-s/.[4] Such variation in the phonemic composition of allomorphs of the same morpheme is called morphophonemic alternation, and systematic statements of such alternations comprise the portion of grammar known as *morphophonemics*. Some alternations occur in all instances in a language regardless of the particular morphemes in which the phonemes occur. Such alternations are called automatic. There are others which are unique. These are called irregular. Others are intermediate in that they apply to classes of morphemes of various sizes. In English, morphemes which have *s*, *z* and *əz* as variants exhibit automatic alternation, *əz* occurring after sibilants (and affricates), *s* after unvoiced non-sibilants and *z* after voiced non-sibilants. Thus the same rule applies both for the third person singular present of the verb and the nominative plural. On the other hand, the variation between /čajld/ 'child' and /čildr-/ of the plural 'childr-en' is a unique irregularity. Psychologically, there would seem to be a real difference between these extremes.

Having distinguished morphemic units, there remains the basic task of grammatical description—the setting up of rules of permitted combinations of morphemes to form sentences. Generality of statement is here obviously a prime requirement. Languages vary widely in number of morphemes, from some hundreds to many thousands. Their possible sequences in constructions can only be stated in practice by the setting up of classes whose members have the same privilege of occurrence. In setting up such classes, modern linguistics characteristically uses a formal, rather than semantic approach. Classes of morphemes or classes of sequences of morphemes (word classes, phrase types, etc.) are defined in terms of mutual substitutability in a given frame. Any utterance and the morpheme or morpheme sequence within it, for which substitutions are made, defines a class. Thus, in English, among other criteria, substitution of single words for *house* in the frame 'I see the house' determines the class of nouns. This contrasts with the traditional *a priori* semantic approach according to which all languages have the same basic grammatical categories (actually based on Latin grammar) and a noun, for example is defined as the name of a person, place, or thing. Actually, formal criteria have always been used in grammars, although often tacitly. 'Lightning' is a noun in traditional English grammar also, although it names an event, because it functions in the same constructions as other nouns.

It is customary to regard sentences as the largest normalized units,[5] and these are successively decomposed into clauses, phrases, words, and morphemes. These units constitute a hierarchy which is also reflected in the speech event by *configurational features*, which, like the distinctive features of phonemic analysis, are assumed to operate on a strictly binary, 'yes-no' basis. Configurational features include such distinctions as those of pitch, stress, rhythm, and juncture, and

[4] This is too simple a formulation. Many problems arise at this point which cannot be discussed here.

[5] However, discourse analysis, being currently developed by Zellig S. Harris, carries linguistic techniques beyond the boundary of the sentence, and Thomas A. Sebeok has attempted to study the construction of sets of whole texts of folkloristic character in this manner (16).

provide appropriate signals as to construction. The sentence is so complex a unit that it cannot be described directly in terms of morpheme constructions. Rather, the description is built up in layers. On any particular level, the combinations are practically always accounted for in terms of *immediate constituents*. In the sentence 'unlikely events may actually occur,' the morpheme *un-* and the morpheme sequence *-likely* are the two immediate constituents which make up the word *unlikely*. In turn, *likely* has as immediate binary constituents the morphemes '*like-*' and '*ly*.' On a higher level *unlikely* enters as a whole in a construction with *events* while *events* itself has *event-* and *-s* as immediate constituents.

It is usual to distinguish as primary divisions of grammar all constructions of morphemes to form words as *morphology* and all constructions using words as units to form phrases, clauses, and sentences as *syntax*. Although no generally accepted definition of the word-unit exists, in fact very nearly every grammar written makes use of the word as a fundamental unit and describes morphological and syntactic constructions separately.[6] In spite of traditional differences of terminology in morphology and syntax, it is generally agreed that the same fundamental principles of analysis apply.

2.1.4. *Problem of Meaning in Linguistics*

Besides specifying meaningful units and their constructions, a complete linguistic description must state the meanings of these units and of the constructions into which they enter. The status of meaning has been a crucial point in contemporary linguistic theory. The statements of Bloomfield concerning meaning in his influential book (2) have sometimes been interpreted both by followers and opponents as indicating that the field of linguistic science only includes a logical syntax of language without reference to meanings. The definition of meanings, on this view, rests with other sciences which deal with the subject matters which speakers talk about. Thus, the definition of 'moon' is the business of the astronomer, not the linguist. The actual practice of linguists both here and in Europe, however, indicates that semantic problems are in fact dealt with and cannot well be excluded from scientific linguistics.

Without entering into the exegetical problem of what Bloomfield meant, which is irrelevant to the present purpose, it may be pointed out that Bloomfield coined the technical terms 'sememe' for the meaning of a morpheme and 'episememe' for the meaning of a construction, both of which are current in American linguistics. Moreover, problems of historical meaning change are discussed at length in his book. This would imply that scientific linguistics does not exclude semantics. It is evident that historical linguistics draws conclusions regarding relationships by comparisons of cognates, that is, forms with both formal and semantic resemblances, so that in this branch, at least, meanings must be dealt with. It is likewise clear that the compiling of dictionaries has traditionally fallen within the linguist's province and continues to do so. No linguist has ever written a grammar in which the forms cited were not accompanied by translations.

The linguist deals with meaning by the bilingual method of translation or the unilingual method of paraphrase, that is, by the apparatus of traditional lexi-

---

[6] For a discussion of the word as a unit see section 3.3. of this report.

cography. In keeping with the general orientation of linguistics as a social science, the linguist defines the socially shared denotative meanings. Avoiding as far as possible controversial issues in the domain of epistemology, it may perhaps be ventured that a distinction may be, and in practice is, drawn between definitions which embody our scientific knowledge about a thing and nominal definitions which are observed rules of use in a given speech community. The linguist practices the latter type of definition. His methods up to now have been the more or less rough and ready methods of lexicography based on the traditional logical concepts of definition. The difficulties involved in the vagueness of actual usage of all linguistic terms in a speech community (if we exclude some scientific discourse in a few societies) are in practice circumvented by the not altogether happy devices of translation and paraphrase, which, involving as they do, language in its everyday use, are equally as vague as the terms which are to be defined. Ambiguity is dealt with by multiple listings of separate meanings based primarily on common-sense analysis. The boundary between the same form with synonymous meanings and separate homonymous forms has never been clearly determined, since it has not been possible to specify *how* different meanings must be in order to justify treatment as homonyms. Nor, in this instance, does an approach in terms of purely formal differences in distribution prove more successful.

2.1.5. *Historical Linguistics*

Thus far all our consideration of linguistic topics has omitted the basic dimension of change in time. This is the field of historical and of comparative linguistics which form a single sub-discipline. The investigation of the history of a specific language may be considered as a comparative study of its sequential synchronic states, while one result of comparing related, contemporaneous languages is a reconstruction of their history. History and comparison are thus, for the most part, inseparable in practice, though a much less frequently employed non-historical comparative approach, the so-called 'typological,' will be considered below.

It was the recognition of certain facts about language change that ushered in the modern scientific period in linguistics. The most fundamental of these were (a) the universality of language change, (b) the fact that changes in the same linguistic structure when they occur independently, as through geographical isolation, always lead to different total end results, and finally (c) that certain of those changes, particularly in the area of phonology, show a high degree of regularity. The acceptance of these three principles—universality, differential character, and regularity of language change—add up to a historical and evolutionary interpretation of language similarities and differences which contrast with the older notion based on the Babel-legend that, as with organic species, languages were types fixed from the time of creation and only subject to haphazard, degenerative changes.

The second and third of these principles, those concerning the differential nature of independent changes and their regularity, in combination, lead to the concept of genetic relationship among languages. Whenever a language continues to be spoken over a long period of time, weaknesses in communication through migration, geographical and political barriers and other factors, result in a pattern of dialect cleavage as linguistic innovations starting in one part of the speech community fail habitually at certain points to diffuse to the remainder. As this continues, the dialects drift farther and farther apart until they become mutually unintelligible languages. However, they continue to show evidence of their common origin for a very long period. In fact, a number of successive series of cleavages may occur within a period short enough for the whole set of events to be inferred. For example, the Proto-Indo-European speech community was differentiated into a number of separate speech communities, one of which was the Proto-Italic. The Proto-Italic in turn split into the Latin, Venetic, Oscan, Umbrian and other separate language-communities in ancient Italy. One of these, Latin, survived, but it in turn developed into the various Romance languages, French, Italian, Spanish, etc. Sometimes, as in the case of Latin, the original speech from which the descendant forms branched off is attested from written records. In other cases we legitimately assume that such a language must once have existed although no direct evidence is available. Such an inferred language is called a *proto-language* ('Ursprache').

Because of the regular nature of much linguistic change, it is possible under favorable circumstances to reconstruct much of the actual content of such extinct languages. In particular, the reconstruction of the ancestral language of the Indo-European family has been a highly successful enterprise which has occupied a major proportion of the interest of linguists up to the present day. Thus far, linguistic relationships are well-established only in certain portions of the world and reconstruction has been carried out for only a limited number of linguistic families, particularly Indo-European, Uralic, Semitic, Bantu, Malayo-Polynesian, and Algonquian. Reconstruction is most successful, probably, in phonology, somewhat less so in grammar, and least of all in semantics. Forms which resemble each other in related languages because of common origin from a single ancestral form are called *cognates*, e.g., English *foot* and German *Fuss*. The history of such a particular cognate is called its *etymology* and it has both a phonological and semantic aspect.

The difficulties of semantic reconstruction may be appreciated from the following artificial example which illustrates, however, the real difficulties often encountered. If in three related languages, a cognate form means 'day' in A, 'sun' in B, and 'light' in C, here are some of the possibilities among which it is impossible to make a rational choice. (1) The original meaning was 'day' which remained in A, shifted to 'sun' in B and to 'light' in C. (2) The original meaning was 'sun' which shifted to 'day' in A, remained in B and shifted to 'light' in C. (3) The original meaning included both 'sun' and 'day.' It narrowed to 'day' in A, to 'sun' in B, while in C it narrowed to 'sun' and then shifted to 'light.' These and others are all possible, and in the present stage of our knowledge, about equally plausible. On the other hand, various Indo-European languages do have cognates all of which mean approximately 'horse,' which can therefore be safely reconstructed for the parent language.

The changes undergone by languages whether documented or inferred can be classified under various universally applicable processes such as sound change, borrowing and analogy. Such processes show a high degree of specific similarity. To cite an example from phonology, *au* has become *o* in many different languages independently. Similar highly specific parallel changes occur in grammar and semantics. In spite of this, our second postulate of differential change shows that there are always a number of possible changes from a given state and our knowledge is not yet sufficient to predict which one will ensue or indeed whether the system will change or remain stable in some particular aspect. Parallel changes within related languages, called 'drift' by Sapir, are probably especially frequent and presumably strongly conditioned by internal linguistic factors.[7]

2.1.6. *Typological Comparison*

The ascertaining of historic relationships and the reconstruction of processes of change is not the only possible motive for the comparison of languages. We can examine the languages of the world, comparing both related and unrelated ones, in order to discover language universals, the greater than chance occurrence of certain traits, and the significant tendencies of traits to cluster in the same languages. The isolation of such clusters leads to the setting up of criteria for classifying language types. The classical nineteenth century typologies rested primarily on considerations of the morphological structure of the word. Because of the relatively unadvanced state of descriptive theory, it suffered from lack of precise definitions for the units employed and was, moreover, tied to an ethnocentric outmoded type of evolutionism. Recently text ratios of more rigidly defined units have been employed in order to construct a more refined typology.

The problems of typology are of intimate concern to psycholinguistics. The universal or more than chance occurrence of certain traits is in need of correlation with our psychological knowledge. More data on languages in many parts of the world and some effort at cross-linguistic cataloguing are probably necessary prerequisites for any considerable advance in this area. One paper growing out of The Symposium on American Indian Linguistics at the 1951 Linguistic Institute (Voegelin's 17a) and two papers published subsequent to the Conference on Archiving at the 1953 Linguistic Institute (Allen's and Wells' 1a, 18) are concerned primarily with typology.

2.1.7. *Bibliography*

1a. Allen, W. S., 1954, Statements for the conference on archiving. *International Journal of American Linguistics* **20**. 83–84.
1b. Bloch, B. and G. L. Trager, 1942, *Outline of linguistic analysis*, Linguistic Society of America, Baltimore.
   A concise summary of linguistic techniques for the general reader. An excellent, if somewhat outmoded, introduction.
2. Bloomfield, L., 1933, *Language*, New York.
   The most important technical introduction to linguistic science as a whole; a classic of the field.
3. Carroll, J. B., 1953, *The study of language*, Cambridge.

---

[7] The various processes of linguistic change are discussed in detail in section 6.

A survey of linguistics and related disciplines, including chapters on linguistics, psychology, communication engineering, and the study of speech.

4. Fries, C. C., 1952, *The structure of English*, New York.

A formal analysis of English syntax presented in readable form. Useful presentation dealing with a language familiar to the reader.

5. Greenberg, J. H., 1953, Historical linguistics and unwritten languages, in *Anthropology today*, 265–86, Chicago.

Deals with the establishment of linguistic relationships and historical reconstruction.

6. Hall, R. A., Jr., 1950, *Leave your language alone!*, Ithaca.

A good popularization of the fundamentals of linguistic science; recommended as a starting point for the novice in this field.

7. Harris, Z. S., 1951, *Methods in structural linguistics*, Chicago.

The procedures of descriptive linguistics are presented from an extremely formalistic point of view.

8. Hoijer, Harry, and others, 1946, *Linguistic structures of native America*, Viking Fund Publications in Anthropology 6. New York.

Descriptive sketches of diverse American Indian languages illustrate a variety of linguistic techniques and structures.

9. Jakobson, R., C. G. Fant, and M. Halle, 1952, *Preliminaries to speech analysis: the distinctive features and their correlates*, Acoustic Laboratory, Massachusetts Institute of Technology, Technical report No. 13, Cambridge.

The binary principle is employed to present phonemic solutions of phonetic data.

10. Joos, M., 1948, *Acoustic phonetics*, Language Monograph, No. 23, Baltimore.

This contribution indicates results and possibilities of instruments in linguistics.

11. Lotz, J., 1950, Speech and language, *Journal of the Acoustical Society of America* **22**. 712–17.

An outline of the principal theoretical problems of modern linguistics.

12. Lounsbury, F. G., 1953, Field method and techniques of linguistics, in *Anthropology today*, 401–16, Chicago.

Review of the various ways in which linguists gather their data.

13. Martinet, A., 1953, Structural linguistics, in *Anthropology today*, 574–86, Chicago.

The three principal schools of structural linguistics are compared and evaluated.

14. Nida, E. A., 1949, *Morphology*², University of Michigan Publications in Linguistics, Ann Arbor.

A presentation of methods for identification of morphemes with useful sections of problems to be worked on by reader.

15. Pike, K. L., 1947, *Phonemics*, University of Michigan Publications in Linguistics, Ann Arbor.

Techniques for phonemic analysis with examples from widely different languages.

16. Sebeok, T. A., and Frances J. Ingemann, Structural analysis and content analysis in folklore research, in *Studies in Cheremis*, Vol. 2: *The Supernatural*, Part Two. Viking Fund Publications in Anthropology, forthcoming.

Some techniques of psycholinguistics are applied to collections of texts of folkloristic character.

17a. Voegelin, C. F., 1954, Inductively arrived at models for cross-genetic comparisons of American Indian languages, *University of California Publications in Linguistics* **10**. 27–45.

17b. Voegelin, C. F. and Z. S. Harris, 1947, The scope of linguistics, *American Anthropologist* **49**. 588–600.

The data and techniques of linguistics and cultural anthropology are compared and contrasted, and trends in linguistics sketched.

18. Wells, R. S., 1954, Archiving and language typology, *International Journal of American Linguistics* **20**. 101–107.

2.2. *The Learning Theory Approach*[8]

Language is perhaps the most complex behavior displayed by the human organism, and, in the main, it is learned behavior. It is understandable, therefore, that linguists should find learning theory of special interest. Although linguists have for many years refrained from 'psychologizing' within their science, it now appears that more interaction between psychologists and linguists would be fruitful. Even while Bloomfield was espousing the separation of the fields, he felt it desirable from time to time to deal with linguistic matters in the framework of early psychological behaviorism (chiefly as structured by A. P. Weiss). Fortunately, this has been an aspect of psychology which has seen tremendous development in the last 20 years. At the present time, probably more experimental work is being done in learning than in any other psychological field. This section of the report attempts to do two things: first, to present some of the major phenomena of learning and, second, to discuss briefly some of the major theories of learning or ways of organizing and explaining the phenomena.

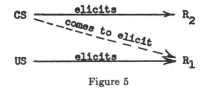

Figure 5

2.2.1. *Phenomena of Learning*

In order to discuss the phenomena of learning most meaningfully and fruitfully, two paradigms will be presented and discussed to reveal the major variables which affect the learning process. These models are phenotypes, and it may be argued that they are in some ultimate sense different kinds of learning or it may be argued that they are explicable under one system. This is not our concern here. It is sufficient for our purposes that they act as convenient vehicles for illustration and discussion.

2.2.1.1. *Classical conditioning.* The first model is taken directly from the famous work of the Russian physiologist Pavlov. It is diagrammatically represented in Figure 5. In its simplest form this learning proceeds as follows: A given stimulus (the unconditioned stimulus or US) is found to be followed by a characteristic response (R_1); another stimulus (the conditioned stimulus or CS) is inadequate with respect to eliciting R_1 but may be followed by some other response (R_2) irrelevant to the experiment; a long series of trials is given in which the US is always preceded by the CS; finally, it is noted that the CS alone elicits some of the response characteristics which normally would occur only after the US; at this point we say that learning has occurred—an initially neutral stimulus now has acquired the ability to elicit a response which originally occurred only in the presence of another stimulus. Suppose we have a dog in our laboratory.

[8] James J. Jenkins.

We know that he salivates when we place meat powder in his mouth. (This is the US [meat powder] → R₁ [salivation] connection.) We decide to condition the response of salivation to the stimulus of ringing a bell. We note before experimentation that ringing the bell (CS) results in extraneous responses (R₂) (moving the head, pricking up ears, etc.), but not salivation. In the training series we ring the bell and, while it is still ringing, place meat powder in the dog's mouth, eliciting salivation. After, say, 100 trials, we ring the bell and note that the dog salivates without the stimulus of the meat powder. The bell (CS) now elicits the response (R₁) (or part of the response) elicited by the meat powder. The conditioning is completed.

To illustrate the manner in which different factors influence this learning process, we may now begin to alter the situation by changing first one and then another variable.

The first thing we might notice is that the number of trials pairing the bell and the meat powder is important. If we only pair the stimuli once, we may not detect any effect. If we have more trials, we see a slight effect. With a great number of trials we get maximum response (most like the original response). Our first important variable, then, is *frequency*. The number of times the experimental situation occurs is important.

Secondly, we might experiment with the temporal relation between the presentation of the bell and the meat powder. If the meat powder precedes the bell-ringing, we discover (perhaps to our surprise) that little or no learning takes place even after a long series of trials. There is practically no *backward conditioning*. Further experimentation shows that simultaneous presentation of the CS and US is "learnable" but not optimal. Maximum conditioning occurs when the bell begins to ring about half a second before the meat powder is presented. We find that the onset of the bell can be moved further and further ahead of the presentation of the meat powder. For example, we might have the bell ring for 30 seconds before the US; with enough training we will find that the dog salivates just 30 seconds after the onset of the bell. Such learning is called *delayed conditioning*. We may even let the bell ring for a few seconds, stop it, wait for 20 seconds, and then present the US—conditioning requires still more trials, but is attainable. This is called *trace conditioning*. If we were very persevering, we might even set up *temporal conditioning*, in which the dog is fed periodically on a short time cycle and the CS is the time lapse itself. Our conditioned dog would salivate periodically like a short term alarm clock.

A third discovery might occur accidentally: when a buzzer was inadvertently pressed, or a glass fell off a shelf or some other noise intruded in the experimental situation, the conditioned animal started salivating. Exploring this systematically, we would find whole classes of stimuli which could be substituted with greater or less success for the original CS, the bell. This is called *stimulus generalization*. In the main, the more alike two stimuli are, the greater is the likelihood that they will function for each other. If we originally condition to a tone, say middle C, we find that, as we move away from C up or down the scale, the conditioned response decreases. In our example we would expect the most salivation to C itself, the next most to B and D, less to A and E, etc.

If we proceed with the generalization experiments, but always pair the US with tone C and never with tone A, we can discover a related phenomenon. Soon tone A loses its power to elicit the conditioned response and it is said that *stimulus discrimination* has taken place. In effect, we have systematically cut down the gradient of stimulus generalization. By this technique we can discover the limits of discrimination of which the organism is capable.

This 'damping out' of a response suggests still another question. What happens in general when the CS is no longer followed by the US? If we tried this in our example, ringing the bell repeatedly but never following it with the meat powder, we would note that the magnitude of the response decreased over successive trials and finally disappeared altogether. The response is said to have been *extinguished*. At this point we might naively assume that our experiment was at an end and the dog was now unconditioned, but if we happened on some subsequent day to bring the dog into the laboratory and again rang the bell, we would find that the conditioned response was still observable, reduced in magnitude but still there. If we extinguished the response again (in fewer trials this time), let a day elapse and again brought the dog into the laboratory, we would still find some residual of the conditioned response. This apparently mysterious revitalization of an extinguished response is called *spontaneous recovery* and indicates a need to postulate something other than 'forgetting' to account for the decline in responses which we observed in the extinction trials. Most psychologists prefer to treat this as a case of 'learning-not-to-respond' or *inhibition*.

In this model we may measure learning in a variety of ways. We may take the occurrence of a response or the frequency of occurrence as an index of learning. Alternatively, we may measure the amplitude or magnitude of the response, or the resistance of a response to extinction as other indices of strength. Depending on the response in question, one measure may be more appropriate than another. It should be noted, however, that in many special cases the indices may not be in perfect agreement and it may be important to specify exactly what aspect of behavior is being considered.

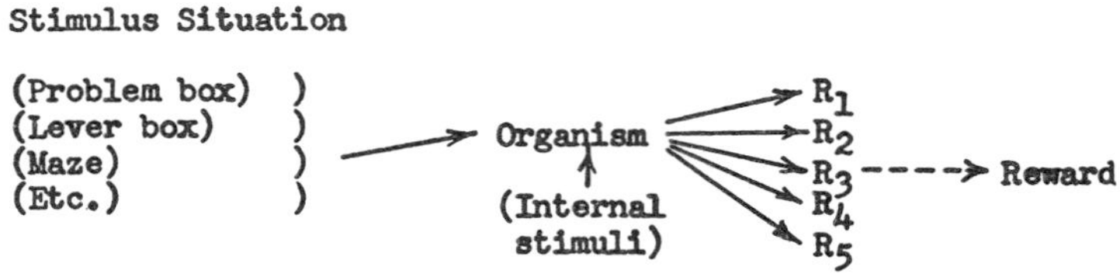

Stimulus Situation

Figure 6

2.2.1.2. *Instrumental learning.* The second model considered here is markedly different (at least phenotypically) from the first. It has been called variously 'trial and error' learning, 'operant,' and 'instrumental' conditioning and descends most directly perhaps from the work of Thorndike. While instrumental conditioning does not readily lend itself to neat diagramming, it can perhaps be roughly portrayed as in Figure 6. In this learning model the organism is placed in a situation in which a variety of responses can be made. The organism is usually assumed to be motivated, that is, some state of need (hunger, thirst, etc.) is presumed to exist on the basis of prior knowledge (hours of food deprivation, water deprivation, etc.). A 'correct' response is followed by reward which is appropriate to the need state of the organism. The probability of the re-occurrence of the rewarded response increases with each rewarded trial up to some limit. The response is said to be learned when it occurs with high probability.

When contrasted with classical conditioning, several different features stand out. The first difference is that the response is *emitted*, not *elicited* by an unconditioned stimulus. This is not to say that responses take place without reference to the stimuli present but rather that we cannot specify the configurations of stimuli which lead to the various complex responses. A second, and presumably important, difference is that the response is *instrumental* in obtaining reward. If the correct response does not occur, the organism is not rewarded. This model seems to entail more 'active' learning than classical conditioning. It goes without saying, of course, that the correct response must be in the behavior repertory of the organism prior to conditioning. Finally, motivation ('drive') and reward ('reinforcement') are much more prominent in this model than in the first one. If the organism is well-fed and comfortable, he is more likely to go to sleep than to learn to solve the experimental problem.

A simple example of this model of learning is one made famous by Skinner. Let us assume that we have a simple box with a small lever in one end of it. The apparatus may be so arranged as to cause a pellet of food to drop into the box when the lever is pressed. If we now put a rat which has not been fed for 24 hours into the box we can observe marked changes in his behavior. At first the rat runs around the box, sniffs in the corners, washes his face, rears on his hind legs, scratches at the walls, etc. Sooner or later the rat 'accidentally' pushes the lever and a pellet is discharged into the box. After an interval the rat discovers and eats the pellet. Sometime thereafter he may blunder onto the lever again. If we chart the rat's behavior we discover that after scattered lever presses the time between presses gets much shorter. In an hour or so we may find the rat industriously pressing the lever, eating, pressing the lever, eating, etc., with great speed and regularity. We say that the instrumental response of lever pressing has been learned.

If we manipulate this situation as we did the first one, we find many of the same variables controlling the modification of behavior. Again we might notice that *frequency* is important. Here, however, it is not the frequency of pairing of CS and US but rather the frequency of response and reward occurring. Similarly, we would find *contiguity* or time relations to be important, but it is response-reward contiguity. We would discover again that order is important, the response must precede the reward, and that the longer the interval between the response and the reward, the less learning takes place. Thus, the responses which occur immediately prior to the reward (whether they are relevant or irrelevant) will be strengthened more than those which were considerably in advance of the reward. (To take a different case, this explains why a maze is learned from the back to the front, errors being reduced in the vicinity of the goal box before being reduced in the middle of the maze, etc.) In this model, too, we may demonstrate *extinction* (if we cease giving pellets for lever pressing) and *spontaneous recovery*. If we alter our situation to include a new stimulus (say a small light over the lever), we can train the rat to respond only when the light is on and thus introduce the phenomena of *discrimination* and *generalization* discussed above.

Other variables not noted in the first model are more clearly revealed in the instrumental situation. It becomes apparent, for example, that the reward functions optimally when it is relevant to the need. Giving water to a hungry rat or food to a thirsty rat does not result in rapid learning if any learning at all. The amount of reinforcement likewise plays a role. All other things being equal, the speed of learning tends to increase as the amount of reward is increased. One of the most important phenomena which may be disclosed and studied most clearly and easily in this second model is *secondary reinforcement*. This is the name given to the reinforcing power which a neutral stimulus may acquire by virtue of having been associated with primary reinforcement. If we put a rat into the experimental box without a lever present, we may train him to approach the food box and eat every time the food mechanism clicks. Then we may introduce a lever which will produce the click when pressed, but empty the mechanism so that it provides no food. In this case in spite of the fact that lever pressing is never rewarded by food, the rat will learn to press the lever and will make a good many responses before extinguishing. We must conclude here that the click of the mechanism itself has acquired reinforcing power. In more dramatic and publicized experiments it has been demonstrated that chimpanzees will work for, collect, and hoard poker chips after experience with the chimp-o-mat—a slot machine arrangement in which the poker chips may be traded for food. It seems likely that most human learning is obtained under conditions of secondary reinforcement (money, praise, smiles, approval, etc.), and it seems especially likely that secondary reinforcement plays an important role in language learning.

In this model, as before, we may measure the extent of learning by frequency of response, amplitude, latency, or resistance to extinction. In certain cases we may also be interested in error scores. A word of caution is necessary here, however. Because these situations differ from each other and from the situation in the first model, measures having the same names may require different interpretations. For example, in classical conditioning amplitude might be a positive function of learning (e.g., drops of saliva) while in instrumental conditioning it might be a negative function (e.g., as lever pressing becomes more skilled, it may be executed with less force).

In a rather great oversimplification we might generalize that the first model presents a picture of the conditioning to an arbitrary stimulus of a highly specific, elicitable response, while the second model describes the differentiation and discrimination of a response out of a mass of behavior emitted in response to a complex stimulus field. The first model stresses time and stimulus controls and the second model stresses the role of motivation and reward. It should be remembered, however, that the models are not independent and the phenomena observed in one are observable (with more or less effort) in the other.

2.2.1.3. *Some additional descriptive statements.* While the models given serve excellently as pedagogical devices, they do not, of course, do justice to the wide areas in which learning studies have been carried on. The development of many complex human skills (typewriting, sending and receiving codes, memorizing verbal material—both meaningful and nonsense, etc.) has been carefully studied and described under a staggering variety of conditions. A few of the many findings which may be of relevance to us can be briefly described. They are explicable in terms of the phenomena described above, but may be of special interest as molar phenomena themselves.

A good deal of attention has been devoted by psychologists to *learning curves* (more properly, *performance curves*). In general, such curves are negatively accelerated, that is, large gains are made initially, then smaller and smaller gains until no appreciable improvement is noted. It is likely that most tasks, however, are approached with considerable residues of skill and experience. For a few tasks 'S' curves may be noted, positively accelerated then negatively accelerated. Such tasks appear to be those in which subjects have had little experience (e.g., tight rope walking, juggling, etc.). Perhaps the 'S' curves are the 'true' performance curves and the 'typical' negatively accelerated curves are only those portions which we see because our subjects already have considerable response repertories available to them.

	First Learning	Second Learning	Test
Case 1 Divergent	S_1————R_1	S_1————R_2	S_1————R_1
Case 2 Convergent	S_1————R_1	S_2————R_1	S_1————R_1
Case 3 Unrelated	S_1————R_1	S_2————R_2	S_1————R_1

Figure 7

Work with *skill sequences* has revealed both in the lower animals and in man an extraordinary capacity for eliminating waste motion and executing a highly polished and tremendously rapid series of responses. A brief consideration of the movements made by a skilled typist or piano player is sufficient to demonstrate the high degree of integration of elements into a smooth series which may be attained. It may be further shown that these are actual integrations, not merely a rapid sequencing of discrete responses. While the beginner types 't-h-e,' the skilled typist writes 'the' or larger units such as 'the next meeting' with such speed that she could not be aware (by virtue of the time lag in the nervous system) that the 't' had printed before the 'e' had been struck. This kind of short-circuiting, grouping and executing of serial responses plays an important role in all frequently executed response chains, including language.

Finally, a considerable body of research has been devoted to questions concerning the effects of prior training on subsequent training and vice versa—the problems of facilitation and interference. In general, we may consider here three cases as illustrated in Figure 7.

In the first case we observe a *divergent* structure. To one stimulus, two (or more) responses must be made. If the responses are highly similar, there will be little interference in the second learning and in the test, but if they are quite different (antagonistic) maximum *interference* will result in both places. In the second case a *convergent* structure is found. Here the response will be *facilitated* in both the second learning and the test situation, and the amount of facilitation will be a function of the similarity of the stimuli. In the third case, we can expect little interference beyond that contributed by any interposed activity and little facilitation beyond adaptation to the experimental setting. In general, what is being said here is: making different responses to the same stimulus is more difficult than making the same response to different stimuli. The first situation gives rise to conflicting response tendencies and demands more information about the occasion, while the second situation broadens the occasion for the use of a single response and, hence, requires less information.

2.2.2. *Learning Theories*

Since 'theory' is a somewhat ambiguous word, it seems advisable to outline briefly the conceptual framework which the seminar utilized in its discussion of learning theory.

2.2.2.1. *General nature of psychological theories.* A fully developed scientific theory contains three distinguishable levels. *Level I* contains the relatively raw 'immediately apprehended' sense data (e.g., the speech sounds, the observations of a dial reading, the perceived movements of a rat). All sciences contain this level, but they differ in their selection of events. *Level II* contains the concepts which are the special concerns of the science (e.g., the stimulus, the phoneme, energy) and laws which are summaries of their observed relations or hypotheses predicting relations not yet observed. Such concepts are meaningful only if they are unambiguously related directly or indirectly to Level I events. Such a relation is equivalent to an *operational definition.* Concepts which are not operationally defined, and systems containing many such concepts, are called *meaningless.* The criterion of meaningfulness is related to that of testability since only meaningful concepts can be used in stating testable hypotheses and laws. *Level III* contains a formal mathematical or logical system. All concepts on this hypothetical level are purely formal or logical in contrast to those of Level II, which are 'descriptive' of Level I events. Level III ordinarily consists of statements defining the elements in the hypothetical system, statements defining operations and relations in terms of the elements, and statements of rules of inference to be used in deriving the theorems of the system. The theorems may be regarded as the logical results of the assumed relations in the postulate set. The *interpretation* of this formal system consists of placing its entities and relations into correspondence with the concepts of Level II. Thus, a theorem on Level III leads directly to an hypothesis on Level II by means of translation of terms indicated by the interpretation. In turn, the laws or hypotheses of Level II are summaries of observed or predicted Level I events. Because of these relations between the levels of a theory, the formal system of Level III is said to explain the laws of Level II which, in turn, explain the events of Level I.

A scientist is free to select or develop any mathematical or logical system which he desires to use. The utility of his choice is then determined by examining the correspondence between his model or system and the concepts or empirical data which he observes. Ordinarily, it is desired that the experimental model be *testable* (that it generate meaningful predictions), *reliable* (that it generate consistent predictions), *coherent* (not in conflict with itself), *comprehensive* (that it explain a wide variety of phenomena) and *simple.* Obviously, both comprehensiveness and simplicity are subjective and debatable, but the other requirements are relatively clear.

Theory-building in psychology has not, of course, proceeded self-consciously to develop level by level as our description above might imply. Psychology developed as a branch of philosophy, as did the other sciences, but the weaning was longer than for most. As late as 1900 most psychology departments were subdivisions within philosophy departments; some still are. Along with the mentalistic tradition of the 19th century, psychologists and pseudo-psychologists were prone to 'theorize' by sticking into the organism whatever faculties, aptitudes, instincts, etc., seemed to serve their immediate purpose. There were practically as many intervening 'explanatory' constructs as there were things to be explained. This has been aptly entitled 'junk shop' psychology.

In the early part of the present century there was a general revulsion against this kind of theorizing, typified by the writings of such men as Watson, Kantor, Weiss, and more recently, Skinner. This stress on objectivity paralleled a similar revolution taking place in linguistics through the same period. These men went to the other extreme, the 'empty organism' position. This view held that the psychologist should concentrate on exploring the many functional relations between objectively verifiable S (stimulus) events and objectively verifiable R (response) events, avoiding intervening variables which involve 'going into' the organism. Thus, Skinner is content to study the behavior of the rat in the lever box under various stimulus conditions where the only observations are tracings on a recording drum—the actual movements of the animal itself not even being observed. If all variations in R were in fact predictable from knowledge of the current stimulus field, then this model would be sufficient. It is quite apparent, however, that with S conditions constant, the characteristics of R will still vary as functions of factors like past history (previous learning), individual differences in aptitudes, motivation, personality, and so forth. Facts of this order led Woodworth in the middle 30's, for example, to insert an O in the formula, i.e., S—O—R, where the O refers rather vaguely to gross classes of intervening 'organismic' variables.

Most contemporary learning theorists utilize models which introduce certain terms between the S and R. These terms may be thought of as falling roughly into two classes: *first*, terms which imply nothing about the internal mechanics of the organism but act as convenient summary terms, for example, 'drive' defined only in terms of hours since last feeding, 'habit' defined in terms of response probabilities or histories, etc.; and *second*, terms which are intended to describe internal states or activities, such as 'drive' defined in terms of blood chemistry, neural and muscular activity, 'habit' defined in terms of neural connections and strengths, etc. Most systems use both types of concepts and attempt to avoid the 'junk shop' kind of psychology by introducing such terms only when they are unavoidable and by anchoring these variables firmly to antecedent (S) and subsequent (R) observable conditions.

At present, the models of learning theory are sets of Level II concepts and laws —some of which are little better than plausible hypotheses. There have been no acceptable attempts to develop or apply formal Level III systems except on a very limited basis.

2.2.2.2. *Four current theories of learning.* While it is obviously impossible to develop in detail even one theory of learning in the space available here, an attempt will be made to outline, and present the contrasts between, four current theories which have great influence at the present time. These are the theories of Guthrie, Tolman, Skinner, and Hull. The interested reader is referred to the more adequate accounts of these and other systems given in the list of references following this section.

Guthrie's Association Theory

Of the theories to be considered here, perhaps the system which is simplest in appearance is that of E. R. Guthrie. This system, which is one of the early off-shoots of Watsonian Behaviorism, reduces all learning to a simple associative rule: *any combination or totality of stimuli which has accompanied a movement will be followed by that movement when the combination occurs again.* Complete learning thus occurs on the first occasion on which a stimulus is paired with a response.

At first glance this simple association rule may seem to be in direct disagreement with the phenomena discussed previously, but this is not at all the case. Guthrie is concerned with stimuli and responses at a 'molecular' level. Viewed in minute detail, no total stimulus pattern is ever exactly like another. Even if all external stimuli were rigidly controlled, changes are taking place within the organism (it is getting hungrier, thirstier, older, weaker, etc.; it is tense, relaxed, asleep, etc.; ad infinitum). Similarly, no two movements are ever exactly alike. They differ in the precise musculature involved, the state of the musculature, etc. The consequences of this infinite shading and change in both stimuli and responses is that learning appears to increase gradually through practice and time as more and more of the total possible stimuli and patterns of stimuli become associated with more and more of the relevant responses or muscle actions.

Generalization is taken care of by thinking of similar gross stimuli as actually consisting of overlapping pools of minute stimuli. As the stimuli become more dissimilar, the pools of stimuli overlap less and less until finally there are too few common elements to mediate the appropriate response. In order to handle *temporal delays and sequences*, Guthrie makes extensive use of movement-produced-stimulation as the actual stimulus field to which the responses are associated. *Motivation and reward* have no primary status in Guthrie's system. They operate only as they affect the central principle. Motivation is important in that it determines and intensifies sets of movements which then are available for associative connections. It supplies members to both the stimulus and response pools. Reward is important in that it terminates a class of movements and changes the stimulus situation— removing the organism, so-to-speak, from the situation before other movements can be associated with the stimuli. Thus, reward acts to prevent associations being formed with incompatible responses; it has no 'positive' function. *Extinction* occurs, according to Guthrie, when the 'correct' response no longer terminates the situation. Other movements follow and in turn are associated with the stimuli. In this manner on successive trials more and more stimuli are related to other movements and responses until finally the 'correct' response disappears. With ever changing stimulus pools, *competing responses* which are close to the same strength will occur in various alternations, depending on the exact number of stimulus-movement associations present, until one of them gains a clear superiority.

It may be seen even in this brief presentation that Guthrie's theory deals with inferred elements of external and internal stimuli and inferred elements of responses. If everything is exactly the same, the organism will do exactly as it did the previous time. If it does not, then it may be argued that things really were not all the same. This amounts to saying that critical tests of the theory are difficult, if not impossible, to devise. The theory is facile in explanation but weak in prediction; it can be used to explain almost any (even directly opposite) outcomes.

Its generality and simplicity are advantages, but it leaves much to be desired in the way of precision, reliability, and testability.

Tolman's Sign-Gestalt Theory

A sharp contrast to Guthrie's theory both as to sources and complexity is the sign-gestalt theory of E. C. Tolman. Drawing from virtually all psychology, from Watson's behaviorism on one side to Lewin's gestalt psychology on the other, Tolman builds a purposive, behavioristic theory of learning. The theory breaks sharply with the association of elemental stimuli and elemental movements and attempts to deal with goal-directed, whole acts of the organism. The level of description employed is molar, showing the relation of the organism to the goal. Most significantly perhaps, Tolman insists that what is learned is not movements or responses but 'sign-significate expectations.' The organism learns meanings and 'what-leads-to-what' relationships. The relationship between a sign and its significate (an early stimulus and a later stimulus) is established in accord with the usual contiguity rule of association, and this relation is the 'expectation.' Thus, to Tolman, classical conditioning may be interpreted by saying that the buzzer comes to mean food-in-the-mouth and the salivation is a consequence of this meaning or expectancy.

This system stresses contiguity of stimuli in building up expectations. The closer in time two stimuli occur the greater the likelihood that an expectation will be set up. Practice plays a role in confirming and strengthening expectations. The more often S_2 follows S_1 the higher is the expectancy. It may be seen that expectancy can be viewed as a cognition of the probability that a given event will follow another. What increases, then, is not response potentials or habits but cognitions, which may be acted on in a variety of ways depending on the cumulative past experiences of the organism with objects and situations in its environment. This gives Tolman's system flexibility and allows him to predict the striking changes which are sometimes observed in the behavior of organisms when the learning situation is radically changed (such as providing alternative routes to a goal, changing the goal object, etc.).

Generalization is regarded as the result of stimulus sign-equivalence. Alterations in stimuli only affect performance by changing the expectancies of the organism. *Reward and motivation* have no direct effect upon *learning* in this system but affect *performance*, which is regarded as clearly different from learning. Thus, a rat may 'know' how to run a maze (i.e., he may know the sign-significate relationships of all of the pathways) but not demonstrate this in performance until he is rewarded for it, at which time his 'knowledge' should suddenly become evident. Reward does, of course, enter in as a stimulus significate whose presence or absence confirms or weakens an expectation. Motivation enters in as a sensitizer or emphasizer of certain significates or sign-significate relations which have been associated with it. *Extinction* is treated as a progressive disconfirmation of expectancies which cumulatively couples with the pattern of preceding situations to eliminate the learned performance. *Spontaneous recovery* takes place because the pattern of preceding situations is changed and the expectancy is still at some strength. When alternative responses are available, the pattern of behavior will ensue which is in accord with the strongest expectancy, and when that expectancy is disconfirmed the next strongest will control behavior and so on.

Tolman also points out that individual differences in organisms (heredity, age, training, special physical conditions) act to define particular behaviors on any occasion. He is thus one of the few learning theorists to comment on capacity laws, but even he has done little with them. In general, Tolman's position is a very broad one. He recognizes levels of learning and lately has come to suggest that there may be several kinds of learning. His system has stimulated much research, especially in the area of cognition. He has been criticized for vagueness and non-quantitativeness, but in part this is true of all of these theories.

Skinner's Descriptive Account

B. F. Skinner himself would deny that his approach is a theory or that psychology needs theories. He prefers, as indicated above, to collect and classify phenomena on Level II, using the most rigorous and simple descriptive categories he can develop, toward the end of systematizing knowledge about the basic phenomena of learning. The first major difference between Skinner and the other theorists discussed here is that he regards the two paradigms, conditioning and instrumental learning, as representing different kinds of learning.

Pavlovian conditioning is regarded as a highly specialized form of learning which plays little part in most human behavior. Skinner terms it *respondent* conditioning, emphasizing that it utilizes a response which can be *elicited* by a specific stimulus. The laws of respondent conditioning state (1) that contiguity of stimulation is the condition for increasing the strength of the CS-R relation and (2) that the exercise of the CS-R without the US results in decreased strength. These laws are summary descriptive statements with little elaboration, and in general Skinner has little concern with this kind of learning.

In instrumental conditioning stimulus conditions sufficient to elicit the behavior cannot be specified and are in fact irrelevant to the understanding of this behavior. The important aspect in this model is that responses are *emitted* and that they generate consequences. Skinner calls this *operant* behavior, stressing the role of the response. He is most concerned with the laws of this model and is convinced that most human behavior (including specifically language behavior) is dependent on this kind of learning. The basic laws of operant conditioning state that (1) if an operant is followed by the presentation of a reinforcing stimulus, its strength is increased and (2) if an operant is not followed by a reinforcing stimulus, its strength is decreased. In most situations an operant does become related to the stimulus field. It may come to occur, for example, only in the presence or absence of given stimuli. It is then termed a *discriminated operant*, but it is still not elicited. The stimulus conditions merely furnish the occasion for the appearance of the operant.

Skinner's system is somewhat like Tolman's in that it tends to deal with acts (not specific muscle movements) but unlike it in that it stresses the role of reinforcement. The all-important contiguity is that of the response and the reward, and one of the major determinants of the strength of an operant is the number of times the response-reward pairing occurs. These pairings summate in a non-linear but increasing fashion to increase the probability of occurrence or rate of occurrence of the operant.

Skinner introduces the concept of a reflex reserve[9] which may be defined loosely as the amount of 'available activity' of a given sort which the organism is

[9] This concept was used in *Behavior of organisms* but has been dropped in later work.

capable of emitting. Rewarding an operant increases the size of the reserve and non-reward decreases it. The rate of responding at any given moment is the function of the size of the reserve. Responses are emitted as some proportion of the total reserve remaining.

The size of the reserve is not a simple function of the number of reinforcements, however. Skinner has found that periodic reinforcement (one rewarded response every few minutes), aperiodic reinforcement (rewards on a random time schedule), fixed ratio reinforcement (reward every n^{th} response), etc., generate very great reserves. His theory lays considerable stress on the important role played by secondary reinforcement (the discriminatory stimuli), and he finds this quite useful in discussing language behavior.

The proportionality which exists between the reserve and the rate of responding may be altered by differing 'states' of the organism. 'States' are carefully defined intervening variables such as drive, emotion, etc. The hypothetical term 'state' is introduced when it can be shown that several operations affect several reflexes in a similar fashion. States are defined by the operations and their effects and imply no physiological correlates. (It is this aspect of the system which has led to its being labeled as an 'empty organism' approach.) Certain states increase the proportionality; others decrease it, but none of them are said to change the size of the reserve. As an example, in a state of high drive a rapid rate of responding would be established and, if the operant were not rewarded, rapid extinction would take place; in a state of low drive the rate of response would be low and extinction slow. Presumably, the same number of responses would be made in either case.

Skinner has studied stimulus discrimination and response differentiation extensively. When reward is made experimentally dependent on stimulus conditions, discrimination takes place. When it is dependent on response characteristics, differentiation of response takes place. Skinner's view is roughly one of mass behavior in a context of generalized stimuli, both becoming progressively more defined as the situation demands it. The problem, as he sees it, is not explaining generalization but rather the lack of it and, similarly, not response variability but lack of it. This aspect of his approach has some great advantages in dealing with progressively changing behaviors. In situations in which alternative responses are available, the response of highest strength has the greatest probability of occurrence. Alternative responses become available as earlier responses are weakened.

Skinner's system has been criticized on the grounds of its narrowness, its concern with only the lever box situation as an experimental base, and its use of the reflex reserve concept. It is, however, basically an empirical, descriptive approach and in the main there can be little argument with its basic laws. It has been valuable and stimulating in its somewhat different analysis of the learning process and in the attention it has directed towards special facets of learning phenomena.

Hull's Deductive System

The most ambitious attempt to develop a rigorous, formal learning theory is unquestionably that of C. L. Hull. This system consists of a basic set of postulates from which, it is hoped, the laws of learning may be deduced in clear and quantitative form. The system stems most directly from Watsonian behaviorism and Thorndike's connectionism.

At the center of the Hullian system are two notions: habit strength and drive reduction. *Habit* is a tendency for a given stimulus discharge in the nervous system to evoke a given response. It is what is learned. *Drive reduction* is the diminution of the neural state accompanying a need. It is the condition which effects learning; it is reinforcement. It is apparent that Hull does not hesitate, as some other theorists discussed here, to 'get inside' the organism and to make positive claims about the nature of physiological events. It should be kept in mind, however, that he anchors these variables (in their role as constructs) to observable events.

Step by step Hull's postulates describe the process of learning as follows:

Stimuli impinge on the organism and generate neural activity which persists for some time before disappearing (P-1).[10] Complex stimuli interact in the nervous system to produce modified stimulus patterns (P-2). Organisms have innate general responses which are set in action by needs. These are not random responses but are selectively sensitized responses which have relatively high probabilities of terminating the specific need (e.g., withdrawal from pain, general movement and locomotion when hungry, etc.) (P-3). When a stimulus trace and a response occur in close contiguity and, at the same time, need is reduced, an increment is added to the habit strength of the particular stimulus-response pair (P-4). This constitutes learning.

Stimuli which are similar evoke the same responses, and the amount of generalization is a function of the difference between the stimuli in terms of 'just noticeable differences' (a commonly used form of measurement in psychology of sensation) (P-5). Drives have stimulus properties and the intensity of a drive stimulus increases with intensity of the drive (P-6). Reaction potential is a product of habit strength and drive (P-7), but does not in itself lead directly to responding. Reaction potential to be effective must be greater than the resistances to response, reactive inhibition (similar to fatigue), conditioned inhibition (learned nonresponding) and the oscillating inhibitory potential associated with the reaction potential (P-8, 9, 10). If the momentary effective reaction potential is above the reaction threshold and stronger than competing responses, the response will occur (P-11). The remaining postulates discuss response measurement and incompatible responses.

Since Hull's system embraces both of the paradigms given above and is at the same time a reinforcement theory, his concern with contiguity is two-fold. He is concerned with the contiguity of the stimulus and the response and the response and reward. Learning is a function of the time lapse between the stimulus and the response according to a rather steep gradient and also a function of the time lapse between the response and the reward according to a gradient of reinforcement. This gradient of reinforcement is believed to be quite short. The gradient of reinforcement, however, can in effect be lengthened into a goal gradient. Stimuli within the range of the gradient of reinforcement acquire secondary reinforcing power and develop reinforcement gradients of their own. These small overlapping gradients summate to produce a major gradient extending considerable distances in space and time from the primary reinforcement itself. This complex treatment of contiguity proves to be a very useful tool in discussing many learning situations.

Habits are formed and increase in strength as a function of the number of reinforcements and the amount of need reduction. Since Hull specifies his position on generalization, it is easy to see how the summation can take place even though

---

[10] This is the postulate number, here Postulate 1. The postulates themselves are quite lengthy and detailed. The sentences here are crude approximations.

exact conditions are not reproduced. One interesting facet of Hull's theory is that habits are never 'unlearned.' Habit strength can only increase or remain the same since it is a function only of rewarded trials. Unrewarded trials do decrease responses, however, because they lead to increased reactive and conditioned inhibition. A response which had been 'completely learned' and 'completely extinguished' would be represented here by maximum habit strength and maximum conditioned inhibition with the net result that it would not appear. Drive and drive reduction are also obviously important in this system. Drive has an activational role through its multiplicative relation with habit strength and in addition exercises a stimulus role. Emphasis of this stimulus role permits Hull to explain experiments which otherwise would be classed as cognitions and has led to interesting work on generalization gradients and discriminative characteristics of drives.

At every step Hull attempts to state at least tentatively the nature of the mathematical functions relating his constructs to each other and to the observable antecedent and subsequent conditions. He also derives corollaries or secondary principles which amplify the basic principles. Hull's position is that all behavior should be deducible from the system. He urges that such attempts be made and, when confirmation is not obtained, the postulate set be appropriately revised. He (as indeed all other theorists) regards the system as a self-correcting one, continuously predicting, verifying, and altering until it is complete.

Hull's system has been criticized for a variety of reasons—its excursions into the nervous system, its insistence upon reinforcement as a necessary condition for all learning, its lack of adequate definition of response, its peculiar mixture of levels in postulates, etc. In the main, however, it has proved to be quite durable. The system has been tremendously successful in stimulating research and providing a frame of reference for new material. It has been, and is being, widely extended to applications in social psychology, personality, and language behavior.

All of the theories outlined above are part of the behavioristic and functionalist tradition. As such they are primarily concerned with the phenomena of learning as manifested in overt behavior and, with the partial exception of Tolman, they all use 'mechanistic' terms in describing their concepts. Some critics believe that these theorists have not sufficiently considered physiological knowledge in developing their concepts. A seemingly larger group of critics object to the apparently 'mechanistic' and 'atomistic' nature of these concepts and feel that such concepts cannot do justice to the full range of human and animal behavior. While such criticism has been expressed in many diverse ways, much of the basis for such objections may be found in the work of the gestalt psychologists, whose name comes from the emphasis they have placed on 'wholes' and 'organizing principles.' Because the primary concern of this group has been the study of perception and problem solving rather than learning, a summary of their theorizing has not been included in this section. (A brief discussion of some of the gestalt phenomena in perception may be found in section 3.1. of this report.)

2.2.3. *Bibliography*

1. Guthrie, E. R., 1935, *The psychology of learning*, New York.
    A presentation of Guthrie's theory along with applications to many everyday behavioral situations. Highly readable.
2. Hilgard, E. R., 1948, *Theories of learning*, New York.
    A fairly recent and comprehensive survey and evaluation of various contemporary conceptions of learning, including gestalt and behavioristic theories.
3. Hilgard, E. R. and D. G. Marquis, 1940, *Conditioning and learning*, New York.
    A more advanced and tightly argued analysis of the fundamental concepts and phenomena of learning. One of the most important critical books in the field.
4. Hull, C. L., 1945, *Principles of behavior*, New York.
    A systematic presentation of Hull's learning postulates and their application to phenomena. Although more recent revisions have appeared, this is probably the best comprehensive statement.
5. Koffka, K., 1935, *Principles of gestalt psychology*, New York.
    Probably the most detailed and extensive presentation of the gestalt point of view, including materials on perception and learning.
6. Lewin, K., 1936, *Principles of topological psychology*, New York.
    Behavior of organisms treated in terms of field theory.
7. McGeoch, J. A. and A. L. Irion, 1952, *The psychology of human learning*, New York.
    An extensive coverage of the facts and theories of learning as applied particularly to human behavior.
8. Miller, N. E., 1951, Learnable drives and rewards, in *Handbook of experimental psychology* (Ed., Stevens), New York.
    A penetrating analysis of the nature and development of secondary motivation and reward mechanisms, with presentation of experimental findings.
9. Miller, N. E. and J. Dollard, 1941, *Social learning and imitation*, New Haven.
    An application of Hull-type learning theory to a variety of social problems. Provides a very readable introduction.
10. Mowrer, O. H., 1950, *Learning theory and personality dynamics*, New York.
    A collection of Mowrer's best papers relating learning theory to personality dynamics. Also presents Mowrer's two-factor theory of learning.
11. National Society for the Study of Education, 1942, *The psychology of learning*, 41st Yearbook, Part II.
    Presents in careful, systematic form several important summaries of contemporary theories as written by their sponsors.
12. Osgood, C. E., 1953, *Method and theory in experimental psychology*, New York.
    A graduate text in experimental psychology, including sections on sensory processes, perception, learning, and symbolic processes. Includes critical analyses of contemporary learning theories and a presentation of the author's mediation hypothesis.
13. Skinner, B. F., 1938, *The behavior of organisms*, New York.
    The most complete presentation of Skinner's conception of learning and data derived from his type of instrumental situation. Important for its methodological contributions as well as for its viewpoint.
14. Spence, K. W., 1951, Theoretical interpretations of learning, in *Handbook of experimental psychology* (Ed., Stevens), New York.
    A critical comparative evaluation of contemporary theories of learning by one of the most active theorists and investigators on the scene today.
15. Tolman, E. C., 1932, *Purposive behavior in animals and men*, New York.
    A systematic presentation of Tolman's early views along with results of numerous experiments. A classic in the field, and a book which has had great influence upon contemporary psychology.
16. Wertheimer, M., 1945, *Productive thinking*, New York.

A delightful little book, published posthumously, by one of the founders of the gestalt movement. It presents Wertheimer's insightful analysis of the process of insight and problem-solving in humans.

2.3. The Information Theory Approach[11]

Strictly speaking, the term *information theory* is a misnomer. As the following discussion will indicate, it is not a theory of 'information,' *per se*, but of information transmission, and then only in situations where a message input may be said to contain 'information' in something like the usual sense of the word. It is concerned with characterizing the entropy or uncertainty of sequences of events. It was with such considerations in mind that it was suggested[12] that the label *information theory* be replaced by *theory of signal transmission*. At any rate, information theory is essentially an extension of the general mathematical theory of probability which has provided some useful descriptive measures in several areas of scientific research. Therefore, it is necessary to be acquainted with some of the fundamentals of the concept of probability and probability theory in order to properly understand information theory.

2.3.1. *Probability Theory*

Despite the seeming simplicity of the concept of probability, there has been much controversy among mathematicians and logicians over its definition. The reader interested in the details of this controversy, as well as the development of a mathematical theory of probability from a postulational system, may be referred to works by Nagel (14) and Feller (4), listed in the references appended hereto. There is general agreement, however, that for most practical and theoretical purposes the probability of an event may be defined as the limit of the relative frequency of its occurrence. In mathematical symbolism,

$$p'(i) = \lim_{n \to \infty} \frac{f(i)}{n},$$

where $p'(i)$ is the 'true' probability of event i, $\lim_{n \to \infty}$ symbolizes the limit of the following expression as n becomes indefinitely large, n is the number of events, $f(i)$ is the frequency of occurrence of event i. In other words, if we have n events, and a particular class of event, symbolized i, occurs $f(i)$ times, the true probability of event i is the value towards which the ratio of $f(i)$ to n tends as we allow n to become indefinitely large.

In practice, of course, we cannot determine probability in this fashion since we can never have an indefinitely large (i.e., infinite) number of events. Therefore, we simply compute

$$p(i) = \frac{f(i)}{n}$$

[11] Kellogg Wilson.

[12] By Y. Bar-Hillel, in a talk at Massachusetts Institute of Technology, 1952.

for some reasonably large but finite value of n. In this case $p\ (i)$ may be called an empirical estimate of the true probability. If $p(i)$ tends to become nearer and nearer to $p'(i)$ as n increases, then we say that the process generating our sequences of n events is a *stochastic process*. For example, if we spin a fair roulette wheel we should find that the probability of any number tends to become closer to 1/38 as n, the number of spins or trials, increases. This would be a stochastic process. Now suppose that there is a magnet under the wheel that tends to attract the ball to the O or OO position and which is turned off and on randomly. In this case, we would find that the probabilities of O and OO would tend to decrease toward 1/38 when the magnet is off and increase away from 1/38 when the magnet is on. This would not be a stochastic process since the estimates of probabilities would not converge toward any particular value. However, if the magnet were left on constantly we would most likely find that our probability estimates would converge to some values greater than 1/38 for O and OO and less than 1/38 for the remaining events and we would again have a stochastic process. Since some such severe fluctuation in the condition of sam-

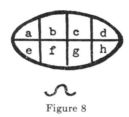

Figure 8

pling is required to make a process non-stochastic, we may generally assume that we are dealing with stochastic processes.

In scientific work we choose certain features of our empirical events as a basis for classification and disregard others. In this manner we create *sets* or *classes* of events (e.g., a 'response,' which may include all the minute variants of a bar-pressing response, or a 'phoneme,' which is a class of allophones). Such sets are *sub-sets* of the class of all events. We will here consider only events which may fall in only a finite number of classes or sets, since such discrete classes are nearly always used in psychology and in linguistics. We will use the symbol Ω to refer to the class of all events, which is divided into a finite number of sub-classes or sub-sets as in Figure 8. The sub-classes in Figure 8 are mutually exclusive; that is, no event may fall in more than one sub-class, and therefore no two sub-classes have any events in common. We will use S to refer to the class of all such sub-sets. We will let i refer to any of the sets in S and $p(i)$ to the probability of an event being in set i. When Ω and S are defined, and $p(i)$ determined (or estimated) for each set in S, we have defined a *probability space*. Before we employ probability or information theory in dealing with empirical data, we should make sure that we have a completely defined probability space.

We can now introduce the notions of joint probability, conditional probability, and independence which are so crucial to information theory. If we have a set of simultaneous or successive events, each of which may fall into one of the classes in the probability space, it is often useful to consider the probability of a joint occurrence of events. The *joint probability*, $p(i, j)$, of events in classes i and j is the probability of their joint occurrence, that is, the relative frequency of a joint event involving both i and j in a large number (or an indefinitely large number) of joint events. The *conditional probability*, $p_i(j)$, of class j is the probability of j when it is given that an event in class i had also occurred; thus, it is the relative frequency of j in the class of all joint events involving i. In mathematical symbolism,

$$p_i(j) = \frac{p(i, j)}{p(i)},$$

and therefore $p(i, j) = p(i) \cdot p_i(j)$. We say that classes i and j are independent if and only if the probability of an event being in class j is unaffected by its being in class i; i.e., if $p(j) = p_i(j)$, then i and j are independent. If i and j are independent, then $p(i, j) = p(i) \cdot p(j)$, and this formula, or an extension of it, $p(i, j, \cdots, s) = p(i)p(j) \cdots p(s)$, may be used to compute the joint probability of a set of independent events.

Languages appear to be structured so that in a sequence of language events, subsequent events are rarely independent of antecedent events, and not all the possible sequences occur. The so-called Markov process is appropriate as a model for representing such sequences. Suppose, for example, that A, B, C, D, and E represent all possible events in a set of sequences. Suppose also that the conditional probabilities of these events are as represented in Figure 9. O represents the state of the system while at its starting point and is merely a convention which indicates the point at which sequential dependency begins and ends; in this example, sequential dependency begins when A or B occurs and ends whenever C, D, or E occurs. The arrows indicate the sequential order of the alternative events and the figures within the arrows indicate the conditional probabilities of the subsequent events. The complete set of sequences which may be generated in this example and their probabilities are as follows:

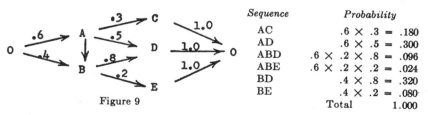

	Sequence	Probability			
	AC		.6 × .3	=	.180
	AD		.6 × .5	=	.300
	ABD	.6 × .2 × .8		=	.096
	ABE	.6 × .2 × .2		=	.024
	BD		.4 × .8	=	.320
	BE		.4 × .2	=	.080

Figure 9

Total   1.000

The probability of each sequence is the product of the conditional probabilities of each event in the sequence, and may also be said to be the joint probability of the events in the sequence. The sum of these probabilities equals unity. In general, a Markov process may be used to represent any set of sequences of events such that the probabilities of subsequent events are dependent on particular antecedent events.

2.3.2. Basic Concepts of Information Theory

In the subsequent portions of this presentation, we will be concerned with probability spaces for which Ω (the class of all events) is a restricted class of physical events—e.g., sounds of speech, energy changes which serve as stimulus inputs. S (the class of all sub-sets of events) for these probability spaces is some 'convenient' or 'suitable' ordering of these events into a finite number of sub-classes. Henceforth, we shall refer to the entire set of events in Ω as a *system* and each of the sub-classes of events in S will be referred to as a *state* of the system.

Comparable systems may differ in 'randomness' due to differences in the probabilities of their states or in the degree to which their states are dependent on prior states. The measures of information theory are extensions of the entropy measures of thermodynamics and measure the degree of entropy—i.e., 'randomness'—of a system's states. A system possesses maximum entropy when its states are equiprobable and independent of previous states—uncertainty is maximal and predictions can be no better than chance. For example, consider a system consisting of a tossed coin which has two states, H (heads) and T (tails): if the coin is 'fair,' and $p(\text{H}) = p(\text{T}) = .5$, the system has maximal entropy and we are maximally uncertain of the outcome of each toss. The entropy of a system is decreased when the probability of some of its states is greater than others—we are less uncertain about what states will occur and predictions can be better than chance. If our coin is 'biased,' and $p(\text{H}) = .75$ and $p(\text{T}) = .25$, the system possesses less than maximal entropy and we are less uncertain about the outcome. Entropy can also be reduced by making subsequent events dependent upon antecedent events, which will be discussed in greater detail at a later point.

The term *information* in information theory is identified with the concept of entropy and so has a meaning that differs somewhat from ordinary usage. The term is not entirely unjustified since a system with little entropy has highly predictable states and the occurrence of any particular state is therefore not very 'informative.' The use of the term, information, may also be justified in another manner. The unit of entropy measure, the *bit*, may be defined as the amount of information needed to specify one of two classes of equally probable events. In the case of our 'fair' coin, H and T constitute two equiprobable classes of events so that we would need only one bit of information to determine if H or T has occurred. Now let us consider a system consisting of two such coins whose states are independent. Here, we would require one bit of information to specify the state of each coin so that two bits of information would be required to specify the state of the total system (i.e., the particular combination of positions, HH, HT, TH, TT, assumed by the coins).

If our system consists of m fair and independent coins, then we would require

m bits of information to specify the state of the total system. Since such a system can assume $k = 2^m$ states, the amount of information needed to specify the state of the system, is $\log_2 k$.[13] Since more information is required to specify the state of a system as the number of states of the system increases, assuming that the states of the system are equiprobable and the states of sub-systems are independent, it is apparent that this amount of information grows with our uncertainty of predicting states of the system. Hence, amount of information may be regarded as equal to the entropy of the system. If a system has k states, its maximal entropy, H_{max}, is given by the equation: $H_{max} = \log_2 k$. If the states of a system can be divided into m pairs of subclasses, then it is apparent that the system has maximal entropy when these subclasses are independent and equiprobable and the amount of this entropy may be determined by the same reasoning as was applied above to the system consisting of m coins. If k is not an integral power of 2, then the applicability of the argument above is not obvious but it suffices to say that H_{max} would then be the average amount of information needed to specify the state of the system if these states *were* equiprobable and the subsystems *were* independent. More rigorous mathematical treatments of such considerations may be found in Fano (3) and Shannon (18).

Let i be any event, or state of a system, in the set of events, I, and let $p(i)$ be its probability. If $p(i)$ equals a particular value, say $1/a$, we can regard this statement as equivalent to stating that i falls into one of a equiprobable classes. Hence, there will be $\log_2 a$ bits of information needed to specify i. Let $h(i)$ be this amount of information, so $h(i) = \log_2 a = \log_2 [1/p(i)] = -\log_2 p(i)$. We may express the average, $\bar{X}$, of a sample of numbers, as

$$\bar{X} = \sum_x x \frac{f(x)}{n},$$

where x is the numerical value of any class of members in the sample, $f(x)$ is the frequency of that class, and n is the sample size. In other words, the average

---

[13] A logarithm (abbreviated 'log') is most simply defined as an exponent. In mathematical symbolism: if $x^y = z$, then $\log x^z = y$, by definition, and x is the *base* of the logarithm. A base of 2 is most widely used in information theory. The examples below, using logs to the base 2, may make the concept of a logarithm clearer.

$2^0 = 1$; therefore, $\log_2 1 = 0$ $2^3 = 8$; therefore, $\log_2 8 = 3$
$2^1 = 2$; therefore, $\log_2 2 = 1$ $2^4 = 16$; therefore, $\log_2 16 = 4$
$2^2 = 4$; therefore, $\log_2 4 = 2$ $2^5 = 32$; therefore, $\log_2 32 = 5$

Logs of numbers which are not integral powers of 2 can be readily obtained from a table of base 2 logs such as that of Dolansky (2). Since logs to any base are proportional to logs to any other base, we may convert base 10 logs to base 2 logs by the formula $\log_2 x = (1/\log_{10} 2) \log_{10} x = 3.3219 \log_{10} x$.

Logs to any base have the properties indicated in the three equations below. The base is not indicated but is assumed to be the same in all cases:

$$\log (xy) = \log x + \log y;$$
$$\log (x/y) = \log x - \log y;$$
$$\log x^y = y \log x.$$

(or arithmetical mean) is the sum (Σ) of the values found in the sample, each weighted by its proportional frequency. Now, we have previously defined our probability estimate as

$$p(x) = \frac{f(x)}{n},$$

so that

$$\bar{X} = \sum_x x\,p(x).$$

We may define the entropy of a system $H(I)$, with a set of states, I, as the average amount of entropy associated with its states. Thus,

$$H(I) = \sum_i h(i)\,p(i)$$
$$= -\sum_i p(i)\,\log_2 p(i).$$

The second form of this equation is the expression usually given as the measure of the entropy of a system.

The measure, $H(I)$, has the following characteristics, all of which are in keeping with our intuitive feelings about the notion of entropy or uncertainty:

(a) If one $p(i) = 1$ and all others are zero, then $H(I) = 0$. In other words, if one state always occurs, then the behavior of our system is completely predictable and its entropy is zero.

(b) If a system consists of k independent sub-systems, each with entropy $H(I)$, then the entropy of the total system is $k\,H(I)$. This theorem follows from the same sort of argument that was applied to the system consisting of k coins. This characteristic is one of the justifications for using a logarithmic measure.

(c) If a system has m equiprobable states, then $H(I) = H_{max} = \log_2 m$. It is apparent that $H(I)$ will approach H_{max} as the set of $p(i)$ approaches equiprobability.

(d) If a system has m equiprobable states, then $H(I)$ increases when m increases. Because of this last characteristic, it is desirable to have a measure which may be used to compare systems with different numbers of states. This measure, $H_{rel}(I)$, relative entropy, is

$$H_{rel}(I) = \frac{H(I)}{H_{max}} = \frac{H(I)}{\log_2 m}.$$

$H_{rel}(I)$ is zero when $H(I)$ is zero and equals one when $H(I)$ equals H_{max}.

A more complex situation is that in which we deal with associated pairs of events. In applications of information theory these pairs of events fall into two main classes: (a) Pairs of events in antecedent (input) and subsequent (output) systems, e.g., the stimulus and the response of behavioristic psychology, the speech sound and the hearer's interpretation; (b) pairs of antecedent and subsequent events in the same system, e.g., sequences of responses, sequences of phonemes or morphemes. The main value of information theory to linguistic and psycholinguistic problems lies in the application of entropy measures suitable for such situations. In general, these measures indicate how much effect the pattern of antecedent events has on the occurrence of subsequent events, and hence they indicate the degree to which sequences of such events are structured (i.e., non-random).

Let I be a set of antecedent or input states and let J be a set of subsequent or output states and let i and j, respectively, be any member of these sets. We may compute $H(I)$ and $H(J)$ for these sets as shown above. Let I, J be a set of associated pairs of states, let i, j be any member of this set, and let $p(i, j)$ be its probability. For every antecedent or input state, i, there will be a conditional distribution of associated j's. We may apply the measure of entropy developed above to these distributions and obtain

$$H_i(J) = -\sum_j p_i(j) \log_2 p_i(j)$$

where $p_i(j)$ is the probability of the subsequent or output state, j, when the associated i has occurred. We may define the *conditional entropy*, $H_I(J)$, of the set I, J as the average amount of entropy associated with these conditional distributions.

$$H_I(J) = -\sum_i p(i) \sum_j p_i(j) \log_2 p_i(j)$$

$$= -\sum_{i,j} p(i, j) \log_2 p_i(j).$$

In effect, this measure weights the entropy of the conditional distribution of each i by the value of $p(i)$.

$H_I(J)$ has the following characteristics:

(a) If one and only one j occurs with every i, i.e., if for every i, one $p_i(j) = 1$ and all others are zero, then $H_I(J) = 0$. We have already found that $H(I) = 0$ if but one state of the system occurs. Similarly, all $H_i(J) = 0$ if but one j occurs with every i and their average, $H_I(J)$, will also be zero.

(b) If the set J is independent of the set I, i.e., if all $p_i(j) = p(j)$ and $p(i, j) = p(i)p(j)$, then $H_I(J) = H(J)$. This theorem follows directly from the definition of independence, i.e., that all $p_i(j) = p(j)$, and from the definition of $H_I(J)$.

Because of these two characteristics, conditional entropy, $H_I(J)$, is used to measure the amount of random error or 'noise' in a communication channel, where we are concerned with pairs of input and output events. If output events are independent of input events, and the distribution of output events is the same regardless of the input events, then 'noise' is maximal and $H_I(J)$ is equal to $H(J)$. If a particular input event always produces a particular output event, then the system is 'noiseless' and $H_I(J)$ equals 0. There is no requirement here that output events correspond in any way, or be related to, input events; for example, a 'scrambler' such as is used in trans-oceanic telegraph communication, which reliably changes the input sounds into some arbitrary but predictable pattern of electrical energy, is a 'noiseless' channel. Thus it can be seen that $H_I(J)$ is a measure of random error and not systematic error. It is possible to devise measures of systematic error, e.g., measures of the validity of signal transmission rather than reliability of the transmission,[14] but they do not derive readily from entropy estimates. The *amount of information transmitted*, I_t, is defined as the amount of information in the output or subsequent system minus the 'information' contributed by noise: $I_t = H(J) - H_I(J)$.

Conditional entropy, $H_I(J)$, is also of value in measuring *redundancy* in sequences of states of the same system. If a particular antecedent state always occurs prior to a particular subsequent state, the sequence is completely redundant, and $H_I(J)$ equals 0. If the antecedent states are independent of the subsequent states, then there is no redundancy and $H_I(J) = H(J)$. There is no reason to suppose that a subsequent state should be dependent on the single antecedent state only. Rather, it is quite conceivable that this dependency could extend for sequences of several states. In determining the extent of this dependency, we redefine I as the class of all possible sequences of r antecedent states, where $r = 1,2,3,4,5, \ldots$, and J is the class of all subsequent states as before. Under these conditions, $H_I(J)$ has an additional characteristic.

(c) If all sequences of length s are independent of all such prior sequences in a longer sequence of states, then $H_I(J)$ will approach its minimum value as r approaches s and will remain at that value for larger values of r. This characteristic is actually a generalization of characteristic (b) and is based on essentially the same line of reasoning.

Characteristic (c) permits us to use entropy measures to determine the size of the 'structured' (i.e., non-random) sequences in any longer sequence of message states: e.g., a linguistic text transcribed phonetically, phonemically, or morphemically. For example, if $H_I(J)$ were computed for the example of a Markov process given above, it should reach its minimum for $r = 3$. However, it is not always practical to use any but small values of r (usually less than 10) because of the difficulty of tabulation and the large sample required to obtain adequate estimates of the probabilities of such a large number of sequences. For sequences consisting of m different states and r units long the number of possible sequences is m^r; e.g., for $m = 2$ and $r = 10$, $m^r = 1024$. An alternative approach has been to determine the conditional entropy of pairs of states r units apart in a sequence (15).

In order to compare two systems with differing numbers of states, it is useful to have a measure of *relative conditional entropy*, $H_I \text{rel} (J)$:

$$H_I rel(J) = \frac{H_I(J)}{H(J)} \cdot$$

[14] Measures termed 'fidelity' and 'communication,' based on the proportion of total transmission which involves *corresponding* states of antecedent and subsequent systems, have been described by Osgood and Wilson in a mimeographed paper.

This measure will vary from a minimum of zero when $H_I(J) = 0$ and each antecedent state is associated with only one subsequent state to a maximum of 1.00 when $H_I(J) = H(J)$ and the subsequent states are independent of the antecedent states. A useful measure of *redundancy*, R, may be obtained by subtracting $H_{Irel}(J)$ from 1; $R = 1 - H_{Irel}(J)$. This measure will vary from a maximum of 1.00 when $H_I(J) = 0$ to a minimum of zero when $H_I(J) = H(J)$.

The measure of *joint entropy*, $H(I, J)$, is closely related to the entropy measures discussed above. Just as we have the measure $H(I)$ defined for a class of single states I, with $H(I) = - \sum_i p(i) \log_2 p(i)$, we have the measure $H(I, J)$ defined for a class of pairs of states, I, J, with $H(I, J) = - \sum_{i,j} p(i, j) \log_2 p(i, j)$. It will then be true of $H(I, J)$ that $H(I, J) = H(I) + H_I(J)$. The proof of this theorem is based on the analogous relation, $p(i, j) = p(i)p_i(j)$, as derived earlier.

In computing the entropy measures described above it is often convenient to prepare a table of $p(i, j)$'s of the form illustrated in Figure 10. The values of $p(i)$ and $p(j)$ in the margins of the table may be obtained by simply adding across appropriate rows or columns. $H(I)$ and $H(J)$ may easily be obtained from these marginal figures by simply adding appropriate values of $-p \log_2 p$ which may be found in Newman's (15) or Dolansky's (2) tables. $H(I, J)$ may be computed by carrying out the same operation on the values of $p(i, j)$ in the main body of the table. $H_I(J)$ and $H_J(I)$ may be directly obtained by using the equation below.

$$H_I(J) = H(I, J) - H(I)$$
$$H_J(I) = H(I, J) - H(J)$$

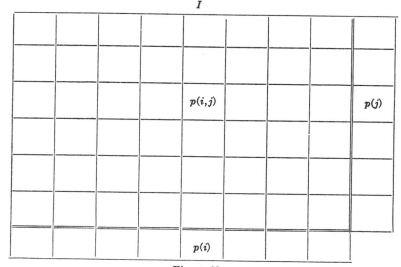

Figure 10

These computational procedures are best used when entropy measures are being applied to pairs of input and output events or to sequences of no more than two events. The computational method described by Newman (15) is more suitable for longer sequences.

Since most of information theory has been developed to deal with problems of electronic communications systems, only those aspects which seem most applicable to language research have been included above. All discussion of entropy measures for continuous data has been omitted, for example. However, the concept of *channel capacity* seems to be of potential value to language research. Shannon (19) defines channel capacity, C, essentially, as the maximum rate (in bits per unit time) at which a communications channel can transmit information. His fundamental theorem for a channel with noise states, in effect, that for rates of transmission of less than C it is possible to make $H_I(J)$ (i.e., 'noise') as small as desired by coding information in some 'optimal' fashion but that for rates of transmission greater than C, we can never decrease $H_I(J)$ below the amount by which the rate of transmission exceeds C. In other words, error can be reduced as much as desired for transmission rates less than C but increases linearly for rates greater than C. If we regard the human organism as a communications channel and responses as output states, this theorem seems of great theoretical and practical interest to students of human communication.[15]

2.3.3. *Some Applications of Information Theory*

Two main classes of application of entropy measures were indicated briefly in section 2.3.2. At this point new symbols for sets of states will be substituted for the general I and J symbols in order to more sharply distinguish the measures used in these two types of situation.

(a) *Conditional Relations between Systems.* In many cases we are interested in describing the degree to which events in one antecedent system influence events in another subsequent system to which it is directly or indirectly coupled. We may symbolize the class of events in the antecedent system as I (input) and the class of events in the subsequent system as O (output). Here $H_I(O)$ may measure the degree of 'noise' in the communication channel between the two systems or the randomness introduced by the channel. If I were a class of stimuli and O were a class of responses, $H_I(O)$ would indicate the average randomness of response tendencies to these stimuli. Conversely, $H(O) - H_I(O)$ would index the *dependency* of output upon input events, e.g., the lack of randomness in the channel.

Nearly all studies involving measurement of information transmission have closely followed the familiar communication channel model developed by Shannon (19). The states of the input are usually simple stimuli such as alternative light patterns or spoken commands. The experimental subjects are treated as communication channels and their responses to the alternative

---

[15] Research proposals relating to the empirical determination of channel capacities in human language behavior are suggested in section 5.5.

stimuli are treated as output states. The conditional entropy of responses to stimuli is the usual measure. Garner and Hake (5) describe the basic methodology of such studies and have written a later series of experimental reports. Since, on the content side, these studies are mainly of interest to those concerned with perception and the design of control system displays, they will not be discussed any further here. However, it should be noted that such methods can be used in psycholinguistic studies where the subject makes an immediate overt response to the message stimuli—i.e., in situations where the message stimuli serve as 'signals' rather than 'symbols.'

In situations where the message stimuli serve as 'symbols,' their effect is generally to change response tendencies in some later situation. For reasons discussed in another portion of this report (section 7), the conventional methods of measuring information transmission do not seem suitable. Rather, the reduction of the conditional entropy of responses in some extra-message situation seems to be a more appropriate measure. Bendig's interesting experimental study (1) is the only one to date which has used this type of measurement.

There is one important caution which should be observed in the application of entropy measures to measurement of information transmission. The meaning of the entropy measures is obviously confounded if the probability of the events we are considering changes during the period of measurement—i.e., if these events cannot be regarded as a stochastic process. It is apparent that such changes will occur if any learning occurs and affects response tendencies during the period of measurement. The contaminating effects of learning may be avoided in any of the three following ways: (I) using groups of similar subjects for short periods of measurement rather than single or small groups of subjects for extended periods of measurement; (II) making several measurements over relatively short periods during the learning process or before and after learning; and (III) using responses which are relatively well learned and which can safely be assumed to be unaffected by learning during the period of measurement. Bendig (1) has used a combination of methods (I) and (II) while Garner and Hake (5) have used method (III) in their experimental studies.

(b) *Transitional relations within systems.* In other cases we are interested in describing the extent to which antecedent events in a system influence subsequent events in the same system. We may symbolize the class of antecedent events as A and the class of subsequent events as S. Here $H_A(S)$ indicates the degree to which on the average particular subsequent events are independent of particular antecedent events, i.e., the degree of randomness in the sequencing. Conversely, $H(S) - H_A(S)$ indexes the degree to which antecedent events predict or lead to subsequent events, i.e., the redundancy in the sequencing. If A is a class of antecedent phonemes and S is a class of subsequent phonemes, $H(S) - H_A(S)$ indicates the degree to which sequences of these phonemes are structured or organized.

Miller and Frick (11) made an early application of a measure of relative redundancy to measure response stereotypy in learning situations. Newman (16) has analysed the entropy of vowels and consonants in sequences of orthography in a number of languages. Shannon (18) and Newman and Gerstman (17) have examined entropy relations in sequences of English orthography. Shannon (19) and Miller (9) discuss the interesting concept of the *order of approximation* to the statistical structure of English orthography: a zero-order approximation consists of sequences generated from the assumption that letters have equal probability of occurrence; a first-order approximation is a sequence generated from the assumption that letters occur with the same probability as in English; a second-order approximation is generated from the assumption that sequences of two letters occur with the same probability as in English; an *n*th-order approximation has the same characteristic for all sequences of *n* letters. The same techniques have been applied to sequences of words, e.g., by Miller and Selfridge (13). The latter investigators have found that the retention of such sequences after rote learning is directly related to the order of approximation, sequences of higher order approximation being more easily retained. It is perhaps unfortunate that so much attention has been devoted to orthography and so little to spoken language in these studies; it is difficult to relate the results of these researches to linguistic theory. The studies cited above demonstrate the potentialities of these relatively new techniques of measurement, and proposals for further study of entropy relations with special reference to linguistic structure are given elsewhere in this report (particularly section 5.1).

2.3.4. *Some Limiting Considerations*

Information theory concepts and measures are particularly liable to misinterpretation and misapplication. For one thing, the term, *amount of information*, has been used to mean amount of entropy in both situations (a) and (b) above. It is necessary to draw a sharp distinction between information in this sense and its common referential sense—we commonly regard a message as 'informative' only if it has some dependable relation to events outside of the message, i.e., an 'informative' message is so because it is indicative of some other state of affairs. Thus, we regard language messages with external referential meaning as 'informative' but arbitrarily selected sequences, such as random numbers or nonsense syllables, as 'uninformative.' When considering sequences of message events we can only measure the degree of randomness, not relations to external events. In this case, entropy measures only indicate how many binary decisions we need to make in order to predict subsequent message states, not how much 'information' in the referential sense the message contains. On the other hand, when we are considering pairs of input and output events in the channel connecting different systems, we can determine the relation of the events in the message output to the external events of the input. Also, the entropy produced by the channel, $H_I(J)$ or 'noise,' is distinguishable from that attributable to the informational content of the input. Only in this case is it possible to measure the amount of information, in the referential sense, in a message by the use of entropy measures, and thus allow the term 'information' to retain something like its conventional meaning.

The distinction made above may be clarified by considering the following example. Suppose that a 'mechanical oracle' has been constructed which answers any inquiry with a set of randomly selected words such that the choice of words is independent of the inquiry and any previously selected words. The entropy within the sequences of the answer is high due to the absence of redundancy, and the conditional entropy of the answers given the inquiries is also high due to the independence of the answers and the inquiries. Thus, we may have high sequential entropy and low information transmission (due to the high conditional entropy) at the same time. This example demonstrates that the two types of measures are sensitive to different aspects of messages and that we should not indiscriminately equate the amount of entropy with the amount of information in a message if the term information is to retain anything like its conventional meaning. To date, nearly all of the applications of information theory to psycholinguistic problems have been concerned with the measurement of entropy of single message events or sequences of events rather than with the measurement of referential information in messages. This is probably due to the greater ease of direct application of entropy measures in the former situations.

Another frequent misconception probably stems from the term 'information theory.' As the previous discussion has indicated, the chief contribution made by this 'theory' to the study of language is a set of descriptive measures and a unit, the *bit*, which are much more broadly applicable than to language processes themselves. It serves chiefly, therefore, as a quantitative tool for describing language processes. It is not a theory of information in the usual sense, nor does it provide us with a theoretical model which can provide hypotheses about or explain the phenomena of human language communication.

Two limitations of a statistical nature must also be mentioned. In the first place, these entropy measures are as yet of little value in *hypothesis testing and statistical inference*. This is because so little is known about their sampling distributions. However, a recent paper by Miller and Madow (12) provides a valuable initial step in the derivation of these distributions. It is also possible to test hypotheses concerning the probabilities on which the entropy measures are based by using the well-known Chi-square test. Secondly, entropy measures take no account of *similarity among states of a system*. Suppose we are studying communication via facial expressions and use $H_I(O)$ as a measure of the degree to which observer judgments (O) are dependent upon actor intentions (I). Within the limited number of judgmental categories provided, conditional entropy measures the degree of uncertainty of judgments made in response to facial poses, but it does not reflect similarity or clustering among judgments since each alternative state is treated as unique. It is possible to reclassify output states on some similarity basis, but procedures for doing this do not involve entropy estimates.

2.3.5. *Bibliography*

1. Bendig, A., 1953, Twenty questions: an information analysis, *Journal of Experimental Psychology* **46**. 345–348.

   An experimental study of the reduction of response entropy (i.e., amount of information transmitted) by each of a series of statements in a modified game of Twenty Questions.

2. Dolansky, L. and M. P. Dolansky, 1952, *Table of $\log_2 1/p$, $p \log_2 1/p$, and $p \log_2 +$ $(1 - p) \log_2 (1 - p)$*, Research Laboratory of Electronics, Massachusetts Institute of Technology, Technical Report no. 277, Cambridge.

   Use of this table reduces computation of entropy measures to the addition of a set of numbers.

3. Fano, R. M., 1949–50, *The transmission of information: I and II*. Research Laboratory of Electronics, Massachusetts Institute of Technology, Technical reports Nos. 65 and 149, Cambridge.

   The first of these papers covers much the same ground as Shannon and Weaver, but the basic theorems are developed in a different way. The second paper contains a valuable discussion of the problem of coding information for transmission through a noisy channel.

4. Feller, W., 1950, *Introduction to probability theory and its applications*.

   This is one of the best available treatments of probability theory, and it contains an excellent discussion of Markov processes.

5. Garner, W. H. and H. W. Hake, 1951, The amount of information in absolute judgments, *Psychological Review* **58**. 446–59.

   A valuable description of application of measures of joint and conditional entropy to a situation where I is a set of stimuli and J is a set of responses. The computational illustrations are also of value.

6. Hockett, C. F., 1953, Review of Shannon and Weaver: The mathematical theory of communication, *Language* **29**. 69–92.

   This paper is actually much more than a review. It is rather an introduction to Information Theory for linguists and contains an excellent discussion of potential applications to linguistic problems.

7. Jakobson, R., H. Halle and E. C. Cherry, 1953, Towards the logical description of languages in their phonemic aspect, *Language* **29**. 34–46.

   The entropy of the set of Russian phonemes is estimated and the problem of optimal coding in terms of a set of binary distinctive features is discussed.

8. Miller, G. A., 1950, Language engineering, *Journal of the Acoustic Society of America* **22**. 720–25.

   The problem of designing a language for special purposes is discussed and the relation between information theory variables and results obtained in intelligibility experiments is discussed.

9. Miller, G. A., 1951, *Language and communication*, New York.

   The chapter titled "The Statistical Approach" contains some interesting material on frequency counts of English phonemes, letters and words, and some examples of various degrees of 'statistical approximation' to English.

10. Miller, G. A., 1953, What is information measurement?, *American Psychologist* **8**. 3–11.

    A good elementary and non-technical introduction and contains an excellent annotated bibliography.

11. Miller, G. A., and F. C. Frick, 1949, Statistical behavioristics and sequences of responses, *Psychological Review* **56**. 311–24.

    Contains an elementary development of the theory of measuring sequences of responses.

12. Miller, G. A., and W. G. Madow, On the limiting distribution and asymptotic moments of the maximum likelihood estimate of the Shannon-Wiener measure of amount of information (Unpublished dittoed manuscript).

    This is an attempt to derive the sampling distributions of entropy measures and it requires a good deal of mathematical sophistication in order to follow the derivations.

13. Miller, G. A., and Selfridge, 1950, Verbal context and the recall of meaningful material, *American Journal of Psychology* **63.** 176–85.

    An experimental study of the rote learning of written material with various orders of statistical approximation to English. It was found that the amount recalled was directly related to the order of statistical approximation.

14. Nagel, Ernest, 1939, Principles of the theory of probability, *International Encyclopedia of Unified Sciences*, **1.** No. 6, Chicago.

    This work is an excellent review of the development and current theoretical status of the concept of probability. The treatment is mainly logical rather than mathematically formal and includes a discussion of some of the more basic theorems of probability theory.

15. Newman, E. B., 1951, Computational methods useful in analyzing series of binary data, *American Journal of Psychology* **64.** 252–62.

    Contains a table of $-p \log_2 p$ that is not as complete as Dolansky's but may be more readily available. Also, detailed computational illustrations are given for $H(I, J)$ for sequences of various lengths, and a valuable recursion relationship for obtaining $H_I(J)$ for these sequences is included. There is also a design for an apparatus to be used in tabulating sequences of binary data.

16. Newman, E. B., 1951, The pattern of vowels and constants in various languages, *American Journal of Psychology* **64.** 369–79.

    The redundancy of constants and vowels in the orthography of eleven languages is given.

17. Newman, E. B. and L. S. Gerstman, 1952, A new method for analyzing printed English, *Journal of Experimental Psychology* **44.** 114–25.

    This is an extension of Shannon's discussion of redundancy in English orthography. (See 18 below.)

18. Shannon, C. E., 1951, Prediction and entropy of printed English, *Bell System Technical Journal*, **30.** 50–64.

    The conditional entropy of the rth letter, given the first letter, in sequences of printed English letters is computed for various values of r.

19. Shannon, C. E. and W. Weaver, 1949, *The mathematical theory of communication*, Urbana.

    The section by Shannon contains the derivation of the entropy measures which marked the beginning of information theory as a separate area. This is still the most basic reference in the field, although the reader who is not mathematically sophisticated would be well advised to begin elsewhere. Weaver's section is essentially a restatement of Shannon's section with a few additional comments and without the mathematical proofs.

20. Weiner, N., 1948, *Cybernetics*, New York.

    This book contains much of the basis for Shannon's later development, and the chapter on "Time Series, Information and Communication" contains the original identification of information with entropy. However, both the prose and the mathematics are difficult to follow, and there is little apparent continuity in the whole work. An expository chapter titled "Information, Language and Society" is provocative.

3. PSYCHOLINGUISTIC UNITS

The linguist is in a relatively fortunate position as compared with other social scientists in being able to analyse his raw data—the sound materials that constitute spoken messages—into discrete units. Virtually all schools of linguistics are in agreement as to the two fundamental building blocks of all natural languages, the phoneme and the morpheme. About lesser as well as more comprehensive units—the distinctive feature at one end of the spectrum and the constructive feature at the other—there is far less agreement and indeed much controversy.

In the early days of modern linguistics much was written about the psychological reality of the phoneme. Much of this was purely speculative, the evident futility of which led to the abandonment of this problem in favor of purely descriptive investigation. Now, in the framework of psycholinguistics, it seems worthwhile to reopen the question in an atmosphere of frank experimentalism. Are the fundamental linguistic units, the phoneme and the morpheme, also the 'natural' units of decoding and encoding? In the process of decoding, a listener or reader can be thought of as making a series of decisions (significances) in terms of input signals; similarly, in the process of encoding, a speaker or writer makes a series of decisions (intentions) in terms of which he produces output signals. What segments of the message correspond to these non-linguistic events in decoder and encoder? Are the units which characterize decoding necessarily appropriate for encoding? In this section we try to clarify the nature of this problem and to suggest some research procedures that might lead to definitive answers— the answers themselves are probably more matters of empirical than of logical decision.

The first question we ask is a strictly psychological one—what are the mechanisms of unit formation in both perceiving and behaving? The second question we ask is whether the basic units with which the linguist operates are merely his convenient and productive fictions or perhaps also have their psychological correlates. Whatever the answer may turn out to be here, we continue to seek the answer to a third question—is it possible that some of the vaguer units linguists argue about, such as the syllable, word, and sentence, may turn out actually to have psychological relevance and thus lead to sharpening of linguistic analysis in addition to mere clarification of ancient conundrums? In what follows an attempt is made to abandon *a priori* methods and avoid circularity; instead, proposals for empirical testing of the adequacy of various possible psycholinguistic units are made.

3.1. *Psychological Bases of Unit Formation*[16]

Psychologists differ widely among themselves in their conceptions of units. That psychology as a science has prospered without resolution of this problem, whereas linguistics gave priority to the definition of units, probably reflects a

[16] Susan M. Ervin, Donald E. Walker, and Charles E. Osgood.

basic difference in purpose—psychologists are more concerned with interpretation and prediction whereas linguists are more concerned with description. Furthermore, psychologists do not find their material already formed into discretely coded events as is language; sensory and behavioral events, at least on the level at which psychologists work, seem to be continuous rather than discrete. So it has been possible for psychologists to vary in their definitions of units from the minutely molecular (e.g., the stimulus elements and muscle fiber contractions of Guthrie and Hull) to the grossly molar (e.g., the purposeful acts of Tolman and Lewin).

On the input side of the equation, gestalt psychologists have been most active in concern about units; gestalt psychology developed out of perception studies and derives its principles from this area. The notion of patterning or 'structure' of stimuli is treated as given, based on the postulated dynamic properties of the field distribution of physical stimuli on receptors and the isomorphic relation of this physical field to psychological processes. Units are segregated as self-integrated aspects of the environment which stand out as figures on a more or less homogeneous ground. Figures are characterized by shaped boundedness (contour), dynamic properties (e.g., obedience to gestalt laws), and constancy. Many of the accepted empirical laws of perceptual organization have resulted from observations under the gestalt impetus. On the output side of the equation, gestaltists have had little to say—appropriate behavior is more or less taken for granted, given adequate structuring of the perceptual field.

Behaviorists, on the other hand, have been particularly concerned with the output side (responses) in relation to comparatively unanalysed input (stimuli). They have dealt with the learning of responses, their differentiation and discrimination, and their amalgamation into skills. Only recently have behavioristically trained psychologists begun to give attention to perceptual organization. Hebb[17] in particular has offered stimulating ideas on the organization of input events, as will be discussed below, and Osgood has been attempting to relate the significance aspects of perception to semantic processes via a general mediation theory.

3.1.1. *Unit Formation in Perceiving (Decoding)*

It is unfortunate for our present purposes that so much of the work on perception has been concerned with vision; it would probably be correct to say that over 90 per cent of the research here has dealt with one aspect or another of vision. Most of the work done on audition has dealt with sensory rather than perceptual processes. This being the case, we shall have to assume a general analogy between visual and auditory modalities.

3.1.1.1. *Phenomena of perceptual organization.* It is apparent that for the most part responses are not made to unorganized masses of stimuli or to stimuli in isolation, but rather to patterns or groups of stimuli. This patterning of stimulus input is not dictated by physical properties of the stimuli themselves but is imposed upon physical events by both innate and learned properties of the organism. The general ways in which the organism imposes an order upon the environment can be determined by observing the characteristic phenomena of perceiving.

(1) *Grouping.* Looking about us, we see objects (books, pictures, hands, doors, and so on), not conglomerations of color points, i.e., sensory input is organized

into wholes by perceptual processes. Similarly, when we listen to speech, we hear significant signals, words, not conglomerations of sound. This distinction is particularly clear when listening to one's own language as compared to an unknown language—the former 'breaks' readily into pieces while the latter does not, these pieces typically corresponding to meaningful units. What factors in stimulus events facilitate grouping? (a) *Nearness* (in time or space). Those constellations of star-points in the heavens which receive labels are nearly always near together in visual space; it is almost trite to say that nearness in time operates to determine units in messages—the longer the pause between two speech events, the less likely they are to belong to the same unit. Similarly, nearness in time is a determinant of visual unity, e.g., in producing the phi-phenomenon. (b) *Similarity*. It is actually nearness in time or space of similar processes, not nearness per se, that determines grouping. The basis of the Ishahara color blindness test is perceiving a form of a given hue (for example, making up the number '9') amongst a conglomeration of multi-hued dots. Similarly, it is presumably the continuity in time of auditory components of a given quality that makes a phoneme stand out as a unit, despite the overlapping of phones (e.g., in hearing /hard/ the /a/ phoneme is a persisting similarity of quality throughout much of the sequence). (c) *Continuity*. The more stimulus events dispersed in either space or time tend to follow regular or predictable sequences, the more likely are they to be perceived as a group. In an X there is directional continuity in seeing two crossed lines rather than an upright and an inverted V. Any violation of continuity increases the probability of disunity in perception. The continuity which characterizes diphthongs presumably is the reason for perceiving them as single units.

(2) *Closure*. Perceptual processes manifest *holistic*, all-or-nothing properties. A group of arcs may be perceived as a complete circle under certain conditions; a pattern of lines in two dimensions may be perceived as a solid cube. Familiar sequences of spoken speech can be mutilated to considerable degrees in transmission without markedly affected intelligibility. In all of these cases the organism's nervous system, either on the basis of innate tendencies toward completion (gestalt) or on the basis of past experience (behaviorism), acts to 'fill in' the input events which are missing at the peripheral level, provided enough of a pattern is given. In general, stimuli which frequently occur together or in close sequence tend to be perceived as wholes. The same thing can be illustrated in language: the sequence *thelittlegirlrodeonahorse* is presumably easier to decode than a sequence of less familiar units, e.g., *thepetitebipedelopedonamare*.

The above are all conditions for *unambiguous* figure and ground. It is also possible to set up conditions under which several alternative groupings are nearly equiprobable, e.g., *ambiguous* figures. The famous Rubin figure, which can be seen either as a vase or as two faces, is a visual example. In the auditory field, the same progression of notes can be made to seem either like two intersecting melodies (e.g., an X) or like two separate melodies, upper and lower (e.g., our upright and inverted V's), by manipulating the timbre, pitch, or some other characteristic of the instruments playing them—and with the same instruments playing through the same mid-point, an ambiguous auditory experience is produced. Ambiguous orthographic patterns could be produced by omission of spaces (e.g.,—*asinaga-tean*), ambiguous linguistic patterns by omission of pauses and junctures, and both could be used to study grouping tendencies in decoding. Furthermore, various cues can be magnified or reduced in clarity so as to vary the speed with which organization takes place. It is suggested that in most speech situations redundancies in organizational cues are necessary to account for the apparent discreteness of acoustic decoding.

(3) *Constancy and transposition.* When a person reacts to an object as 'the same' despite variations in illumination, in angle of regard, in distance, and so forth, he is showing constancy—each stimulus pattern is different, but his perceptual response is constant. When a person learns to respond to that one of two objects which is the brighter (larger, nearer, heavier, and so on) and continues to respond correctly despite wide changes in the absolute stimulus values, he is displaying transposition. Both of these phenomena are the same at base. The subject must have cues available that the context has changed (e.g., that the illumination has been lowered, that a disk is being held at something other than right angles to his line of regard, etc.) in order to show constancy of perception; in transposition one object provides the context for the other. If such contextual cues are eliminated constancy is eliminated, and what is perceived corresponds to what is given peripherally (and the object changes in brightness, in shape, and in size in accordance with actual stimulus values). Again, this phenomenon has been studied almost exclusively in connection with vision, but its analogies in hearing—particularly speech decoding—are apparent and probably of great significance for the problem of psycholinguistic units.

Constancy in decoding is evident in the fact that phonemes have a constant 'significance' in the code regardless of the phonetic environments in which they appear (allophones). Transposition is operating whenever intonation and stress is correctly interpreted by the hearer *in relation to* the context or mean value of the utterance in which it occurs—the rising intonation of a question is not differently interpreted because a deep-pitched rather than a high-pitched voice is producing it. Perceptual constancies are basic to the operation of language *as a code;* the classes of unique events which have a constant significance in perception are what the descriptive linguist analyses as the phonemic structure of a language.

The usual experimental situation for measuring constancy requires a *standard object*, viewed under some contextual condition such as a shadow or at some obvious angle of regard, and a *comparison object*, viewed under 'normal' conditions and capable of being varied through degrees of brightness, angles of regard, and so on. The subject first adjusts the comparison object under open field conditions until it looks just like the standard; he then repeats this adjustment, but using a *reduction screen* which eliminates the context. If the match made under open field conditions is identical with that made with the reduction screen, he is said to show 0 per cent constancy (i.e., the context had no effect on, was not taken into account in, his perceptual judgment); if the comparison object 'looks the same' as the standard without any such adjustment, (e.g., without being darkened to account for the shadow), perfect constancy is shown. Some general facts about constancy are the following:

(a) *The use of a reduction screen eliminates the constancy effect.* The analogous expectation for speech decoding would be that allophones and allomorphs should tend to sound more and more different as environmental context is reduced. The terminal past tense allomorphs should seem more like /t/ and /d/ when restricted (e.g., by tape cutting) to these sounds than when heard as parts of meaningful words, such as *faked* /feykt/ vs. *played* /pleyd/, where both endings should sound like /d/.

(b) *What is perceived in experimental conditions is usually a compromise between perfect constancy and absolute stimulus equation.* Since it would be difficult to get subjects to report *how* similar speech sounds appear, the percentage of listeners giving 'same' as a report could be used to indicate the extent of compromise. (Cf. Section 4.1.1.2.)

(c) *The greater the contextual difference between standard and comparison objects, the greater the constancy effect.* In speech decoding this would mean that the greater the difference in phonetic environment, the *more similar* allophones and allomorphs should sound. The /t/ and /d/ allomorphs should sound more similar in the comparison *napped* /napt/ vs. *waved* /weyvd/ than in the very close environments of *napped* /napt/ vs. *nabbed* /nabd/.

(d) *Only object-tied stimulus characteristics* (e.g., surface colors) *display constancy.* The more meaningful the segments in which speech sounds occur, the greater should be the constancy effect. The past tense allomorphs should sound more alike in the meaningful comparison *ached* /eykt/ vs. *aimed* /eymd/ than in the meaningless comparison /ikt/ vs. /imd/.

(e) *The more cues available that standard and comparison objects are 'the same'* (albeit under different contexts), *the greater the constancy.* This again implies that constancy effects are strongest under natural conditions. Presumably, constancy among allophones and allomorphs should be enhanced by orthographic identity and diminished by orthographic distinction.

(f) *The direction of the constancy effect is typically a 'regression toward the real object'* (Thouless). In other words, what is perceived tends to be more like the object as known under 'normal' conditions of inspection, e.g., ordinary daylight illumination, normal angle of regard, inspection distance, etc. Isn't it the case that /t/ sounds like /d/ in the past tense signal position, rather than the reverse; and that /z/ sounds like /s/ in the nominative plural signal position, rather than the reverse? Is the 'real' sound psychologically /d/ or /s/ here because of frequency of usage? Is it the one that corresponds to orthography?

Most of the evidence on visual constancies suggests that these are *learned* phenomena; certainly, perceptual constancies in language are learned. It seems likely that the users of a given language learn to discriminate those differences in the sound material that make a difference in the code and to *not* discriminate (pay no attention to) differences that do not make a difference in the code, the latter type of learning contributing to constancy effects. In a later section of this report (section 4), an experiment is described which gets at this prediction.

3.1.1.2. *General principles of perceptual organization.* The empirical phenomena of perceptual organization described above seem to reflect the operation of a limited number of underlying principles of organization. Drawing on a great deal of evidence which cannot be included here, three general levels of organization of sensory input may be postulated.

I. *Projection level: summation of points of maximal stimulation and suppression of other activity.* Marshall and Talbot[18] and others have provided evidence for such processes in the visual projection system and indicated how they contribute to the formation of sharp contours on the visual cortex. Similar processes seem to operate in audition (e.g., *masking* in relation to pure tone resolution). These

---

[18] In *Biological Symposia*, Klüver, ed. (Ronald Press, 1942).

mechanisms contribute to a general 'sharpening' of sensory signals; however, although constituting a significant aspect of total reception, they seem to be innately determined and 'sensory' rather than 'perceptual' in character.

II. *Integrative level: central correlates of redundant and frequently occurring sensory events become integrated at this level.* Hebb has described a general principle of neural organization which fits this situation: if two or more neurones in fibrous contact, either directly or mediately, are simultaneously active, the synaptic junctures associating them are strengthened, so that the occurrence of one becomes a condition for either evoking (high frequency of repetition) or at least 'tuning up' (lower frequency of repetition) the other. Since density of fibrous contact is probably both a function of nearness in neural space and of similarity of fiber type (due to anatomical organization), we can see a basis for two of the major determinants of *perceptual grouping*, nearness in space and similarity in physical quality. Reverberation in neural circuits provides for integration of neural events over short time intervals, giving a basis for another determinant of grouping, nearness in time. The general import of this principle is that sensory events will tend to be perceived in groups dependent upon redundancy and frequency in past experience. Thus things seen or heard together or in close temporal sequence in past experience will come to function as wholes in subsequent experience. The phenomena of *closure* and *continuity* become nothing more than demonstrations of this principle—parts of redundant and frequently experienced wholes serve to activate central representations of the whole. Figure experiences, whether visual or auditory, and their resistance to breaking up, are also phenomenal effects of the operation of this general integrative principle. Elsewhere in this report, this type of principle is applied to an analysis of grammatical mechanisms in language decoding and encoding (section 6.1).

III. *Representational level: surrogates of total behaviors to objects become associated with signs of these objects, serving both as the significance of these signs and as mediators of instrumental behaviors appropriate to the objects represented.* The development of representational mediators is discussed in some detail elsewhere in this report (section 6.1). Suffice it here to say that distinctive portions of the total behavior elicited by proximal object stimulation (e.g., taste, texture, eating, etc., of APPLE) come to be called forth in anticipatory fashion by the distal cues from the object (e.g., visual color, shape, etc. of APPLE). According to theory, it is by virtue of the association of visual and auditory patterns with these distinctive mediating processes that they serve as signs of the objects as palpably experienced (e.g., this particular visual pattern of rounded-redness is a perceptual sign of APPLE because it now elicits a minimal but distinctive part of the same behavior originally elicited by direct contact with APPLE). Since the various distal appearances of APPLE (under different illuminations, at different distances, and hence different visual angles, and so forth) are all associated with the same proximal stimulations and terminal behaviors, they come to constitute a class of signs having the same significance. Organisms learn to disregard the non-significant contextual differences. This association of a class of varied distal stimulations with a common significance is the essence of the constancy phenomenon.

Presumably the same type of analysis would apply to linguistic constancies, at least at the 'word' level. The word *apple* is heard with a variety of intonations, in a variety of constructions, and in a variety of voice timbres, but it is associated with a common perceptual sign and/or proximal experience (e.g., is accompanied by seeing and/or manipulating the same object APPLE). The question of phonemic and morphemic (grammatical) constancies presents more difficulty, since they do not have 'significance' in any representational sense. However, the same underlying principle of learning constancies probably applies—language users learn to pay attention to the constant features which are significant (in the code) and to disregard the variable features which are not significant. Actually, the same distinction between constant (significant) and variable (non-significant) features arises in connection with perceptual constancies—enough of the features of APPLE must be present, such as shape and color, to elicit the common mediating process or significance, which then provides for constancy in perception despite the variable, contextual features, such as size and illumination. The parallel between linguistic analysis of language constancies and psychological analysis of perceptual constancies is an intriguing one and deserves attention.

3.1.1.3. *Some research proposals.* (1) *Phonemic and morphemic constancies.* Following the close analogy between visual and linguistic constancies, one would want to study the perceived similarities of allophones and allomorphs under varying degrees of linguistic context—complete meaningful utterances, single meaningful words, conditioning phonetic environments, and isolated speech sounds. Rather than asking the subject to make a judgment of degree of similarity, one should either require judgments of 'same' or 'different' with percentages of subjects indicating the degree of constancy, or use a forced choice technique, e.g., given [tʰal], choose either [stʰal] or [stal] as the more similar. Another experimental possibility here comes from the known characteristics of orthography: having taught speakers of an unwritten language the alphabetic notion along with a partial alphabet, their own perceived constancies should appear in use of the same symbols for what are allophones in their language.

(2) *Study of perceptual grouping in language decoding.* At an earlier point in this section it was suggested that ambiguous spoken or written materials (the former produced by deleting between-word junctures by tape cutting and the latter by omission of between-word spaces) could be used to study spontaneous grouping tendencies. If subjects were given a sample of such material and instructed to segment it, the relative strengths of alternative grouping tendencies should appear in the frequencies of common cutting points. The use of anagrams (and equivalent 'anvocs'—jumbled vocalizations) offers another approach, applicable to smaller units than words. The stronger the transitional probabilities (e.g., sensory integrations) binding parts of the given anagram together, which must be separated for solution, the more difficult and time-consuming should be the solution. The stronger the transitional probabilities of the correct letter sequences, to be discovered, the less difficult and time-consuming should be the solution.[19] Such

[19] Research along these lines is now being conducted by Charles Solley at the University of Illinois.

analysis requires computation of transitional probabilities for samples of both English orthography and phonemes.

(3) *Study of 'communication units.'* It might be appropriate to begin with an approximation to the normal linguistic situation—face-to-face conversations between two speakers of a language. The grossest unit of language perception would seem to be the shortest consecutive sequence of speech produced by one individual to which another can make a discriminative response, e.g., the minimal sequence that makes a difference in behavior. The effects of increased context upon shortening of this minimal sequence could also be investigated. Utterance completion could be used as a tool here, for example.

3.1.2. *Unit Formation in Behaving (Encoding)*

The 'flow of speech' is a rather apt simile. In the midst of ordinary conversation the adult speaker is operating rapidly, smoothly, and largely unconsciously upon the outward-moving columns of air by alternately contracting and relaxing a set of muscles into varying postures which modulate the rates and amplitudes at which this air vibrates. These muscles are always in flux, always approaching some posture and leaving another, never in static pose. This flow of behavior is analysable into over-learned, well-integrated *vocalic skill sequences* (probably individual words and trite phrases) which are encoded as units and run themselves once initiated. These skill sequences are themselves further analysable into *vocalic skill components*, which we tentatively identify with syllables rather than phonemes—if a speaker is asked to slow down his output to a very low rate, he typically inserts longer pauses between syllabic units without changing to any great extent the intervals between the phonemes constituting syllabic units. This is, of course, an hypothesis in need of test.

3.1.2.1. *Vocalic skill components.* The basis for formation of motor output units is probably the same as that involved in the formation of sensory input units— central neural integration based upon peripheral motor redundancy and frequency. As a matter of fact, the evidence for central integration or programming of motor skills is clearer than in the case of sensory events.

A three stage process of skill formation can be envisaged: (1) The starting point is repetition of a regular sequence of motor responses on the basis of direct, intentional encoding, imitation of adult models, or some other basis. (2) Since under these conditions each movement produces proprioceptive self-stimulation (feedback) which can become conditioned to the succeeding movement, a chain of simple stimulus-response associations is set up, and the developing skill 'runs itself' at a much more rapid rate. However, as Lashley pointed out many years ago, there is just simply not time enough in a rapidly executed skill (e.g., playing a cadenza or speaking) for impulses to travel in feedback fashion from periphery to center and back again between each movement. (3) Once a sequence of movements is being executed repeatedly on a proprioceptive feedback basis, the time intervals between successive reactions are short enough to permit the formation of *central integrations* (presumably in the motor cortex) among the neural events that are the necessary antecedent of these movements. Again, following Hebb's general notion, when cells having nervous interconnections are caused to be simultaneously active, there results an increase in the probability that subsequent activation of any one of them will lead to activation of the next in sequence and so on. In other words, a short-circuiting within the motor system is accomplished and a greater speed and stability of execution becomes possible.

The phoneme has been defined as a bundle of distinctive features, these features including such characteristics as tongue-tip position, rounding or flattening of the lips, vibration or non-vibration of the vocal cords, and so forth. This definition spells out the fact that the phoneme is a *spatial* pattern of motor activity, but it is also a *temporal* pattern of activity. As a bit of skilled behavior it includes the temporal effects of approaching toward its typical posture from a diversity of other postures (antecedent environments) and receding from this to a diversity of other postures (subsequent environments). Since central motor programming in the nervous system is much more rapid than peripheral execution, there is always a tendency to anticipate features of subsequent phonemes and persist in features of antecedent phonemes. These skill modifications are at once the basis of allophones and evidence of the formation of encoding units.

The tightness with which the elements of a skill component (or a skill sequence, cf. below) are welded is a function of both redundancy and frequency. Due to the relatively high order of redundancy *within* phonemic units, the spatial pattern of events here should be highly evocative, e.g., occur as synchronous bursts as wholes; due to the lower order of redundancy *between* phonemic units (e.g., /b/ can be followed by /i/, /e/, /a/, /o/, and other vowels as well as by the consonants /l/ and /r/), one would expect the temporal sequences of phonemic events within syllables to be merely predictive of one another, and thus less tightly welded. This expectation, however, does not take into account the possibility of forming higher order units on the basis of extremely high *frequency*, e.g., syllables which become a 'pool' of alternate wholes in encoding. Casual observation suggests the syllable as the minimal unit in encoding—not only is there the fact that slowed down speech is accomplished by syllabic spacing, as noted earlier, but babbling behavior in infants is typically syllabic in nature. The work of Stetson on the relation of the chest-pulse to syllable formation also seems to support this view. It should be noted that this does *not* imply that the syllable is also the minimal unit in decoding.

3.1.2.2. *Vocalic skill sequences.* The model in which proprioceptive and auditory feedback is a controlling factor in skill execution is probably preserved in the more loosely welded vocalic skill sequences, the sequences of syllables that constitute words and trite phrases. The rapidly executed pattern of responses within each syllabic unit produces distinctive sensory feedback; to the extent that certain sequences of syllabic units are redundant and of frequent occurrence, this distinctive stimulus pattern will become predictive of certain subsequent syllabic units. Thus familiar syllabic sequences should run themselves off more rapidly in encoding than unfamiliar syllabic sequences, and frequency of errors in encoding should be predictable as substitutions of high frequency sequences for low frequency ones at points of high antecedent similarity.

Suggestive evidence for this analysis is provided by the research of Grant Fairbanks on the effects of delayed auditory feedback. He has been able to show that the interval of delay in feedback at which the greatest interference is produced in both spontaneous encoding and reading aloud (e.g., stuttering, reduplication of preceding sounds, omissions, and the like) is about 0.25 seconds. This corresponds closely to the average rate of syllable production, about four per second. Attempts to disclose finer 'ripples' of interference corresponding to the average rate of phonemic production have been unsuccessful.

The general import of this analysis is that functional units of encoding are flexible with respect to standard linguistic units; they depend for their formation upon redundancy and frequency factors in the main and may span sequences of varying length. Units may be as small as the syllable and as large as a phrase (e.g., "Howd'ya-do?", "B'lieve-'t-'r-not"). The behavioral correlates of tightness of unit formation should be latencies between elements in production and the existence of skill modifications, such as truncation, amalgamation, and anticipatory and perseverative alteration.

3.1.2.3. *Some research proposals.* A number of research proposals related to units in encoding are included in section 5 on transitional psycholinguistics. Certain general possibilities may be suggested here.

(1) *Detailed latency measurement.* Modern instruments make it feasible to analyse juncture and pausal phenomena in close detail. The general prediction is that the distribution of within-syllable intervals should be of minimal duration, if evident at all, and significantly shorter than between-syllable intervals. Between-syllable intervals in turn should vary with redundancy and frequency factors, being shortest between syllables within common words and trite phrases and longer between syllables in rarer words and less predictable phrases. Intervals between morphemic boundaries, and the effects of stress and intonation upon type of juncture can also be investigated in this manner.

(2) *Delayed auditory feedback.* Given measurements of transitional probabilities in English, particularly as between syllables, the delayed feedback technique could be employed to check the prediction that weaker links in the encoding chain, e.g., points of low transitional probability, are more susceptible to interference.

(3) *Slowed speech.* A similarly detailed analysis should be made of intentionally slowed speech on the part of native speakers. The expectation offered here is that increases in latency will be chiefly apparent between syllables rather than within —accomplished, perhaps, by elongation of the terminal voiced phoneme of each syllable.

(4) *Interruption technique.* If a spontaneously encoding speaker or a reader is interrupted at unpredictable intervals (by some ingenious technique not specified at present), he would be expected to begin again at the nearest 'natural' unit onset, e.g., *"interruption te//—technique is a metho//—od of stud//—ying,"* etc. The expectation is that these units would be syllabic or larger.

(5) *Backward-working skill modifications.* Probably one of the best indices of encoding units is the existence of backward-working (e.g., anticipatory) skill modifications. When the speaker modifies his articulation of the /k/ in *cool* as compared with the /k/ in *key* to anticipate the following vowel, it is uncontrovertible evidence that this much, at least, is being encoded as a unit. In other

words, the encoder must have already selected the vowel aspect of the syllable at the time of executing the initial phoneme. The same sort of logic applies to encoding units operating over larger segments of the message. When a Spanish-speaking encoder, for example, produces *las bonitas casas*, the grammatical marker for the feminine gender, *-as*, which appears in the article depends upon the noun form, *casas*—again, it is certain that at least this much must have been selected at some level of organization as a single unit. A detailed analysis of such backward-working adaptations should be a very profitable enterprise. It would probably provide evidence for a hierarchical structure of units-within-units in encoding (cf., section 3.4).

3.2. *Relations between Psychological and Linguistic Units*[20]

3.2.1. *The Problem*

By application of the logically rigorous methods described earlier (section 2.1), the linguist has been able to determine minimal units on each of the levels into which language is usually divided. The unit on the phonological level is the *phoneme*; the unit on the morphological level is the *morpheme*; and most linguists would probably admit the validity of the *function class* as a meaningful and useful unit at the syntactical level. These units can be rigorously defined in terms of linguistic method and have proven useful for descriptive purposes.

However, the speaker of a language is also aware of certain units in its structure. At least he uses certain terms consistently in talking about his language which indicate perception of units roughly at each of these levels. Sapir has pointed out that speakers of Indian languages which have no orthography at all have no difficulty in dictating a text to a field worker 'word by word.' The same speaker, probably, could dictate his text 'one sentence at a time' if asked to. This implies an implicit set of criteria for defining words and sentences. For languages which have a written form, these criteria are usually reflected in the orthography. A 'word' is a unit which, when written, appears between spaces. A 'sentence' is a unit which, when written, starts with a capital and ends with a period. But, obviously, the orthography is merely a representation of what, at one time at least, were felt to be criteria that operated in speech—that is, the criteria which govern our Indian informant who has no prejudices because of orthography. With his concepts of 'word' and 'sentence' the speaker indicates his awareness of units at the levels of morphology and syntax. Regarding phonology, there would be less agreement in identifying the number of 'sounds' in a given utterance, but speakers would probably agree on 'syllable' counts, if not on syllable boundaries. The three psychological units which emerge from a native speaker's analysis, then, are the *syllable*, the *word*, and the *sentence*.

If we use the dichotomy of 'linguist units' and 'psychological units' to apply respectively to the units determined by the linguist and the native speaker, our immediate problem becomes one of relating them. In other words, we are con-

---

[20] Sol Saporta.

cerned with the psychological validity or reality of existing linguistic units and with the linguistic feasibility or productivity of 'natural' psychological units. There is the further problem that what we might call 'psycholinguistic units' need not correspond precisely to either those arrived at by deliberate linguistic analysis or those arrived at by casual lay analysis. Psycholinguistic units would be those segments of the message shown to be *functionally operative* as wholes in the processes of decoding and encoding, and these too are capable of analysis into levels. For example, the units operating in correlation with events at the semantic or representational level are probably different than those operating at the grammatical or integrative level, and both of these in turn are probably both different and larger than the units correlated with skill components in encoding.

3.2.2. *Linguistic Feasibility of Psychological Units*

The linguist, aware that syllable, word, and sentence are functional concepts to the native speaker of a language, has felt obliged to define them rigorously, but he has met with little success.

(a) He has been reasonably successful in incorporating the concept of the *syllable* into his descriptions, but only for some languages. In some dialects of Spanish, for example, the quality of a vowel (open vs. closed) is determined by its position in the syllable (non-final vs. final). We have, then, objective criteria for determining syllable boundaries. Most attempts to define the syllable have been made in terms of the presence or absence of a vowel, or some similar criterion. However, too often linguists have ended with the kind of circularity by which a syllable is defined as that unit which contains one and only one vowel (or diphthong) and the vowel is defined as that unit which may function as a syllable. Other definitions have been attempted in terms of chest pulses, etc., but there apparently is no definition which is entirely satisfactory. It has also been suggested that even if definable, the syllable as a concept may be irrelevant in a formal system of analysis.

(b) The *word* has met with even less success. Some linguists maintain the position that defining the 'word' is a pseudo-problem, that there is no unit in language which correlates with the traditional unit we call 'a word.' Other linguists maintain that there is no general definition, but merely a definition for a particular language. In Czech, for example, each word is stressed on the first syllable. Word boundaries can then be determined. This obviously does not apply to most other languages. The next part of this report (3.3) outlines a new, and apparently successful, linguistic solution of this problem by Greenberg.

(c) The *sentence* likewise has not been clearly defined in linguistics. The most meaningful definitions have been in terms of intonation features and juncture phenomena. A sentence end is usually marked by one of several 'final junctures' accompanied by a certain intonation pattern. After listening to impromptu conversations in several languages, one suspects that even these criteria apply only in 'cleaned-up' texts, and may not really apply in the everyday communication situation.

The result is that the linguists for the most part have been unable to operate profitably with these units of language which speakers intuitively understand and use.

3.2.3. *Psychological Reality of Linguistic Units*

We come now to the reverse problem of determining whether the units which the linguist can isolate are psychologically valid.

(a) The *phoneme* is probably the one unit which can be demonstrated to exist both linguistically and psychologically. (A specific experimental technique is suggested below.) Under normal circumstances, in the decoding process, people do not distinguish differences between allophones. They are, of course, noticed when incorrectly used by a foreigner speaking with an accent. Likewise, speakers in encoding are not conscious of selecting among allophone classes—this is automatic. Consequently the allophone is too small to be a unit in the encoding or decoding process, implying that the phoneme is. But here, apparently, is a contradiction. If the selection of an allophone is determined, say, by the following phoneme, it implies that at least for the *encoder*, a group of two phonemes is a unit—that one selects at least two phonemes (possibly a syllable) at a time. On the other hand, however, two words or two messages may differ by only one phoneme, which means that the one phoneme has been selected independent of the environment and likewise that the *decoder* must distinguish between phonemes.

If we consider the initial sound in 'key,' we must conclude that it plays a dual role. The particular allophone [kʰ-] is a part of a larger unit in the flow of speech. However, the phoneme to which this sound is assigned, /k/, is itself a unit, and as a unit it serves as a basis for distinguishing this lexical item from, say, 'tea.' In trying to relate units to points of decision, then, we conclude that whereas the abstraction, i.e., the phoneme, corresponds to a unit of decision, the particular manifestation or actualization of the phoneme, i.e., the allophone, is only part of a unit. Our problem then is to determine what is this larger unit. There are two possibilities. 'Key' may have been chosen either as a phonological unit (a syllable), or as a morphological unit, (a morpheme). Obviously the two levels need not exclude one another. A discussion of the hierarchies of levels appears further on in this section (3.4).

(b) There is evidence for the justification of larger units as well. Just as allophones are encoded and decoded automatically, *allomorphs* may be selected automatically, indicating the same process on the morphological level. For example, an English speaker, and particularly a listener, is not aware of the phonemic difference between the singular 'house' /haws/ and the corresponding allomorph in the plural 'houses' /hawz-/. In other words, it is as though the phonemic difference between /s/ and /z/ were neutralized, indicating that a unit larger than the phoneme is being decoded.

Again the abstraction, i.e., the morpheme *house*, is a unit because of the obvious decision not to say, for example, *churches*. However, the particular allomorph is a part of a larger unit in the flow of speech. This may be a morphological unit, the word, or some syntactic unit, perhaps the noun phrase.

(c) On the *syntactic level*, the category of agreement indicates selection of word groups. A Spanish speaker who begins a phrase with the feminine article 'la' indicates by this choice that he has already selected a feminine noun, so that, on the syntactical level, perhaps the whole noun phrase is a unit in encoding. There is an interesting difference here also between encoder and decoder: for the *encoder*, the subsequent unit (in this case the noun) determines the antecedent (the article); for the *decoder*, the antecedent limits the probabilities of the subsequent. It is as though in one case the article 'agreed' with the noun ('agreed' here is equivalent to 'is determined by') while in the other case, from the point of view of the listener, the noun 'agrees' with the article. The question of agreement has not been clearly treated in linguistics, and this is possibly because it is difficult to find one explanation which will cover what seem to be two different processes.

In this connection, it is tempting to hypothesize a relation across languages between the expression of agreement by adjectives and the position of the adjective in relation to the noun. For example, one might suspect that if the selection of the noun determines the form of the adjective, then the adjective is more likely to follow the noun. This is generally true in the Romance languages, where many adjectives must follow, and others may follow or precede. On the other hand, if there is only one form of the adjective, as in English, it may very easily precede since the selection of the noun cannot affect the form of the adjective. German, of course, would be an obvious exception. Before such a hypothesis could be seriously considered, a large number of languages would have to be investigated. If such a relation appeared, it would imply that the units of encoding differ from language to language, that the larger the role played by agreement, the larger the unit of encoding.

Our preliminary survey suggests that: (1) for the most part, linguists have been unable to operate profitably with 'natural' folk units, and (2) there may be some basis for concluding that the linguistic units are psychologically valid. The latter must, however, be tested by suitable experimental situations.

3.2.4. *Research proposals*

Research should be directed at setting up situations designed to yield independent results which can then be compared with the two sets of units described above. It may develop, for example, that on the phonological level, both the syllable and the phoneme are valid.

3.2.4.1. *Child language.* One field for such investigations might be in child language. The order in which distinctions and contrasts are made should be carefully analyzed. For example, if it turned out that a child learned a series of monosyllabic items, no two of which formed a minimal contrast (e.g., if, when a child learned the word 'pa', he did not then learn 'ma', but first learned 'me'), then one might conclude that learning was on a syllable basis rather than on a phonemic basis. On the morphological level, the writer has heard of cases where children have confused the items 'yesterday' and 'to-morrow,' indicating that each is a minimal unit of meaning and has been learned as such. This error is in terms of 'words,' not morphemes, and apparently would conflict with the analysis of those linguists who would insist on dividing 'yesterday' into two meaningful units (morphemes) on the basis of contrasts with such items as '*yester*year' and 'Mon*day*,' 'Tues*day*,' and perhaps even 'to-*day*.'[21] This is not to be interpreted as indicating that the morpheme is not a unit in language learning. A child's use of a form such as 'runned' or a formation such as 'monk' from 'monkey,' in analogy to a pair like 'dog—doggie,' indicates an awareness of morphemes. Nevertheless, it seems reasonable to conclude that an analysis of the learning process would indicate both the morpheme and the word as valid units.

3.2.4.2. *Reversed speech.* Another possible technique might be the use of reversed speech in a controlled experimental situation. The purpose would be to ascertain those points where mistakes are made, the hypothesis being that from these points some indication may be had of the units into which the speaker divides speech. The next step would be to correlate these units with the psychological and the linguistic units previously mentioned. We assume that any features that are encoded simultaneously are being treated as indivisible units, either in the perception of the item as presented or in the production of the item in reversal.

It is apparent from even the most superficial observation that any native speaker of English, instructed to reverse the sounds of the word 'net' will respond with /ten/, and he will also be of the opinion that his answer is 'correct.' The linguist is of course aware that the speaker has modified all three sounds, perhaps, substituting one allophone for another. The fact that allophones are thus changed automatically indicates that, at this level at least, not allophones but phonemes are functioning as units. The examples selected for experimentation here would have to be carefully chosen to test the units being considered. For example, given the word 'mate,' most subjects can be expected to respond with /teym/, thus indicating that on this level dipthongs are a psycholinguistic unit.

If English is used for these experiments, one problem that comes up immediately is the influence of orthography. Two possibilities suggest themselves: (1) The effects of spelling may theoretically at least be eliminated by using either illiterates or pre-school children as subjects. (2) The effect of spelling may be so considerable that it might be advisable to measure it directly in an attempt to ascertain whether it has any effect on the perception of units by speakers.[22] For example, one might ask subjects to reverse a series of words given orally, amongst which were included the pair 'wrong,' 'right,' and then some time later, the pair 'read,' 'write.' By comparing the two reversals for the sequence /rayt/ one might determine to what extent mistakes were a result of orthography. The same results might be obtained by asking them to reverse other pairs of homonyms presented in slightly different form. For example, one might expect different results from subjects told to reverse the last words in the sentences 'I don't like to pay my income /taks/,' and 'I always

---

[21] For a discussion of the suggestion that morphemic analyses, like phonemic analyses, can only be based on individual idiolects, see Nida, *Word*, 7. 1–14 (1951).

[22] It seems reasonable to assume that spelling does affect the analysis of some speakers. Most speakers, for example, do not readily associate 'cat' and the element 'kit' of 'kitten,' whereas they do associate 'goose' with the element 'gos' of 'gosling.' It seems that the orthography here overbalances the phonetic relation.

use nails, but rarely use /taks/.' For our purposes, we may assume that the influence of orthography has been eliminated by using either illiterates or pre-school children.

The hypothesis, then, is that it may be possible to determine psycholinguistic units by analyzing those places where subjects make 'mistakes,' i.e., where the reversal does not coincide with the actual reversal of phonemes and would not 'sound right' if played back in reverse on tape. It seems likely that these places may coincide with the various linguistic and psychological boundaries as defined above—namely, boundaries of phonemes, morphemes, syllables, words and so forth. Still assuming that orthography has no influence, subjects might be asked to reverse the words 'boys' /boyz/ and 'noise' /noyz/. Linguistically, the /z/ is different in these two cases, in one case being a morph in itself; furthermore, the morpheme 'plural' has an allomorph with the phonemic shape /s/ as well as the one /z/. If we extend the process by which allophones were substituted in the example 'net'—'ten,' we may reasonably assume that there will be competition between allomorphs in the reversal of 'boys,' whereas no such competition should exist in the reversal of 'noise.' We might expect 'soyb' (rather than 'zoyb') as a significantly more common response than 'soyn'[23] because of the conflict of /s/ and /z/ in the former case. Another typical mistake might be 'yobz,' where the sequence of morphemes is maintained with reversal occurring within the morpheme. Another possible measure of the effect of this linguistic boundary might be the relative latency of similar responses. Those responding to 'boys' with /zoyb/ would be expected to have taken more time than those responding /zoyn/ to 'noise.' We suggest, then, that at those places where there are clear linguistic boundaries, subjects will indicate that, to a certain extent, linguistic units correspond to (or influence the determination of) psycholinguistic units.

We have thus far limited ourselves to monosyllabic units. It would be interesting to see what would be the effect of increasing to, say, four syllables, but without changing the instructions. Would subjects automatically try to reverse syllables instead of phonemes? In other words, is the unit of perception in part determined by the length of the utterance? A further possibility is to instruct subjects to reverse the syllables in a series of words of two syllables, which differ in their linguistic units. One would expect, for example, significant differences between a pair such as 'boyish' and 'parish,'[24] where the co-occurrence of syllable and morpheme boundaries in the first case should facilitate reversal. This procedure could be carried out on all levels of linguistic analysis. For example, subjects could be requested to reverse the words in the sentence 'The boy went home.' The most common error one would expect would be 'home went *the boy*,' where 'the' and 'boy' are considered as forming a unit, in accordance with the usual linguistic analysis. Carefully chosen examples and accurate interpretation of results might reveal interesting correlations between the linguistic (formal), the psychological (intuitive) and the psycholinguistic (functional) levels of unit analysis.

---

[23] Notice that it is likely that diphthongs will not be reversed.

[24] The relative frequency of the words might be a factor in facilitating reversal, in which case the words would have to be chosen in accordance with a reliable frequency list.

3.3. *The Word as a Linguistic Unit*[25]

The word as a unit occupies a paradoxical situation in present-day linguistic science. Such a unit, roughly coinciding with the usage of the term in every day language and in the discourse of sciences other than linguistics, is actually employed as a fundamental dividing line between the two levels of morphological (infra-word) constructions and syntactic (supra-word) constructions. Yet no generally accepted and satisfactory definition exists, and some linguists deny validity of the word altogether, relegating it to folk-linguistics. Others believe that the word must be defined separately for each language and that there are probabably languages to which the concept is inapplicable. Some define the word in phonological terms, as when a word in Czech is defined as a sequence with stress on its initial syllable. Other definitions depend on the distribution of meaningful units and may be qualified as morphological or grammatical. Here belongs Bloomfield's well-known definition of the word as a minimal free form. This definition has the advantage, lacking in so many others, of being operational. Unfortunately it leads to results not at all like the traditional notion, although it was manifestly intended to correspond at least roughly to ordinary conceptions of the word. For example, 'the' in English would not be a word, but 'the king of England's' in the sentence 'the king of England's realm includes land on several continents' would. This is not in itself a fatal objection to its acceptance as defining *some* unit but it cannot be considered an adequate explication of the ordinary usage. Nida, for example, who adopts it, finds it necessary to supplement it with additional criteria, an indication of its unsatisfactory status.[26]

3.3.1. *Criteria for 'Word' Units*

Before proceeding with the definition to be proposed, we must ask what requirements must be fulfilled by a definition for it to be considered satisfactory. The popular conception of the word as indicated by the use of space in orthographies of various languages is not in itself sufficiently consistent to make a definition possible which will justify every word division in every existing orthography. This would be an unfair, and one might add, an impossible, requirement. As generally in problems of scientific explication, we take the popular non-scientific use as a point of departure, and one to which our results must, in general, conform. We require of our definition that it involve procedures that can actually be carried out (i.e., that it be operational), be free of logical contradiction, and give results in general agreement with the popular notion of what a word is.

Among the requirements that must be satisfied for the word to correspond to the usual notions regarding it, are the following: it should consist of a continuous sequence of phonemes such that every utterance in a language may be divided into a finite number of words exhaustively (i.e., with nothing left over) and unambiguously (ever phoneme' should belong to only one word). Otherwise stated,

[25] Joseph H. Greenberg.

[26] See Eugene Nida, *Morphology: the descriptive analysis of words*[1] (Ann Arbor, 1946). For a convenient review of the history of the subject, not discussed here, see Knud Togeby, Qu'est-ce qu'un mot? in *Travaux du Cercle Linguistique de Copenhague* 5. 97–111 (1949).

the division of an utterance into words should involve the assignment of each phoneme to one of a set of mutually exclusive classes which exhaust the universe of the particular utterance. It would also be expected that every word boundary should be a morph boundary, that is, the constituent phonemes of a morph, the minimal meaningful sequence, should never be divided between two or more words. On the other hand, it would be expected that many morph boundaries would not be word boundaries.

3.3.2. *Overview of this Analysis*

To aid in clarifying procedures, which must otherwise seem obscure at many points without some knowledge of the end-result and the major difficulties to be overcome, an informal account of the nature of the solution attempted here will first be given. The continuity, or non-interruptibility of the word, has been mentioned above as a desideratum of a successful definition. This might suggest immediately that a word be defined simply as a sequence within which another sequence cannot be inserted. However, it will soon appear that while in general this is true, it does not constitute an adequate definition. For example, we can insert 'r' in 'gate' to get 'grate,' but we wish 'gate' to be a word in English. We can insert 'house' in 'schools' to get 'schoolhouses' but we would certainly want 'schools' to be a word. The first example shows the necessity of eliminating insertions between non-meaningful elements (i.e., between 'g' and 'ate'). The second example shows that even this is not enough, for here the insertion takes place between 'school' and 's,' in other words, at a morph boundary. Much of the procedure is motivated by the attempt to discover a unit which permits only certain specifiable insertions. The result is the determination of a unit here called the 'nucleus,' intermediate between the morph and the word in length. For any utterance, $m \geq n \geq w$ where 'm' is the number of morphs, 'n' the number of nuclei and 'w' the number of words. Having defined the nucleus, we test all nucleus boundaries to see if they are word boundaries. Unlimited possible insertion of nuclei at a nucleus boundary makes it a word boundary. Since our procedure gives us word boundaries, and words are defined simply as the stretches between boundaries, the requirement of continuity is necessarily fulfilled.

Another feature of the procedure which perhaps requires some preliminary explanation is that it is entirely contextual in the sense that it provides a method for dividing a particular utterance into word units. We do not ask, as is sometimes done, whether 'hand' is a word in English but whether, in the utterance 'the hand is quicker than the eye,' the sequence 'hand' constitutes a word. This is because in many instances we want a sequence (e.g., Latin 'trans') sometimes to be a word, as the preposition meaning 'across' in 'coelum non mentem mutant qui trans mare vehunt' but sometimes to be part of a word, as when compounded with a verb in 'sic transit gloria mundi.'

3.3.3. *Definition and Clarification of Terms*

The first unit to be considered is the *morph substitution class* (MSC) in terms of which it will be possible to define the key nucleus unit referred to above. A morph substitution class is a set of single morphs (minimal units with a meaning) which in a given context may substitute for each other. For example, in the sentence 'the singer broke the contract' the morph 'sing-' in 'singer' belongs to an MSC which contains 'sing-,' 'play-,' 'min-' and other members, since 'the player broke the contract' and 'the miner broke the contract' are possible utterances; 'reform-' does not belong to the class since 're-form' consists of two morphs. It might be thought that the use of the concept of the MSC in defining the word involves a vicious circularity in that the definition of morph implies the comparison of word units in order to isolate minimal components. In fact, however, the notion of the word is not necessary here, and Harris and others have specified procedures for defining the morph while ignoring the word as a unit.[27]

The varying methods of defining morphs will almost all turn out to have no effect on our end result. The only exception is that the type of discontinuous morphemes described by Harris in his "Discontinuous Morphemes"[28] is naturally excluded, since such discontinuous elements are known to belong to different 'words' before we begin. We do not allow discontinuous morphs except such as have constantly numbered sequences of phonemes in their gaps. For example, in classical Arabic we have a morph q—t—l 'kill' in 'qatala zaydan' 'He killed Zaid,' but the number of dashes is restricted. Most disputed cases of morph division involve combinations such as 'receive' or 'huckleberry,' in which each of the elements belongs to such a small and unique MSC that nothing can be inserted anyway and either solution, as one morph or two morphs, leads to the same result.

Another proviso must be made: sometimes a substitution can apparently be made but the two morphs are not members of the same class.

One further limitation is necessary regarding what may be accepted as a morph. Sometimes intonational and other features extending over phrases or sentences are considered as morphs. Only prosodic elements simultaneous with a single segmental element, for example, tone in Chinese or stress in English is accepted here. It is self-evident that a unit which extends over a whole sequence such as a sentence cannot be relevant to the problem of its internal subdivision into words.

The next notion to be defined is that of a *thematic sequence*. In the example of 'sing-er' above we saw that 're-form,' although a sequence of two morphs and representing two MSC's, behaved in the construction 'reform-er' like a single MSC, that containing 'sing-,' 'play-,' etc. A sequence of two or more MSC's will be said to constitute a thematic sequence (1) if there is some single MSC for which it may always substitute and yield a grammatical utterance and (2) if none of the MSC's of the sequence is equivalent to, that is, has exactly the same membership as this single MSC for which the sequence may substitute. The thematic sequence may be said to form a theme and to be an expansion of the single MSC for which it may substitute.

Thematic expansion includes both what is usually called derivation and what is called compounding. Thus 'duck-ling' is a sequence of two morphs which is called a derivational construction. It consists of the MSC containing 'duck-,' 'gos-,' etc. and the MSC containing '-ling' as its only member. It may substitute for the single MSC containing 'hen,' 'chicken,' 'goose,' etc. among its members, and neither of its constituent MSC's is equiva-

---

[27] Z. Harris, From morpheme to utterance, *Language* **22.** 161–83 (1946).

[28] Z. Harris, Discontinuous morphemes, *Language* **21.** 121–7 (1945).

lent to this latter class since both contain members 'gos-, -ling' not found in the MSC of 'hen,' 'chicken,' etc.

We are now ready to define *nucleus*. A nucleus is either (1) a single MSC which is not part of a thematic sequence or (2) a thematic sequence of MSC's. Among single MSC's are some which are expandible into thematic sequences but are not expanded in the particular construction analyzed, and some which are not. In the sentence 'the farmer killed the ugly duckling' there are nine morphs: (1) the (2) farm- (3) -er (4) kill- (5) -ed (6) the (7) ugly (8) duck- (9) -ling. There are seven nuclei: (1) the (a nonexpandible MSC) (2) farm-er (a thematic expansion containing two MSC's) (3) kill- (a single MSC expandible e.g. into 'un-hook-') (4) -ed (a nonexpandible MSC) (5) the (as above) (6) ugly (a single MSC expandible into 'un-god-ly') (7) duck-ling (a thematic expansion consisting of two MSC's).

There remains finally the distinction between nucleus boundaries which are also word boundaries and those which are not. There are a number of ways of stating the distinction which give practically the same results. The one adopted here is as follows: a nucleus boundary is an infraword boundary if and only if a fixed number of nuclei may be inserted including those with zero members. Often nothing may be inserted. (Zero can be considered a limiting instance of a fixed and finite number.) It is a word boundary in the excluded instance, that is, when insertions are possible and they are not fixed in number, e.g., if both three and five are possible. Usually an indefinitely increasing number of insertions is possible, that is, there is 'infinite' insertion at word boundaries. In the above sentence no nucleus can be inserted between (3) kill- and (4) -ed and therefore it is not a word boundary. Between all the others, sequences of nuclei may be inserted of varying length and, in fact, without limit. Thus between (1) 'the' and (2) 'farm-er' we can insert 'very, headstrong, cruel, unloveable, etc.;' between (2) 'farm-er' and (3) 'kill-' can be inserted 'who lives in the house which is on the road that leads into the highway,' etc.

There is one kind of insertion which must be forbidden by a special rule since it can be carried out at any nucleus boundary whatever. This consists of one whose initial nucleus is the same as the nucleus after the boundary and whose final nucleus is the same as the nucleus before the boundary. In the above sentence, we might insert between (4) kill- and (5) -ed '-ed and slaughter-' producing 'the farmer killed and slaughtered the ugly duckling,' but '-ed,' the initial morph of the insertion, belongs to the same nucleus as (5) -ed and 'slaughter-' is a member of the same nucleus as (4) kill-. An indefinite number of such insertions of varying lengths is always possible.

Phoneme modifications at word boundaries, often known as *word sandhi*, make no difference to the analysis if they are regular. Whenever the modification can be stated in terms of the occurrence of phonemes, that is, is phonologically regular, the result is merely to restrict the insertion at any boundary to the subclass which begins with one of a particular set of phonemes. But by a well-known theorem in set theory, an indefinite enumerable set subtracted from an indefinite enumerable set still leaves an indefinite enumerable set. For example, the exclusion of all odd numbers still leaves an infinite set of integers. There is one rare type of occurrence in which *sandhi* gives rise to a single phoneme in place of the final of one nucleus and the initial of the next.

In Sanskrit if a nucleus ends in basic /-n/ and the next begins with basic /l-/, the result is a single phoneme /l̃/, a nasalized lateral. In this case the number of words is determinate, but the ascription of /ĭ/ to the former or latter *is* arbitrary. If we changed our phonemic analysis to make /ː/ a supra-segmental phoneme we could divide /ĭ/ into two phonemes and assign /ː/ to the former word and /l/ to the latter. A similar argument applies to junctural phonemes. In the example from English used here the junctures have not been written. They would not affect the analysis.

The present definition of nucleus resolves the contradiction between phonological and grammatical definitions of words. In the former, it is not the presence of stress or some other marker which demarcates the word, but the existence of stress or other *variation* or shift which produces different classes whose analysis by the present distributional (grammatical) method generally justifies such an apparently phonological procedure.

For example, in Latin, what is usually called a word is stressed on the penultimate syllabic if this is long, on the antepenultimate if it is short. This suggests a phonological definition of the word unit on the basis of this rule of stress. The enclitic -*que* ('and') is reckoned as a syllable with any preceding sequence in locating the stress which serves as a marker of word boundaries under this definition. Thus, traditionally *dŏminus* ('lord') and *dŏminúsque* ('and the lord') are both single words. Under the present purely distributional analysis likewise, *dŏminúsque* will be one word, and not two. *Dōminús*- belongs to the same nucleus as *legatús*-, *puér*- and all other stress-shifted nominative singular masculine substantives which may be substituted for it. Since no nucleus can be interposed between the nucleus of *dŏminús*- and that of -*que*, -*ve* and other enclitics, *dŏminúsque* is a single word. Even in monosyllables where there is no stress shift, *mŭs* ('mouse') and the *mŭs* of *mŭsque* ('and the mouse') are members of different nuclei since the former can only be substituted by *dŏminus*, *puér*, etc. and the latter by *dominús*-, *puér*-.

3.3.4. *Some Psycholinguistic Implications*

The concept of nucleus as defined here is essentially a unit of which there is always a single fixed number in the class of words which are mutually substitutable in the same construction. As such it corresponds to the notion of positions in the word as developed by Boas in connection with the description of American Indian languages. It may find application beyond that of its utility in the present definition. For example, it might well be investigated psychologically as a possible fundamental encoding or decoding unit.

It has been seen that intraword nucleus boundaries and those which coincide with word boundaries are different in the choices presented to the speaker. In the former, the next nucleus is determined, or passed over if it has a zero member, by the next one not represented by zero in the context. At a word boundary, on the contrary, the speaker has a choice among a number of different nuclei. It has been noted elsewhere in this report that pauses tend to occur at word boundaries rather than within the word. Indeed, it may be proposed that the presence of potential pause be employed as an independent definition of the word-unit (cf., section 5). This phenomenon is probably connected with the greater latency which occurs in psychological experimental situations when a subject is faced with choices referring to different bases of judgment even where the number of alternatives are the same as a set all involving the same basis of judgment (cf., section 5). At every boundary in speech we must make choices, but within a word we choose a particular member of a determined class. At word boundaries we must, in addition, make a semantic selection, the choosing among alternative nuclei. Indeed, it seems quite possible that the nucleus corresponds to the minimal semantic unit.

Finally, a possible application of the present analysis to the development of child language may be pointed out. It has been remarked as paradoxical that, in the child's speech development, syntactic constructions, supposedly on a higher level, occur at a period when morphological distinctions are not yet developed. Thus the child says 'boy run,' which involves an actor-goal construction but ignores the morphological distinction between singular and plural. At this period of the child's development, however, all utterances have a maximum of two 'words,' later on three 'words.' In accordance with our definition, however, 'boy' and 'run' are not words since there is no possibility of indefinite—in fact, of any—insertion at their boundary. Hence at this stage the child does not have syntax since he does not have word sequences. What he has, since he may substitute 'girl' for 'boy' or 'eat' for 'run,' are fixed sequences of nuclei whose rules of combination are therefore analogous to that within the adult word. When he learns boundary expansion, his former morphology becomes syntax and a new morphology of intraword constructions appears. Hence the paradox is only apparent. The child develops a morphology before he handles syntactic constructions.

3.4. *Hierarchies of Psycholinguistic Units*[29]

The various research techniques for getting at psycholinguistic units suggested both here and elsewhere in this report will probably yield evidence for a number of different types of units. The larger will include clusters of the smaller in the same way that function classes include morphemes and morphemes include phonemes, but they will also overlap to varying degrees in all probability. These units will be found to be related to certain levels of organization within the human nervous system, which may be tentatively identified as motivational, semantic, sequential, and integrational. The first of these levels, motivational, is discussed further in section 7.1. The other three, semantic, sequential and integrational, are discussed in some detail in section 6.1 in connection with the development of language behavior.

In general, the question we ask is this: *how much of the message is related to decisions or choices made at each of these levels of organization and what features in messages serve as boundary markers of these units?* In the case of encoding, we want to know what segments of messages (output) depend upon *intentional decisions* made at motivational and semantic levels as well as what segments represent sequential and integrational organization of vocal skills. In the case of decoding, we want to know what segments of messages (input) determine *significance decisions* about both emotional state and meaning as well as what segments contribute to sequential and integrational organization in language perception. There is no requirement that the units of messages discovered be the same for

[29] Charles E. Osgood.

both encoding and decoding, and the evidence already presented at least implies that they are not.

The *motivational level*, as we are using the term here, is concerned with decisions of a gross nature—whether to speak or not to speak, and if the former, whether to make a statement, answer a question just received, ask a question, give a command, or so forth, and within these decisions whether to use an active or passive form of address, what to emphasize, and so on. The functional unit here would seem to be the 'sentence' in a broad, non-grammarian sense or the 'construction' in the linguistic sense. There are features which mark these units as being wholes at a gross level, including *intonation pattern, stress pattern*, and certain *construction markers*. These three types of features tend to be somewhat redundant with respect to one another, which would be expected if they depend upon the same decisions; for example, construction markers like 'who,' 'when,' 'do,' 'have,' 'will' at the beginning of an utterance signal that the encoder has already selected a question form, and the usual rising intonation is redundantly related to this selection to a considerable degree. Motivation obviously influences the location of primary stress, but it also modulates relative stress throughout a construction. (There are undoubtedly effects which go beyond the bounds of the single construction or sentence, but we have enough complexity to worry about within this unit!) On the reciprocal decoding side, units for interpreting motivational significances are probably the same as above for intonation and stress patterns, since decoding here requires the complete utterance (e.g., 'The boy walked down the street alone' can be suddenly shifted from statement to question by a rising intonation between, roughly, 'a-' and '-lone'). On the other hand, construction markers that occur at the beginnings of utterances, like 'How . . . ,' can function as sufficient segments for decoding motivational significance in themselves.

The *semantic level* is concerned with discriminations among possible meanings (or among alternative representational mediators, if one prefers this less mentalistic language). What segments of messages as produced by an *encoder* correspond to decisions on this level? We suggest the *function class* as the encoding unit here. This would mean that 'the new car' would be a single unit in encoding, not two or three units. Some languages provide evidence for such functional units, e.g., when the Spanish speaker encodes 'las bonitas casas' he must have selected the head of the phrase at the time of initiating 'las.' It seems likely that the semantic unit for the decoder, on the other hand, will be much smaller. We suggest Greenberg's ¬*nucleus* as a candidate here. Unlike the encoder, who 'knows' he is going to say 'the little girl with the red hair' when he starts, the decoder must react sequentially to the sound material as it is unreeled, modifying his interpretation as new material comes along—'the' must be discriminated from other possibilities, such as 'a,' 'some,' 'all' and so on, 'little' must set up a process different than what would be started by receiving 'big,' 'hairy,' 'green,' and so forth. The same is true for grammatical tags—the /-t/ in 'walked' must be distinguished from '-s,' '-ing,' and even 'zero' endings.

The *sequential level*, as we have called it here, concerns the tying together of either input or output events on the basis of their redundancy and frequency, e.g., their transitional dependencies. It would seem that it is here that the *word* appears as a unit in both encoding and decoding. On the encoding side the features characterizing the word as a unit would be *backward-working skill modifications* (e.g., the fact that the terminal phone in /haws/ is changed across morph boundaries to make /hawz-/ in the plural)—these seem to operate clearly within word units but not beyond, except in trite phrases—and *length of junctures* (we expect that detailed analysis will show intervals between words to be significantly longer on the average than junctures within words, even at morph boundaries). On the decoding side, the significant feature is probably length of juncture, which corresponds to spacing between words in orthography. There are also *grammatical* sequencing mechanisms that work over larger segments for both encoder and decoder.

At the *integrational level* we are dealing with the smallest building blocks of language which, because of their extremely high internal redundancy, high frequency of occurrence, and limited number, become very tightly welded and indivisible units. Again, we feel reason to believe these units are different for encoding than for decoding. In encoding this minimal building block seems to be the *syllable*, i.e., these are the minimal motor skill components which are variously compounded into words and utterances. Only by considerable effort, if at all, can the native speaker produce separate phones—witness his way of 'saying the alphabet,' in which every 'letter' (with the possible exception of the vowels) is produced as a syllable (e.g., /ey/, /biy/, /siy/, /diy/, etc.). In decoding, on the other hand, the *phoneme* seems to be the minimal unit. As we have already seen, allophones are typically not perceived by the native speaker, but he does make decoding discriminations in terms of minimal phonemic contrasts, as between /haws/ and /maws/.

What goes on in the rapid interplay of conversation between an encoder and decoder must be tremendously complicated, since it involves operations on all these levels simultaneously and in relation to all of these types of units and their distinguishing features. In the process of encoding, for example, a speaker may be motivated toward obtaining some butter for his bread, which influences his selection of a "command' construction; the automatisms associated with this intention select the verb form first, and 'Pass me,' 'Gimme,' 'Hand me,' or some other is encoded; this is followed by the encoding of 'the butter,' that member of the form class which is associated with the representational process established in butter-using situations. Mechanisms at lower levels in the motor system are presumably concerned with the calling forth and ordering of word units, each of which includes one or more syllabic components tightly welded as motor skills. The decoding process is equally complex. It should be stressed that the hierarchical analysis suggested here, and particularly the identifications of units and correlated features, is entirely tentative in nature. A great deal more empirical evidence is needed.

4. SYNCHRONIC PSYCHOLINGUISTICS I: MICROSTRUCTURE

Speech communities are knit into systems of social organization by the transfer of messages over interpersonal communication channels. These channels are made up of a number of different bands over which messages can move synchronously. There is, of course, the *vocal-auditory band* which couples movements of vocal muscles with stimulation of auditory receptors. It is axiomatic that speech is independent of a light source, which is one of its great advantages over most other avenues of communication. There is also a *gestural-visual band* which couples movements of facial and bodily muscles with stimulation of visual receptors. Interpersonal messages in everyday communication travel simultaneously over these auditory and visual avenues, typically reinforcing one another but occasionally being in contrast for certain purposes. Other sensory modalities (such as smell, touch, taste, and temperature) may participate in communication —they certainly do with other species, and the remarkable feats of Helen Keller show that they can be highly discriminating even in the human—but they usually contribute in limited and unintentional ways, since they are seldom under the voluntary control of the encoder. There is finally what we may call the *manipulational-situational band*, which via the mediation of 'things' that the encoder manipulates and the decoder observes also couples the two. In this chapter we explore both organization *within* these bands and interaction *between* them. The result is essentially the outline of a broad area and serves to etch the gaps that exist in our empirical knowledge.

4.1. *Within Band Organization*

Each of the bands in the interpersonal channel can be studied internally to determine its organization. To what extent is its coding *discrete* or *continuous*? To what extent *arbitrary* (in terms of learned social agreements) or *natural* (in terms of innate biological necessities)? What is the organization or *structure* of the code? What classes of events have common significance and reflect common intentions (like allophones)? How do the continuously coded signals interact with the discretely coded signals? Questions of this sort have been asked and answered in some detail for the vocal-auditory band, since this is the central area of operation of the structural linguist. A little work has been done in the gestural-visual band, as we shall see, but practically nothing in other bands. We shall therefore use work that has been done on the vocal-auditory band as a model for potential application elsewhere.

4.1.1. *The Vocal-auditory Band*

The study of synchronous bands as a psycholinguistic problem cannot fruitfully begin on the global level depicted above. Here we restrict our attention to information carried within the auditory band. The organization of synchronous bands within the auditory channel is not itself well understood. Some of the variables are, of course, linguistic in the narrow sense—bundles of distinctive features and hierarchies of configurational features which contribute to the formal aspects of the message. The auditory channel also includes variables which convey information as to the code being used, social relations between the communicators, their geographic origin and physiological states, and their evanescent emotional attitudes. These variables are sometimes called 'voice qualifiers.'

4.1.1.1. *Non-linguistic organization.*[30] The discretely coded signals in this band have been explored by linguists and should not concern us here, except as they contribute to communication in a fashion which is not subsumed under their purely linguistic function. This distinction between linguistic and non-linguistic variables is unfortunately not so clear theoretically as it might appear to be from the particular scope of the work in which linguists engage. It seems to be possible to distinguish linguistic features as discrete and quantized in contrast to the continuity of the non-linguistic. But this may reduce in the last analysis to the fact that the former have been studied systematically by linguists from a particular point of view, e.g., the discreteness may be imposed on the material, while the others have not been so treated. Some of the problems discussed here may eventually be subsumed under linguistic methodology proper.

(1) *A variety of views.* There are several ways in which the non-linguistic features can be categorized. Sapir, in an article on "Speech as a Personality Trait" suggested two interrelated analyses differentiating the individual from the social aspects on the one hand, and distinguishing levels of speech on the other. The particular levels which he found relevant are the following: 1) *Voice* is the lowest and most fundamental level. 2) On the next level is *voice dynamics,* which subsumes intonation, rhythm, continuity, and speed. 3) *Pronunciation* concerns those variations, individual or social, made upon the phonemes of a language. 4) *Vocabulary* involves the particular selection made by speakers or groups of speakers from the lexical pool of a language. 5) Finally, on the highest level, *style* characterizes those typical arrangements that are made of the vocabulary elements. This classification suggests a number of the variables which may be treated.

Sebeok, following, in part, Lótz, has approached this analysis from a somewhat different point of view. Tentatively, he has suggested the following features as particularly relevant: 1) *Manner of speaking.* This is a constant feature of the individual speaker and may be shared with either the entire speech community (Japanese is spoken in a higher pitch than, say, English) or with a particular social group. 2) *Speech organ characteristics.* These may be long range as in the case of a speaker with cleft palate or short range, as when the speaker has a full mouth or a cold. 3) *Pragmatic* (emotive or expressive) *features.* These can be broken down into a) statements about codification used to bring people into implicit agreement as to the meaning of their messages and, of course, as to the code they are using, and b) statements about interpersonal relationships reflecting the emotional relationship of the speakers, their mutual status and role, and the felt success of their communicative efforts.

[30] Thomas A. Sebeok, Donald E. Walker, and Joseph H. Greenberg.

Another categorization which could be used has been suggested by Greenberg and Walker. This involves a series of binary distinctions between learned vs. unlearned, voluntary vs. involuntary, and constant vs. intermittent features. The unlearned features are by definition not susceptible to the voluntary-involuntary differentiation. 1) *Unlearned:* a) *Constant*—this includes such factors as voice quality, the effects of cleft palate, deviated nasal septum, and the absolute range of vocalization. b) *Intermittent*—the effects of cough, fatigue, full mouth, and of colds and other temporary physiological conditions. 2) *Learned:* a) *Involuntary*—the following features are those not usually varied voluntarily by the individual for specific vocal effects: (i) *constant*—average tempo of speech, vigor of articulation, normal range of speaking, normal distribution of allophonic features; (ii) *intermittent*—variations in the above introduced by moods or emotions. b) *Voluntary*—features introduced into the message specifically as vocal modifications: (i) *constant*—some characteristic referring to success of communication, interpersonal relationships, and statements about codification; (ii) *intermittent*—variations induced by emphasis, intonations for sarcasm, encouragement, irony, etc.

Given some such scheme as the three presented above, two problems must be considered. The first involves the utility of the classification itself, but, independent of any particular means of categorization, it should be possible to specify relevant variables by the consistency of their identification in experimental situations. The second problem involves specification of the particular phenomena in the sound material which represent these variables and determination of the ranges of variation permitted. Once such identifications have been made, it should be possible to study relations of linguistic to non-linguistic features.

(2) *Sketches of specific systems.* In *Hungarian*, there is a distinctive feature of length. Expressively, it is possible to distort this feature so that long is substituted for short, and over-long for long. There is no phonemic stress. Expressively, also, it is possible to stress a syllable other than the first, usually the third. This illustrates the fact that expressive features can be superimposed on distinctive features, or, again, a distinction can be introduced which is not phonemic. A third possibility consists of the substitution of a contrast already in the language in a position where it does not ordinarily occur. Fourth, it is possible to introduce an entirely new (from a phonemic point of view) phone into the language for expressive purposes. The above are all carried on the vocal-auditory band but are not phonemic. *Spanish.* One might consider these bands as consisting of levels of information. For example, the information, 'relative social position' is usually expressed in Spanish by the morphemic contrast between 'tú' and 'usted,' indicating the categories of familiarity and politeness. However, in addition, this same information may be carried on another level, namely by the use of the diminutive morpheme '-ito' under certain conditions. This morpheme may be used in any conversation with the meaning 'diminutive' or 'endearment.' When added to a word like 'Adios,' however, the information carried is merely that there is relative familiarity between the speakers. In terms of the problem being considered here, one may consider this use of the morpheme as an introduction of a new contrast into the code, a contrast expressed not by any morphemic distinction, but expressed by use of a certain morpheme in special environments. *English.* Similarly, in English, the use of a particular allophone in special environment, may be considered as giving additional information. The distribution of the voiceless aspirated stop, e.g., [tʰ] is usually limited to initial position. It is used, however, by some speakers in final position

instead of the customary unreleased stop. The usual effect of such usage is an unfavorable one on the listener, which is usually expressed as 'an attempt at putting it on' or 'over-careful enunciation,' etc. This then may be considered as the use of a non-phonemic contrast as an expressive feature.

(3) *Research proposal: Determination of non-linguistic features and correlated variations in the sound material.* The experimental situation here requires elimination of all communication bands other than the vocal-auditory. This can be accomplished by having subjects speak through screens, in the dark, over the radio, or onto tape recordings. The latter recommends itself as permitting the most control, delayed uses of the material, and sampling of the most natural situations. The experimental situation also requires deliberate variation in the physiological, emotional, social and other characteristics of speakers that are assumed to be transmitted as information by non-linguistic features. The general proposal below is to (A) obtain judgments as to these characteristics of speakers from representative hearers, based on tape recordings, and correlate them with observable features in the sound material, and then (B) experimentally vary what seem to be the relevant features on a series of tapes and see if in fact these variations are accompanied by changes in the judgments presumably dependent on them.

(A) Record the conversation of two individuals in natural encounter (as in someone's office, in role playing situations, in therapy sessions, and so forth). Play the consecutive, uninterrupted remarks of one speaker to a group of subjects and ask for spontaneous comments about the characteristics of the individual. Then ask for specifications of age, sex, physical condition, emotional state, the apparent audience, social status, etc. Then request the same subjects to indicate as best they can the basis, *in the sound material*, for each of these judgments. Check communality of judgment and correlate with both the original speaker's judgments about himself and those of independent judges who have witnessed the original communication situation. This experiment could be varied by using conversational material in which both speakers are heard. Another variation would be to use artificially structured situations, with participants instructed to act out particular relationships under particular assumed emotions.

(B) Having obtained evidence in (A) as to what variables in the sound material seem to function as cues for such judgments, it should then be possible to introduce electronic modifications in samples of the same speech which alter certain of these variables systematically (at least those variables which can be so modified). If our identifications are valid, then the consistency and extremeness of judgments about, say, 'anger' should be continuously variable by modifying, say, pitch, amplitude, and rate of speech in some combination. There is a considerable body of research already available[31] which would guide and sharpen experiments on this problem.

4.1.1.2. *Linguistic organization.*[32] Early students of language described speech sounds as similar if they gave the 'impression' of similarity, i.e., if they were perceived as similar. Such judgments are influenced by the physical characteristics of sound, but also by the perceptual characteristics of hearers. More recently, phoneticians have defined speech sound similarity in terms of either spectro-

[31] See particularly Cantril and Allport, *The psychology of radio* (Harper, 1935), and a series of research papers by Grant Fairbanks on quantitative vocal correlates of emotion.
[32] Kellogg Wilson and Sol Saporta.

graphic analysis (acoustical phonetics) or positions of the articulatory organs (motor phonetics). In this section we suggest a general logic and procedure that may be applicable to analyzing the internal structure of any band of human communication, even though it is discussed here in relation to linguistic sound material.

(1) *Phonetic, phonemic and psychological spaces.* While the exact nature and number of variables needed for adequate description are not agreed upon, it seems reasonable to suppose that speech sounds can be regarded as occupying positions in a multidimensional space in which each of the variables used in describing the sounds corresponds to a dimension of the space. The dimensions of such a space are defined in physical terms and may correspond to either discrete or continuous variables, or a combination of both; however, the categories of a discrete variable should be ordered in such a way (e.g., four degrees of increasing length) that they can be regarded as a quantized continuous variable. We shall regard the position of a sound in this *phonetic space* as constituting its *phonetic reality.* The phonetic space is *invariable* in the sense that the language of the speaker or hearer of a sound does not affect it. The phonetic space is *continuous* in an operational sense, since no sound could conceivably be assigned to the same position as another if measurement were sufficiently refined. The physical similarity of speech sounds is measured by the distance between their positions in this multi-dimensional phonetic space.

Phonemic analysis results in another—and more convenient—way of describing the speech sounds of a language. We can regard the analysis of a language into a set of k phonemes as defining a space consisting of k mutually exclusive regions which correspond to the phoneme classes. The position of a sound in this *phonemic space* will be regarded as constituting its *phonemic reality.* The phonemic space is *variable* in the sense that the position of any sound depends on the divisions imposed by the language code of its users. Also, the phonemic space is *discrete* and *unordered* in the sense that two sounds are either in the same or different regions (i.e., in the same or different phoneme classes), and a statement that one pair of sounds is 'more alike' than another is meaningless.[33] Thus, two sounds are either phonemically the same or phonemically different.

Conceptually, the simplest possible relation between the phonetic and phonemic realities would be one in which the regions of the phonemic space correspond to clusters of sounds in the phonetic space. Thus, phonetically similar sounds would be phonemically identical. However, we would not necessarily find such a simple relationship as the following example indicates: let us consider the vowel [ʌ·] in the word 'buzz,' the unstressed vowel [ə] of 'Rosa's,' and the unstressed vowel [ɪ] of 'roses' in the dialect of speakers who distinguish between the last two. Laboratory measurement would probably indicate that the last two are more

[33] The technique of phonemic analysis used by Jakobson and his associates, in which phoneme classes are determined by sets of binary distinctive features, gives a *discrete* but *ordered* phonetic space, since similarity of phones may be regarded as varying with the number of distinctive features shared by their phoneme classes.

phonetically similar than the first two. On the other hand, a phonemic analysis is very likely to assign the first two to /ə/ and the third to /ɨ/.[34]

The lack of exact correlation between the phonetic and phonemic similarity·of sounds can be at least partially attributed to the perceptual habits of the speakers of a language. These habits permit their possessors to respond differentially to some phonetic differences and to ignore others. The effects of these habits are most evident in the accents and misinterpretations of people who are learning a foreign language. The use of impressionistic judgments of 'similarity' by the linguist is justified if such judgments approximate these perceptual habits. Nevertheless, we need an objective technique of describing these habits which is not affected by the results of a phonetic or phonemic analysis of the speech sounds of a language. Our purpose here is to outline such a technique and to suggest experimental procedures needed to apply it.

The end result of the technique to be proposed below will be to generate a *psychological space* containing a set of speech sounds. A measure of *psychological similarity*, which indicates the degree to which a pair of speech sounds are perceived as similar by a group of subjects, will form the basis of this psychological space, which will be *continuous* like the phonetic space but *variable* like the phonemic space. The dimensions of this space should indicate the bases for discrimination between the speech sounds employed by the subjects, these dimensions constituting a minimum set of 'distinctive features' needed to make the discriminations involved in the ordering of the speech sounds.

While determination of the psychological space is independent of the associated phonetic and phonemic spaces, we can expect the *results* expressed in the psychological space to be dependent on the results expressed in the phonetic and phonemic spaces. The psychological space must be related directly to at least some sub-space of the phonetic space, since at least some of the dimensions of the phonetic space must correspond to the differential stimuli to which the subjects respond. The psychological space must also be related to the phonemic space, since two sounds cannot contrast and be used to indicate differential 'meaning' in the same phonetic environment if they are not discriminated. Thus, the difference between the phonetic and psychological spaces represents a transformation in the ordering of speech sounds produced by the perceptual habits of a set of speakers of a given language; it may be regarded as the result of a sort of phonemic analysis in which each cluster is a group of psychologically similar sounds sharing 'distinctive features' with similar values, but where distributional criteria are ignored. The difference between the psychological and phonemic spaces represents a transformation in ordering produced by considering distributional criteria alone.

(2) *Experimental proposal.* The human perceptual apparatus operates so that the same speech sound does not always produce the same perception. Thus it may be said to behave like a communication channel with some degree of noise, where the distribution of output events is not perfectly predictable for each input event. Following this analogy, it seems reasonable to say that two input events (speech sounds) are *similar* to the extent that they produce similar conditional distribu-

[34] Cf. the vowel phonemes as presented by Smith and Trager in *Outline of English structure* (1951). The phonetic and phonemic symbolism used here is from the same source.

tions of output events (perceptual discriminations). The first experimental problem discussed below (A) concerns a method of determining similarity of perceptual judgments of speech sound, a modification of the psychophysical *method of paired comparisons* being finally selected. Experimental procedure and selection of materials is then described under (B); for demonstration purposes, the suggested analysis is limited to the cardinal vowels. Finally, under (C), we suggest a possible way of treating such data, essentially a computation of 'distances' between speech sounds as perceived based upon the conditional distributions of forced-choice judgments.

(A) *Method for determining psychological similarity.* We need to select some differential response pattern which is indicative of our subjects' perceptions. The obvious method is to simply ask them what they hear when a particular sound is presented, but there is no reason to suppose that untrained native speakers could make a coherent report. On the other hand, phonetic training would probably change the similarities the subjects have learned to perceive as native speakers and hence destroy the very condition we wish to study. Articulation tests—in which subjects select a spoken word from several written alternatives—can be used with naive subjects, but they have several disadvantages for our purposes:

    (a) It is necessary to use a different set of words for each group speaking a different language or dialect, making it impossible to compare the pattern of perceived similarities of different language or dialect groups under identical conditions.

    (b) Since all possible phonetic environments are not found in the words of a given language, our results would be confounded by the dissimilar environments in which the sounds we are studying occur.

These objections could be avoided by use of one of the psychophysical techniques. It would be possible to present the same group of stimuli to any group of subjects and to present each sound in a particular phonetic environment or set of environments.

The most applicable of the conventional psychophysical techniques is the *method of paired comparisons*, in which the subject is presented with a pair of speech sounds and asked to state whether they are the 'same' or 'different.' However, it is a common observation that subjects do not have the same criteria of 'sameness,' so we might well have some subjects saying that two sounds are the same because they appear to be 'similar' and others who would say that two sounds are 'different' because they are only similar. We may avoid this limitation of the method by presenting our subjects with sequences of three instead of two sounds. The subjects would be given response sheets with the letters *a b c* opposite the number corresponding to each sequence, and they would be asked to cross out the position of the sound *least like* the other two. Thus, the responses of the subjects will be based on a simple and relatively unequivocal forced choice rather than on the rather complex judgment of 'sameness.'

The main disadvantage of this technique is the large number of sequences which it is necessary to use. If we use all possible orders, i.e., all permutations, of *n* speech sounds in sequences of three different sounds and in sequences where two sounds are the same,[35] there would be

$$\frac{n!}{(n-3)!} + \frac{2(n!)}{(n-2)!}$$

---

[35] The reasons for using each sound paired with itself will be made clear later when the measure of similarity is introduced.

sequences. For n = 14, this quantity is 2,548. If we use only all possible combinations, each combination being represented by but one of its possible orders, there would be

$$\frac{n!}{3!\,(n-3)!} + \frac{(2n!)}{2!\,(n-2)!}$$

sequences. For n = 14, this quantity is 686. Obviously, there would be considerable saving of time if it were feasible to only use all combinations. Therefore, it would be well to run at least one pilot study using all possible permutations of a small number of speech sounds to determine if the order of presentation has any effect on the patterns of judgments made by the subjects.

(B) *Procedure and materials.* The temporal order of events given below for the presentation of each sequence seems to be adequate:

1 sec.	Announcement of no. of sequence
1 sec.	Silence
½ sec.	First speech sound
½ sec.	Silence
½ sec.	Second speech sound
½ sec.	Silence
½ sec.	Third speech sound
3 sec.	Recording of judgment

At this rate, it would be possible to complete 686 sequences in 85.75 minutes and 2548 sequences in 318.50 minutes. In order to preserve uniformity of the sounds employed, it would be desirable to record each sound but once and 'assemble' sounds for experimental presentation by re-recording them on magnetic tape.

Because there is more agreement concerning the articulatory position, the distinctive features, and the role of the formants in the production and reception of the vowel sounds, it would be advisable to begin this type of analysis with a set of cardinal vowels. The use of cardinal vowels has the additional advantage that this material may be used with speakers of various languages to determine the effect of language on perception of phonetic similarity. In order to be sure of their exact acoustic qualities it would be well to have these sounds produced by some electronic apparatus.

(C) *Treatment of data.* Let i, j and k represent any of the set of n speech sounds and let $p(i; j/k)$ represent the estimated probability that k will be judged the most dissimilar member of the sequence i j k.

Let $p(i; j) = \sum_k p(i; j/k)$. The measure $p(i; j)$ appears to be related to the joint probability of the production of sound i and the perception of sound j, $p(i, j)$. However, it differs from $p(i, j)$ in that:

(a) $p(i; j) = p(j; i)$ while $p(i, j)$ does not necessarily equal $p(j, i)$.

(b) $p(i; j)$ is relative to the choice of sounds with which i and j co-occur.

Point (a) is not an overly serious objection since a relation of similarity should be symmetric; i.e., a should be just as similar to b as b is similar to a. Point (b) merely states that $p(i; j)$ is relative to the situation in which it is determined—a limitation equally true of any estimate of $p(i, j)$, although the precise nature of the limitations differ.

We shall define the distance between sounds i and j, $D(i, j)$,[36] as

$$D(i, j) = \sqrt{\sum_r [p(i; r) - p(j; r)]^2}$$

where r is any of the complete set of speech sounds of which the sequences are composed. If two sounds are similar, they should be judged as similar to other sounds to the same

---

[36] Cf., Osgood and Suci, A measure of relation determined by both profile and mean difference information, *Psychological Bulletin* **49** (1952).

degree. In this case, all of the differences, p(i; r) − p(j; r), should be zero or near zero so that D(i, j) is small. If i and j are usually perceived as dissimilar we would expect all of these differences to be large so that D(i, j) would be large. If three sounds, i, j and k, are ordered along the same dimension, the distances between the three possible pairs will be such that D(i, j) + D(j, k) will be equal to D(i, k) within the limits of sampling error.

If the number of dimensions in the psychological space is three or less we should be able to simply construct a physical model which preserves the proportionality of the distance measures. The nature of the dimensions could be determined from the clusterings of the sounds along the dimensions or at their end-points. If the number of dimensions is greater than three, it would be necessary to apply some factor analytic procedure. Suci has developed a technique which can be directly applied to distance measures, and other factor analytic techniques could be applied to correlation matrices of p(i; r) with p(j; r) for all pairs of i and j.[37]

(3) *Some applications of psychological space.* The technique indicated above is tedious and can be applied only to small sets of sounds at one time. However, we were unable to devise any simpler technique which is compatible with the demands of scientific rigor.[38] Even with these limitations, it can be a valuable research tool.

The psychological space serves as a sort of transition stage between the phonetic and phonemic ordering of speech sounds and can serve to clarify the nature of phonemic analysis. It also might provide a more objective measure of the perceived similarity of speech sounds than the impressionistic judgment of even an expert linguist. The ordering of a language's sounds in a psychological space could be used as a standard to select between two equally simple, exhaustive and non-contradictory phonemic analyses. Furthermore, we may use this technique to test Jakobson's hypothesis concerning the binary nature of the distinctive feature. If he is correct, we would expect the sounds to form clusters in the psychological space such that each cluster marks the end of one of the dimensions.

There are other potential applications to linguistic theory. Consider, for example, the contrast between voiced and voiceless consonants in Spanish and English. In Spanish, the contrast between voiced and voiceless is phonemic between [p] and [b] and [t] and [d], but allophonic in [s] and [z]. Therefore, we would expect that the psychological space for a group of Spanish speakers would

---

[37] Cf. an unpublished paper by Suci; and R. B. Cattell, *Factor analysis.* After the statistical technique above had been devised, we found that a similar technique had been devised by Warren S. Torgenson (*Psychometrika*, 17. 401-19 [1952]). Torgenson introduces some refinements not present in our technique which require additional assumptions about the nature of his measures and their distribution and which lead to lengthy and laborious computation. It should be noted that Torgenson seems concerned with developing a psychometric measuring device while we are concerned with the less demanding task of determining the ordering of speech sounds in an exploratory fashion.

[38] In the discussion of the seminar group it was suggested that the sounds may have to be put in specific phonetic environments to obtain the desired relation to the phonemic space. There is nothing in the nature of the technique or the basic theory to prevent this being done, but it is evident that the use of particular environments would severely restrict the generality of the results. Therefore, the more general technique was suggested in the hope that phonetic environments will have generally slight effects.

reflect this linguistic fact by placing the allophonic pair closer together than the phonemic pairs. Another situation arises when Spanish speakers are asked to distinguish between [f] and [v], since the latter sound does not occur in their language. The most likely outcome here would seem to be that [v] will be psychologically similar to another sound in Spanish so that the relation between [f] and [v] will correspond to the relation between [f] and [b]. This effect is suggested by the errors made by Spanish speakers in learning English. It is possible that the nature of the psychological space may indicate the effect of morphophonemic relations. For example, the fact that in English /t/ and /d/ are alternates of a very common 'past tense' morpheme should make them more psychologically similar than corresponding pairs such as /p/ and /b/ or /k/ and /g/.

Another set of hypotheses may be explored by obtaining psychological spaces for the same set of speech sounds from speakers of various languages. As mentioned above, it seems likely that speakers of different languages will show differences in their psychological spaces which correspond to differences in the phonemic spaces of the language. The effect of learning a second language, or of bilingualism, on the psychological space could also be investigated; our example concerning Spanish speakers would imply that a relatively greater distance between /f/ and /v/, indicative of a phonemic distinction, should be associated with Spanish-English bilingualism. Finally, it would be of interest to obtain a sort of 'asymptotic' psychological space, using subjects highly trained in distinguishing between speech sounds. Such a space should indicate the complete set of discriminations which the human perceptual apparatus is capable of making.

4.1.1.3. *Levels of awareness of linguistic differences*. [39] Utterances differ at many different levels—phonetically, phonemically, in word order, stress, intonation pattern, and grammatical construction. It is usually assumed that native speakers can identify some of these differences but not others. In particular, it is said that they cannot hear allophonic differences. The following analysis is intended to describe some procedures for testing whether discrimination has occurred between two utterances which are similar in all respects but one. If it can be demonstrated, for example, that speakers consistently *report* no difference between allophones, but that their responses to allophones differ in some other way, then we will be better able to infer the nature of the decoding processes involved.

(1) *Verbalization about differences*. These may be of two varieties: (a) The subject points out the linguistic feature that is different. (b) The subject reports how he feels about the difference, what different information it gives him either about the content of the utterance or about the speaker. Differences in word order and grammatical construction, for instance, may be recognizable as features for subjects even though they may differ in their report about the information the differences give them. Shifts in phonetic aspects, while not specifically identifiable, may by many subjects be reported to indicate that the speaker has a certain dialect, comes from a certain group, etc.

(2) *Indirect verbal indices*. In certain cases, subjects may report no difference, or they may report a difference but not know whether or in what way it affects them. Free association methods, or the semantic differential (cf., section 7.2.2.), could be used to specify these affects. For example, one could take clusters of words, such as 'young strong man,' vary

---

[39] Susan M. Ervin.

the stress or intonation pattern, and test the effects on these indices. Voice qualifiers might be studied in this way also. One of the problems here would be that a whole utterance is somewhat difficult to use as a stimulus, but subjects might be instructed to respond only to the last word, as they have been in some context studies using word clusters.

(3) *Non-verbal responses.* The subject would be conditioned to some sound, in a certain context, and generalization to other sounds or to contexts containing the same sound would be measured. Or, conversely, one could determine how easily discrimination is learned. PGR and finger movements in response to shock might be appropriate to use here. This technique would be particularly useful for phonetic and allophonic discrimination studies. For example, it could be used to test generalization between phonetically dissimilar allophones which are not similar in sensory features.

These techniques could be used with several variations, such as varying the degree of audibility to see effects on level of awareness. Also, the location of the difference in the utterance could be varied. It might be hypothesized that differences occurring at points of high transitional entropy are more likely to be noticeable. Other variables which should be related to level of awareness of differences are the following: age, education, amount of contact with other languages and dialects, types of personality (presumably intellectualizers are more aware of language differences than repressors), characteristics of the language itself, and so on.

4.1.2. *The Gestural-visual Band*

It is apparent from casual observation that distinctive movements of facial and bodily musculature are part of the total communication process—one can get a considerable amount of information from a completely silent movie, for example. This band of the communication channel is strictly equatable with the linguistic band: a set of responses on the part of one individual (encoder) produces stimuli which can be interpreted by another individual (decoder). This band is capable of the same type of analysis that has been given the vocal-auditory system, but relatively little has been done.[40] Such study would require (1) descriptive analysis of the gestural-visual code itself—which is coming to be known as *kinesics*—and (2) analysis of the relations of these messages to the intentions (encoding) and significances (decoding) of communicators—which might be called *psycho-kinesics.*

4.1.2.1. *Kinesics.* A very promising beginning in the study of gestural communication has been made by Birdwhistell in strict analogy with the techniques of linguistics. A particular motion or posture of a given part of the organism (facial or bodily) is called a *kine* (equivalent to *phone*). The first step in the analysis of any gestural system would be a complete 'transcription' of the kines in their sequential context of one or more 'informants' from a given language-culture community. Birdwhistell describes a notation system for transcribing or recording kines which is unfortunately (but perhaps necessarily) very complex and cumbersome. In just the same sense that phoneticians require training in objective

---

[40] See, however, Ruesch and Bateson, *Communication*, and a series of articles by the same authors; D. Efron, *Gesture and environment* (1941); R. L. Birdwhistell, *Introduction to kinesics* (Foreign Service Institute, 1952), and the references he cites.

listening, so kinesiologists require training in objective looking—the untrained observer will be likely to perceive only those movements which are significant in his own 'language.'

The second step in analysing any gestural 'language'—again, in parallel with linguistics—would be to determine what movements are significant in the code, i.e., what classes of kines constitute *kinemes* (equivalent to *phonemes*) by virtue of having the same significance. The movements which constitute such classes would be called *allokines* (cf., *allophones*), and they would also be characterized by either conditioned variation (e.g., types of smiles varying somewhat with antecedent facial posture) or free variation (e.g., winking with right or left eyes being equivalent in significance and independent of context). Individual members of a gestural community would be expected to vary somewhat (cf., *idiolects*), particularly in the features allowing free variation, and to show some constant transpositions, e.g., variations in the general amplitude of gestures. The general procedures of the kinesiologist, as described by Birdwhistell, would be to try out various 'minimal pairs' of kine patterns (for example, variations in eyebrow position with the rest of the facial pattern constant) and get from 'informants' judgments of 'same' and 'different' in meaning. The equivalent of *morphemes*, or perhaps words, in gestural language would be total patterns of facial and bodily posture which, as wholes, have distinctive significance but lose this significance when broken up. To the best of our knowledge, there has been as yet no complete analysis of any gestural language by this method.

There are, of course, a great many questions that need to be answered about kinesics. For one thing, the direct application of linguistic methods implies that events in the gestural-visual material are discretely coded at some level, e.g., that elevation of the eyebrows is either present or absent and thus either does or does not signal something; it seems quite possible, however, that we are dealing here with continuously coded materials, e.g., that the *degree* of judged 'surprise' or 'horror' or other kinemorph including this feature will be found to vary continuously with the *degree* of eyebrow elevation. Another question concerns the innate vs. learned nature of the signs here. Birdwhistell takes the position that all kinemes are learned, but there is considerable evidence for cross-cultural similarities of expressions of at least certain intense emotions going back to the work of Darwin. And there is, of course, the question of whether or not there *is* any communication via the gestural-visual medium, and whether or not this band is completely redundant with respect to linguistic and situational contexts. There are the well-known psychological studies on judgment of emotion from facial expressions which seem to show that when the situational context is removed, accuracy of judgment approaches zero—if you do not see the baby being pricked with a pin, you're as likely to call his expression 'joy' as you are 'pain.'

4.1.2.2. *Psychokinesics.* This brings us to the problem of psychokinesics, relations between the characteristics of communicators and the characteristics of the gestural-visual messages they exchange. The question raised above as to the validity of the gestural-visual band as a communication medium is actually a psychokinesic problem: *to what extents are particular gestures, facial and bodily, conditionally dependent upon 'intentional' states of encoders and to what extent are 'significance' states of decoders conditionally dependent upon particular gestures?* One way of getting at this problem experimentally would be to have the same communicator repeatedly produce gestures appropriate to the same intention (e.g., repeatedly pose 'anger,' 'consternation,' 'boredom,' and the like); we would anticipate certain variable kines and perhaps certain constant kines to appear, the latter being critical to encoding. Similarly, we could repeatedly present moving or still pictures of the same gestures to the same individuals for interpretation, to determine the degree of consistency in decoding. The question of whether or not we are dealing with a 'language' in the interpersonal sense would require replicating individuals in the same design above, i.e., do different encoders and decoders drawn from 'the same community agree in the gestures used to represent certain intentional states and in the interpretations of certain gestures? Questions of this sort apparently have not been considered by Birdwhistell.

Psychologists have been interested in these problems over a considerable period,[41] but have limited themselves pretty much to facial gestures as 'expressions of the emotions.'[42] The issue has generally been phrased as follows: (1) are facial expressions valid indices of the actual emotional states of the encoder? In other words, can judges accurately infer emotional states from facial gestures? The results obtained here are rather discouraging. Although accuracy is reasonably high when facial gestures appear in situational and linguistic contexts (e.g., a picture of a woman running from a fire and heard screaming, "Save me! Save me!"), it is very poor when these supports are removed. However, many studies purporting to get at this question have actually been designed to answer a quite different one: (2) is there social agreement on the *meaning* of facial expressions, quite apart from what the 'real' emotional state of the encoder may be? That this was actually the question being asked is evident from the fact that many studies have used professional or amateur actors deliberately posing certain facial expressions on demand. Even here, however, results have been inconsistent, partly because of difficulties in scoring 'correctness' (e.g., should we count a judgment of 'scorn' in the same category with 'contempt'?) but also because there are still two different issues being confused. (3) Do facial expressions validly communicate the *intended* states of the encoder, regardless of his 'real' feelings? Here correctness of judgment by observers is determined by the instructions given the actors. (4) Regardless of what the intention of the encoder may be, do observers in a given culture agree on the meanings of the facial gestures they perceive? This final question eliminates the skills of the encoder entirely, and we merely look for evidence for structure or agreement among decoders.

An experiment on question (4) above provides evidence for a considerable degree of communication via facial expressions.[43] Numbers of different college student subjects

---

[41] See Woodworth, *Experimental psychology* (1938).

[42] However, see the work of M. Krout on other gestures.

[43] Osgood, Suci, and Heyer, The validity of posed facial expressions as gestural signs in interpersonal communication. Paper delivered at American Psychological Association meetings, Pennsylvania State College, 1950.

posed 40 different emotional states (from the labels given them) under lighting conditions that emphasized the lines and shadows of the face. The labels for these same 40 states were written on the blackboard and student observers were instructed to select that one label which seemed to best fit each seen facial posture. Each state was posed by five different actors and judged by five different groups of observers, orders of presentation being randomized between groups. Since correlation with the 'intent' of the actor was not involved at this point, the 40 samples of judgments for the intended states were treated simply as reactions to that many independent facial stimulus situations. If the expressor intended 'anxiety' but most observers perceived states like 'dreaming sadness' and 'quiet pleasure,' it made no difference in the computations. The question was: to what degree are variations in the use of one label correlated with the use of other labels? If 'disgust' and 'contempt' are similar in meaning—and if facial expressions do have different effects as stimuli—then any facial stimulus that calls forth one label should also tend to call forth the other, and vice versa.

Coefficients of agreement were computed for each label with every other label, yielding a 40/40 matrix which was analysed by the difference method and the results represented in a solid model.[44] The distances between all of these labels were reproducible in only three dimensions with a high degree of accuracy, indicating the existence of only three major factors. The structure had a roughly pyramidal form: going upward and out from one corner at 'complacency' was a series of increasingly pleasant expressions terminating at another corner with 'joy;' going outward and left along the base of the pyramid from 'complacency' was a series of increasingly compressed or grim expressions, running through 'contempt' and 'cynical bitterness' and terminating on 'sullen anger;' outward from 'complacency' and toward the right along the base of the pyramid was a series of increasingly open and traumatic expressions, running through 'expectancy,' 'awe,' and 'anxiety,' and terminating at the front right corner in 'horror;' finally, running across the front face of the model was a series of equally traumatic and tense expressions, but from 'sullen anger' through 'rage,' 'dismay,' and 'fear' over to 'horror.' Given this structured character of the decoded significance of expressions, it becomes possible to experimentally manipulate gestural components (e.g., kines relating to the mouth, eyes, nose, and so forth) and determine what variations in the encoding correspond to variations in significance. That facial gestures *do* have considerable validity as signs in communication is indicated by the existence of structure in the judgments—only to the extent that the changing stimulus characteristics of the face did have commonly accepted meanings which restricted judgmental categories could anything other than chaos (unplotability) have resulted from this method.

4.1.3. *The Manipulational-situational Band*

All we can do here is to sketch in the types of communication materials which would be included under this rubric. Again, we may divide this band into the discretely and arbitrarily coded materials vs. the naturally and continuously coded (discreteness and arbitrariness do not necessarily go together in opposition to continuousness and naturalness, but we suspect that they usually do). The whole field of *orthography* could be treated in this context—the writer (encoder) produces a product via his manipulations and this product, in a letter or a printed page, constitutes the object-situation to which the reader (decoder) responds. In this case we would be dealing with arbitrary and discrete coding. Somewhat less arbitrary and certainly less discrete would be the use of *symbolism*, as in cartoons, the 'V' for 'victory,' 'thumbs up,' the political elephant, and so on. On the same continuum is *aesthetics*—again, encoders (artists, musicians, and the like) produce

[44] Cf., Osgood and Suci, *Psychological Bulletin* **49**. (1952).

certain products via their specialized manipulations and these products serve as the source of aesthetic stimulation for decoders (appreciators and critics). Here, although there may be a certain arbitrariness or conventionality in the code (witness the fact that 'primitive' peoples often have great difficulty perceiving the objects in drawings that are to us quite realistic), it certainly is continuously organized—the mood of 'excitement,' say, probably varies continuously with the brightness of color, shape of forms, and so forth. Perhaps more obviously manipulational-situational are many of the acts of everyday communicating—leaving a key under the doormat, hanging mistletoe above the archway, moving your castle to a position where it confronts your opponent's queen, and even breaking and bending twigs and grass in a way that unintentionally communicates your course to a pursuer.

4.2. Between Band Organization[45]

The notion of sequential redundancy between parts of a message as serially unreeled is now a fairly common one, particularly as a result of the work of Shannon, Miller, and others. The notion that there can also be synchronic redundancy among simultaneous events within the same band or between bands is less familiar but equally reasonable. Both linguists and information theorists have taken cognizance of redundancies within the linguistic band per se, the former observing that phonemes are for the most part overdetermined (in terms of clusters of correlated features) and the latter reporting that one can experimentally cut out 50 per cent or more of the total information in the auditory channel without seriously hampering intelligibility. There is also redundancy between discretely and continuously coded signals in the vocal-auditory band—witness how stress is typically accompanied by lengthening of vowels, how stress and raised pitch tend to go together, and so forth. Redundancy between bands, e.g., between vocal-auditory and gestural-visual bands, has been for the most part neglected, although Ray Birdwhistell and H. L. Smith[46] have made some very interesting observations along these lines. Informal observation indicates at least two types of relation between communication bands: (1) *synchronic complementation*, the usual situation in which gestural signals have the same significance as vocal signals and hence complement one another; (2) *synchronic contrast*, the more informational situation in which gestural and vocal signals have different (usually opposed) significance and hence change each other in some fashion.

4.2.1. Synchronic Complementation

At the lowest level, of course, there is constant between-band complementation between the vocal-auditory channel and the visible gestures of the speech apparatus itself—the fact that people can learn to 'read lips' with high proficiency testifies to this. The rest of us do much the same thing in traumatic interpersonal

---

[45] Charles E. Osgood.

[46] See Claude Lévi-Strauss, Roman Jakobson, C. F. Voegelin and Thomas A. Sebeok, *Results of the conference of anthropologists and linguists*, Indiana University Publications in Anthropology and Linguistics, Memoir 8 (Baltimore, 1953).

exchanges in which the speaker, under strong emotion, typically exaggerates the speech motions. Less obvious and more in need of experimental verification are possible ways in which both facial and bodily gestures may complement those parts of the linguistic band related to motivational and semantic information. Are there any facial and gestural concomitants of stress, for example—is there a tendency toward raising of the eyebrows with rising intonation (e.g., at the end of a question)? It should be possible to study these and other possible relations by the careful analysis of sound-film recordings. Unquestionably gestures are related to semantic events in the sound channel—in fact, this is probably the primary correlate. The meaning of negation is synchronously encoded in the vocal "No" and the shaking head; the meaning of agreement is synchronously encoded in the vocal "Yes" and the nodding head. The meaning of 'being completely at sea' is often expressed by the shrugging of the shoulders while saying "How should I know?" or some related sequence. For the more motor expressive individual, at least, movements of hands, face and trunk keep up a running commentary on his verbal output—"a *big* boat" is accompanied by cupped, spreading hands, "I was *shocked*" is accompanied, perhaps, by retraction of the head and popping of the eyes.

Similar synchronic redundancies can be observed between the manipulational-situational band and the vocal-auditory band. The very common use of 'doodling' and diagramming on a pad as a means of facilitating interpersonal communication about objects and events is an example. Another illustration, here of the intimate redundancy between auditory and orthographic inputs, is the following: Once while listening to some recordings of Gilbert and Sullivan, with the verbal libretto in hand, the writer noticed that by alternately reading the words in parallel with listening to them sung and then just listening, he could make the *auditory* material alternately seem perfectly clear and then perfectly ambiguous—without the printed guide the sounds were literally meaningless, but with the printed material before him, it seemed that the *speech sounds* suddenly became completely intelligible. This demonstration is rather striking when experienced, and it has additional implications for the close relation between perception and meaning. Other examples of redundancy between situational cues and verbal decoding are legend and often humorous—in a situation where a knife is needed and you are handing another person this implement, you may actually say, "Here, use this plate," without his noticing the error at all; when entering an elevator in the morning and greeting someone with a tip of your hat, you may actually say something quite insulting without its usually being noticed.

The psychological basis for complementation between bands seems to be quite simple and apparent. From the encoder's point of view, both the vocal response of saying, "No, . . ." for example, and the head-shaking gestural response are in a hierarchy associated with the *same* mediation process of intention, e.g., both reactions have been learned in similar situations and associated with the same significances. Since these reactions are not incompatible or competing, they will tend to be elicited synchronously by occurrence of the negation semantic state. Presumably the stronger the *motivation* operating, the greater will be the tendency to overflow into these parallel reaction pathways. From the decoder's point of view, in his own development of decoding behavior he has been exposed to many people who use such gestures, and thus repeatedly the elicitation of the negation semantic process by the words 'no' and 'not' and the like have been accompanied by the head-shaking visual pattern and thereby associated. Here again, the decoder has learned to interpret synchrony of correlated signs in several bands as increased intensity of motivation on the part of the encoder—if he says "no" and shakes not only his head but his whole body in saying it, he must really mean it! This analysis, of course, does not explain the *origin* (in culture or language community) of this parellelism. In general, then, complementation between bands is based upon the association of reactions (encoder) and cues (decoder) in different systems or modalities with the same intentions or significances.

4.2.2. *Synchronic conflict*

It is possible for the encoder to produce gestural signs incompatible with his vocal signs. These gestural signs may be in *direct contrast*, may be unrelated or *irrelevant*, or may be simply *suppressed*, and quite different effects upon decoders seem to be produced.

(a) *Direct contrast.* One of the standard phenomena of sensory psychology is that of intensification by contrast. A patch of black cloth looks even blacker when set against a field of white; a bit of yellow becomes more deeply saturated when seen against blue; a man of ordinary height looks dwarfed when standing with the members of a basketball team. In all these cases, contrast is maximal when figure and ground are directly opposite in quality, and the same law seems to hold for synchronic contrasts in communication, which is probably the most common non-complementary relation. "Fine!" the man says with a wry expression while looking at his deflated tire. "That's one of the most brilliant arguments I've ever been subjected to," says the professor, his voice 'loaded with sarcasm.' In such cases of irony or sarcasm, the significance of the verbal signs is directly reversed in keeping with some other set of cues, either facial (wry expression) or voice qualifiers ('loaded with sarcasm'). Why are the vocal signs in these examples more susceptible to reversal than signs in the other bands? It may be that verbal signs are more abstract and hence more susceptible to such modifications; another hypothesis would be that compatibility or incompatibility with events in the *situational* band determine the shift—in both cases above the verbal materials were in conflict with the situational context (the flat tire, the obviously inadequate argument).

(b) *Irrelevant.* It is possible, although admittedly difficult in the normal person, to produce gestural or facial signs which are simply unrelated to the intention underlying verbal encoding. Thus, a person may grimace and repeatedly clench his hands while saying, "Oh, we had an interesting trip to New York . . . saw a new show and bought some clothes we really needed." To the decoder, this is evidence of *conflict* in the encoder, as if one set of meanings were directing one encoding system while another were directing the other. And this, of course, is one of the clues used by the psychiatrist in diagnosing dissociation. The other effect upon the decoder is probably to dilute or make ambiguous the significance of what is being said.

(c) *Suppression.* The encoder may completely eliminate information via either the vocal-auditory or the gestural-visual band. In the former case we say the person is being 'secretive,' is 'daydreaming,' or 'has something on his mind'—in other words, we interpret his gestural display as indicative of active mediational states and interpret his general mood therefrom. In the latter case, we speak of the person as being 'dead-pan' or 'poker-faced,' and in general take the lack of normal complementary gestural behavior as indicative of inhibition—which of course it is. The typical effect of suppression of information in any one of these bands is to make the decoder question the validity of information in the other bands.

As we have seen above, the association of gestural and vocal signs with common mediators in decoding and the association of these common mediators with equivalent gestural and vocal acts in encoding provides a psychological basis for synchronic complementation as the 'normal' situation in interpersonal communication. Conflict between vocal and gestural bands, whether in the form of contrast irrelevance, or suppression, necessarily involves·some degree of potential confusion on the part of the decoder. For normal communicators, therefore, production and interpretation of such effects as sarcasm and irony, deliberate irrelevance and band suppression implies a certain degree of intelligence—greater discrimination among overt responses (encoder) or among mediators (decoder) is required. In this connection it is interesting that the only 'coded' type of dissociation between bands is that of direct contrast or opposition, as found in irony and sarcasm. It is as though only the complete 'flip-flop' from one motor reaction to its direct opposite in all-or-nothing fashion can be readily handled—note the parallel here with tendencies in languages to select binary oppositions in phonemic signals. The synchronic conflicts introduced by abnormal psychological disturbances may involve irrelevance and suppression (but probably not intentional contrast) and clearly indicate underlying conflict.

4.2.3. Research Proposals

The type of research on synchronic interactions will depend upon whether encoding or decoding is being studied. (A) *Encoding.* Here one might study the relative difficulties of deliberately 'acting out' instructions which involve complementation, contrast, irrelevance and suppression—presumbably complementation would be the easiest, 'most normal' task and intentional irrelevance the most difficult. Another research direction would be to experimentally produce states of motivation and emotion in which complementation, contrast, and so on are relevant, and study encoding with intelligence, for example, as a variable. (B) *Decoding.* Here one immediately thinks of sound-motion movie recording as the basic technique, with cutting, splicing, and elimination of bands as means of experimental manipulation. In producing the original materials, one could use either trained actors (in which case a specific series of 'intentional' states could be expressed and recorded, with or without situational context) or set up experimental situations with untrained and unknowing actors. The general procedure might be to present the recorded materials under various experimental conditions and record judgments from decoders as to their interpretations of encoder intentional states. One experimental treatment would be to successively eliminate bands of information—how does masking out the situational band (leaving gestural and vocal) affect the decoder? Eliminating the vocal band? The gestural band? Which band by itself carries the most information and what kind of information? Does one get evidence for complementation (i.e., enhancement of effects) or mere redundancy? Another experimental treatment, particularly with a series of particular emotional states acted out by trained actors, would be to deliberately change the normal between-band complementation. One could, for example, have the words originally accompanying a joyful gestural pattern occur with a graded series of other gestural patterns, including that for gloom; or one could vary the words accompanying a constant gestural pattern. In both of these cases, one would have to take care to use verbal materials whose automatic speaking gestures were sufficiently similar to each other. Judgment as to 'sarcasm,' 'mental disturbance,' 'secretiveness' and the like could be secured from the decoding subjects.

5. SEQUENTIAL PSYCHOLINGUISTICS

Study of the sequential or transitional structure of language behavior provides a meeting ground for linguists, information theorists, and learning theorists. The linguist, applying his own methods of analysis, discovers hierarchies of more and more inclusive units; the information theorist, usually starting with lower-level units such as letters or words, finds evidence for rather regular oscillations in transitional uncertainty in message sequences, the points of highest uncertainty often corresponding to unit boundaries as linguistically determined; and the learning theorist, working with notions like the habit-family hierarchy, finds it possible to make predictions about sequential psycholinguistic phenomena that can be tested with information theory techniques. Here we come back once again to the problem of units in encoding and decoding, the general notion being that at any given level of selection by speaker or hearer both the transitional probabilities and the correlated indices of habit strength will be higher *within* units appropriate to that level than *between* such units. And we again find it necessary to think in terms of interactions between hierarchical levels in the processess of encoding and decoding, a sort of 'super-Markov process' in which selection of higher-order, more inclusive units results in a reloading of the transitional probabilities obtaining among lower-order units.

5.1. *Transitional Probability, Linguistic Structure, and Systems of Habit-family Hierarchies*[47]

This section offers a general picture of how our three approaches intersect and facilitate one another in understanding sequential mechanisms. It also provides, by way of concrete illustration, a discussion of hesitation phenomena in ordinary conversation and lecturing and some hypotheses about such phenomena which are capable of empirical testing.

5.1.1. *Statistical Structure of Messages*

Transitional structural analysis assumes units of a given order (phonemes, morphemes, words) and seeks to ascertain their transitional probabilities: "Given an occurrence of the unit x, what is the probability that y will be the next unit to follow?" "That z will be?" Etc. for first-order probability. Or: "Given the sequence of units xy, what is the probability that z will be the next?" "That w will be?" Etc. for second-order probability. Similarly for higher-order probabilities. Or, stated in information-theory terms: "In the case of the occurrence of a sequence xy, what is the 'amount of information' in the occurrence of y, given the previous occurrence of x?" (first order). "In the case of the occurrence of the sequence xyw, what is the 'amount of information' in the occurrence of w, given the previous occurrence of xy?" (second order).

The units with which this type of analysis may operate are various. The most readily available units are letters of conventional orthography. This choice may

---

[47] Floyd G. Lounsbury.

be purposeful, as when the investigator is concerned with the statistical properties of telegraph messages (e.g., Shannon), or it may represent some linguistic naïveté (e.g., Newman's Samoan Bible). Where interest is in speech behavior, the units chosen should be phonemes rather than orthographic symbols. Morphemes are also possible units for this type of analysis, as are words. Zipf did some simple counting with these orders of units, but he did not obtain transitional probabilities. To the best of our knowledge no one has yet carried out any systematic transitional analysis involving morphemes or words.

Transitional probabilities are determined generally from natural data, i.e., from records of the normal flow of speech. When the units of analysis are words, however, recourse can be had to the experimental device of the word-association test and other short-cut procedures (see sections 5.3, 5.4, 5.5). The transitional probabilities determined in this manner appear to correspond well with those which might be determined from the analysis of a necessarily large amount of natural data, though there is not yet conclusive evidence for this. When the units of analysis are anything less than minimal free forms of a language, no such experimental short-cut appears to be possible.

5.1.2. *Statistical vs. Linguistic Structure*

We must distinguish between 'transitional structure' and 'linguistic structure.' The former is a product of statistical analysis; the latter, of linguistic analysis. They reflect important differences in statistical and linguistic procedures. In the procedure of contemporary structural linguistic analysis, frequency of occurrence (of a given unit in a given context, or of a given contrast) is not a relevant criterion. Only the *possibility* of occurrence—as represented by some one instance or by many instances of it—is relevant. The answers which are sought from data are of a simple yes-or-no type rather than of a how-much type. In statistical analysis on the other hand, frequencies are the immediate goal of analysis, e.g., the *probability* of occurrence. Statistical procedure usually ignores, however, a matter which is basic to linguistics—the distinguishing of levels of structure. Linguistic analysis is directed toward the discovery of these and their combinatory and hierarchical arrangements. The structure of particular utterances is stated in terms of these, and the structural pattern, or grammar, of a whole language consists of generalized summary statements of the same. Discovery of the hierarchical structure in a language is by means of 'immediate-constituent' analysis. The boundaries between constituents on the same level of structure are established. A sentence—any one on this page for example—is not to be broken down simply into all of the units of a given order, such as words or morphemes. Rather, the process of immediate-constituent analysis is carried out, proceeding from level to level of structure, so that constructions on one level are established as constituting the units of structure on the next higher level. The criterion for establishing the boundaries between two different units on the same level is generally that of maximum substitutibility of possible replacement parts (Wells, Nida, Harris).

Statistical analysis ignores the differing hierarchical values of these boundaries.

All boundaries, for purposes of statistical procedure, are taken as equivalent. Thus, in the sentence just preceding this one, the boundary between *are* and *taken*, that between *taken* and *as*, and that between *as* and *equivalent* are not accorded the different statuses which linguistic analysis would ascribe to them. They are lumped together as cases of the same sort of thing. The differences between them which are initially ignored do, however, get reflected in a certain fashion in the statistical results. These different 'transitions' will often be found to have different probabilities of occurrence. The different transitional probabilities are in a way indexical of the different linguistic statuses of the boundaries between the words of each pair. The correspondence is only rough, however, and many other factors besides the linguistic hierarchical statuses of the boundaries affect the transitional probabilities. The former cannot be derived from the latter, nor vice versa.

'Statistical structure,' then, is to be understood as denoting the system of transitional-probability relationships between the units of a given order in a language. (Care should be taken not to confuse the terms 'order' and 'level.' Words, morphemes, and phonemes are different *orders* of units. Between units of the same order strung along in sequence there are boundaries, or 'transitions,' belonging to different *levels* of construction.) 'Linguistic structure,' on the other hand, may be understood as the system of hierarchical combinatory possibilities between the units of a given order.

5.1.3. *Behavioral Levels in Encoding and Decoding*

There are behavioral data of various kinds which support the inference of at least three psychological levels of organization of linguistic responses (see section 6.1). Osgood has distinguished a 'representational level,' an 'integrational level,' and a 'skill level.' The triggering of linguistic responses appears to be accomplished by a complex of internal stimuli deriving from each of these levels. (It should be noted that the use of the word 'level' in the present context is independent of its use in the different context of the preceding paragraphs.) Stimuli from the representational level derive from the meanings or significances of incoming stimuli and have been labeled with the roughly characteristic term, 'intentions.' (Meanings and significances of incoming stimuli, of course, derive not only from the external sources, but also from the internal emotive and evaluative systems which in turn derive from past experience and learning.) Intentions are probably more synthetic than their relatively analytic expression in speech. The process of selecting the larger semantic units of language for the expression of intentions has been called 'semantic encoding.'

Much of the triggering of linguistic responses, however, is accomplished at a lower organizational level of greater automaticity and less conscious awareness. Ordering of semantic units, concrete-relational classification of these, concordal agreement and certain other relational phenomena appear to belong to the 'integrational level.' This process has been called 'grammatical encoding.' The final triggering of the motor acts which produce the sounds of speech appears to be accomplished on the still lower level of motor skill organization. The sequenced triggering of the individual motor acts in speech is accomplished at a rate of speed which Lashley showed to be, like the individual motor acts in piano playing, too great for each such act to be under specific cortical control via feedback mechanisms. This process may be called 'motor encoding.' Speech pathology, particularly aphasia, shows examples of disturbances in each of the above described systems.

5.1.4. Habit-family Hierarchies and Transitional Probabilities

Whenever a variety of stimuli terminate in a common response, we have a convergent habit-family hierarchy; whenever a given stimulus is associated with a variety of responses, we have a divergent habit-family hierarchy. In other words, a habit-family hierarchy is a cluster of associations in which one of the members, S or R, is common. Associations (habits) vary in strength, and variations in habit strength are known to correlate with probability of occurrence of responses (as well as with other indices, such as latency and amplitude). Habit strength, in turn, is known to depend upon variations in both the frequency and contiguity of S–R associations. Information theory measurements deal with the probability of occurrence of one event among the class of possible events of the same order. If we conceive of an antecedent message event (of any order or size of unit) as constituting or indexing a stimulus situation and the subsequent message event (of the same order or size of unit) as constituting a response, then the transitional probability measurements of information theory can be viewed as reflections of the systems of encoding or decoding habit strengths.

Since the linguistic structure of the language and the 'semantic structure' of the culture is such that certain message events co-occur more often than others (frequency of S–R) and certain message events appear closer together in the temporal sequence than others (contiguity of S–R), it must follow that at each level of organization hierarchies of habits of varying strength will be developed, and these will correspond to sets of transitional probabilities. Assuming a constant and limited number of alternative events of a given order (phonemes, morphemes, words, constructions, etc.), transitions characterized by convergent hierarchies should correspond to points of relatively low transitional entropy or uncertainty (e.g., where a wide variety of stem morphemes converge upon a limited number of suffixes) and transitions characterized by divergent hierarchies should correspond to points of relatively high transitional entropy or uncertainty (e.g., initial phonemes of words following junctures).

Beyond these general determinants, the habit strengths of associations within hierarchies will vary with frequency and contiguity factors, and so therefore will vary the entropy characteristics of sequential sets of message events. If frequency and contiguity factors are such that all of the alternatives following a given event are of about equal habit strength, uncertainty will be maximal for that number of alternatives; if frequency and contiguity factors are such that one event is highly associated with another and other events only remotely, a relatively low degree of uncertainty will exist. A number of observations of behavioral stereotypy, including the masses of highly regular data about languages assembled by Zipf, lead one to the hypothesis that habit-family hierarchies tend toward a structure such that habits strengths of the member associations decrease according to a logarithmic function of their rank in strength. Further discussion of transitional entropy measurements and entropy profiles will be found in section 5.3.

As was pointed out above, it seems necessary to view language behavior as organized simultaneously on at least three levels, a semantic (representational) level, a grammatical (integrational) level, and a receptive-expressive (sensory-motor skill) level. Each of these levels is assumed to deal with units of decreasing size, hierarchically arranged such that the units at a higher level include units of the next lower level. We assume also that habit-family hierarchies of the sort we have been discussing operate at each of these levels. A given antecedent event at the semantic level (e.g., the meaning of a stimulus word in free association tests) will tend to elicit a hierarchy of subsequent semantic events (e.g., meanings of associates of variable strength), as indexed by the hierarchical frequencies of overt responses—arranged, interestingly enough, according to a Zipf-type function. Similarly, reception or production of an antecedent syntactical unit (e.g., a nominal phrase, such as *the little red schoolhouse* . . .) will set up readinesses, based on past redundancies, for a variety of subsequent syntactical units (such as . . . *sat on a hill*, or . . . *I love is still there*, or . . . *and barn were painted*), and these alternative constructions constitute syntactical hierarchies which, although there is no evidence available, probably have a Zipf-type distribution. Similar hierarchical arrangements have been demonstrated for phoneme sequences.

Finally, mention should be made of the conditioning or restricting effect of context upon selection within hierarchies and hence upon transitional probabilities. Given only knowledge of the immediately antecedent event at any one of these levels, uncertainty as to the subsequent event is maximal (within limits imposed by the structure of the hierarchy). As we increase our knowledge by taking into account more and more of the sequence of antecedent events—as well as subsequent events, in the case of decoding—uncertainty as to the subsequent event decreases. Psychologically, this is due to stimulus patterning, e.g., the stimulus, including traces from past events, becomes more specific and hence more precisely associated with a given response than with the others. The association of a subject to the single stimulus word, BLUE, is less predictable than to the sequence, I'M ALL BLACK AND BLUE. The way in which events at superordinate levels reshuffle transitional probabilities at subordinate levels (see particularly section 5.3.) can also be understood in terms of the effects of contextual stimuli upon modulating the 'average' structure of hierarchies. Thus the cue effects of a given semantic decision persist through some period of time and serve to modify the actual eliciting stimulus pattern at each of a series of hierarchical choice points at some lower level of encoding or decoding. This conception helps explain an apparent paradox—the fact that a speaker's sequencing is almost perfectly dependable, e.g., he 'says what he meant to say and it always makes sense,' despite the uncertainty present from the point of view of the observer with his entropy measurement. The point is that, from the speaker's point of view, selection at each hierarchy is a simultaneous function of *all* of the preceding sequence and of regulating inputs from *all* levels of organization, whereas, from the entropy estimater's point of view, selection at each hierarchy is being predicted from only first and second order segmental probabilities (usually) and takes only a single level of organization into account (usually).

5.1.5. *Pausal, Juncture, and Hesitation Phenomena*

Encoding and decoding processes being as complex as they are, it is always difficult to discover easy checks on the type of model described above. The fact that *habit strength is inversely correlated with the latency between S and R* seems to offer one avenue of approach, however. At any level of the model just described, the stronger the transitional habits, and hence the lower the transitional entropy or uncertainty, the shorter should be the pausal durations separating sequential events. This means that within syllables, within familiar morphemes, and even within familiar words and phrases the durations of pauses (latencies) separating successive events should be minimal, if measureable at all. On the other hand, pauses should be somewhat longer, and hence measureable, at boundaries between units where transitional habits are weak, the number of alternatives large, and hence the transitional probabilities low. The boundaries of constructive units might be of this sort. As will be discussed below, what we are calling 'hesitation phenomena' seem to reflect transitions of low probability at the *semantic* level, and these do not seem to correspond in any simple fashion to standard linguistic boundaries.

Hesitations which interrupt the continuous flow of speech are anything from very brief pauses to extended periods of halting, often filled with 'hemming and hawing.' The phenomena we are speaking of are not to be identified with linguistic 'junctures.' A variety of phonetic phenomena, including such things as brief pauses, *ritardando* effect, slight articulatory shifts, and even morphophonemic alternations have at one time or another, or by one writer or another, been set up as 'juncture phonemes.' But we are not referring to these. Even if 'junctures' sometimes consist of short pauses, the pauses under consideration here are not the same. For one thing, there is a difference in duration. Juncture pauses which we have seen in spectrographic analysis of speech were in the order of a hundredth of a second or less in length. The pauses referred to here, however, are appreciably longer. We are not sure of the lower limit in duration of these pauses, for measurements have not been made, but in general, certainly, they are longer. They often, of course, may last as much as several seconds. Another and more important difference is that they do not characteristically fall at the points in a sentence where junctures are presumed to fall.

This last point may be made clearer by means of an illustration. Consider the speech of a man lecturing or speaking on a difficult and not too familiar subject and, as we say, 'thinking on his feet.' There are pauses and perhaps quite a bit of hemming and hawing as he 'organizes his thoughts' or 'gropes for the right expression.' Compare his output under these conditions with his output if he is reading a prepared and rehearsed typescript on a familiar subject, or if he is delivering it after having committed it to memory. In the latter case the pauses which we note are those which fall at the boundaries of syntactic units, the so-called syntactic junctures. They may be fleetingly brief and few in number, or they may be exaggerated, longer, and more frequent for emphasis and stylistic effect, but in any case they are distributed systematically in some sort of conformity with the linguistic structure of the sentence as revealed by immediate-constituent analysis. This is not so in the first case where the man was thinking on his feet. To be sure, the syntactic junctures appear also here. But in addition there are frequent hesitation pauses. These would vary considerably in length, some would be dead-ends from which the speaker re-treats to start over, some might be filled with hem-and-haw to mark time, etc. But the significant thing about these is that the majority of them do not fall at syntactic juncture points. Instead of occurring at the boundaries of major syntactic units, they typically fall at minor structural boundaries and within, rather than at the ends or beginnings, of larger syntactic constructions. Whereas juncture pauses are an aid to the hearer and help to put across the structure of a sentence, these hesitation pauses are often an annoyance to the hearer and interfere with rather than aid in grasping the sentence as a whole. Reading the material after sufficient rehearsal, or speaking it after memorization, would eliminate most of these hesitation pauses. Even the practised and fluent lecturer, however, apparently cannot entirely eliminate these in unrehearsed discourse. He may reduce them to such a point that neither he nor his hearers are aware of them, but a listener who is concentrating upon these rather than on the content of the lecture will find them very marked though brief.

Hesitation pauses have figured very little in linguistic analysis. Probably one reason for this is the way in which the informant technique has been made use of in the past. Whether the informant be an American Indian speaking a strange language to an inquiring linguist, or whether he be a linguist speaking his own language to himself, the time-con-suming task of committing the observations to paper has necessitated a great many repeti-tions of stretches of speech a sentence or less in length. The repetitions demanded of the informant amount to rehearsal and result in his memorization of the phrase or sentence, and thus the hesitation pauses are weeded out. Only nowadays, with the advent of easy-to-use recording machines, are records of speech possible which preserve these little 'defects' for the investigator. One group of linguists has recently given particular attention to these pauses, preserving them in their transcriptions. But they have not been clearly enough distinguished from junctures. In some cases they have in fact been regarded as junctures.

Hesitation pauses in speech need much more study. We have hunches as to some of the results which such a study might show. These may be put in the form of hypotheses to be tested. The hypotheses have to do with the suspected relationships between hesitation pauses, transitional structure, and units of encoding. More conjectural are some which have to do with linguistic structure and units of decoding.

Hypothesis 1: Hesitation pauses correspond to the points of highest statistical uncertainty in the sequencing of units of any given order. (High statistical un-certainty = high transitional entropy.) The observations which lead us to formulate this hypothesis have been focused on the sequencing of words. We are relatively hopeful for the substantiation of the hypothesis when the units are of this order. Whether the same may hold true for some sort of hesitation or tempo phenomenon when the units are morphemes or phonemes, or perhaps some higher-order phrase units is a completely open question.

Testing of this hypothesis will require accumulation of two sorts of data: measurements of hesitation pauses, and transitional probabilities. It should be done for a single speaker, since the values of these would vary considerably with the speaker and his familiarity with various possible subjects of discourse. Our observations suggest to us that magnetic recordings of the class performances of a good lecturer would make excellent material for the identification and measurement of hesitation pauses. The measurement of transi-tional probabilities, on the other hand, would be more laborious. There are two theoretically possible methods. The one might make use of a large amount of natural data, e.g., a semes-ter's lectures in a particular course. The calculation of all transitional probabilities for every pertinent word in its various contexts, or for every pertinent context and the various words which may follow, would be an impossible task. A limited sampling could be done, however. A more practical short-cut in establishing transitional probabilities would be to administer word-association tests to the speaker of the recorded material. An interesting experiment could be worked out combining these two methods of getting at transitional probabilities. The 'Cloze' procedure being developed by Wilson Taylor should also be useful here, in this case given to the speaker himself.

Hypothesis 2: Hesitation pauses and points of high statistical uncertainty correspond to the beginning of units of encoding. Evidence on this point will be of an indirect sort, since the encoding process is not open to observation. The psychological theory would have a unit of encoding begin with semantic encoding in a higher mediational system and set off a train of more automatic responses in the lower dispositional and motor skill systems. Automaticity of response is a product of frequent repetitions. A response which originally is consciously directed is transformed with sufficient repetition into an automatic unconscious response. (To understand the point, one need only think of a person learning to drive an automobile or to type or to execute immediately and 'without thinking' any prescribed response to a given stimulus.) If it should be shown that the stretch of speech from one hesitation pause to the next is a convergent one, i.e., one characterized by decreasing statistical uncertainty (increasing transitional probabilities), then we would have strong support for claiming this as a unit of encoding.

Hypothesis 3: Hesitation pauses and points of high statistical uncertainty frequently do not fall at the points where immediate-constituent analysis would establish boundaries between higher-order linguistic units or where syntactic junctures or 'facultative pauses' would occur. Evidence on this question would be relatively easy to assemble, given the recordings and analysis of data proposed under Hyp. 1 above. It would be necessary only to add linguistic analysis of the same material.

Hypothesis 4: The units given by immediate-constituent analysis, and especially those bounded by facultative pause points, do correspond to units of decoding, however. (These do not necessarily coincide with units of encoding: see Hyp. 5.) A definition of 'unit of decoding' would have to be given in terms of speech comprehension. It is a common English-class dogma that carefully phrased speech, with pauses, etc. 'for expression,' is more comprehensible than either 'slurred' or 'chopped-up' speech. The phrasing pauses here referred to are characteristically inserted at points which immediate-constituent analysis establishes as the boundaries between larger units. Conceivably an experiment might be designed to test the facilitation or hindrance of comprehension with different distributions of pauses in speech material. Among the experimental distributions would be included the two which we have discussed and which we suspect correspond to units of encoding and to units of decoding, respectively.

Hypothesis 5: Units of encoding for easy oft-repeated combinations approach coincidence with those of decoding. In such material (e.g., the favorite oft-repeated assertions of a professor in his university lectures) hesitation pauses will tend to be eliminated. The frequent repetitions increase very highly the transitional probabilities between the units of which it is composed and reduce the statistical uncertainty at all points within it. The pauses which remain in the delivery of such material are those which fall at major syntactic juncture points and which may be magnified for stylistic effect or diminished for speed and economy of effort, depending on the content of utterance. A test of this hypothesis could be achieved fairly simply by choosing from a large collection of recordings a number of the most frequently repeated sentences, series of sentences, or parts of sentences, and examining these and comparing them with other less frequent sentences.

5.2. *Certain Characteristics of Phoneme Sequences*[48]

A few applications of entropy measures have already been made on the level of phonemic analysis. The probabilities of English phonemes and of all possible sequences of two such phonemes have been estimated from a text of 20,000 phonemes, and appropriate entropy measures have been computed.[49] Similar analyses will probably be carried out in the near future on other languages. Such studies would be of great value in describing and comparing the structures of various languages. However, since the factors governing the choice of phonemes extend over long sequences of phonemes, and even morphemes, these entropy measures can at best be regarded as averages over a large set of conditions and so only partial descriptions. Jakobson and his co-workers[50] go at this descriptive problem in a different fashion. Here the phoneme is treated as a class of sounds defined by a set of distinctive features. This sort of analysis permits one to estimate the degree to which all of the potential combinations of distinctive features are used. Both of these approaches are utilized in the following analysis.

Whereas the descriptive linguist has usually limited his interest to those combinations which *can* occur in a language, it appears that analysis of *relative frequencies* of combinations may reveal data which can be more meaningfully interpreted and lead to more fruitful hypotheses. One such hypothesis is based on the assumption that a message will tend to be produced in such a way as to take into consideration the effort of both the speaker and the hearer (cf., Zipf). For example, in any *cluster of consonant phonemes*, the minimum effort for the encoder would be the one in which any two successive phonemes would be most similar; this, however, would cause a maximum effort on the part of the listener, who would be forced to make a series of very fine distinctions. For the decoder, the simplest situation is the one in which two succeeding phonemes differ as much as possible, thus making the distinction easy to make. If speech does re-

[48] Sol Saporta.

[49] This tabulation was carried out under the direction of John B. Carroll at the Summer Seminar on Psychology and Linguistics held at Cornell University in 1951. Only a privately distributed mimeographed summary of the results is available so far.

[50] Jakobson, Fant, and Halle, *Preliminaries to speech analysis* (Cambridge, 1952). Cherry, Halle, and Jakobson, Toward a logical description of languages in their phonemic aspect, *Language* **29**. 34–46 (1953).

flect both factors, then we would expect low frequencies of both extremely similar clusters and extremely different clusters, i.e., a normal distribution curve, where frequency of a cluster is a function of the difference between the two phonemes in the cluster.

Roman Jakobson's distinctive feature analysis offers a meaningful measure of differences between phonemes. If we compare the English phonemes /p/, /t/, and /θ/, we can establish that /t/ and /θ/ have the same distinctive features, except for their contrast as to continuant/interrupted. This − vs. + contrast is here counted as being a difference of 2 units. On the other hand, while /t/ and /p/ contrast as to grave/acute, which is two units of difference, they also differ in that the feature of strident/mellow is irrelevant in /p/ but is − in /t/. This kind of a difference is here counted as one unit of difference, so that /p/ and /t/ differ by a total of 3 units. In this way, the units of difference between any given phoneme and all other phonemes may be established. The series of 20,000 phonemes analysed by Carroll, showing the frequency with which each phoneme is followed by every other phoneme, provides data for a test of our hypothesis. We would predict that lowest frequencies of clustering would be between phonemes maximally similar or maximally different. The results for 845 consonant clusters are as follows:

Difference between phonemes in number of units	Average frequency of clustering
0	0.0 (by definition)
1	0.0
2	0.2
3	1.2
4	5.1
5	5.4
6	0.4
7	1.9
8	0.7
9	0.2
10	0.0

It is apparent, then, that clustering does tend to follow a normal curve, except for the disproportionately low occurrence of clusters differing by 6 units. This is based on an analysis whereby /č/ and /ǰ/ are considered unit phonemes. If one accepts a phonemic analysis whereby these affricates are considered to be clusters of /tš/ and /dž/ respectively, each occurrence of /č/ and /ǰ/ becomes a cluster. The resulting analysis into distinctive features indicates that these clusters differ by a total of 6 units difference. The average frequency of clusters differing by 6 units would then be 3.6 ,which is quite in keeping with the normal curve. It seems justified, then, to assume that at least in consonant clusters, maximum efforts for either encoder or decoder are avoided in favor of those situations where the effort is more or less equally divided. If our hypothesis is correct, it should apply to all languages. Phonemic transcriptions for diverse languages must be analyzed in terms of transitional frequencies, as well as in terms of distinctive features, to determine whether or not this is a general principle.

The above is merely one particular analysis. The investigation of factors which may determine transitional frequencies, however, can be extended to cover all types of data. A further examination of the same material used above indicates other possible fields for investigation. For example, a significantly higher percentage of voiceless stops is found to occur before juncture than the corresponding voiced stop. The fact that this is due to a well-known historical change in Germanic is of no relevance here. Precisely the same psychological factor which might tend to cause this on the synchronic level would also operate in affecting change. Exactly what this factor is, of course, is difficult to determine. One possible explanation is the seemingly reasonable assumption that less information need be given in final position of word units. This would then assume that voiceless gives less information than the corresponding voiced. It has been suggested by Zipf that the voiceless is easier than the corresponding voiced, so that if the information value is not a factor, the system might tend to choose the unit requiring the least effort. This is, of course, merely a hypothesis which would have to be tested in various languages.

Leopold has suggested that in child language there seems to be a tendency for a stop to be replaced by the corresponding fricative in word final position but not in word initial position. This immediately suggests that a correlation might be found in adult speech. The available corpus of transitional frequencies for English does indicate a tendency for this to be true, but it is not significant with this amount of data. In any case, it seems that this method may have many fruitful applications. The immediate need is for similar data in diverse languages, so that general principles, if any, may be disclosed.

5.3. *Applications of Entropy Measures to Problems of Sequential Structure*[51]

Because of the frequently observed effects of antecedent events on the choice of subsequent events in language, the Markov Process has been regarded as an ideal conceptual tool in the study of linguistic structure. The Whorf and Harris models of the English monosyllable could be readily used in such an analysis and lack only the conditional probabilities of passing from one state to another to be complete Markov processes. Likewise, knowledge of syntactical structure can guide us in applying entropy measures to morphemes or words and setting up appropriate Markov processes. However, it seems that existing knowledge cannot do more than provide us with guides for describing such relatively simple phenomena, leaving the more complex and less well understood aspects of linguistic structure untouched.

The most obvious way to approach these more complex aspects would be to apply entropy measures to extended sequences of phonemes taken from a large sample of texts. By increasing the length, r, of the sequences of phonemes in A, the class of all possible sequences of antecedent phonemes, we should be

[51] Kellogg Wilson and John B. Carroll.

able to find a minimum sequence length, say n, for which $H_A(S)$ ceases to decrease significantly, S being the class of subsequent events. The set of joint and conditional probabilities obtained for all sequences of length n or less should enable us to set up a Markov Process which completely represents linguistic structure within the limits of sampling error. While such a procedure is feasible in theory, it is hardly practical because of the enormous effort needed to sample and tabulate the very large number of sequences in A.[52] Moreover, the results of such an analysis would be of such a bewildering complexity that they would be practically unusable.

5.3.1. *Higher-order Markov Processes*

A more practical conceptual scheme can be devised using the concept of a higher-order Markov Process—a Markov Process such that each of its states is itself a Markov Process. Such a scheme can allow incorporation of the existing units of linguistic analysis. For example, the states of a higher-order Markov Process could be morpheme classes, each of which is represented by a Markov Process whose states are phonemes. Such a representation has additional advantages in clarifying the entropy analysis of phonemes. It is easily demonstrated that the probability of a phoneme may be expressed as a sum, over all the morpheme classes, of the probability of a morpheme class times the probability of the phoneme in that morpheme class.[53] In other words, the probability of a phoneme is a weighted average of its probability within each of the morpheme classes. Thus, a highly probable phoneme could be highly probable in just a few morpheme classes or moderately probable in nearly all morpheme classes. In English, the phoneme $/\theta/$ is highly probable only in words including a definite article morpheme (e.g., 'the', 'these,' 'those') while the high probability of the vowel phonemes is most likely due to their moderate probability in a large number of morpheme classes. A simple count of phonemes over a large sample of texts would be incapable of indicating these phonemena whereas the analysis suggested above should. Thus, the more complex analysis proposed here is potentially more capable of indicating the details of linguistic structure.

Eventually, it will probably be necessary to establish a hierarchy of Markov Processes where each level contains some of the processes of the next lower level as states. For the time being, however, it would probably be best to confine the setting up of such a hierarchy to linguistic units which are relatively well understood, such as the phoneme and some classes of morphemes. It should be realized that the choice of levels in the hierarchy of Markov Processes is largely a matter of convenience in conceptualizing linguistic structure

---

[52] This number is relatively small for very small values of r, say 1 or 2, but increases very rapidly as r increases. For example, if our phonemic transcription used 34 phonemes, the number of sequences in A for $r = 4$ would be $34^4 = 1,367,500$ (approx.). This state of affairs would be much worse if a full phonetic transcription were used.

[53] Using mathematical symbolism, if $p(a)$ is the probability of phoneme a, $p(B)$ the probability of a morpheme class B which is any of a set of morpheme classes, and $p_B(a)$ the probability of a in B, it is easily shown that

$$p(a) = \sum_B p(B)\ p_B(a).$$

and that there can be no serious objections to using any particular set of categories so long as the categories on each level provide a probability space with mutually exclusive divisions. In fact, the use of categories established by various schools of linguists may well indicate a hitherto unrealized agreement in the nature of linguistic structure.

5.3.2. *Entropy Analysis of a Small Scale Artificial Language*[54]

The analysis of a small scale artificial language given here is meant as a demonstration of a potentially valuable technique. The demonstration hinges on the fact that, given the rules of its construction and the number of its interchangeable states, the total number of messages that can be transmitted is known and finite. This is, of course, not true of natural languages. However, artificial languages can be so designed as to incorporate any particular aspects of language in which the investigator is interested without contamination with the many complexities of natural languages. Moreover, such languages permit the study of phenomena which may not be found in any natural language. While it is correct to point out that we can 'only get out what we put in' such an artificial language, this technique allows us to explore the implications of certain aspects of linguistic structure which we may not have been aware of previously.

Structure of small scale language.
(1)
Phonology:

Vowels: a, i
Consonants: b, d

(2)
Morpheme classes and exhaustive lists thereof:

Nouns: bab 'man'
(N)   bad 'woman'
       bib 'boy'
       bid 'girl'   [Each of these may be used as either subject (N_s) or object (N_o)]
       dab 'dog'
       dad 'cat'
       dib 'wolf'
       did 'bird'

Verbs: *Transitive* (V_t)   *Intransitive* (V_i)
      aba 'see'   iba 'go'
      abi 'kill'   ibi 'come'
      ada 'find'   ida 'walk'
      adi 'lose'   idi 'fly'

Truth-value markers: (T)
  ba 'yes'   (approximate translation)
  bi 'no, not' (approximate translation)

---

[54] This analysis has been described elsewhere by John B. Carroll and is included here because of the remarkably clear way in which it illustrates many of the problems with which this section is concerned.

(3)
Syntax:
The following is an exhaustive classification of the sentences of this language:

Statements:		No. of possible sentences		
N_sV_iT	(with intrans. vb.)	$8 \times 4 \times 2$	$= 64$	
$N_sV_tN_oT$	(with trans. vb. and obj.)	$8 \times 4 \times 8 \times 2$	$= 512$	

Questions (parallel to above)
V_iN_sT $4 \times 8 \times 2$ $= 64$
$V_tN_sN_oT$ $4 \times 8 \times 8 \times 2$ $= 512$

Total No. of possible sentences: 1152

(4) Juncture, stress, intonation, etc.: there is no stress or intonation in this language, at least not phonemically. There are no junctures between 'words,' so that all sentences are simply strings of phonemes.

Sample sentence: dadabididbi. 'Cat kill bird not.'

(5) Non-linguistic considerations. We will assume that all of the 1152 sentences in this language are equiprobable, and that there are no dependencies *between* sentences in a string.

Application of entropy measurement

(1) Entropy of a single sentence: $H_S = \log_2 1152 = 10.17$.
(2) Entropy reduction of each phoneme, considered with respect to its position in the sentence is: $H_P = H_S - H_R$, where H_R is the entropy of the statements which are still possible after the transmission of phoneme P.

To illustrate: Consider the successive phonemes of the sentence abibibbabbi 'see boy man not' or 'does not the boy see the man?' (Free translation.)

Phoneme	Remarks	No. Possible Sentences Remaining	H	H_P
—	Any sentence possible before transmission begins	1152	10.17	—
a	Must be question with trans. vb., of which the no. of possibilities is	512	9.	1.17
b	Verb either *see* or *kill*	256	8.	1.0
a	Verb must be *see*	128	7.	1.0
b	N_s must be either *man, woman, boy* or *girl*	64	6.	1.0
i	Must be either *boy* or *girl*	32	5.	1.0
b	Must be *boy*	16	4.	1.0
b	N_o is *man, woman, boy,* or *girl*	8	3.	1.0
a	*Man* or *woman*	4	2.	1.0
b	*Man;* sentence either pos. or neg.	2	1.	1.0
b	Redundant; gives no information	2	1.	0.0
i	Sentence is negative	1	0.0	1.0

                                                10.17

(3) Entropy reduction of each morpheme, also considered in relation to its position in the sentence, is $H_M = H_S - H_R$ where H_S and H_R are as defined previously. The same sentence is used here as in the example above.

Morpheme	Remarks	N_R	H	H_M
—	Any sentence possible initially	1152	10.17	—
aba	Verb *see*; sentence is question with V_t	128	7.00	3.17
bib	This is noun *boy*	16	4.00	3.00
bab	This is noun *man*	2	1.00	3.00
bi	Sentence is negative	1	0.00	1.00
				10.17

Note that this analysis can be obtained from that in section 2 above by summing across the phonemes in each morpheme.

Sometimes variations in structure allow for a greater entropy reduction for particular morphemes. For example, consider the sentence, ibiadbi—translated 'Come woman not.'

Morpheme	Remarks	N_R	H	H_M
—	Any sentence possible	1152	10.17	—
ibi	Question with V_i *come*	16	4.00	6.17
bad	This is noun *woman*	2	1.00	3.00
bi	Sentence is negative	1	0.00	1.00
				10.17

Note that the entropy reduction of the first phoneme here is 4.17.

The entropy analysis of the language described above seems to justify the following conclusions:

(1) The amount of entropy of any message in the language is constant regardless of what type of units are being analysed. However, the amount of redundancy depends upon the characteristics of the symbols in which the message is coded.

(2) The amount of entropy of a message with specified structural boundaries is a function of the ensemble of all possible messages within these boundaries. This ensemble is determinable from the grammar of the language and the inventory of its form classes. It would be possible to test the validity of this conclusion for English sentences of a limited structural type—say of the form Noun-Verb-Noun. This also could be done for similarly limited classes of words, but in both cases we would have to account for the differential probabilities of the units within the language.

(3) The entropy of a given symbol at a given point in a message is a function of the extent to which its transmission narrows the range of possible messages. The average amount of entropy per symbol is an average of such measures.

5.3.3. *Entropy Profiles*

The analysis of the amount of entropy reduction for every unit in the model language above seems to be closely related to the entropy profile analysis to be described here. However, there are two important differences which should be noted:

(a) An entropy reduction analysis presupposes that the number of possible messages is finite and that the probabilities of each of the messages is known. An entropy profile analysis involves no assumption concerning the number of possible messages or their probabilities, but requires only that the various component units which can occur in the environment of the message and their probabilities be known. Thus, it appears that entropy reduction analysis could be applied only to limited classes of natural language messages since the number of messages in nearly all languages is indefinitely large.

(b) An entropy reduction analysis of the type above presupposes that the structural units of the language are known. Such an analysis indicates the contribution of these units to entropy reduction. An entropy profile analysis involves no such assumption about the higher order units of a language, but serves in the selection of the most appropriate higher order units.

Let 1, 2, 3, 4 . . . n represent a set of sequentially ordered phonemes in a text of n units length. Let x and y be any pair of antecedent and subsequent phonemes in this sequence. Let A be the class of antecedent phonemes which may be selected before any y and let S be the class of subsequent phonemes which may be selected after any x. Let a be any member of A and s be any member of S. Finally, let $p_x(S)$ and $p_y(A)$ represent the conditional probabilities of the s's and a's for particular x's and y's.

It is possible to measure the entropy of class S after any x and the entropy of the class A before any y by means of the equations $H_x(S) = -\sum_s p_x(s) \log_2 p_x(s)$ and $H_y(A) = -\sum_a p_y(a) \log_2 p_y(a)$.[44] The total amount of entropy between any x and y, $E(x, y)$, is given by $E(x, y) = H_x(S) + H_y(A)$.

Let us examine the behavior of $E(x, y)$ in four extreme cases.

(1) Only one phoneme follows x and only one phoneme precedes y. In other words x and y always occur together.

$$x \text{———————} y$$

Obviously, $H_x(S) = H_y(A) = 0$, so $E(x, y) = 0$.

(2) (a) Only one phoneme, y, follows x but k different phonemes can precede y equiprobably.

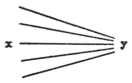

Obviously, $H_x(S) = 0$ and $H_y(A) = \log_2 k$, and $E(x, y) = \log_2 k$.

(b) l different phonemes follow x equiprobably but only one phoneme, x, can precede y.

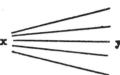

---

[44] It should be noted that $H_x(S)$ and $H_y(A)$ are measures of entropy in particular conditions and so correspond to the measure $H_i(J)$ discussed in section 2.3. They are not measures of conditional entropy which average measures corresponding to $H_i(J)$ over a number of conditions.

Obviously, $H_x(S) = \log_2 l$ and $H_y(A) = 0$, so $E(x, y) = \log_2 l$.

(3) l different phonemes can follow x equiprobably and k different phonemes can precede y equiprobably.

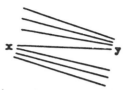

Obviously, $H_x(S) = \log_2 l$ and $H_y(A) = \log_2 k$ so that $E(x, y) = \log_2 l + \log_2 k$.[56]

Once $E(x, y)$ has been computed for all pairs (x, y) for the sequentially ordered phonemes 1, 2, 3 ... n, an entropy profile may be plotted from these values. We would expect this profile to be near zero for instances of high redundancy like case 1, to be moderately high for instances of partial redundancy like cases 2 (a) and (b), and to be maximally high for instances of minimal redundancy like case 3. We may further distinguish between the two types of case 2 instances by plotting $H_x(S)$ on the same graph as $E(x, y)$ since $H_x(S)$ will be low for instances like case 2 (a) and high for instances like 2 (b). The resulting profile will appear as in Fig. 11. The two data points between phonemes 1 and 2 represent $E(1, 2)$ and $H_1(S)$; the two points between phonemes 2 and 3 represent $E(2, 3)$ and $H_2(S)$, etc. The underlined numbers beneath the points on the graph indicate the class type most nearly represented by the entropy relations.

So far, we have not mentioned the most tedious part of the computation of entropy profiles—the estimation of the $p_x(s)$'s and the $p_y(a)$'s. This estimation can be carried out in at least two distinctly different ways which will naturally lead to somewhat different interpretations:

(1) *Estimation from sample texts.* Such estimation would require a large sample of texts in a given language with a variety of semantic contents. Since all the phonemes of a language will be included in any sizeable sample, one such estimation should suffice for the computation of entropy profiles for any text in the sampled language. However, this conclusion would not necessarily apply to morphemes or any larger linguistic units. An entropy profile based on such an estimate should indicate only the effect of the formal structure of the language and should be relatively independent of the semantic content of the text.

(2) *Estimation from subjects' anticipations.* This technique would require a group of homogeneous subjects—all speakers of the language of the text—to anticipate the phonemes of the text. In obtaining the $p_x(s)$'s, the text would be given in a forward direction and the subjects would be asked to anticipate what the next phoneme would be. In obtaining the $p_y(a)$'s, the text would be given in a reverse direction and the subjects would be asked to anticipate the

[56] Naturally, we can expect to find such extreme cases only rarely in actual texts. Nevertheless, these cases are pure examples of the four general kinds of relationships we can expect to find among sequentially ordered message events and so we can expect that they will be approximated by empirical data.

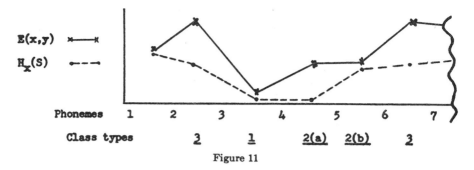

Figure 11

preceding phoneme. In both cases, it would probably be necessary to repeat the portion of the message already given to control for differential memory effects. Also, sufficient instruction concerning the semantic content of the message should be given before the first anticipations are made to insure that the effect of semantic content is relatively constant throughout. This method is rather cumbersome if the units are phonemes, since it only could be used for short texts in one experimental session and because of the difficulty in recording the responses of linguistically naive subjects. Regardless of the units used, it would be necessary to make a new estimation for every next text analysed. Nevertheless, this method of estimation should reflect both the effect of the structure of the language (assuming that the subjects respond in terms of this structure) and the semantic content of the message. While this sort of analysis is of little importance to linguistics, *per se*, it is of great potential value to the determination of the psycholinguistic units of decoding.

Once entropy profiles have been computed for a variety of texts, it would be of interest to determine the degree to which the points of high entropy in the texts coincide with the morpheme boundaries. If such a correspondence is found, it would be possible to define morphemes objectively in terms of entropy relations and perhaps it would be possible to distinguish various types of morphemes in terms of these entropy relations. If such a correspondence does not occur, we can only hope that the points of high entropy have enough common characteristics to permit the identification of new linguistic units. The discussion of entropy profiles has been mainly concerned with the isolation of morphemic or morpheme-like units as states of some higher order Markov Process. Once these units have been determined, we could transcribe our texts in terms of these known units and repeat the analysis, with the aim of determining yet higher order units.

5.3.4. The 'Cloze' Procedure[57]

While not strictly an application of entropy measurements, a new method of measuring 'comprehensibility' of relatively large scale texts being developed

[57] Cf. W. Taylor, Cloze procedure: A new tool for measuring readability, *Journalism Quarterly* **30**. 415–33 (1953).

by Wilson Taylor is certainly relevant here and could be translated into information theory statistics. The underlying logic of the method is as follows: In the process of encoding, transitional dependencies among semantic events, among grammatical and syntactical regularities, and also (although less importantly here) within skill sequences are simultaneously contributing to a rather precise selection among hierarchies of alternatives at each choice point. If the encoder producing a message and the decoder receiving it happen to have highly similar semantic and grammatical habit systems, the decoder ought to be able to predict or anticipate what the encoder will produce at each moment with considerable accuracy. In other words, if both members of the communication act share common associations and common constructive tendencies, they should be able to anticipate each other's verbalization.

The term 'cloze' is derived from the gestalt notion of *closure*, e.g., the tendency to fill in a missing gap in a well-structured whole. Given the sequence 'Chickens cackle and————quack,' almost anyone would immediately supply the missing 'ducks.' Similarly, given 'The old man————along the dusty road,' almost everyone will supply some verb form (grammatical disposition) and most will be affected by the 'old' element semantically and choose an appropriate verb, such as 'hobbled,' 'crept,' or 'limped.' As the actual procedure has been worked out, the experimenter deletes every n^{th} word in a text (it has been shown that this automatic procedure works as well or better than either deleting specific categories of words or words at random, providing one is using a text of sufficient size), leaving equal sized blanks in their places, and decoding subjects read through the passage filling in the missing words. The more closely the totality of sequential cues in the passage elicits at each test point the same word selection as the original author's, the higher will be the decoder's 'cloze' score (only absolutely correct fill-ins are counted, judging synonyms proving too difficult and not materially affecting results):

Taylor has demonstrated the feasibility of this technique as an index of 'readability'—in fact, it behaves much more satisfactorily than either the Flesch or Dale-Chall formulas. Not only does it order the same materials used as demonstrations by the authors of these standard formulas in the same way, but on some special test materials it alone yields sensible results. For example, both Flesch and Dale-Chall indicate a passage from Gertrude Stein as being very 'easy'! Taylor's 'Cloze' score shows Stein, more appropriately, as very difficult. In other words, this method takes into account the highly unpredictable semantic and grammatical sequencing characteristic of Stein. Taylor has also tested the assumption that his method is essentially a measure of degree of 'comprehension.' In a very carefully designed experiment using Air Force training materials for which comprehension tests were already available, he showed that 'Cloze' scores correlated very highly with initial comprehension scores (pre-message) and also predicted terminal comprehension (post-message).

There are many possible applications of this technique to psycholinguistic problems. For example, it is possible to construct alternatively coded messages on the same topic and use the 'Cloze' method to determine which form produces

the most information transfer (cf., section 7.3 for discussion of an entropy measure of information transfer which could be combined with the Taylor procedure).
Along similar lines, one may construct messages which vary in the transitional
dependency of either their semantic or grammatical sequencing, or both, and
use the 'Cloze' procedure to measure the effects produced on decoders (cf.,
section 5.4 for discussion of a method for constructing such messages). Using
the same message and deleting every, say, fifth word, but using five equated
groups to cover the entire message (e.g., group I having words 1, 6, 11, etc.
deleted, group II having words 2, 7, 12, etc. deleted, and so forth) it should be
possible to use this method to construct an entropy profile at the word unit level.
The significant advantage of Taylor's 'Cloze' procedure is that it taps simultaneously all of the complex determinants affecting word choice, both at various
levels of organization and through long stretches of sequencing; it is applicable
to comparing encoders (e.g., readability), messages (comprehensibility), and
decoders (e.g., individual differences in reading skills, second language mastery,
information about topic, etc.).

5.4. *Transitional Organization: Association Techniques*[58]

In any empirical analysis of verbal behavior as it occurs 'naturally' (in a
conversation, an interview, a letter, a book, an oration or what have you) the
investigator is likely to feel overwhelmed with problems of multiple causation
affecting the production of utterances. In an effort to simplify the analysis,
one might (following Skinner) divide the 'causes' into four major groups: (1)
States of the speaker. Here one might study such variables as drives or needs,
attitudes, beliefs, fatigue, etc. (2) *Audience variables.* The language or sub-
language spoken or understood by the audience, the stimuli from the audience
indicating approval or disapproval, the ease with which the audience can hear
the speaker, etc., are important considerations within this category. (3) *Verbal
and non-verbal referential stimuli.* Under this heading one might investigate the
effects of presence or absence of things being talked about, past experiences in
the presence of given stimuli, discriminative reinforcement histories, etc. (4)
Intraverbal connections. In this category one might study the tendencies of a
speaker's responses to influence his future responses; i.e., the tendency of the
choice of one word to lead to the choice of a related word later, the choice of one
form of utterance to lead to the choice of a particular subsequent one, etc. Since
we are concerned here with transitional organization of language behavior, the
fourth category is the one to which we may turn our attention.

The general assumption being made here is that emission of any antecedent
response increases the probability of occurrence of a hierarchy of interrelated
subsequent responses. It is also assumed, of course, that these intraverbal connections arise in the same manner in which any skill sequence arises, through
repetition, contiguity, differential reinforcement. It should be recognized that
this analysis does not lead immediately to a tool for breaking down contextual
effects. Any utterance (especially a single word) may be thought of as belonging

[58] James J. Jenkins.

to a large number of response hierarchies, sound classes, form classes, sequence classes, frequency classes, etc. The analysis does suggest, however, experimental techniques for dealing with fragments of context in simple situations in which their specific influences may be more precisely studied.

5.4.1. *The Word Association Technique*

A first approach to the examination of interrelationships between word units may be found in the classic word association test. In this kind of test the subject is instructed to respond to a stimulus word with the first word (other than the stimulus word) that occurs to him. Substantial amounts of data have been collected on the responses of groups of people to small sets of stimulus words. For stimulus words occurring with high frequency in a given culture hierarchies of response words have been observed. For a given stimulus word a large number of subjects (sometimes as high as 80 per cent) may give the same response word; a much smaller number of subjects give a second response word; a slightly smaller number gives a third word, and so on down to responses which are made only by individual subjects. Thus, for a stimulus word the probabilities of given responses may be specified for cultural groups. While there is some evidence that the response hierarchies obtained from a group of subjects are related to individual hierarchies of response, this has not been clearly established.

It is possible, then, with this technique to ascertain the transitional probability between stimulus words and response words for a given group under these restricted conditions. This amounts to specifying a divergent hierarchy of responses to each given stimulus word.

In addition, it has recently been shown that these probabilities are directly related to the transitional probabilities between the same words when they are both produced by the subject himself in a restricted recall situation. If S–R words from the association test are scrambled in a list and read to subjects who are asked to recall them, it can be observed that in recalling the list, the subjects tend markedly to recall the words of the pairs together. It appears that recalling one word of a pair acts as a stimulus for the recall of the second word of the pair. As the strength of the word pairs on the association test norms is increased, the amount of pairing in recall increases. To a considerable extent the order (apparently freely determined by the subject) is predictable from a knowledge of the cultural S–R pairs. Our information is thus extended from a knowledge of responses made to outside stimuli to a prediction of responses made to previous responses. This is an important step, since it suggests that we may use the word association test data in constructing experiments to examine the effect of high and low transitional probabilities on the performance of a variety of verbal tasks.

Past experiments in free association have also demonstrated the importance of instructions given the subject in the determination of the response words made to the stimuli. If, for example, the suggestion is made that opposites may be given or even more directly the subjects are requested to respond with opposites, the variety of response words decreases markedly and the frequencies of a few responses rise correspondingly. In this situation also the responses are in general more rapid. It is as if a major portion of the response hierarchy were removed and only the specific subportion designated by dual class membership (related to stimulus word and opposition) were available. The existence of this phenomenon illustrates the possibility of determining transitional probabilities under special limiting conditions.

It has also been shown that speed of response to a stimulus word in free association is an index to the rarity of the response word (although it may also indicate emotional involvement or competition of response words). In like manner, speed of response is also a function of the familiarity or rarity of the stimulus word. This is additional evidence supporting the notion that the free association test measures transitional probabilities in a manner which should be useful in experimentation which moves closer to 'real life' situations and the problems of context.

5.4.2. Word Association in the Study of Language Structure

The above characteristics of the word association test suggested a major experiment designed to evaluate the effect of varied transitional probabilities measured in this manner. In brief, the experiment would consist of three stages: (1) building up networks of high and low transitional probabilities by word association techniques, (2) using these networks to construct stories or essays of very high and very low average transitions, and (3) testing these stories against each other for differences in comprehension, reading or speaking ease, ability to withstand mutilation ('Cloze' procedure), etc. This would constitute a full-scale test of the efficacy of this approach to transitional probabilities.

Stage one could be accomplished by capitalizing on the control of set and the measurement of association strength which have been pointed out above. A group of subjects could be asked to respond with the first *verb* they think of when a particular *noun* is given; the first *noun* they think of for a given *adjective*, the first *adverb* for a given *verb*, etc. The most popular and most rapidly given words would be paired with the stimulus words to construct high probability sentences. The very infrequent and delayed responses would be used for the low probability sentences. While the stories or essays resulting from the manipulation of these rather sizeable amounts of data might not be great literature, it seems likely that fairly parallel texts (in content) could be developed. In stage two these texts would be assembled and tested to exclude extraneous variables, such as differences in the basic frequency of occurrence of words in the culture, the sentence constructions, order of presentation of material, etc. In stage three the texts would be presented to new groups of subjects in controlled reading situations. It would be predicted that the high transitional probability text would be read faster (both silently and aloud), would require fewer eye fixations, would be more completely understood (as determined by a comprehension test), would be more accurately recalled after a lapse of time, and would be more easily read after mutilation (i.e., when every fifth or tenth word is deleted). All of these predictions can be readily appraised.

It might be of further interest and lend verification to this study if another group of subjects were simply given the lists of words and asked to construct stories. It would be predicted that these subjects would use the combinations found to be of high transitional probability and avoid the low transitional probability combinations. This would constitute further evidence for the similarity of the stimulus-response and response-response conditions and would increase our information concerning these phenomena. If these predictions are borne out, the word association test would appear to be an instrument *par excellence* for the study and examination of transitional probabilities as they effect context.

Other suggestions appear relevant both for the understanding of context and for the understanding of the phenomenon of word association itself. The linguist looks at free association data or serial associations and notes that stimuli and responses often fall in the same form classes. The data presently available on free associations are not sufficient to determine if this is the case, since for the most part stimuli have been nouns and adjectives with a very few verbs. It is proposed that a large body of associative data be built up, systematically sampling grammatical classes, grammatical 'tags' and various lexical units. Pronouns, verbs, adverbs, prepositions, conjunctions, relative pronouns, etc. must be studied. Various changes in the stimuli (from singular to plural, present to past tense, etc.) need to be explored. This simple kind of experimentation may contribute markedly to our understanding of language habits which are essential to mature language behavior. Cross linguistic studies would be of interest and may further embody suggestions for second language learning.

A straightforward linguistic analysis of free association also may contribute to a clarification of 'normal' response categories. In spite of the long history of use of free association tests, a satisfactory method of classification has not been found. The most common attempts have been an unsystematic mixture of semantic, psychological and linguistic criteria. The inadequacy of these measures is indicated by the following example: in one system the response 'length' to the stimulus 'long' is classified as an example of 'compounding;' however, the pair 'height-high' is an example of 'phonetic similarity' and is the same as the response 'able' to 'table.' Perhaps purely linguistic criteria may be found which will classify possible responses. While it is unlikely that any system will 'explain' *all* of the responses, a suggestion for classification is presented here. It is intended to apply it to the broad collection of associations proposed above. It seems probable that refinements may be included as the work progresses.

Word associations may be interpreted as a result of relative distribution of the stimuli and responses. The similarity between any two words can be conceived linguistically as the degree of similarity in distribution. However, it seems apparent that this similarity may be profitably divided into two classes, *paradigmatic* and *syntagmatic*. Two words are considered paradigmatically similar to the extent that they are substitutable in the identical frame (this corresponds rather closely to Zellig Harris' use of the term 'selection') and syntagmatic to the extent that they follow one another in utterances.

For example, if we were to measure the paradigmatic similarity between 'table' and its most common response in word association tests, i.e., 'chair,' we would investigate to what extent they occurred in the same frame. 'Table' and 'chair,' as well as almost any other member of the noun class, such as man, woman, dog, cat, etc., occur, for example, in the frame, 'I saw a _____.' If we then consider the frame, 'I bought a _____ ,' we have eliminated 'man' and 'woman,' but our class still includes, 'table,' 'chair,' 'cat,' 'dog,' etc. At the other extreme is the frame 'My favorite piece of furniture is _____.' in which 'table' and 'chair' occur, but not the others. Furthermore, 'chair' and not 'table' occurs in the frame 'I like to sit in an easy _____.' We would then hypothesize that one factor in any word association test would be the relative paradigmatic similarity of the hierarchy of responses, so that frequency of responses would be a function of paradigmatic similarity.

Another factor in forming word associations is the relative frequency with which words follow one another in a sequence. The frame 'I saw a _____.' may obviously be completed by a larger number of possibilities than 'I bought a _____.' or 'I sat on a _____.' Consequently, the associative strength of 'sat-chair' will be greater than 'saw-chair.' We can then define syntagmatic similarity as the probability with which any one word will be followed immediately by the second. It seems reasonable to exclude from this analysis the grammatical morphemes, or function words, such as 'a,' 'and,' etc.

As presented up to this point, paradigmatic similarity is restricted almost exclusively to words of the same form class. Syntagmatic similarity, however, can be extended to include both words of the same as well as of different form classes. The example above is one of association between verb and noun. If we include the frame 'I bought a table and _____.' we can establish a syntagmatic similarity between words of the same form class.

If both paradigmatic and syntagmatic similarity may be factors in strength of association, it follows that the highest associative strength will be between words of the same form class, insofar as only these words can be similar both paradigmatically and syntagmatically. It is not surprising, then, to find that the most frequent types of responses among adults are 'coordination' (e.g., table-chair) and 'contrast' (e.g., black-white).[59] Certain related hypotheses present themselves regarding what might be expected in word association tests. For example, if, as seems likely, the sequence 'black and white' is more frequent than 'white and black' in our culture, this difference should manifest itself in word association tests in that 'black' would tend to elicit 'white' significantly more than the reverse. In this light, the Kent-Rosanoff tests[60] were re-examined and yield the following cases (out of 1000 responses): table-chair, 844 vs. chair-table, 494; black-white, 706 vs. white-black, 605; hand-foot, 156 vs. foot-hand, 198; long-short, 758 vs. short-long, 336. The latter is an example of a word, in this case 'short,' with two competing responses, namely, 'tall' and 'long;' 'long,' however, has just one main response. A series of words of this kind might be used in experiments to test the validity of this hypothesis.

It seems likely that a few special categories may have to be invoked for a complete analysis of associations. For example, the 'phonetic similarity' class (e.g., table-able) may be indispensable, although it accounts for a very small percentage of associations. Even here it seems likely that one might get a higher percentage of this type of response by selecting words which are either paradigmatically or syntagmatically similar as well as phonetically similar.

A basic problem for this analysis, of course, is the determination of objective measures of paradigmatic and syntagmatic similarity. As a beginning, paradigmatic similarity might be defined simply as common form class membership, but a stronger measure of similarity might be developed through judges' ratings or sentence completion techniques. Syntagmatic similarity is even more difficult to measure. Ideally, an extensive count of spoken and written English might provide it, but the task is too great for practicality. Again, perhaps judges' ratings or sentence completions will be required. Further work here is sorely needed.

    [59] The terms are those used by Miller, *Language and communication*, based on work done by Woodrow and Lowell, *Psychological monograph* **22**. 97 (1916).
    [60] W. A. Russell and J. J. Jenkins, Kent-Rosanoff norms for Minnesota college students (in press).

5.4.3. *Context and Association*

Two experiments which have brought the word association work closer to context problems are given here to illustrate the uses of the technique as an experimental tool.

Howes and Osgood[61] have made a careful study of word associations in the determination of responses to a complex of four stimulus words. Subjects were told that they would be given four words and that they were to respond to the last word by writing the first other word it made them think of. Control sets used nonsense words or numbers preceding the last word. The experimental sets were devised to study the influence of adjacent words on the responses to the last word. Variables studied were the distance (in time) of an experimental word from the last word, the density of the experimental words (whether they were all calculated to influence the stimulus word in the same way; whether two of them were; whether only one of them was) and the cultural frequency (by Thorndike-Lorge count) of the experimental words used. As an example, consider the stimulus word 'man.' Used alone it evokes 'woman,' 'boy,' 'child,' etc. If the word 'yellow' is inserted before it, does the response 'Chinese,' 'Japanese,' Jap,' etc. appear? If so, does this response decrease as the word 'yellow' is moved one or two words away from the stimulus word 'man?' If the word 'alien' or 'eastern' is added instead of the other neutral words in addition to 'yellow' does this increase the number of 'Chinese' responses? If in place of 'yellow' some rare synonym were used, would it achieve the same result?

This experiment clearly demonstrated that all of these were significant variables. The subjects did respond to the compound stimuli. The influence of an experimental word decreased as it moved away from the last word. Increasing density increased the number of influenced responses. Words of high cultural frequency exercised more influence than words of low cultural frequency. This experiment is an excellent example of the use of a simple tool to attack this complicated problem. Its implications are immediately obvious.

A second experiment is one undertaken by MacCorquodale and others as part of the Minnesota Studies in Verbal Behavior. While the research is not as yet complete, the influence of associative bonds in context appears to have been demonstrated. In an attempt to reveal 'thematic strengthening,' alternate sets of sentences were constructed to have the 'same meaning.' In one pair of such sentences a word was changed to a substitutable word, but one which it was felt strengthened a different response hierarchy. The sentences were left incomplete and given to different groups of subjects for completion. For example, one sentence (in its control form) read, 'The children noticed that the snow was beginning to *hide* the ground as they got out of ——.' In its experimental form this sentence read, 'The children noticed that the snow was beginning to *blanket* the ground as they got out of ——.' The difference between the sentences, then, lies in the response hierarchies evoked by the two words 'hide' and 'blanket.'

---

[61] D. H. Howes and C. E. Osgood, The effect of linguistic context on associative word probabilities, *American Journal of Psychology* (forthcoming).

The sentence exercises only the control that the children must be getting out of something or somewhere. Any difference in the determination of what or where must be the result of the associations strengthened by the changed words. In this example, the control sentence elicited many references to 'school,' 'the bus,' 'the house,' etc., and the experimental sentence in contrast elicited, as hypothesized, a large number of references to 'bed' which were almost totally lacking in the control group. Further experimentation with this technique should reveal in actual context the operation of the significant variables dealt with by Howes and Osgood.

In summary it appears that many important questions regarding 'language in action' may be attacked with one of the oldest tools in the psychological repertoire, the free association test and its derivatives, and that many challenging hypotheses are available for research.

5.5 *Channel Capacity in Semantic Decoding*[62]

In Shannon's development of information theory, *channel capacity* is defined as the maximum rate (expressed in bits per second) at which a communication channel can transmit messages with a minimal amount of error. When the rate at which messages are presented to a channel (i.e., the rate of input) exceeds its capacity, the amount of random error in transmission increases with the amount of excessive information. Comparable phenomena seem to occur in ordinary language communication. When a radio announcer spins through a series of baseball scores—Yankees 2, Browns 4; Red Sox 12, Senators 5; Indians 3, Tigers 7; White Sox 3, Athletics 2—what is a simple task for the encoder may be an impossible task for the decoder (who wants to know who played whom and with what result). If the decoder does hold onto one particular game and its result, he loses both what went before and what followed. In this case, the channel capacity of the decoder has been passed.

Experimentally, it is necessary to deal with the human communicator as a single system intervening between manipulatable states of some physical input system and recordable states of some physical output system, e.g., as intervening between observable stimuli and responses. However, this total communicating unit is comprised of many sub-systems whose limits, or capacities, may vary one from the other. One experimental problem is immediately apparent: in order to study the characteristics of any system in a communication chain, it is necessary to devise conditions under which the capacities of the other systems are not limiting factors.

5.5.1 *Theoretical Analysis*

For present purposes we shall eliminate by our choice of stimulus materials and response categories grammatical aspects of decoding. As shown in Figure 12, the semantic system is here conceived as a set of mediating processes $(r_1\text{———}s_1, \ldots r_n\text{———}s_n)$ which, as implicit reactions, are dependent to variable degrees upon states of the input system $(S_1, \ldots S_n)$. We shall assume

[62] Charles E. Osgood.

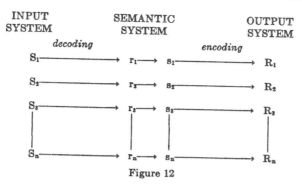

Figure 12

that, as with any system, mechanical or organic, the semantic system is limited in the number of different states which it can assume during any finite time, e.g., its rate of shifting from state to state is finite. The capacity of a system under optimal conditions will be called its *maximum capacity*. We shall also assume that the output system in human language behavior has a lower maximum capacity than the semantic system, e.g., that sequences of 'ideas' can proceed at a faster rate than the sequences of vocalizations with which they are associated. What we shall call the *functional capacity* of a system—that which it displays under a given set of conditions—is always equal to or less than its maximum capacity.

What are some of the conditions affecting functional capacity? (1) *The greater the conditional dependencies of states in a given system upon states in its antecedent system, the greater its functional capacity.* Conditional dependency in this context is assumed to be equivalent to habit strength. Since latency of reaction is an inverse function of habit strength, the stronger the decoding habits the more rapidly each mediating reaction will follow presentation of the appropriate sign. One of Baseball's Faithful, for whom the signs 'Athletics' and 'Red Sox' are strongly associated with differential mediators, would have less difficulty keeping up with the announcer's stream of scores than a casual follower of the sport.

Referring back to Figure 12, in decoding the conditional dependencies are those between members of the set S_n and members of the set r_n. In ordinary language communication, of course, these conditional dependencies are very high (e.g., heard or seen words as physical stimuli are strongly associated with particular significances and not with others); under these conditions, therefore, functional capacities should tend to approach their maxima.

The question of the effect of transitional dependencies within a given system, e.g., the tendency for certain states of the system to follow others with non-chance probabilities, raises a number of complicated problems. Transitional dependency (or redundancy) is assumed to be equivalent to 'associations' when dealing with sequences in the semantic system (e.g., predictability of subsequent members of the set r_n given knowledge of the occurrence of antecedent members of this set). Certainly, on a practical level, it seems obvious that the rate of decoding will be faster when the sequence required of the semantic system is one for which it is already 'set' on the basis of past experience—the Lord's Prayer is presumably easier to decode than a series of baseball scores.

In the first place, it should be noted that the example given in the preceding paragraph involves high conditional dependencies as well—the sequence 'impressed' on the test system by its input happens to correspond to already established transitional probabilities within the test system. If the conditional dependencies between input and semantic systems were near zero (for example, with a series of low association value nonsense syllables as stimuli), only random output could result, and the transitional organization of the semantic system would seem to be irrelevant. On the other hand, with high degrees of conditional dependency between input and semantic systems the amount of transitional dependency operative can be varied independently by manipulating the sequences of input signals (e.g., from a random sequence of signs like AGAINST WOULD IT THE FOLLOWED SET to one of high transitional predictability like A ROLLING STONE GATHERS NO MOSS). This was essentially the variable investigated by Miller and Selfridge in studying the case of learning verbal materials chosen with varying approximations to English syntactical structure.

Taking into account conditional dependency, we may then state that (2) *the more the sequences of states impressed on a system by the input correspond to existing transitional dependencies within the system itself, the greater will be its functional capacity.* Assuming equally strong decoding habits, the rate at which A ROLLING STONE GATHERS NO MOSS can be handled by the semantic system would be faster than the rate of handling messages like STONE A NO MOSS ROLLING GATHERS.

So far we have assumed that the number of *units* in messages, as determined objectively from the input or output, necessarily corresponds to the number of states assumed by the semantic system in any sequence, e.g., A ROLLING STONE GATHERS NO MOSS contains six units because there are six 'words' separated by white spaces. But let us suppose for the sake of argument that in English ROLLING is always followed by STONE and STONE is always preceded by ROLLING, i.e., maximum transitional dependency or redundancy—would ROLLING STONE represent one state or two sequential states in the semantic system? Conversely, does everything within the brackets defined by either white spaces (orthography) or pauses of certain length (speech) constitute a single unit semantically? Since GATHERS is divisible linguistically into GATHER and S in morphemic analysis, aren't there at least two semantic units here?

We do not as yet have any satisfactory ways for identifying semantic units and correlating them with message units (cf., discussion of psycholinguistic units, section 3). It seems likely, however, that high orders of transitional dependency within systems will be equivalent to reduction in numbers of units or states. The 'short circuiting process' envisaged here is presumably more feasible in the semantic system than in the motor skill output system. If r_1 is highly predictive of r_n, the required indexing responses can be initiated by s_1 rather than waiting for s_n; but just because R_1 (e.g., saying A ROLLING STONE . . .) is highly predictive of R_n (saying . . . MOSS) does not mean that the encoder will skip the intervening vocalization. Such a 'short circuiting process' may, of course, underlie the empirical law associated with Zipf to the effect that frequently used forms tend to become reduced in length.

So far nothing has been said about the number of alternative states among which a system must choose, the variable most often dealt with in information theory studies. The usual observation is that performance, as indexed by latency, errors, or some other measure, decreases as number of alternatives is increased. In such experiments, however, *conditional dependencies have been low.* In intelligibility studies, for example (cf., Miller's *Language and Communication*), it is necessary to work with a signal/noise ratio near discrimination threshold for number of alternatives to have its maximum effect. Obviously, if the signal were clear, it would make little difference how many alternatives were allowed. In ordinary communication, the number of alternative semantic states or meanings is extremely large, but we have no trouble in decoding as long as the peripheral signals are clear.

In effect, such studies have used the number of alternatives as a means of manipulating the conditional and transitional dependencies in their decoding and encoding. Such manipulation is feasible if conditional dependencies are low so that all of the possible states of a system follow a given state of the antecedent system with nearly equal probabilities. In such a situation, where habit strengths for all responses are nearly equal, additional alternatives have the effect of increasing response randomness or entropy. However, if conditional dependencies are generally high so that given states of the antecedent system reliably lead to particular states of the subsequent system, then one habit strength is so much larger than the others that additional alternatives can have little effect on response entropy.

Similarly, number of alternatives should become a less important determiner of channel capacity as transitional dependencies within the system increase—if alternative *b* is highly dependent upon occurrence of alternative *a* and alternative *d* is highly dependent upon occurrence of alternative *c*, we have effectively reduced the alternatives from four to two. Assuming these arguments to be valid, (3) *the greater the number of alternative states required of a system, the lower will be its functional capacity; the effectiveness of this factor varies inversely with both the conditional and transitional dependencies involved, having no effect when either is maximal.* In other words, channel capacity becomes independent of number of alternatives when either conditional dependency (predictability of states of the subsequent system from those of the antecedent system) or transitional dependency (prediction of subsequent states of the test system from antecedent states of the same system) becomes maximal.

A final general variable to be considered is *the nature of the alternatives* representing various dimensions. It should be easier, for example, for a subject to choose among four objects differing only in color than to choose among four objects differing simultaneously in shape and color, e.g., among red circle, green circle, yellow circle and blue circle as compared with among red circle, green circle, red square, and green square. Generalizing, (4) *if total number of alternatives is held constant, the slope of channel capacity as a function of number of alternatives should be steeper as the dimensionality of the alternatives is increased.* All of the hypotheses described above are susceptible to experimental test, as well as a number of secondary hypotheses to be described in course.

5.5.2. *Experimental Requirements*

In most psychological experiments dealing with intact human subjects we manipulate input (stimuli) and observe output (responses). Therefore we are necessarily dealing with the complete decoding-encoding sequence and all of the systems intervening between S and R. In the information theory sense, we are necessarily treating the individual as a channel connecting input and output systems. If we are interested in the capacity of any particular system, it is necessary that the contribution of other systems be minimal and roughly constant. If we are studying *decoding time*, we want to be able to segregate *encoding time*. There seems to be no direct way to index decoding time as a separable portion of *total time* (e.g., time between presentation of stimulus and occurrence of reaction). On the other hand, this does seem to be possible in the case of encoding time. Therefore we would start with decoding time as the variable and encoding time as the constant.

The general nature of the research proposal is as follows: (1) We provide the subject with an extremely simple and overly practiced encoding response (e.g., reaching out and touching an object). (2) Using optimally coded input, we give him practice at the encoding alternatives until conditional dependency under this condition is maximal (e.g., the 'locations' of the objects to be touched perfectly established). Optimal coding in this case might be flashing pictures of the objects to be touched on the screen one at a time (e.g., shown a picture of the *round, red, tall* object, he must touch it as soon as possible). Encoding time under these conditions should quickly reach a stable minimum. (3) The subject is now presented with *serial* verbal information, either spoken or written, such as ROUND ... RED ... TALL, and must react by touching the correct object as soon as possible after hearing the last signal. (4) The rate of presentation of this serial information is gradually increased. Measurement is made of both *total time* (from onset of first signal to termination of encoding reaction) and *encoding time* (from end of last signal to termination of encoding reaction).

The general nature of the results to be expected is shown diagrammatically in Figure 13. Up to a certain critical rate of input (*range a*), total time will be a decreasing function of increasing rate of presentation and encoding time will be a constant. Encoding time is constant through this range because it depends solely upon decoding of the last signal plus the constant encoding time—prior signals are completely decoded before the next appears. Total time decreases through this range because the rate of presentation is becoming faster. For a certain range beyond this critical point (*range b*), total time will remain at some constant value while encoding time gradually increases. Encoding time increases because it now includes increasing time spent in decoding prior signals (e.g., the subject is still decoding ROUND when RED appears and is still decoding RED when TALL appears, starting the measurement of encoding time). Total time remains constant through this range because the increase in encoding time is compensated for by the more rapid rate of input. At some further point, total time should become variable, and this should be accompanied by appearance of frequent errors (*range c*).

At the first critical point—that at which total time becomes constant and encoding time begins to increase—the *difference* between total time and encoding time should provide a measure of *decoding time* under these particular conditions,

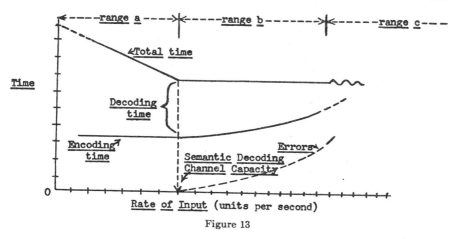

Figure 13

e.g., that amount of time required for decoding $n-1$ input signals. The projection of this critical point of the base line (shown by dashed arrow in Figure 13) should indicate the *decoding channel capacity* under these conditions, e.g., the rate of input events in units per second which can be handled by the system.

Design 1. Materials might consist of a set of objects variable in four ways through two dimensions (SHAPE: circular, square, triangular, oval; COLOR: red, yellow, green, blue) and in two ways through two other dimensions (CROSS-SECTIONAL SIZE: wide, narrow; HEIGHT: tall, short). At any one time, a maximum of 16 alternatives may be set in the panel, either each of 4 shapes in each of 4 colors (16 alternatives, but only two dimensions) or each combination of 2 shapes, in 2 colors, of 2 sizes, and having 2 heights (16 alternatives involving 4 binary choices). In this way one may investigate the effects of varying the number of alternatives when dimensionality is either held constant or varied with number of alternatives. These objects would probably be displayed in a panel against electrical contact switches, so arranged that a mere touch against any one will stop the timers for total and encoding time.

Design 2. A closer approach to typical linguistic materials could be obtained with a panel of 'nominal' objects arranged in 1 to 4 rows or columns, these objects being BALL, WHEEL, HAND, FACE, for example, and being set on levers. Each row could be in a different color or some other 'adjectival' variable. Each object could be capable of movement in 4 'verbal' ways, e.g., PUSH, RAISE, TURN, SHAKE, and in 4 'adverbial' modes, e.g., QUICKLY, SLOWLY, SMOOTHLY, ROUGHLY. Again, the input information could be recorded on tape and could be varied in both rate and complexity with respect to the response board. At the simplest level would be commands involving only two variables, e.g., PUSH A WHEEL, SHAKE A BALL; this could be extended to RAISE THE RED FACE and TURN THE BLUE WHEEL, etc.; and extended further to four alternative linguistic dimensions, e.g., SHAKE THE YELLOW HAND SLOWLY or TURN THE GREEN BALL SMOOTHLY.

Design 3. This general type of method could probably be extended to decoding of pictorial materials. We might first give the subject a statement, e.g., THE CIRCLE IS RED, then flash on the screen a simple picture with the subject to respond either *true* or *false* as quickly as possible. The picture shown could vary from the simplest case of being a red (or not red) circle, to a binary situation showing a circle and a square, one red and the other not red; similarly, the statement to be tested against the picture could be varied from THE CIRCLE

IS RED to THE LARGE CIRCLE IS RED (with appropriate samples of objects shown), and so forth. Even more complex linguistic combinations could be used with appropriate pictures, such as THE LARGE BALL UNDER THE ROUND TABLE IS GREEN. Extrinsic variables would be such things as frequency of usage of the labels used (e.g., decoding habit strengths), amount of relevant and irrelevant information, transitional predictability of the sequences use (e.g., THE MAN IS SMOKING A PIPE should be decoded correctly more quickly than THE WOMAN IS SMOKING A PIPE).

5.5.3. *Test of Predictions*

(1) *The rate of presentation at which encoding time begins to increase will always be equal to that at which total time becomes constant.* This applies to all situations and is important because it makes possible the specification of empirical units of decoding channel capacity. If this prediction does not hold, it means that our theoretical analysis of this general situation has been wrong. If it does hold, then we are in a position to explore the effects of many other variables upon decoding time, using this critical rate as an index.

(2) *Channel capacity will be an increasing function of the strength of the decoding habits involved*—e.g., *of conditional dependencies.* In the sample material given above, conditional dependencies were maximal—the decoding significances of GREEN, ROUND and so forth are maximal—and this condition therefore serves as a control. If nonsense syllables were substituted for these words with other groups of subjects, and different groups were given varying amounts of pre-training in decoding (seeing particular nonsense items with appropriate objects), it would be possible to test this prediction. The greater the amount of pre-training (and hence, theoretically, the greater the conditional dependency), the greater should become the decoding channel capacity. The function derived would presumably be typical of other learning phenomena, e.g., a negatively accelerated growth curve. Another way of testing this prediction would be to use meaningful materials varying in familiarity or frequency of usage. If VERMIL-LION, MAUVE, TURQUOISE, and so on were substituted for familiar color labels, one would expect decoding channel capacity to decrease.

(3) *Channel capacity will be an increasing function of the strengths of associations between sequential semantic states,* e.g., *transitional dependency.* Here one could manipulate *external redundancy* (for example, man vs. woman smoking pipe as discussed above or "turn wheel" vs. "turn face" in another design) or *pre-experimental training* (for example, by giving training in which certain sequences of nonsense syllables were highly probable and others unlikely). The manipulation of pre-experimental training would permit the greatest control and hence presumably yield the most stable functions.

(4) *Channel capacity will decrease with number of alternatives.* (5) *Channel capacity will be a steeper function of number of alternatives when number of dimensions of variation also increases than when dimensionality is constant.* The materials described under *design 1* provide a means of testing these predictions. The total number of alternatives can be increased from 4 to 16 with dimensionality either constant (from 2 shapes in 2 colors to 4 shapes in 4 colors) or increasing (from 2 shapes in 2 colors to 2 shapes in 2 colors of 2 sizes and of 2 heights). If this

source of variation is combined with degree of pre-training on nonsense substitutes for meaningful words, then the additional prediction—that number of alternatives as a variable has decreasing effect as conditional dependencies increase—can be tested.

One additional possibility in this line of study may be mentioned, and that it its relation to the problem of *psycholinguistic units*. If stability of the decoding-time index for a given condition and abrupt changes in its value for varying conditions can be demonstrated, it should then be possible to determine what sorts of linguistic variations involve the addition or subtraction of semantic decoding units. If changing numbers of phonemes or syllables or even grammatical morphemes do not change the decoding channel capacity, it would be apparent that these are not relevant psycholinguistic units as far as semantic decoding is concerned. On the other hand, if adding or subtracting lexical morphemes did regularly produce correlated shifts in decoding time, this would be evidence for the lexical morpheme as a semantic decoding unit. It is realized, of course, that what has been suggested in these few pages on channel capacity represents close to a lifetime of research for the person who undertakes to investigate this problem fully. On the other hand, it should not take long to determine whether or not the basic experimental notion—that total time can be separated experimentally into measurable decoding and encoding times in the manner indicated—is itself valid.

6. DIACHRONIC PSYCHOLINGUISTICS

In this section we discuss a variety of topics, all of which have in common the fact that they involve comparison between two or more stages in language development. Attention is first directed toward development of language behavior in the individual member of a speech community, *first language learning*; a general theoretical model of the process is described, a possible experimental analogue is suggested, and various research problems are discussed. A second topic is *second language learning and bilingualism*. Although these are important problems, they came under only tangential discussion in the seminar and hence are only treated briefly here. They are already areas of concentration for many specialists. The third general topic in this section is *language change*. Although this term refers to the speech community rather than the individual, it will become apparent that the processes at work have their loci in the nervous systems of many similarly constituted individuals. The treatment of each of these problems is 'psycholinguistic' in that relationships between the changing structures of messages and changing behavioral organizations of message users are stressed, and the underlying commonness of these problems will be apparent from the reappearance of identical principles, chiefly learning principles.

6.1. *First Language Learning*

This section attempts to apply learning theory to the development of language behavior. The major concern will be with modifications produced by the actions of persons in a given language-speaking culture in setting up models of verbal behavior, administering reinforcements, etc. This account does not give attention to the maturational or genetic features which presumably operate across all cultures and may influence rates of development, sequence, individual differences, and the like. This, of course, in no way implies that these are not important, but reflects, rather, limitations in seminar time and report space. Findings in the area of motor skill development mark this as an important area of research, and it is being carried on by such men as Jakobson, Leopold, Grégoire, Ohnesorg, and Cohen. In other words, we have arbitrarily limited ourselves to the *learning* of language decoding and encoding behavior.

6.1.1. *A Psycholinguistic Analysis of Decoding and Encoding*[63]

6.1.1.1. *Language decoding.* In human communication decoding refers to the process whereby certain patterns of stimulation (usually auditory or visual) elicit certain representational mechanisms (ideas or meanings) via the opera-

---

[63] Charles E. Osgood and James J. Jenkins. While members of the seminar were of somewhat different theoretical persuasions, it was agreed that theoretical differences are not critical at this point. This analysis follows Osgood's mediational theory in the main. For alternative (but not necessarily contradictory) views of language learning cf. B. F. Skinner, *Verbal behavior*, William James Lectures, Harvard University, 1947, or Roger W. Brown and Don E. Dulaney, A stimulus-response analysis of language and meaning (privately distributed).

tions of a complicated central nervous system. The basic question here is, how do certain stimulus patterns (signs) come to represent other stimulus patterns (objects), i.e., how are meanings acquired?

The first steps in the development of meaning, and hence in learning to decode the environment, are inseparable from the first steps in the development of perception. We infer that intimate 'knowledge' about common objects in the environment is first obtained from their *proximal cues*—the sensations of warm milk in the mouth and stomach, the feeling of a wooden block in the hand, the experience of being cuddled. We further infer that, since *distal cues* (visual, auditory) of objects can antedate their palpable presence, these cues will tend to become signs of these objects. The unique visual cues from the infant's bottle will become signs of milk-object, the sounds of mother's voice will become signs of her palpable presence, and so on. The general mechanism here can be seen by reference to Figure 14. Total stimulation from the object ($\dot{S}$) elicits a complex set of reactions (R_T); in the case of the baby's bottle, these reactions would include sucking, salivating, swallowing, and so forth. The distal stimuli ($\boxed{S}$) which regularly antedate or accompany total stimulation from the object will tend to evoke some reduced portion of this total behavior as a representational mediation process (r_m); in the present instance, sight of the bottle may produce anticipatory salivating and lip-pursing movements. The self-stimulation (s_m) arising from the mediating reaction is the conscious awareness of meaning and may become associated with various instrumental sequences (R_X), such as reaching forward with the hands, vocalizing, and so forth (e.g., encoding mechanisms).

Distal cues (perceptual signs) bear a necessary and inevitable physical relation to the objects they represent—not the arbitrary, assigned significance characteristic of most linguistic signs. Since the distal cues of common objects appear in a variety of contexts—at various angles of regard, under various illuminations, at varying distances, and so on—but antedating the same behavioral object, these modes of appearance become a class of signs having the same significance. This is the phenomenon of *perceptual constancy*, and it is only one instance of the intimate relation between perceptual and meaningful processes (cf., section 3.1.1).

In learning the significance of *linguistically coded stimuli*, the representational processes already established in the child's pre-verbal, perceptual experience with common objects and situations are merely transferred (conditioned) to those auditory stimulus patterns which adults arbitrarily assign to these objects. The typical procedure is for the adult to deliberately or unconsciously direct

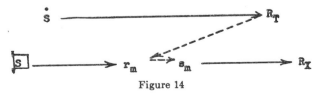

Figure 14

the child's 'attention' (orientation of exteroceptive receptors) to some object while repeating the vocal sequence which for him labels the object. It is characteristic of language that the same noise is usually applied to a class of objects and situations. The large, green, light-weight beach ball, the small, red, dense, rubber ball, the small, white, hard, golf ball and so on are all stimulus situations labelled /bɔhl/ at haphazard intervals. It can be shown that a hierarchy of representational mediation processes will emerge from such experiences. The strongest and most available decoding habits in the hierarchy of the auditory stimulus /bɔhl/ will be those most frequently elicited by the distal cues of the particular objects encountered. Since most ball-objects are round, graspable, resilient, and throwable, representations of these common characteristics will gradually become the stable significance. It should be pointed out that we are dealing here with *concept formation*.

6.1.1.2. *Language encoding*. In human communication encoding is the process whereby a speaker's intentions·become coded into those vocal reactions which produce intelligible sounds in a given language. This is commonly called the 'expression of ideas.' It involves both the formation of complex motor skills and their association with representational mechanisms of the sort discussed above.

(1) *Development of vocal skills*. The development of basic vocal skill components in young infants can probably be viewed as a gradually changing series of stages. The first stage we might typify as 'random' behavior. We know for other easily observed and recorded motor systems that the earliest activity is simply a kind of mass activity. The system does everything it is capable of doing, as if the motor neurons were firing off indiscriminately. This appears to be true of verbal behavior as well. Profiles of sounds produced by new-born infants show no differences over racial, cultural, or language groups. The determiners of frequency of emission of given sounds appear to be physiological rather than situational. When by happenstance the articulators are in a given position, a given sound emerges. As the organism develops, a progressive differentiation seems to take place (again, as with other motor systems). More and more aspects of the verbal production become 'differentiated out' and controllable as indicated by repetitions, predictable variations and the like. It seems probable that the gross features of the behavior are controlled first. Thus, we should expect volume and pitch control much earlier than precise articulations.

As further development occurs, control and the possibility of repetition and persistence extends to the fine musculature of the articulators, and at about this point we begin to talk about the 'babbling stage.' Analysis of sound profiles here indicates that differences are evident between infants in different language groups. How do these arise? One of the phenomena of learning discussed earlier was that of secondary reinforcement. Stimuli which have been present during or preceding reinforcement acquire reinforcing power themselves. We may assume that parents' activities and, indeed, the parents' presence, is reinforcing to an infant, and that this reinforcement has been accompanied by verbalization on the part of the parents in the sounds of their own language. Thus, the language sounds themselves can acquire secondary reinforcing power, e.g., become signs of primary satisfactions. We may predict, then, that when a child utters a sound like one in the language, this act through its auditory feedback is in itself reinforcing. This response is increased in strength over the utterance of sounds which do not appear in the language and hence have less reinforcing power. When we say that the strength of an utterance is increased, we mean that its probability of appearance is raised, and we would predict that a given sound (at this stage) will be made over and over again until it is temporarily extinguished—at which point another rewarding sound will take its place.

It has long been postulated that a 'circular reflex' of some sort accounts for babbling behavior (cf. E. B. Holt or F. Allport), but it is questionable whether this is needed to explain babbling, and it is obviously not sufficient to explain the change in sound patterns toward those of the culture. The writers incline to the notion that secondary reinforcement is a necessary and sufficient condition to explain this phenomenon.

Accepting the fact that gratifying speech sounds tend to be selected from a larger potential pool of skills, how are these particular spatiotemporal integrations established and strengthened? Motor synchronizations and sequences that occur on reflexive, echolallic, or imitative bases with sufficient frequency are a sufficient condition for establishment of proprioceptive, feedback systems. This makes possible more rapid and stable occurrence, which is the necessary condition for organization of these skill components on a central motor level (cf., section 3 of this report). In any case, it seems doubtful if phonemes are ever produced as isolated units, except by a process of abstraction—babbling (the earliest stage of 'deliberate,' repeatable encoding of speech sounds) is typically syllabic rather than phonemic.

The language community exercises continuous control over the variation which is permitted for any speaker. A person's language is susceptible to external pressures as well as to the internal pressures toward modification. If a difference makes a difference (i.e., if it is phonemic), there is a concerted, (though perhaps indirect), effort on the part of the community to enforce a discrimination—people either do not understand or misunderstand. The language community is thus a source of direct differential reinforcement. The learner himself has a source of control in that he gets continuous feedback from his own productions and can compare those productions with those of others in the community. Diverse general social pressures may motivate him to conform, or his past rewards for conformance to models may hold him within certain distortion limits.

It seems likely that variation will be countenanced by the community where the difference does not make a difference in the code. Allophonic variation is permitted since the environmental probabilities make clear what is being said. In a similar manner the community may tolerate considerable degrees of distortion from non-native speakers (foreign accents) when the variation is consistent, predictable and, in effect, translatable. It is interesting to speculate on the effect of variations which might be phonemic in another language but not in the one being spoken at the time (say, the intrusion of a click into English). It seems likely that such variations would simply have the effect of static or 'noise in the system' and, depending on the degree of disruption of communication, might be tolerated.

(2) *Development of semantic encoding.* While it is true that certain automatisms (reading aloud, reciting number series, and the like) may short-circuit the interpretive process, most communicative acts, including voluntary speech, are largely determined by what we may call the 'intentions' of the speaker, for lack of a better term. We identify 'intentions' with the self-stimulations produced by representational mediators. The problem here will be to describe the ways in which representational mediators (meanings, significances, ways of perceiving) become associated with vocalic skill sequences.

We have already noted that the syllabic babbling responses of the infant produce auditory feedback or self-stimulation. If the same response is immediately repeated, as is the case in babbling, this auditory input will tend to become associated with elicitation of the response. This stage in the development of semantic encoding is shown as (a) in Figure 15. S_x refers to the indeterminate conditions which initiate the first occurrence of the vocal skill component (R_V), producing auditory self-stimulation (S_s). The importance of this stage is that it readies the child for imitation of 'other person' speech. Once vocalic self-stimulation is associated with production of the vocal reaction, auditory stimuli received from other people (S_o), particularly if they are similar in stimulus

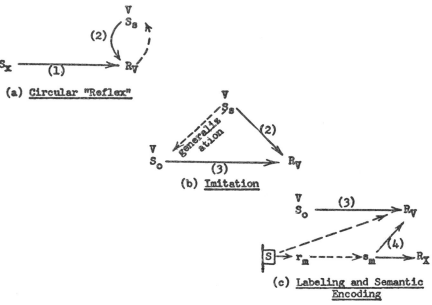

(a) Circular "Reflex"

(b) Imitation

(c) Labeling and Semantic Encoding

Figure 15

quality, will also elicit the reaction, as show in Figure 15(b). This is a case of primary stimulus generalization. If these imitative reactions are rewarded (as they definitely are in the average family situation), the child develops a broad tendency to imitate other people's speech (cf., Miller and Dollard, *Social Learning and Imitation*, 1941, for details here). Given this tendency to imitate vocalic responses, the remainder of the process follows quite simply. As shown symbolically in Figure 15(c), the adult vocalizes the correct label for a common object or situation $(\overset{v}{S_o})$ while directing the child's exteroceptors (usually visual) to the appropriate stimuli. The child imitates this sound (R_v). If, as is likely at this stage in development, the distal stimuli $\boxed{S}$ of the object have already acquired meaning (cf., earlier section on decoding), the self-stimulation from this mediation process $(r_m \text{———} s_m)$ must also be becoming associated with the correct vocalic reaction (step 4 in the diagram). *This is a unit in semantic encoding*, a learned association between an ideational representing process and a particular vocalic skill sequence.

An example is probably in order. Through his babbling practice, the child will imitatively produce /bɔh/ upon hearing his mother say /bɔhl/—note that perfect imitation is not expected, since accuracy depends on the babbling practice the child has had. On repeated occasions mothers and other linguistically sophisticated individuals hold up, point to, hand over, and handle the object BALL while vocalizing the label. Since the distal cues of this object already elicit representational mediators (e.g., have significance) in the child—he has already played with such objects a great deal—these intervening processes tend to become associated with his own imitative vocalization of /bɔh/. Note how the development of such semantic encoding frees the individual from dependence upon immediate external cues—*any* antecedent condition, ideational and motivational as well as external, which gives rise to the appropriate mediation process becomes capable of eliciting this bit of vocal expression (e.g., desire for the object). Being associated with a common mediation process, this vocal skill will also transfer to all those signs which elicit the mediator, i.e., the label 'spreads' to all members of the class, 'ball.'

6.1.1.3. *Grammatical aspects of decoding and encoding.* So far we have dealt with pure semantic decoding (the association of representational mediators *as responses* with more or less isolated signs in various modes of presentation) and pure semantic encoding (the association of representational mediators *as stimuli* with more or less isolated vocal skill sequences). Most messages received and sent by adult communicators, however, involve complex *sequences* of signs, many of which have a largely operative function—the connective matrix within which semantic units are studded. This matrix of non-lexical material follows complicated but largely unconscious rules; neither speaker nor hearer is normally aware of deliberately selecting or noting word orders, appropriate affixes, and the like, yet these phenomena proceed in highly predictable fashion. This is probably part of what Sapir had in mind when he referred to 'the unconscious patterning of language.' These rules are the grammar of the language.

That the decoder *is* reacting to grammatical information, however, is indicated by the sharp awareness to *error* when wrong signals are received. The absence of an *s*-ending on the verbs in *the boy who live next door eat the apple* delivers an error signal to the sophisticated listener. Some process—set in motion by the singular noun form, persisting through reception of the verb form, and predictive of the nature of this verb form—must be postulated to account for this sensitivity to grammatical error. Similar postulation must be made to account for the encoder's unconscious precision in ordering and affixing tags through long conversational sequences.

Grammatical facility is here assumed to be a special case of the formation of *anticipational* (decoding) *and dispositional* (encoding) *mechanisms* in the human nervous system, both dependent upon the frequent repetition of redundant events in sequential inputs or outputs. Following Hebb's general notion about neural integration,[64] according to which near-synchronous activities in neighboring loci tend to become more and more strongly associated by the development of synaptic connections, if two or more input or output events, *a* and *b*, are both redundant (e.g., occur together or in close sequence) and frequently experienced, the central neural representation of one will tend to become a condition for the occurrence of the other. Under conditions of very high frequency and redundancy, *a* may become a sufficient and hence 'evocative' condition for the occurrence of *b* (and certain perceptual errors and illusions may result, for example); under lesser degrees of frequency and redundancy, *a* merely becomes 'predictive' of *b*, by lowering the threshold for the occurrence of *b* in competition with other possible events (and increased stability of decoding or encoding sequences is thereby provided).

(1) *Ordering grammatical mechanisms.* At an intermediary stage in language development the child encodes largely in holophrastic units (e.g., 'pure semantic encoding'). Each expression is a content unit. The 'little words' (connectives, prepositions, articles) are lacking as is grammar in general. Similarly, we find that certain aphasic individuals encode in what has been called a 'telegraphic style,' again lacking connective words and grammatical correctness. The normal adult both orders his semantic units into certain arbitrary constructions and surrounds them with grammatical 'cement.' In the argot of electronic computers, we might say that global impulses from the semantic unit feed into a 'sequence timer' which unreels the message in a certain order and adds certain elements according to the rules of its construction.

Let us take a series of utterances all fitting the same standard syntactical construction: (*the fat man*) (*is walking*) (*on the sidewalk*); (*a black dog*) (*was running*) (*after a car*); (*awful storms*) (*come*) (*in the fall*). Every time the child uses such a construction, perhaps in deliberate imitation of adult speech, definite sequences of events take place—adjectival forms are followed by nominal forms, these in turn being followed by verb forms, which are themselves followed by prepositional phrases. We have here the general condition for formation of an *ordering* type of disposition, whereby activity type *a* in the motor associational

---

[64] D. O. Hebb, *The organization of behavior* (New York, 1949).

area 'tunes up' activity type *b*, and so on. Having said *the big, fat* . . . , we experience a disposition toward encoding *some* nominal form; having encoded an actor-action phrase, e.g., *boys eat* . . . , we experience a hierarchy of multiple readinesses for several subsequent types of phrases—prepositional (*in the woods, with their hands*, etc.), object (*food, meat*, etc.), adverbial (*rapidly, quietly*, etc.), and so on. The comparative strengths of dispositions in such hierarchies could be estimated empirically by presenting incomplete utterances of the type given above. Similar mechanisms operate in sequential decoding.

(2) *Set mechanisms.* In lengthy sequences of encoding the speaker may have to maintain and reiterate, for the hearer's benefit, certain types of information. An entire discourse may be cast in some past *time*, may be concerned with plurality of *number*, deal with feminine *gender*, and require a subjunctive *mood*. It would obviously be convenient for both speaker and hearer to delegate these constancies to some lower-level, automatic mechanism. In computer language, the mechanism here would be analogous to a kind of 'locking device' which sets the computer for some repetitive operation, say, to add two zeros to any number ending in 5. Similarly, when the 'past' oriented human communicator encodes any verb, a dispositional set operates to add some one of the allomorphs of -*d*.

Set dispositions also participate in hierarchial habit systems. Whenever a variety of semantically determined contents (stems or roots of words) channel upon the *same* dispositionally determined suffix, we have a *convergent encoding hierarchy*. Examples would be plurals (lamp/*s*, root/*s*, cat/*s*, stem/*s*, leave/*s*, boy/*s*), verb tags (go/*ing*, sing/*ing*, play/*ing*), adverbial tags (smart/*ly*, casual/*ly*, soft/*ly*), and so forth. Such convergent hierarchies are the psychological condition for *generalization* (transfer, spread of habit); we can immediately see a feasible mechanism here for what linguists refer to as *extension by analogy.* Having established *boy: boys, cat: cats* and so forth for the common signs in early life, this paradigm generalizes promptly to *argot: argots* and *system: systems* as these new nominal contents are encountered. The same generalization mechanism applies to syntactical constructions; a construction formed with such simple contents as *the doggie eats his dinner quickly* generalizes to such complicated contents as *the linguist studies his corpus assiduously.*

Wherever the same semantically determined content terminates in *varied* dispositionally determined suffixes, we have a *divergent encoding hierarchy*. All of the suffixes which can be combined with a given root morpheme constitute such a hierarchy, e.g., play/-, play/*s*, play/*er*, play/*ing*, play/*ed*, play/*fulness*, play/*fully*. Since divergent hierarchies are known psychologically to produce *interference*, the question arises as to why interference is largely lacking here. Encoders rarely substitute erroneous grammatical endings, saying *the child player in the field* for *the child plays in the field*, for example. This highlights the *discriminatory function of dispositional sets* in encoding. Interference occurs within hierarchies only to the extent that highly similar stimulus situations are operative. Note that in each case where a different suffix is applied above, a *different* dispositional set is operative. In other words, in each case the same semantic stimulus input is compounded with a distinctive dispositional input, making it possible to encode different endings discriminatively.

It is clear what should happen in cases where *both* the semantically determined content and the dispositionally determined set are the same (or highly similar), but a divergent set of suffixes must be encoded. This *is* the condition for interference and hence errors. The prime examples of this occur with the irregular forms of a language. With a constant dispositional set (plurality) and semantic determinants similar to other regular forms (*leg*: *legs*; *toe*: *toes*; *hand*: *hands*), the youngster typically encodes *foots* as the plural of *foot*—and similarly for *goose*: *gooses*; *mouse*: *mouses*, and the like. With a constant dispositional set (past tense) and semantic determinants similar to regular forms (*walk*: *walked*; *play*: *played*), the youngster typically encodes *breaked* as the past of *break* and *catched* as the past of *catch*. An interesting prediction arises here: since the shift in such divergent hierarchies is typically from a weaker to a stronger habit, one can predict that errors in encoding irregular verbs will be inversely related to their frequency of usage in the language. Since *go* is a very high frequency verb, there should be less tendency to encode *goed* as the past form than to encode *slayed* (rather than *slew*) as the past of *slay*, a relatively infrequent verb. In other words, only relatively high frequency words should be capable of persisting in their irregularity against the combined onslaughts of regular dispositional tendencies.

(3) *Congruence mechanisms.* There are many characteristics of grammatical encoding and decoding that simply reflect regularities in the message itself. These are the various correspondences or agreements that are maintained between parts of messages—a kind of useful redundancy. Most familiar to English-speaking communicators, perhaps, are the congruences set up between nominal and verbal forms. In the present tense, a singular noun takes a verb form ending in -s while a plural noun takes a verb form with a zero ending (*the boy eats*; *the boys eat.*). We must postulate that such congruence mechanisms have a reverberatory 'holding' characteristic; set in motion by the occurrence of a prior grammatical tag, they persist 'silently' until a second, corresponding tag is encountered, whereupon they release a particular encoding unit and are themselves eliminated. In computer language, this operates much like a condenser, one input signal setting up a cyclical action which is only released into another channel when another input signal of a specified type is received.

One of the characteristics of reverberatory mechanisms in the nervous system is that they tend to extinguish in fairly short order unless reinforced repeatedly from some external source. This leads to the prediction that, other things equal, the longer the delay between congruent elements in a message the greater the probability of error. Whereas the probability of encoding *the boys runs fast* is relatively low, the probability of *the boys whose father used to be a track star runs fast* is greater. Confusion among the prior tags for a congruence relation also produces errors, e.g., singular and plural forms occurring close together and prior to a verb as also illustrated in the sentence above.

6.1.1.4. *Summary.* A model for both decoding and encoding operations in human communicating has been developed on the basis of a mediational type of learning theory. On the decoding side, linguistic messages are viewed as sequences of auditory (or visual) stimuli which include cues for both semantic and grammatical decoding operations; on the encoding side, similarly, the vocalic (or orthographic) skill sequences are jointly elicited by stimulus compounds arising in both semantic and grammatical levels of organization. The semantic or ideational level of organization has been identified with the development of *representational mediation processes*; the grammatical level of organization has been identified with the development of *anticipational* (decoding) and *dispositional* (encoding) *processes*; the motor skill level has been identified with integrations of sequential activities in the motor projection area itself; and the message level comprises either the patterns of auditory and visual stimuli received by the communicator (decoding) or the patterns of vocalic and orthographic skill sequences produced by the communicator (encoding).

6.1.2. An Experimental Analogue for Studying Language Learning[65]

As a means of studying problems of language acquisition, the seminar tried to devise a simplified model of language behavior, such that experimental manipulation and control would be feasible. The experimental model should include the essential characteristics of natural languages, and the following are at least minimal requirements: (1) The model must have both a complete dictionary and a complete grammar. (2) It must be constituted of a hierarchy of units, such that every 'utterance' is completely organized in terms of any of the levels of the hierarchy. (3) There must be units which are sequential and units which are synchronous in respect to each other. (4) Operation of the model must involve both perceptual, receptive processes and activational, responding processes. Corresponding to the aural-oral cycle of speech in natural languages, our model will be based on a visual-manual cycle.

If we want to use our model to study acquisition of first languages, we must eliminate, or at least carefully control, the possibility of mediation by translation. Three suggestions were made as to how this might be done: (1) Use of chimpanzees, or lower primates as subjects. This might be too expensive, too slow for complex problems, and possibly not parallel to human language learning (although it might be of interest in its own right). (2) Human infants might be used as subjects, but their general nonavailability for prolonged and rigidly controlled experimentation makes this possibility infeasible. (3) The solution actually adopted is to put adult humans into a non-translation situation, that is, where mediation by their own language would be not necessarily absent, but constant and trivial. Of course, with adult subjects the problem situation cannot be identical with the situation of infants learning their first language, at least from the point of view of the subjects, but we can control what we believe in theory to be the essential factors of the situation, and the model can easily be changed to follow any necessary modifications in the theory.

The subject (who may suggestively be called 'infant') sits before a panel below which is a set of control knobs or levers. As he sits there, lights of different colors

[65] James J. Jenkins and Leonard D. Newmark.

and in various sequences flash on the panel in front of him. The flashing of lights is controlled by an experimenter ('parent') sitting at a corresponding panel in another room, unseen by the infant. The parent's 'messages' are 'meaningful,' i.e., are in accord with a system of intent as coded in the model language, but it is probably not necessary that the infant be preinformed that the light flashes he is watching are so meaningful. He may respond to the flashes in a variety of ways, but eventually he will probably try moving some of the controls and see the visual result of his own responses (e.g., 'feedback'). This would correspond roughly to the random behavior stage in vocalizing. Some mechanism of reinforcement (say flashing the word 'right,' which we assume has reinforcing properties for the subject) strengthens such responses. While such reinforcement may be used initially just to get the subject to 'say' something, later it serves in the discrimination between proper and improper responses for the code. This parallels the increasingly discriminated reinforcement applied in language learning.

The infant watches the patterns of light on the panel, and with reinforcement presumably will attempt to duplicate these, or make any other reinforcible set of responses, by manipulating the controls at his disposal. Patterns of increasing complexity will be discriminated by the infant, and hierarchy of patterns according to complexity will be established both for his recognition and for his motor manipulation. Eventually, we would suppose that he will learn the entire code, the model language.

The apparatus consists of two light-boards with controls such that operating controls on one board turn on lights on the other board, and if we want visual feedback, lights on the same board as well. The effects of getting feedback which differs from the parent's signals can be studied by building in a different set of relays of the controls to the two boards. The controls are of two types, corresponding approximately to natural language segmental and supra-segmental features: the left hand operates controls which are held constant over more or less larger sequences; the right hand may operate one of two other types—either controls (perhaps press bars) which are operated in sequences, corresponding to segmental phonemes, or a single complex mechanism with independently but synchronously acting elements, corresponding to distinctive phonemic features, e.g., a knob which may be pushed or pulled, raised or lowered, moved right or left, or twisted left or right, with neutral positions possible for any of these operations. Operating these controls produces patterns of light on the boards. Visual qualitative differences between infant's and parent's patterns may be introduced by such modifications as intensity differences or wave-length shifts which contrast the lights produced by parent and those produced by infant. These differences parallel the non-linguistic features which enable us to distinguish one speaker's voice from another or other's voices from our own.

Since the model is to be simpler than natural language in nonessential points, the code may be constructed with a simpler 'phonology' (three or four distinctive features, or perhaps five phonemes, plus two suprasegmental features), morphology (perhaps 30 morphemes in three classes as determined by phonemic constituency or position of occurrence in the sequence), and syntax (two possible orders of morphemes). Of course, the code can be complicated to any desired degree, and the corresponding effect on learning can be measured.

The problem of how subjects can be motivated in the rather laborious set-up proposed here was raised. It was generally agreed that we cannot tell until the experiments have been tried whether the satisfaction of 'solving the problem' would be adequate in maintaining the cooperation of the subjects. It may be true that children in the real situation are subject to the same boredom as the 'infants' in the experimental situation, so this factor might well be studied by experimentally varying the type of reward given the subject for participating in the experiments. In general, however, it appears likely that some sort of relevant reinforcement must be amply provided.

It will be noted that no 'meaning' is attached to the code symbols or patterns of symbols, as they appear in the experiments outlined above, other than that they belong to a code, are recurrent, and are somehow differentially reinforced. If 'referential' meaning is desired in the system, it can be introduced in a number of different ways. One way suggested was to introduce a separate field on the light-board—a field containing a moving light. Certain patterns of light in the vari-colored message-field, could be associated with movements of the light in the 'semantic' field, 'requests' for action on the moving light, etc. Obviously, any simple modifiable visual or auditory stimulus could be used as the referent. Since in natural language, many complicated conversations are carried on by response to linguistic and not referential material completely (note: Hello. How are you? Fine, thanks, etc.), it may be that the mechanism of language can be studied for our purposes without the many complications introduced by reference to extra-linguistic things. Furthermore, as we have previously noted, we may complicate and interfere with the learning process by the mediation of translation.

Although designed primarily for study of problems of first language learning, the apparatus can be used for study of different sorts of problems. For instance, having thoroughly mastered one code, the infant can be given proper instructions and run through the experiments again with a different code. In some ways this situation can be made to resemble second-language learning situations, but it is doubtful that this experimental design is the best suited for study of such problems. It has also been suggested that interesting data might result if two subjects equally ignorant of any prepared code were placed at the two panels, rather than a naive 'infant' and a trained 'parent.' The nature of the communicative code, if any, finally adopted by these subjects might shed some light on their conception of their own natural languages.

Some specific problems in language learning that might be studied in this situation are discussed below. One problem previously referred to is the role of secondary and generalized reinforcement in language learning, particularly their role in the approximating of cultural sound patterns which seem to occur with the babbling stage. In the experimental situation outlined above we might ask what the likelihood is of a subject repeating a 'model' pattern of lights under varying conditions. (1) Repetition when the patterns appear along with nothing else in the stimulus field. This would presumably give a summary measure of the subject's past reinforcement history with respect to imitation in this kind of situation. (2) Repetition when the patterns appear at the same time that reward is given. This would give the patterns the status of secondary reinforcers. (3) Repetition when the patterns appear initially without other stimuli but with reproductions by the subject being reinforced. We would here have a measure of the rate at which the subject learns to imitate initially neutral models. At this stage we would perhaps be most interested in (2), the reproduction of secondary reinforcers. This case seems to be closely parallel to the postulation earlier concerning babbling. While, of course, work with adults (even if successful) would not deny the existence of the circular reflex in infants, it would clarify the possibility of the alternative explanation and might lead to further, more conclusive research.

A second group of problems which might be attacked here would be those related to certain transitional phenomena. For example, it can be hypothesized that set dispositions, ordering dispositions and congruence dispositions (tense, order and agreement) are all dependent on frequencies with which sequences appear in the code and manifest themselves in the same way in association tests, recall situations, etc. Our experimental situation would permit us to study the growth of such dispositions and to control the actual frequencies in any manner we choose. Experimental analogues of association tests and recall tests can be easily constructed.

Further consideration along these lines would lead us to another set of experiments on paradigmatic development (see the section 5.4 for a discussion of the influences of paradigmatic and syntagmatic relationships upon association). One very basic question which might be asked is whether we could build up 'use by analogy' in our experimental model. Suppose in one sequence of learning trials we presented units singly at first and then in later stages began using the units in context. Suppose unit one were rewarded in context one and unit two also rewarded in context one. A new context might be introduced and again both units rewarded when they appear in the context, and so forth. Then, if unit one were presented in context 'X,' would the subject tend to encode unit two in that wholly new context? This learning-by-analogy is often assumed in descriptions of language processes but has rarely been attacked experimentally. If this can be demonstrated, then another very interesting question arises—will unit one evoke unit two in an association test? Here we could have a control over the paradigmatic class which is not at all possible in 'natural language.' On a broader scale, studies of analogy such as these might be extended to verb tenses, sentence forms, etc.

These are only a few examples of the kinds of learning studies which need to be performed. Whether this situation will approximate language in such a manner as to lead to fruitful results is, of course, a matter for empirical confirmation. One seminar member objected that this was 'nothing more than complex instrumental learning' but that is probably exactly the way an arch-behaviorist might describe language itself. In general, we might say that this is a highly flexible coding and learning situation which provides for 'listener,' 'speaker,' and 'listener-speaker' situations. It has advantages over the experimental use of an artificial language in ease of production of the stimuli (it doesn't need a trained speaker or phonetician), ease of control of the code, and ease of precise recording (each response is clearly what it is and can be set to make its own record).

6.2. *Second Language Learning and Bilingualism*[66]

When, after becoming a practical expert in his own, first language, a person starts learning a second language, new sets of decoding and encoding habits are being formed in competition with the old. When the bilingual shifts from language to language, similarly, two systems of decoding and encoding habits come into conflict to a greater or lesser degree. The fact that the same general principles found to be important elsewhere in this section also are significant here justified discussing second language learning and bilingualism in the present context. Since the seminar did not devote much time to these topics, however, only a brief sketch of the thinking of some of us on these problems is offered. The reader is referred to recent books by Uriel Weinreich and Einar Haugen[67] for excellent treatments, undertaken from the linguistic point of view, but with very considerable psychological and sociological sophistication.

6.2.1. *Compound and Coordinate Language Systems*

Both second language learning and bilingualism involve the acquisition and utilization of two linguistic codes. The messages produced in the two or more languages employ differently constructed and organized units, different grammatical rules, and different and equally arbitrary lexical systems, excepting occasional cognates. To the extent that phonemic systems are different, two sets of differentiations and constancies on the decoding side and two sets of vocalic skill components on the encoding side have to be maintained. Since the entire systems of transitional redundancies in two languages are different, alternative anticipational and dispositional integrations have to be established. And since the lexical aspects of messages in two languages are different, alternative sets of semantic decoding and encoding habits have to be maintained—in other words, alternative sets of associations between message events and events in the representational system, or meanings.

Perhaps because of dependence on the model provided by second language learning in school situations, many writers seem to have assumed that *meanings* are constant in second language learning and in bilingualism. The meaning of the object HORSE remains the same as perceptually experienced. Hence the meaning of its alternative linguistic signs, *horse/Pferd*, must be the same—all that is involved is two systems of coding the same meaning. This is the case under certain circumstances, which establish what we shall call a *compound language system*. In such a system, as shown in Figure 16, two sets of linguistic signs, one appropriate to language A ($\boxed{S}_A$), and the other appropriate to lan-

[66] Susan M. Ervin and Charles E. Osgood.

[67] Einar Haugen, *The Norwegian language in America* (1953), and Uriel Weinreich, *Languages in contact* (Linguistic Circle of New York, 1953).

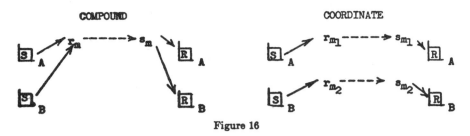

Figure 16

guage B ($\boxed{S}_B$), come to be associated with the *same* set of representational mediation processes or meanings ($r_m \rightarrow s_m$). On the encoding side, likewise, the same set of representational processes comes to be alternatively associated with two sets of linguistic responses, one in language A ($\boxed{R}_A$) and the other in language B ($\boxed{R}_B$). This development is typical of learning a foreign language in the school situation. It is obviously fostered by learning vocabulary lists, which associate a sign from language B with a sign and its meaning in language A. A compound system can, however, also be characteristic of bilingualism acquired by a child who grows up in a home where two languages are spoken more or less interchangeably by the same people and in the same situations. In this instance some compromise representational processes taken from both languages may be established, with neither having pronounced dominance.

A very different kind of relation between two languages in the same nervous system is what we shall call a *coordinate language system*. In this case, as shown on the right-hand side of the diagram, the set of linguistic signs and responses appropriate to one language come to be associated with one set of representational mediating processes ($r_{m_1} \rightarrow s_{m_1}$), but the set of linguistic signs and responses appropriate to the other language become associated with a *somewhat different* set of representational processes ($r_{m_2} \rightarrow s_{m_2}$). This kind of development is typical of the 'true' bilingual, who has learned to speak one language with his parents, for example, and the other language in school and at work. The total situations, both external and emotional, and the total behaviors occurring when one language is being used will differ from those occurring with the other. The kinds of representational processes developed must then also be different and hence the meanings of the signs. This development can also characterize the second language learner, who, relying as little as possible on translation and immersing himself in the living culture of another language community, comes to speak a second tongue well.

Even within a coordinate system there may be interference between the two sets of processes. Given the likenesses throughout human cultures in the situations and objects dealt with by language, it is certain that the representational processes elicited by translation-equivalent signs in two languages will often be similar. In decoding, this produces a constant pressure on the bilingual to confuse meanings, to interpret a sign in language A as its translation-equivalent in language B would be interpreted. The more similar the *signs*—cognates, for instance—and the more similar the *mediators*, the greater this pressure will be. Interference is most likely to occur when the languages are closely related and the cultures or the experiences associated with the languages are alike.

On the encoding side, the more similar the meanings or representational processes, the more errors there will be. These may consist in delays or blocking of response, if the alternative responses in the two languages are quite different. There may be intrusions of responses from the wrong language, if the items in the two languages are similar. These phenomena are often obvious in the compound system, where *identical* mediators must elicit alternative responses. They may take subtle forms in the coordinate bilingual, resulting merely in minute delays or shifts in response frequencies in comparison with monolinguals. Compromise formations usually result, depending upon relative habit strengths in the two languages in vocalic skills, lexical associations, and transitional patterning.

In spite of the pressures for interference, there are many instances of remarkably pure bilingualism, in which the speaker, once launched in a given language, in an appropriate situation, and speaking of events associated with that language, will experience no difficulties and perform like a monolingual. There are at least three general predictive factors to be considered for the coordinate bilingual. In the first place, the *feedback stimuli* from previous utterances in a given language are more associated with mediators appropriate to that language than another, unless considerable language mixture has occurred in past usage. Secondly, the current *interpersonal situation* will affect interference in speech as much as it does features of style or dialect within one language. Hearer bilingualism, the relative prestige of the languages, momentary feelings toward the hearer will alter the general availability of responses in each language or even lead to deliberate use of interference by a speaker. Finally, stimuli arising from the scenes, objects, and people present during the formation of a language will also be associated more strongly with mediators appropriate to that language. Hence bilinguals report that when they are with, or even think about, their parents or their home, the parental language becomes more available. A bilingual under emotional stress may revert to the language spoken when comparable emotions have been experienced in the past.

For any semantic area we would expect speakers of more than one language to distribute themselves along a continuum from a pure compound system to a pure coordinate system. How would one *measure* or index the location of particular individuals along this continuum? At one extreme, the meanings of translation-equivalent signs are identical, and at the other the meanings of translation-equivalent signs are different. Furthermore, the semantic differences involved tend to be connotative rather than denotative. The *semantic differential* (cf., section 7.2.2) seems particularly appropriate as a tool here. It could be used to measure coordinateness within a semantic area or to make a general estimate if appropriate samples could be devised. If a sample of pairs of translation-equivalent signs were given to a varied group of two-language speakers for differentiation against an appropriate form of the semantic instrument, with

D between profiles of the pairs computed for each speaker, the average D (difference in meaning) should vary directly with the degree of 'coordinateness' of the language systems within each speaker. The validity of this measure could be estimated against such criteria as frequency of interference in ordinary conversation, fluency measures, and translation facility, to which we now turn our attention.

6.2.2. *Translation under Compound and Coordinate Systems*

In the process of translating from one language to another, linguistic signs in one language ($\boxed{S}_A$) must be decoded and equivalent or related linguistic responses must be made in the other language ($\boxed{R}_B$). The behavioral situations are quite different, depending on (a) whether the translator maintains compound or coordinate languages in his nervous system, and, if the former, (b) whether he is translating to or from his dominant language. The left-hand diagram in Figure 17 represents the translation process for a compound language system. Solid lines show translation *from* the dominant language, and dashed lines show translation *to* the dominant language. The right-hand diagram represents the translation process for a coordinate language system; the encircled numbers represent alternative translating circuits at different stages in the development of translating fluency in the coordinate system.

Compound system translating. When the product of an ordinary foreign language course in high school, let us say, translates *from* his native English into the other language, we have the situation represented by the solid lines in the left-hand diagram. Encoding the foreign forms involves direct response competition, since both are associated with a single set of American culture meanings. The 'same' mediated stimulus must elicit a response (foreign language output) quite different from the dominant response (English language output) in the habit hierarchy. The task would be impossible were it not for differences in the total stimulus pattern for the translator. Such differences may be brought about by the 'set' to translate, the feedback of foreign cues from preceding output, distinctive dispositional tendencies (once the foreign language grammar and syntax has become sufficiently learned), and unique associations with the use of the second language. These cues must be sufficient to counteract the stronger English response tendencies in the presence of s_m. An analogous situation exists for the

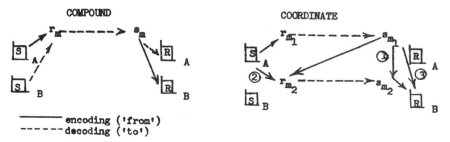

Figure 17

bilingual who has learned to speak both languages in a homogeneous environment. Encodings in either language in response to inputs in either language may be equally reinforced. One would expect more or less continuous interference and intrusion in encoding, in either language. This interference is not due to the pressure of a dominant language, as in the earlier example, but to lack of distinctive cues in previous use of the two languages.

Theoretically, decoding from a foreign language should be facilitative for a compound system, since different inputs are associated with the same representational reactions or meanings. To the extent that signs in the two languages are similar in form, decoding will be made easier. In a sense, the process of decoding the non-dominant language always involves translation, since the representational processes of the compound system are appropriate only to the dominant language. It is interesting to note that the compound system, whether a result of second-language learning or childhood bilingualism, can never translate in a true *cross-cultural* sense, since there is no possibility of comparing meanings in two culture contexts when only one system of representational processes is present.

On the other hand, the coordinate system provides true cross-cultural translation, but with certain theoretical complications, for the system itself is changed by the translation process. Let us take the ideal case of the bilingual in whom both languages are of about equal availability. As shown in the right-hand side of the diagram above, signs in language A must elicit meanings appropriate to language community A, due to the processes of learning to decode in a coordinate system. However, these language A mediation processes are associated with encoding in the same language. How then does the coordinate bilingual translate?

It will be recalled that to the extent that human cultures, situations, and objects are similar, the coordinate system is likely to involve some representational process in language B that is closely similar to that being elicited by the input in language A. This process may not be exactly the same as that elicited by the sign in language A. Translation-equivalent signs in the two languages may elicit slightly different representational processes due to the subtle differences in context or connotation which ordinary translations must lose, e.g. the difference between 'Weltanschauung' and 'philosophy of life.' Or there may be several processes in language B which are similar in different respects to a representational process in language A. Such is the case when a translator must choose between several partially adequate translations, as in the various English translations of 'gemütlich.' In both of these instances, simple generalization between s_{m_1} and s_{m_2} by pathway (1) may make translation possible. Since generalization is most probable between maximally similar representational processes, the result is the encoding of the most adequate cross-cultural translation.

Another possibility is that pathway (2) between s_{m_1} and r_{m_2} is established by learning, which would be necessary if s_{m_1} were so closely associated with a cultural context peculiar to language community A that appropriate generalization to language B processes was inhibited. Such learning might occur, for example, if a bilingual is in a situation which elicits s_{m_1}. This may be due to an appropriate external context, thoughts about events that occurred in the context of language A, or a conversation with a language A monolingual. For learning to occur, r_{m_2} must also be elicited, perhaps because a language B monolingual describes or refers to situations or objects represented by s_{m_1} but using language B signs. Generally, it would appear that a learned association between s_{m_1} and r_{m_2} probably only develops in situations in which some generalization between s_{m_1} and s_{m_2} also occurs. Learning then facilitates the appropriate translation. Whether through generalization, learning, or both, the translation is such that the meanings elicited in *monolinguals* in languages A and B are as similar as possible.

The ideal translator or interpreter accomplishes a transformation of signs through a three-person channel (monolingual A—coordinate translator—monolingual B) such that the representational processes of all three, or the meanings of the signs, remain unchanged. Obviously, the more the cultures, or the situations and objects discussed differ, the less rapidly the interpreter can encode. He is delayed by lack of quick generalization to similar meanings in the other language, or by conflict between several partially appropriate meanings. Interference in decoding may be produced by semi-cognates, similar or identical forms with varying meanings.

The above description treats the coordinate translator as though he were translating for the first time, but the translation process itself brings about new learning. Practice may reduce the capacity for cross-cultural translation, as we will demonstrate. Three different kinds of short-cuts may develop in the proficient translator or interpreter. In encoding, a linguistic response in language B must repeatedly occur in close sequence with the representational process appropriate to language A, as shown by pathway (3). This produces the same kind of interference discussed earlier, in the compound system, since s_{m_1} may elicit different responses depending on whether the speaker is supposed to *speak* language A or to *translate* it. Note that the representational process of language B has not been elicited at all. The second short-cut may consist in direct decoding into language B by pathway (2). The representational process appropriate to language B occurs soon after presentation of the linguistic sign in language A when there is frequent translation. This sign in language A must therefore become associated with a mediation process appropriate to language B, and it will compete with the process appropriate to language A, and, to the extent that they are similar, will lead to elimination of the meaningful discrimination in decoding. Finally, the mediation process may be only secondary, the response in language B being directly associated with hearing of a sign in language A, without intervention of a meaning process. This is most likely to happen for simultaneous interpreters who always use the same translation for the same word or phrase.

If a coordinate bilingual is hired to interpret in *one direction only*, from language A to language B, we must predict that (a) he will gradually develop an appropriate set of translation meanings for the signs in language A, and (b) he will lose his ability to speak language A. In other words, he will become a perfect A-to-B translating machine, while retaining his proficiency in language B—thus, a sort of dual-input speaker of language B. If a coordinate bilingual translates frequently *in both directions*, he must gradually (a) lose the distinctiveness among the mediation processes appropriate to each language and (b) suffer increasing confusion in encoding. In other words, *the very process of two-way translating tends to transform a coordinate system into a compound system.* It would be interesting to test these predictions on a sample of professional translators over time, using the type of experimental design suggested earlier with the semantic differential. This transformation can be minimized by refreshing the monolingual associations in both languages, of course.

6.2.3. *Grammatical and skill levels*

We have emphasized the semantic aspects of second language learning and bilingualism because these aspects have been relatively neglected. There is a great deal of carefully analysed information on purely linguistic aspects of bilingualism, phonemic, morphemic, and grammatical interactions and the like, and the interested reader is referred to the two sources given at the beginning of this portion of the report. For the most part previous work has reported the occurrence of certain phenomena without attempting to relate frequencies of occurrence to the learning experiences of the speaker. Grammatical aspects should be particularly profitable to study from this standpoint. Being organized on largely unconscious levels on the basis of transitional redundancies, these aspects of encoding should be especially difficult to learn and, once learned, should be equally difficult to suppress when trying to master a second language. For the coordinate bilingual, on the other hand, two alternative grammatical systems once established should provide for greater stability and independence between the two language systems.

We have considered here only the aspects of bilingual speech which reflect the influence of two linguistic codes on each other, omitting consideration of such non-linguistic features as pronunciation and style, (cf. section 4.1). Yet further study of these features would probably be rewarding, especially for psychologists who would be interested in their sensitivity to differences in the attitudes of bilinguals and second-language learners toward the respective speech communities.

6.2.4. *Research proposals*

(1) *Indexing degree of coordinateness of language systems.* The possible use of the semantic differential as a means of determining the degree of separateness of meanings for translation-equivalent signs has already been discussed. (A comparison with responses of monolinguals is suggested in section 7.4.3.1. This would determine not only semantic areas in which a compound system exists, but the language community for which the meanings are appropriate.) (2) *Influence of bilingualism on perception and meaning.* One of the writers[68] is now engaged in research of this nature. Subjects varying in degree of bilingualism tell stories in response to the Thematic Apperception Test (a series of rather ambiguous situ-

[68] Susan M. Ervin.

ational pictures), (a) in language A after preliminary instructions in that language, and (b) after an interval of several weeks, in language B after similar preparation. The expectation is that ways of perceiving these pictorial signs, their meaning to the subject, will vary with the language being used, and with the degree of coordinateness of the systems in a given subject. (3) *Measuring the transitional proficiencies of second language learners and bilinguals.* The 'Cloze' procedure developed by Wilson Taylor and described briefly in section 5 seems adaptable to problems in this area. Passages in languages A and B, as translated by maximally facile coordinate translators, could be mutilated (every fifth word deleted, for example) and given to subjects with varying degrees of bilingualism or varying amounts of second language training. In the former case, the more nearly equal the correct 'fill-in' scores for languages A and B, the more 'truly' bilingual in the coordinate sense the subject; in the latter case, the more nearly equal the scores in A and B, the greater the learning of the second language. This technique has two advantages; first, by its nature it samples all of the subtle contextual factors of both semantic associational and grammatical-dispositional levels; second, by using each subject's own performance in his most proficient language as a criterion, it eliminates individual differences in intelligence, language abilities, and the like. (4) *Measuring interference between languages under varying conditions.* Three factors were cited above in accounting for the degree of interference in encoding—feedback, the interpersonal situation, and differential past experience. Encoding with these conditions varied can be studied to see how conditions influence the amount and the kind of borrowing.

6.3. *Language Change*[69]

Languages change in response to both internal dynamics and external pressures. Psycholinguists are interested in both processes, but the present analysis concerns the former. The existence of similar forces operative under similar conditions everywhere in language is indicated by the existence of a limited number of types of change which reoccur in different, historically unconnected languages and at different chronologic periods. Linguists have accumulated an enormous amount of authenticated information relating to such changes and have been able to formulate a number of principles regarding the 'hows' of specific changes. The psychologist, in line with his general orientation, is typically interested in the 'why,' that is, in the isolation of general principles of behavior underlying shifts in linguistic habits. No doubt the interplay of factors in any particular instance is too complex to allow of complete explanation in the foreseeable future, but this does not mean that there are no general laws whose combinations limit the possibilities to the point where at least statistically probable outcomes may be hypothesized.

A striking fact about language change is that although both changes of form and those of meaning are always proceeding simultaneously, each can be extracted by analysis as a set of separate and practically independent processes.

[69] Joseph H. Greenberg, Charles E. Osgood, and Sol Saporta.

Nevertheless, they do impinge on each other at a few points. Each of these two major areas of change, the *formal* in which will be included both phonological and grammatical changes, and the *semantic*, will here be given separate treatment. In each of these two major areas, tentative generalizations concerning the facts of change based on linguistic data will be followed by a discussion of the psychological mechanisms which may be suggested as operative in bringing them about.

6.3.1. *Formal change*

6.3.1.1. *Linguistic facts.* Changes in the phonemes, the basic units of the sound systems of language, may involve (1) replacement of one phoneme by another, (2) loss of a phoneme, (3) transposition or metathesis, (4) insertion of a phoneme. These types have been stated in decreasing order of frequency of occurrence, replacement being by far the most common. Changes in phonemes may further be classified as regular or sporadic. A change is regular if it affects all instances of a given phoneme under specified conditions. Otherwise it is sporadic. Examples of *regular changes* are the following: In early Aramaic þ in all instances was replaced by *t*; in (probably) 18th century Hausa, a West African language, *s* was replaced by *š* in all instances where *e*, *e·*, *i*, or *i·* followed. An example of a *sporadic change*: In the development of Spanish from Latin, *r* was replaced by *l* in the word *arbol* 'tree,' earlier *arbor*. In cases of sporadic change, reference to specific instances is unavoidable.

Regular changes are, in turn, divided into unconditioned and conditioned. In *unconditioned changes*, all instances of a phoneme are affected without limiting conditions. A *conditioned change* involves only some of the occurrences of a phoneme under stated limitations in terms of other phonemes or positions in the utterance. In the above paragraph, the first change mentioned is unconditioned, the second conditioned. Unconditioned changes tend to occur in sets. What is involved is the replacement of some one distinctive feature common to a number of phonemes by another distinctive feature in all its occurrences. Sometimes such changes are, as it were, reversed in midstream. After affecting one or more phonemes, the older form reasserts itself in some instances and the result is somewhat checkered. An example of such a mass shift is Grimm's First Law, a statement of consonant changes from Proto-Indo-European to Proto-Germanic. For instance, /p > f, t > þ, k > x/ among other changes, that is, in the three instances cited, a stop feature was replaced by a fricative feature.

Two types of results may be distinguished here: either a phoneme or group of phonemes through a change in feature may give rise to sounds which did not previously occur in the language, or change may be to sounds which already do exist. In the former eventuality, no change in phoneme inventory (i.e., number of phonemes) or distribution (i.e., occurrence in particular forms) results. In fact, some would call such a change phonetic, rather than phonemic. In the latter case, we have the phenomenon of merger which involves a reduction in phonemic inventory. The following empirical generalizations are offered with regard to merger. Each is understood as being preceded by 'other things being equal':

(1) The more uncommon a phoneme is in human speech in general, the more likely it is to be merged with another phoneme. (2) The lower the frequency of a phoneme in a given language the more likely it is to merge with another phoneme, providing this second phoneme is not itself of excessively high frequency. (3) The closer the points of articulation shared by two phonemes the more likely they are to merge. (4) The more distinctive features shared by two phonemes the more likely they are to merge. (5) The fewer the pairs of different linguistic forms which are distinguished by the phonemes, the more likely they are to merge.

Conditioned changes result typically from conditioned allophonic variations in which by loss or change of the original conditioning factor a formerly nonsignificant contrast becomes phonemic. For example, in the transition from Proto-Indo-European to Sanskrit we reconstruct the following stages:

1. ka ke ki ko ku
2. ka če či ko ku (phonemically as in stage one. We now have an allophone [č] which occurs before e and i. There was no [č] in the language previously.)
3. ka ča či ka ku (a merger of o and e with a has produced a phonemic contrast ka vs. ča which did not exist before).

Another type of result ensues if a phoneme undergoes a conditioned change but the resultant of the change already exists. In this case, there is partial merger. The old instances of the phoneme which were not affected continue but the new variant merges with another previously existing phoneme. It is clear that this type of change affects the distribution but not the inventory. In recent Russian o changed to a under conditions of lack of stress. Since stressed o continued and a already existed, no new phoneme was added to the language. In general, conditioned change is the diachronic aspect of the synchronic problem of conditioned allophonic variation.

The following general facts about regular conditioned changes must be considered: (1) The conditioning factor is more often a phoneme which follows rather than one which precedes. (2) The conditioning factor is almost always immediately following or preceding. Sometimes a vowel is affected by that of a following or preceding syllable. More remote conditioning factors are very rare. (3) The change usually results in an articulation which is more like the conditioning phoneme. That is, it is assimilative rather than dissimilative. In general, then, changes result in a sequence of articulation which abbreviates or eliminates movements. For example, the fronting of a k to č before i eliminates the forward movement from back to mid position. (4) Final positions of syllables, words and utterances are often conditioning factors for change, initial positions only rarely. Changes with final position as their conditioning factor are typically those which result in loss or merger. This, of course, results in fewer phonemes in these positions. We know of few languages which have more distinct phonemes in syllable final than in syllable initial position.

Sporadic changes have the following characteristics: (1) Certain sounds are most frequently affected—liquids (r, l), nasals (n, m) and sibilants (s, š). (2) Dissimilation is probably as frequent as assimilation, contrasting with its rarity in regular changes. (3) The conditioning factor often operates at a distance. Example: Latin *peregrinus* > Italian *pellegrino* 'pilgrim.' Here the succession of two *r*'s has resulted in the dissimilation of the first to *l* even at a distance. The connection of such changes with speech-lapses, championed by Sturtevant, is highly plausible.

As has been stated, regular sound changes proceed in general without regard to the meanings of the forms in which they occur. However, it seems likely that regular changes are encouraged or inhibited depending on their consequences for grammatical structure. Thus, although both Germanic and Romance languages have stress, the unstressed vowels have tended to merge in Germanic languages but to remain distinct in Romance. This may well be connected with the fact that unstressed syllables in Germanic are typically limited to non-root morphemes, while in Romance languages the root may sometimes be unstressed, e.g., Italian *'amo* 'I love' but *a'mo* 'he loved.' In turn, the merger and loss of final vowels in Germanic languages has had repercussion on the grammatical system, in that distinctions based on difference of inflectional morphemes which became homonymous had now to be expressed by other, syntactic, means.

The chief process of *morphological change* is analogy. (1) By alternations between morphs of the same morpheme one pattern is replaced by another, usually more common; or (2) the alternation is effaced completely by extension of one of the forms to the alternant. Such changes are often stated in the form of an analogical proportion. Examples of both types of change are (1) the replacement of 'brought' by 'brang' (sing: sang = bring: brang) and (2) 'calfs' for 'calves' (cliff: cliffs = calf: calfs). The extension of a formative, typically derivational affix, to a combination in which it had not previously existed, or the formation of a new compound out of existing elements may likewise be viewed as a kind of analogical process. Thus the new form *draftee* can be expressed as the consequence of an analogical extension (employ: employee = draft: draftee). The less frequent types of morphological change such as folk-etymology and blending are not considered here specifically. They may be looked upon as partial analogical processes.

6.3.1.2. *Certain general hypotheses relating to change in form.* For convenience in discussion, principles relating to formal language change may be taken up in two categories: (1) those relating to the locus (in utterances) of change; (2) those relating to the process of change.

(1) *Principles Relating to the Locus of Change.* The evidence for generality described above makes it clear that changes in language structure are not haphazard as to locus—to the contrary, there are definite 'stress points' within messages as sequentially unreeled. Are there any general principles, i.e., general cross-linguistically, which would make it possible to specify 'stress points' and hence predict the most probable locus of changes?

I. *Short-circuiting. Features of subsequent phones will tend to be anticipated wherever possible.* The limits suggested by 'wherever possible' are at least the following: (a) To the extent that an articulatory feature of a subsequent phone is incompatible in the motor sense with that of an antecedent phone in its immediate environment, the tendency toward short-circuiting will be reduced; (b) To the extent that an articulatory feature of a subsequent phone would change the phonemic (i.e., code) character of an antecedent phone in its immediate environment, the tendency toward short-circuiting will be reduced. In this case, speaker 'lapses' (see below) will tend to be corrected by hearers. The basis for short-circuiting within the rapidly executed and tightly bound phone sequences that constitute syllabic units probably lies in the nature of skill formation—the central programming of neural events in the motor cortex is much more rapid than the sequential execution of movements, resulting in overlapping excitation patterns and a tendency to anticipate.

II. *Perseveration. Features of antecedent phones will tend to persist wherever possible.* Again, 'wherever possible' is limited at least by (a) articulatory incompatibility, and (b) production of significant (e.g., to hearers) phonemic changes. In the latter connection, it should be noted that shifts from one *distinctive* feature to another are not necessarily significant—there may not exist in the language any meaningful unit (e.g., word) corresponding to the modified signal even though it is phonemic. The basis for perseveration of this kind would seem to be something akin to motor inertia or 'least effort'; it is simply easier for the rapidly operating encoder to persist or remain in whatever articulatory feature happens to be held than to change it. Due to such perseveration, there should be a general tendency, other things equal, for phonemes displaying a certain feature to be followed by phonemes displaying the same feature in a given language. Obviously, this tendency cannot be carried to its logical conclusion, or the code becomes uniform and hence meaningless to the hearer. Elsewhere in this report (section 5.3), Saporta describes some computations on sequential phonemes in English which bear on this matter.

The combination of short-circuiting and perseverative principles in skill execution leads to the following expectations: (a) That the positions of instability in a language with reference to these factors should be those in which the phones both antecedent and subsequent to a given phone include one or more features in common. On this basis, for example, one would predict that voiceless consonants would be more common in initial and terminal positions in words than in medial positions where they would often be surrounded by voiced vowels. (b) That where a given phone is bounded by antecedent and subsequent phones displaying different features within the same dimension (e.g., voicing, tongue position, lip position, etc.), this phone should be characterized by transient or intermediary features between those in its environment. The general fact that subsequent phones have more effect upon sound changes than antecedent phones implies that the short-circuiting mechanism is stronger quantitatively, but this does not derive directly from any theoretical notion. The specification of conditions operative in determining which factor will be dominant remains extremely obscure. There is no doubt a tendency for intervocalic unvoiced consonants to become voiced—we can at least predict that this is more likely to happen than, for example, that they will become glottalized. Still, many languages go through very long periods during which intervocalic voiceless stops remain entirely stable and we are as yet unable to specify what factors, linguistic, cultural or otherwise, determine when the change will take place and when not.

A number of principles derive from analysis of transfer and interference in sequential materials. A great deal of experimental data[70] justify the following summary statements.

III. *Convergent hierarchy. When a variety of antecedent states* (e.g., stimuli) *converge upon a common subsequent state* (e.g., response), *transfer is positive and retroactive effects are facilitative, the degree of facilitation varying directly with the similarity among the antecedent states.* This sets the general condition for extension by analogy at the grammatical level, e.g., having learned *play-ed, walk-ed,* and *fix-ed* it becomes easier to transfer to *crawl-ed, digest-ed,* and *master-ed,* as well as for what might be called error by analogy at any level, e.g., to the extent that a given subsequent acquires high frequency with certain antecedents it should tend to generalize or transfer to other antecedents. The psychological fact that the degree of facilitation varies with similarity among the antecedent states should also have its evidence in language behavior. Certainly it is easier to extend by analogy, from *boyhood, manhood,* and *priesthood* to coinages like *babyhood, warriorhood,* and *scouthood* (semantically similar antecedents) than it would be to *stonehood, lighthood,* or *hillhood* (semantically dissimilar antecedents). On the phonemic level, until appropriate data have been analysed, one can only hypothesize that high frequency subsequents should tend to generalize among similar antecedents, e.g., there should be a tendency for the initial phonemes in sets with common terminus to be separated by fewer distinctive features than chance would dictate (*time, dime* and *lime, rhyme,* for example, are the only sets in English having this particular medial and terminal, and t/d and l/r are separated by few distinctive features). In this connection, it would be useful to have a frequency list of syllables in English as well as other languages.

IV. *Divergent hierarchy. When a common antecedent state diverges upon a variety of subsequent states, transfer is negative and retroactive effects are interfering.* This is the general psychological condition for competition among responses and errors. Having learned to make one reaction to a stimulus, it becomes more difficult to substitute another reaction to the same stimulus. Observe the following:

Initial (Convergent)	*Medial* (Divergent to Convergent)	*Terminal* (Divergent)
pin	pin	pin
sin	pan	pit
tin	pen	pick

Even for the simple task of rapid repetition, initial (convergent), medial (divergent-to-convergent), and terminal (divergent) sets become increasingly difficult in that order. On the same ground, one would expect 'stress points' to be located in positions of divergence rather than convergence, both at phonemic (e.g., /t/ tending toward /d/ in terminal and medial positions in contemporary American) and at grammatical (e.g., irregular nouns or verbs) levels. In all such cases, shifts should be in the direction of the stronger (i.e., more frequently used)

---

[70] See C. E. Osgood, The similarity paradox in human learning: A resolution, *Psychological Review* **56**. 132–143 (1949).

habits in these divergent hierarchies; /t/ should be under greatest stress to shift toward /d/ in those positions where the total probability of /d/ is higher, and 'weak' irregular verbs should be more susceptible to error than 'strong' irregular verbs. The latter prediction has been verified for irregular verbs in English, a significant negative correlation being obtained between frequency of errors in writing past tense forms and frequency of usage in Thorndike-Lorge lists.

In the present paradigm it should be noted that *the greater the similarity among the divergent responses, the less the interference.* This requires some clarification: With increased response similarity there is, to be sure, greater *intrusion* (substitution) of one response for the other; on the other hand, there is less interference in the sense of blocking, or failure to respond, and in terms of latency of response. This effect is maximal with reciprocally antagonistic reactions, where the learning of one is accompanied by inhibition of the other. This also has interesting implications for language change: In the first place, similar phonemes in terminal positions should tend to merge, e.g., intrude upon each other with such frequency and unpredictability that the difference would lose its distinctiveness. This would help explain the general fact that there is greater diversity in initial position than in terminal position. A similar phenomenon should apply to grammatical affixation—there should be greater diversity among prefixes (and hence differential semantic or lexical significance) than among suffixes (where automatic grammatical significance should be the rule). In the second place, antagonistic reactions in competing divergent positions should tend to interfere with each other in the sense of blocking and increased latency. The combination of these two factors—merger among closely similar reactions and reciprocal blocking among antagonistic—leads to the expectation that the sets of phonemes that appear in given positions following a constant should tend toward an average separation in distinctive features, neither too similar nor too disparate, when frequency is studied.

These psychological considerations offer to shed some light on the typological linguistic problems relating to the contrast between prefixing and suffixing languages. Since inflective and derivational elements are few in number compared to the morpheme membership in root position, the general considerations relating to transitions from divergent hierarchy (in this case root classes) to convergent hierarchies (derivational and inflectional) morpheme classes apply here. In accordance with the principles just discussed, there is greatest facilitation when the divergent hierarchy is followed by the convergent. On this basis, one would expect suffixing languages to be more frequent than prefixing ones, a fact noted by Sapir. One would also expect the prefixing languages to be more fusional (i.e., irregular) and suffixing languages to be more agglutinational (i.e., mechanical) in their morphophonemics. The consideration advanced is that in prefixing languages the difficult transition from a class with few members to a class of wide choices will be ameliorated to the extent that there are special variant forms (alternants) each restricted to a small number of subsequent roots. Indeed, in limiting cases this becomes in a sense a single choice since the enunciation of a prior element which can only be followed by some single subsequent, commits one to this subsequent in advance. The longer this process goes on the more the prior element becomes fused with the subsequent until it ceases to be an independent morpheme.

We might therefore advance the developmental typological thesis that prefixing languages tend towards the isolating type. The evidence both for this and the hypothesis of greater irregularity for prefixing languages needs careful examination before any definitive conclusion can be drawn. Our impression regarding this latter thesis of the more fusional nature of prefixing languages is that it holds in general. Very striking is the total absence to our knowledge of nominal inflectional elements in prefixing position, where the disparity of hierarchies is greatest. In support of the thesis of the development of isolating from prefixing languages, there is striking positive evidence in five cases and no contrary instances of which we are aware. Annamite, Chinese, Thai, Zapotec (Mexico), and Ewe (West Africa) are all classical isolating, monosyllabic languages and all are related to languages of a prefixing type of the Austroasiatic, Sino-Tibetan, Thai-Malayo-Polynesian, Oto-Manguey, and Niger-Congo families respectively.

The empirical fact noted earlier—that the smaller the number of features separating two phones, the greater the probability of change from one to the other—seems to be incorporated in the hierarchy analysis above.

Another principle relating to the locus of formal language change derives from information theory:

V. *Sequential redundancy. The more redundant, i.e., predictable, the occurrence of one message element from knowledge of the occurrence of another, the greater the probability of modification of one of them.* Information theory in itself does not indicate the precise locus of change, but since messages are unreeled in only one direction, it seems likely that susceptibility to modification should be greater in the terminal members of such redundant sets. This, incidentally, should be a special condition for *loss* of a phoneme in a language as compared to change. It will probably be necessary to distinguish between inherent redendancy, e.g., where the physiology of the articulatory processes requires it, and incidental redundancy.

(2) *Principles Relating to the Process of Change.* The process of language change is probably best conceived in terms of the total communication act, involving continuous functional interaction between speakers and hearers. In this process the speaker is the petitioner for changes (cf., Sturtevant's notion of 'lapses') and the hearer is the judge who, via social feedback or differential reinforcement, either allows or refuses to allow each particular modification. Given the existence of many 'stress points' in a language, speakers are under more or less continuous, if unconscious, pressures toward modification; to the extent that the process of effective communication in a group is or is not hindered by such modifications, the language will change.

I. *Production of changes. Individual speakers of a language will tend to produce changes in those positions and of those types indicated above in proportion to the degree of stress under which they are communicating.* By 'stress' here is meant any condition of the speaker that reduces his attention to his own self-feedback. Presumably young children in the process of learning language are particularly prone to predictable errors—there seems to be evidence on the rate of change in language suggesting modification in terms of generations of speakers. Similarly, rapid speech, speech under fatigue or any other debilitating condition, speech as it occurs in popular songs, and so forth will be special conditions facilitating change.

II. *Social Feedback. To the extent that a speaker modification (a) makes a difference in the code, (b) is not redundant, and (c) occurs in a position of high information value with respect to appropriate behavior, the hearer will differentially reinforce the existing 'correct' form.* The social relation between the participants in the communication act is also involved here—parents and elders are much more likely to correct children and youths than vice versa, for example. What we are dealing with here are the conditions under which a hearer is likely to notice an erroneous or missing signal and evince this by either a checking verbal response— "What did you say?"—or by unexpected behavior from the speaker's point of view. If I ask my son for the *nail* and am handed the *pail*, to use a crude illustration, I am likely to say, "No, I said *nail*," with appropriate emphasis and clear articulation of the initial phoneme. Obviously the factors indicated above are interactive: a phoneme shift which makes a difference in the code may nevertheless be passed by the censor if it occurs in a position of low information value in the semantic sense and/or if it is redundant with respect to its phonetic environment (e.g., carried by the allophonic variation in surrounding phonemes). Similarly, a shift may occur in a position of high information value if it does not change the code (or, in doing so, does not produce a different word) and/or if it is in redundant relation to its environment. As young individuals in a language community learn the language as well as the culture, they develop self-correcting tendencies based on self-feedback. However, this self correction is clearly dependent upon the pattern of differential reinforcement received from other members of the community and hence should follow the same principles.

III. *Strengthening. Uncorrected modifications, being reinforced as parts of total communicative acts, become stronger habits and compete more and more effectively with 'correct' habits.* The mere fact of occurrence of changes in predictable loci, e.g., non-random modifications, indicates the existence of underlying readinesses at these points. If we accept the general notion that effective communication is typically rewarding (needed objects are brought to the speaker, his social goals are accomplished, and so forth), then it follows that all stimulus-response sequences contributing to the total communicative act will tend to be reinforced.

IV. *Generalization. As the habits producing modifications at 'stress points' become stronger, these new response tendencies will generalize or spread to other positions, initially to similar antecedent environments* (e.g., similar stimuli) *and thence gradually to all environments.* This analysis implies that all changes begin their careers as 'sporadic,' tending to become 'conditional' changes under appropriate conditions, and eventuating as 'unconditional' changes. There is considerable doubt among linguists as to the validity of this notion—most apparently assuming 'sporadic,' 'conditional,' and 'unconditional' changes to be different in kind— but the empirical evidence needs to be re-examined from this point of view.[71] The 'appropriate conditions' under which sporadic modifications become conditional and conditional changes unconditional are *frequency* conditions. The present analysis would assume that where changes of a sporadic nature are recorded, the initial occurrence was in a position of maximal 'stress' or predictability from both environment and competing habit structure, but the tendency toward generalization was blocked by stronger regular or 'correct' habits in other similar environments. Similarly, the restriction of a conditional change to its specific

---

[71] There is also a matter of definition involved here. We are assuming that most 'sporadic' changes occur in environmental stress points of the sort discussed, while many linguists reserve this term for changes of unlawful, haphazard sorts with respect to environmental factors.

environments suggests that continuing generalization tendencies were blocked by stronger regular habits in other environments in which the same speech sounds occur. These strong regular or 'correct' habits represent 'frequency mountains' over which the generalization tendencies cannot pass. Presumably various 'strong irregulars' (such as certain nominative plurals like *child-children* and certain verb forms like *go-went*) are relics of the language's past and survive the onslaughts of generalizing changes because of their high frequencies of usage. It also follows from all that has gone before that positions of emphasis—loudness, initial positions of utterances, positions of high information value, and so forth— will be the most resistant to change since these are positions where modifications produce checking reactions from hearers in the language community.

V. *Social change. Language change in a community will be gradual and cumulative, representing a continuous changing proportion of individuals who do or do not hear and produce a particular feature or set of features.* The process of change in the community would most probably be represented by an S-curve. The rate of change would probably be slow at first, appearing in the speech of innovators, or more likely young children; become relatively rapid as these young people become the agents of differential reinforcement; and taper off as fewer and fewer older and more marginal individuals remain to continue the old forms. On an empirical level, it should be possible to make a comparative study of forms used as a function of age and other sociological variables. It was suggested that the rate of change may be a function of the size of the language community; it is also undoubedly a function of the status of the communication system. The nature of language change *within* the individual is a difficult question—some linguists feel that this is an all-or-nothing matter akin to mutation, whereas most psychologists feel that there should be a period, at least, of oscillation between competing forms. Perhaps, in a manner akin to *imprinting* in birds, individuals never change in the features they hear and produce after early childhood experiences, language changes being purely a matter of sociological shift in the composition of the group. Again, empirical data would have to be collected with this question in mind.

Information theory also generates a very general prediction concerning the direction that language change should take at any given stage. Information theory techniques are readily applicable to phonological changes since we have a unit, the phoneme, which is sharply limited in number for each language and hence susceptible to counting on the basis of texts or lexicon. The same consideration applies to the distinctive features into which phonemes may be analysed. In employing information theory concepts here, two alternatives are available. We may compare two or more stages of the same language attested by written records or we may compare related languages on the basis of assured changes from an ancestral phonological system reconstructed by the well-established techniques of historical linguistics. The comparisons would be in terms of entropy estimates.

Our general hypothesis would be that there are two general factors which influence change in a phonological system: a tendency toward *efficiency* and a competing tendency toward *redundancy* (cf., Zipf's notions of speaker and hearer economies). A phonemic system may be considered as efficient to the degree that all combinations of distinctive features are utilized in the phonemes, that all phonemes are equi-probable, and that their occurrences are independent of neighboring phonemes. In fact, however, there can never be maximum efficiency —not only would articulatory difficulty of certain combinations of features and of certain sequences always be limiting factors, but channel noise would seriously diminish the comprehensibility of such a system. Perhaps, also, the speed of transmission of semantic units would exceed the channel capacity of the decoder. For these reasons, we may think of a language as maintaining an unstable balance between efficiency and redundancy factors.

VI. *Entropy balance. The more the entropy of a given language system deviates from that representing balance between efficiency and redundancy factors the greater will be the tendency to change in the direction of balance.* This 'homeostatic' principle obviously requires some statement about the balance point. If we give speaker and hearer equal weight in the communication situation, then the balance point would be expected to be 50 per cent efficiency. Synchronically, the calculation of entropy measures of phonological units for an adequate sample of contemporary languages should show something like a normal distribution about this 50 per cent balance point. Diachronically, similarly, a sample of the stages of a given language through time should show a normal distribution about 50 per cent efficiency. Finally, if at a given stage a language is either well above or well below the mean 50 per cent entropy level, we should expect to find either a decrease or an increase in entropy to characterize the subsequent process of change in that language.

A phonemic system may be considered efficient to the degree that the number of distinctive features needed to describe the number of phonemes approaches the minimum of $\log_2 n$, where n symbolizes the number of phonemes in the system. For example, a system of 32 phonemes, using 10 distinctive features, would have an efficiency of exactly 50 per cent, since it could be done with only five distinctive features ($\log_2 32 = 5$) under conditions of maximum efficiency. We may define the redundancy as $1 - E$ (efficiency). A system of 32 phonemes and 8 distinctive features would be 62.5 per cent efficient and 37.5 per cent redundant. The general hypothesis is that both the average efficiency of different languages synchronically and of the same language diachronically for different stages in its history should approximate the same mean value when this measure is applied.

Unfortunately, very few languages have been analysed in terms of their distinctive features. Nevertheless, the following data display a surprisingly close approximation to predictions: The phonemes of English have been analysed as being 28 in number and requiring 9 binary oppositions.[72] The efficiency of this system then is 4.80/9 or 53 per cent. Russian phonemes, on the other hand, are 42 in number and employ a total of 11 distinctive features.[73] The efficiency of the Russian system is therefore 5.38/11 or 48.9 per cent.

[72] Jakobson, Fant, and Halle, *Preliminaries to speech analysis* (Cambridge, 1952).

[73] Cherry, Halle, and Jakobson, Toward the logical description of languages in their phonemic aspect, *Language* **29**. 34–46 (1953).

The efficiency of modern Spanish, as shown in the table below, is 50.9%. The tendency of three contemporary languages to cluster about 50 per cent efficiency is apparent. The only available presentation of analyses of successive stages of the same language is that of E. Alarcos Llorach for four periods of Spanish.[74] The inventory of phonemes, distinctive features, and efficiency estimates is given in the following table:

Stages	Phonemes	Distinctive Features	Efficiency
I	21	9	4.39/9 = 48.8%
II	24	8	4.58/8 = 57.3%
III	27	10	4.75/10 = 47.5%
IV	24	9	4.58/9 = 50.9%

The average of these stages is 51.1 per cent and there is a cyclic trend about this value, both of which are consistent with the hypothesis as applied to diachronic data. Needless to say, no secure conclusions can be drawn from such scanty evidence, but the smallness of the deviations from predictions is striking.

The same prediction, interestingly enough, can be reached on *a priori* grounds within information theory itself. If we have n distinctive features of binary form, we would expect 2^n possible phonemes. In addition we would expect the selection of a sub-set of phonemes which are maximally discriminable. If the distinctive features were dimensions of a similarity space, we would expect the phoneme regions to be maximally distant (i.e., maximally discriminable). Such a set would be in diagonally opposite regions. If there are n distinctive features, then there would be 2^{n-1} maximally distinguishable regions. Then the ratio of existing phonemes to possible phonemes would be

$$\frac{2^{n-1}}{2^n} = \frac{1}{2} = 50 \text{ per cent.}$$

The general notion just described says that languages should tend to change in such ways as to return toward a balance between efficiency and redundancy factors, but it does not specify what types of changes would accomplish these ends. In general, it seems likely that *phonemic merger* should tend to increase the entropy and hence efficiency of a language system (by reducing the total number of phonemes relative to the same number of distinctive features) while *phonemic split* should tend to decrease the entropy of a language system. This, of course assumes that the merging phonemes vary in frequency and the result of pooling them will be a more even distribution and hence an increase in absolute entropy. In other words, the preceding analysis assumed approximately equal use of the phonemes in a language. If we had data at our disposal on phoneme sequences, similar predictions could be made with regard to transitional measures, namely, an increase in entropy as a result of merger and a decrease in entropy as a result of splitting.

6.3.1.3. *Proposed experiments.* A number of research suggestions are embodied in the theoretical analyses above. Additional proposals may be noted here. (1) *Prediction of merger and splitting from entropy measures.* The information theory analysis just given suggests certain rather obvious tests. For example, measures of relative entropy for Javanese, which has maintained most Proto-Austronesian consonants intact, should be compared with those for Hawaiian or Samoan, in

[74] *Fonologia Español* (Madrid, 1950).

which there has been widespread merger. The process of splitting could be tested by studies of consonant frequencies in the transition from classical Latin to Italian, during which the number of consonant phonemes increased. (2) *Re-analysis of historical data.* There is an immense amount of evidence available on language change. This should be restudied and sampled in such a way as to test the various hypotheses that have been suggested above. Do we, for example, find that changes tend to occur initially in those positions where anticipatory and perseverative environmental factors combine to modify the intervening phone? Do we find that changes are more probable in terminal and medial positions than in initial? Would a fine enough time series reveal the predicted generalization of changes? (3) *Contingency analysis of languages in general.* Numerous typologies of world languages have been made, but usually without any clear purpose. The various principles discussed above generate certain predictions as to what language characteristics should (a) appear together and (b) shift from one into the other historically. A matrix in which the columns were defined by characteristics (agglutinative, tonal, etc.) and the rows by a random (or perhaps exhaustive) sample of world languages could be analysed to determine empirically what characteristics tend to appear together and what languages tend to be related to more than chance degrees. This analysis presupposes further development and validation of the specific quantitative indices for each characteristic which have recently been advanced. (4) *Experimentally produced lapses.* There are a number of ways in which contemporary speakers can be placed under stress and the locus and nature of their lapses recorded and checked against theory. Some of the possibilities are: (a) enforced rapidity of speaking, with tape recording of the results that can then be stretched for analysis; (b) detailed analysis of the spontaneous speech of children of various ages; (c) speech under the conditions of delayed feedback—will the loci of disturbances be predictable from principles such as those above?; (d) analysis of the changes that occur in popular singing; (e) sampling of deliberate 'humorous' modifications, e.g., 'speakers' to 'speagers,' produced from native speakers on request.

6.3.2. *Semantic Change*

6.3.2.1. *Linguistic facts.* Change in meanings is as constant a feature of linguistic history as change of forms. Changes in the semantic area of language are in many instances motivated by the introduction of new cultural items or changes in old ones. The basic responses to such situations are usually one of the following: (1) *Borrowing* from another language. (2) *Extension* of an old term used to designate something similar either formally or functionally. (3) *Coinage* of a new term, often by compounding or derivation from previous morphemes. A kind of borrowing in which a new formation is based on the traditional resources of a language but modelled after a formation in a foreign language is sometimes called a *calque.* The following examples will illustrate these processes. English borrowed *street* from Latin (*via*) *strata* to designate the paved roads which were new to the Anglo-Saxons. It extended the meaning of the already existing verb *writan* 'to scratch,' to include runes on the bark of trees. English formed a new word *railroad* out of two existing morphemes. An example of calque is the German *Fall* in the meaning of grammatical case. It is a translation of the Latin *casus* which has this same meaning in addition to the literal meaning of 'falling.' It in turn is a loan translation of the Greek *ptōsis*, literally, 'a falling.'

Very many changes in meaning can be shown to occur without any precipitating cause in non-linguistic cultural change. These changes like those listed above can be classified as (1) *coinages*, new forms with new or old meanings whether completely new (*noggin*) or novel combinations of preexisting elements (*big shot*). (2) *Meaning shifts* in preexisting forms. (3) *Obsolescence* (e.g., loss of the term *whither*). Meaning shifts can practically all be covered by the term 'metaphor.' The various figures of speech of traditional rhetoric, synecdoche, metonymy, etc. name a process by which a term is extended through various associations, e.g., part for whole, whole for part, specialization, generalization, weakening, elevation, degradation, etc. The nonce metaphor of the poet or of the ordinary speaker becomes a meaning shift if it spreads to the rest of the speech-community. If the older meaning becomes obsolescent then a complete shift has taken place, usually with an intermediate period in which both senses exist. More often the various meanings all continue in use, some being viewed as primary others as metaphorical. The prevailing polysemy of words and other linguistic forms is the synchronic result of this diachronic process.

Once a shift has taken place, the result may be a chain reaction. The new meaning of the particular form which has undergone a shift may have been covered by some already existing term. This second term may become obsolescent, or may specialize in some narrower meaning, or in turn shift with further results. For this reason a change in meaning should never be considered in isolation but rather in its effect on a set of forms with related meanings. This is the concept of the semantic field, which has been dealt with especially in Europe.[75] Specific parallel changes of meaning tend to occur with high frequency in widely separated areas. Such meaning changes can usually occur in either direction. Thus 'sun' has become 'day' or 'day' has shifted to 'sun' independently in many languages. Often the same term is used for both, and if historical reconstruction is not possible we cannot tell in which direction the shift occurred. Such instances should be assembled and correlated with word association data (see below).

As in other aspects of historical study we can utilize either historical material proper or that derived from comparison of related languages. A form which is the continuation of an older form in the same language, or shares a common origin with one in a related language as shown by resemblance in form and meaning, is called a *cognate*. Examples of cognates are (1) Anglo-Saxon *stan* 'stone' and modern English *stone* in the same meaning. (2) Modern English *bone* and German *Bein* 'leg.' In this case English has generalized while German keeps the earlier restricted meaning.

6.3.2.2. *Theoretical analysis of meaning change.* We start with the assumption that 'semantic change' in the present context refers to change in the reference

---

[75] See particularly Jost Trier, *Der deutsche Wortschatz im Sinnbezirk des Verstandes; die Geschichte eines sprachlichen Feldes* (Heidelberg, 1931).

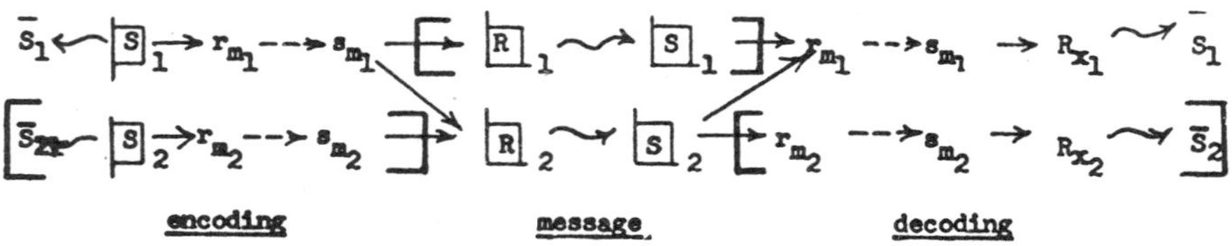

encoding   message   decoding

Figure 18

of a linguistic sign (or in the semantic state associated with a linguistic sign) and not to change in the significance of referends (objects) themselves as distally perceived. In other words, when the object MOUTH comes to be called *mouth* rather than *cheek*, we do not assume that the meaning of this object to human communicators has changed, but rather that the arbitrary linguistic sign by which communicators refer to this object has shifted.

This situation is described in learning theory symbols below and in Figure 18. The distal perceptual sign ($\boxed{S}_1$), deriving from an object ($\bar{S}_1$) elicits its appropriate mediation process (r_{m_1}————s_{m_1}) in the encoder, but rather than mediating the encoding of the original linguistic reaction ($\boxed{R}_1$), it now mediates a different linguistic reaction ($\boxed{R}_2$). There is no change in the significance of the perceptual sign (e.g., the meaning of MOUTH), but there is a new encoding unit associated with this object via the mediation process. Similarly, on the decoding side of the communication equation, the original linguistic sign ($\boxed{S}_1$) as a message event no longer elicits a mediation process ($r_{m_1} \rightarrow s_{m_1}$) capable of mediating behavior (R_{x_1}) appropriate to the same object ($\bar{S}_1$), but another linguistic sign ($\boxed{S}_2$) does elicit this process. Processes previously associated with the new message event, $\boxed{R}_2 \leadsto \boxed{S}_2$, if there were such, are indicated by brackets, as are the displaced message events.

Even a casual survey of materials of semantic change as noted above indicates that these shifts are not haphazard. Rather, the referends of the members of a set of cognates tend to be closely related semantically. What general mechanisms of semantic change can be derived from theory which might account for this lawfulness?

(1) *Association transfer.* The regularities of physics, biology, and culture combine to enforce certain transitional dependencies in sequences of signs. Thus *sun* to *warmth*, *eye* to *see*, *man* to *work*, and vice versa and so forth. As shown in Figure 19, such redundant sequences of signs provide conditions for establishing central associational connections ($s_{m_1} \rightarrow r_{m_2}$). Such intraverbal or associative connections are a major determinant of reactions in free association tests. However, as shown by the arrow ① connecting $\boxed{S}_1$ with r_{m_2}, this transitional redundancy also provides a condition for a shift in meaning, such that the prior sign comes to signify what was initially an associate. Similarly, on the encoding side, under conditions of high redundancy the representational process associated with the prior sign will tend to become an eliciting condition for encoding the subsequent linguistic unit, as shown by the other arrow ② con-

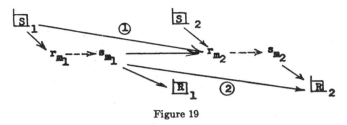

Figure 19

necting s_{m_1} with $\boxed{R}_2$. This represents a response competition situation in both decoding (competing mediators) and encoding (competing expressions), e.g., divergent hierarchies. To the extent that the mediating reactions r_{m_1} and r_{m_2} are similar, the subsequent will tend to intrude in place of the antecedent (e.g., if *ugly-duckling* were a high frequency combination, the heard sign *ugly* might also tend to elicit the representational process originally associated with the sign *duckling*, and *ugly* would be acquiring a different meaning). To the extent that the vocalic expressions $\boxed{R}_1$ and $\boxed{R}_2$ are similar, the subsequent will tend to intrude in place of the antecedent (e.g., if *bright-light* were a high frequency combination, the representational process characteristic of brightness should tend to elicit the encoding unit *light*—the encoder will have a tendency to substitute the linguistic sign *light*, as in "It's a very light day," in situations appropriate to the original meaning of *bright*). Both of these processes, mediator substitution and vocalic substitution, have the same end result—a shift in the sign associated with a particular mediation process. Of course, numerous additional factors would be operative in determining the probabilities of such shifts—for example, whether the redundant items are in same or different grammatical classes, relative frequencies of usage, and so forth.

(2) *Situational context redundancy.* Again by virtue of physical, biological, and cultural regularities, the distal signs associated with certain objects will co-occur with high redundancy. When looking at CHEEK one will nearly always see MOUTH also; when reacting to the COLOR of an object one will also be perceiving its SHAPE. If the male nobility are nearly always seen on horseback, *horseman* will tend to acquire the meaning of *nobility* or *gentleman* (cf., Span. *caballero*); if the material of which something is made is redundantly and rather exclusively experienced in context with its function, the name for the material may substitute for the function (cf., *nickel*). As shown below, the greater the frequency of co-occurrence in common situational context of two distal signs, and hence the greater the probability of co-occurrence of their appropriate mediational processes the greater will be the tendency for substitution of one encoding unit for the other (as shown by the dashed arrows). Note that the same shift in encoding units could be accomplished by a change in meaning of the distal signs (e.g., confusion and substitution between r_{m_1} and r_{m_2}), but this need not be the case—the word originally used for JAW can be substituted for that for MOUTH without implying any change in how people perceive these parts of the physiognomy. The likelihood of *mediator* confusion should depend upon

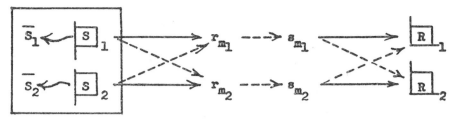

Figure 20

their similarities, and this in turn upon the cultural differentiation between these objects (e.g., to the extent that specific operations, such as chin-beard styling or chin guards for battle, apply to JAW as separate from MOUTH, mediator confusion should be reduced). This distinction between mediator and vocalic skill unit shift verges on the Weltanschauung problem (cf., section 7). It can also be pointed out that situational context redundancy of the sort described here imposes difficulties in the transmission of language from one generation to another, and thus further increases the likelihood of language change—when an adult refers to, and even 'points at' his LIPS, the child is quite likely to be reacting in terms of his MOUTH.

(3) *Physical stimulus generalization.* This is a very straightforward mechanism and simply refers to the tendency for a reaction, in this case mediational, to spread from one stimulus pattern to others, as a function of their physical similarity. Thus the word for SUN should tend to generalize to the object MOON as distally perceived and vice versa; the word for the human EYE should tend to generalize to similar appearing knots in wood, keyholes in doors, and slots in needles; the word for FLOOR should tend to generalize to other level expanses, such as PLAIN and ROAD. The greater the habit strength of a particular mediational and encoding sequence (e.g., the greater its frequency of occurrence), the greater should be its capacity for generalization. Thus, if the name of one carnivorous animal (*cat* in English) acquires a very high frequency of usage as a result of environmental factors, it may generalize so widely as to substitute for carnivorous animals in general.

(4) *Mediated generalization.* The mechanism just described is one means whereby a class of stimulus patterns, in that case physically similar, may become, associated with the same label. Mediated generalization is another mechanism but does not require physical similarity. If one object, as distally perceived (e.g., LEG of a person), acquires a certain significance (e.g., 'stand on') and another object (e.g., that which holds up a table) acquires through independent conditioning a very similar signification, then the instrumental reactions associated with one sign (in this case, the vocalic encoding unit *leg*) will tend to transfer via mediation to the other sign. Other illustrations would be the transfer of the term *ship* to space traveling objects (space*ship*) in science fiction, the use of terms like *chicken* and *filly* to refer to young girls, and reference to *head*

as the top or most important part of something. Some such process as this presumably is basic to metaphor in general.

6.3.2.3. *Research proposals on semantic change.* (1) A first step by way of research would be to summarize and categorize (perhaps in terms of the mechanisms described) the various types of semantic changes that have occurred in language families. This should be done across language families as well. Of course, much of this work has already been done and merely needs to be analysed. (2) Given the above collection of information on historical semantic changes, it would be interesting to compare these data with those obtainable from *association techniques*, using, of course, contemporary subjects. The first mechanism described above, association transfer, involves reactions to linguistic signs, and the usual free association technique should yield data most directly comparable to these types of language change. The other three mechanisms above, situational context redundancy, primary and mediated generalization, involve reaction to the distal or perceptual signs of objects, e.g., labeling operations, and a technique used by Karwoski, Gramlich and Arnott,[76] among others, where people associated to objects themselves as perceived distally, should yield relevant data. The experimental question is this: to what extent can one demonstrate significant correlation between the associations made to words and objects and evidence on semantic changes that have occurred? Will the types of changes that have been known to occur in languages with considerable frequencies be matched by high frequencies of appearance in association tests? Demonstration of this sort would lend general support to the hypotheses generated here. (3) Study of the *verbal paraphasias of aphasics*—the encoding units substituted in the search for the 'correct' units—would be interesting in its own right as well as instructive in the present context. Do verbal paraphasias, when collected in sufficient numbers, also parallel free association and object association frequencies? (4) The conditions for each of the mechanisms described can be manipulated experimentally under laboratory conditions. For example, one can deliberately vary (a) the sequential redundancy of signs, (b) the contextual (situational) redundancy, (c) the physical similarity of objects, and (d) the development of common significances for dissimilar objects, all in a situation using nonsense materials, and, after training in labeling, measure the errors produced and their natures, the difficulties in training itself, the changes that occur in retention of labels, and so forth.

[76] Karwoski, Gramlich, and Arnott, *Journal of Social Psychology* **20**. 233–47 (1944).

7. SYNCHRONIC PSYCHOLINGUISTICS II: MACROSTRUCTURE

Within the general organization of this report into synchronic, sequential, and diachronic problems, the reader has probably noticed a general trend from the molecular toward the molar. Although all three types of problems span this continuum to some extent, it was particularly evident in synchronic psycholinguistics, and for that reason we have made an arbitrary segregation of synchronic problems into 'microstructure' (section 4) and 'macrostructure' (section 7). In this section, then, we are concerned with relations between larger segments of messages and grosser psychological correlates. The effects of *motivational states* upon encoding and decoding is one such relation (7.1). The persistent and important issue of *meaning* is another (7.2). Referring as it does to relations between events in messages (signs) and events in behaving organisms (representational processes), it clearly falls within the area of synchronic psycholinguistics, but we limit ourselves here to an analysis of various ways of defining meaning, and the measurement of certain aspects of meaning. A third problem which seems to fall best in this catetory is that of *information transmission* (7.3), both between individuals using the same code and between individuals using different codes (e.g., translation). Finally, we have a little to say about the very complicated and ill-defined area of *language, cognition, and culture*, which includes the so-called 'Weltanschauung' problem. Here we limit ourselves to an attempt to clarify somewhat the nature of the problem and to presentation of concrete research studies, some completed and some proposed. It was the consensus of the seminar that arm-chair theorizing on this problem has about reached the saturation point and what is needed is experimental data collecting and hypothesis testing.

7.1. *Effects of Motivational States upon Decoding and Encoding*[77]

In the ordinary, everyday uses of language much of the information transmitted concerns emotional states, attitudes, and motives of both speakers and hearers. Malinowski used to refer to this as 'phatic communion.' In this section we wish to analyse both some of the ways in which the motivational states of hearers can influence their decoding of messages and some of the ways in which such states of speakers can influence their encoding of messages. As will be seen, motivational states can influence discrete, linguistic aspects of messages as well as continuously variable, non-linguistic aspects, although the latter are presumably more susceptible to such effects. These are distinctly psycholinguistic problems, concerning relations between states of communicators and states of messages.

7.1.1. *Learning Theory Propositions*

It will be useful to segregate the effects of motives into two classes—their general energizing effects and their more specific cue effects, a distinction made

[77] Charles E. Osgood.

in most psychological discussions (cf., Miller and Dollard, for example). To the extent that drive states are intense, perhaps involving changes in body chemistry (e.g., hormonal changes and the like), they will serve to energize the organism, increasing the strengths of action tendencies; to the extent that drive states are distinctive, e.g., comprise discriminable stimulus patterns which can be selectively associated with reactions, they will serve as cues in the elicitation of those responses to which they have been conditioned. We shall refer to the energizing properties of drive by the symbol D and to the selective, specific stimulus properties of drive by the symbol S_D. The former effects may be either innate or learned (as in acquired drives states like anxiety), whereas the cue effects of drives must be learned like other stimulus-response connections.

7.1.1.1. *Energizing effects.* One of the basic principles of Hull-type learning theory states that drive combines multiplicatively with habit strength to yield reaction potential. In symbolic terms: $_sE_R = {_sH_R} \times D$. Since it is the excitatory potential associating stimulus with response ($_sE_R$) that is directly coupled with behavioral indices in this theory, this means that the amount of drive associated with a response tendency (e.g., on either decoding or encoding sides) will directly influence the probability, latency, and so forth of the behavior concerned. If the learned habit strengths associating stimulus with response ($_sH_R$) of alternative decoding or encoding reactions are near their maxima, and hence of roughly equal strength, it can be seen that motivational variables will become very important in determining what reactions actually occur. This condition is probably typical of most ordinary language behavior, and hence momentary fluctuations in motivation—attitudes of speakers and hearers, 'sets' of one kind or another, interests in one or another aspect of the message, and so forth—will be significant in directing both decoding and encoding activities of communicators.

The postulated multiplicative relation between habit strength and drive has one very significant corollary: if two or more alternative responses to the same stimulus (e.g., a divergent hierarchy) have different habit strengths, the effects of increasing generalized drive (D) will be to further increase the difference between the two reaction potentials. In other words, the effects of increased generalized drive upon habit-family hierarchies will be to further augment the probability of the dominant response and relatively damp the probabilities of weaker reaction tendencies. This has important implications for language behavior under stress conditions.

7.1.1.2. *Cue effects.* The cue effects of specific drive states operate precisely like any other contextual condition—by virtue of having been associated with the elicitation of particular responses, these cues acquire evocative properties and contribute to the total eliciting pattern, e.g., they may serve to 'weight' the stimulus situation in favor of one response rather than another. If the motive state of anger has been associated with swearing responses, subsequent occurrences of this motive state will increase the probability of such responses. If strong fear states were associated with the first, childhood language of a bilingual speaker, but not with the second, adult language, subsequent fear states should 'throw' the speaker back into his childhood tongue. Less traumatic interplays between motive states (interests, attitudes, and the like) are presumably operative continuously in the flow of communicating. What we have referred to elsewhere as the 'intentions' of speakers reflect the integration of such motive states with semantic states.

To this point we have been speaking only of the cue effects of specific drive (e.g., drive states previously and differentially associated with particular reactions). What should be the cue effects of generalized drive (e.g., drive states not previously and differentially associated with particular reactions)? Since the effect of any flood of novel stimulation is to change the pattern eliciting specific reactions, e.g., it shifts the momentary pattern along generalization continua away from the point of maximal habit strength, the effect of nonspecific drive should be to weaken existing habits. Since weaker members of response hierarchies, which are nearer the reaction threshold anyway, will tend to be eliminated in this fashion, the cue effects of non-specific drive (just like the energizing effects above) will be to relatively augment the probability of occurrence of dominant responses.

7.1.1.3. *Language habit-family hierarchies susceptible to motivational effects.* Referring back to the general learning theory model of decoding and encoding processes developed in section 6.1, there are at least four places at which hierarchies susceptible to motivational effects are found.

(1) *Semantic decoding.* Since all signs are to some extent multi-significant, homonyms being only the extreme case, varying the intensity of generalized drive should tend to channel perception and significance into more stereotyped modes and varying specific motivational states should operate selectively to change the probabilities of particular alternative significance or ways of perceiving.

(2) *Anticipational decoding.* Given varying histories of contiguity and redundancy in 'what follows what' in both linguistic and perceptual decoding, the central sensory representations of antecedent events will be differentially associated with hierarchies of subsequent central sensory events, usually as predictive rather than evocative tendencies (e.g., 'tuning up'). Increasing the level of generalized drive (e.g., decoding under anxiety) should operate to stereotype these input sequencing mechanisms, thereby producing errors. Increases in specific drive associated with specific decoding sequences should simply stabilize such sequences, offering resistance to external disturbances (for example, the greater the interest in a particular musical instrument, the better one will follow its line through a complex selection). Whether specific motives operate upon anticipational (and dispositional) mechanisms directly or mediately via feedback from the semantic system would be difficult to ascertain.

(3) *Semantic encoding.* Semantic states, as 'intentions,' are associated with hierarchies of alternative encoding units or 'expressions.' Again, the effect of increased generalized drive should be to further stereotype semantic encoding, and the effect of increased specific drive should be to increase the probability and amplitude (stress, pitch) of those message units associated with such drive states or 'interest,' while decreasing their latencies (e.g., tending to move them

forward in the message sequence, either through choice of alternative constructions or, if drive is high enough, breaking through constructive barriers).

(4) *Dispositional encoding.* By virtue of varying degrees of contiguity and
redundancy between units in sequential encoding, antecedent skill sequences,
as centrally represented, will be variably associated with hierarchies of subsequent skill sequences, as centrally represented. These output redundancies in
language behavior are particularly concerned with grammatical ordering, affixing, and so on. The effects of generalize drive will be to stereotype the structure
of utterances (making the most probable sequences still more probable) and the
effects of specific drive—probably indirectly, through selection of semantic items
—will be to select among alternative constructions those most closely associated
with the motive state operative.

7.1.2. *Research Proposals and Predictions*

It is always easy to note errors in perceptual decoding, misinterpretions of the
significance of signs, and conclude that such and such a motivational state 'must'
have been operative. A young minister was reading a newspaper report on a
speech given by the Bishop in his area; he sat down and wrote a letter to the
editor complaining that, while it was all right for the paper to disagree with the
doddering old Bishop, it was not fair to keep inserting in italics, the word *applesauce*—the editor wrote back pointing out that the word in italics, which the
young minister had repeatedly misread, was *applause*. To conclude that the young
minister 'must' have had no respect·for his superior may be valid, but the argument is circular scientifically if the act of misperception is the only basis for assuming the motive state. Similarly on the encoding side, it is easy to note shifts
in construction from passive to active in what appear to be appropriate motive
conditions, to note a 'primitivisation' of word selection and construction selection
under emotional states, and infer the presence of the independent variable, but
the argument is equally circular. What is needed for research in this area is controlled situations in which the independent variable, motive state, can be manipulated independently of the dependent variable, language behavior, and the effects
upon the latter observed. In other words, we need to devise experimental situations in which either generalized drive level or specific motive state can be made
to be present in one group or at one time and absent in another (control) group
or another (control) time. Whereas this is relatively easy to accomplish as far as
generalized drive level is concerned, it is very difficult to accomplish as far as
specific motive state (attitude, interest, etc.) is concerned.

7.1.2.1. *Decoding operations and motivation.* (A) *Generalized D.* Earlier in this
report (section 5.4) association techniques were described for building up message
materials having either relatively high or relatively low transitional probabilities
for a particular community of people. If one group of subjects from this community were caused to be under general high drive level and another under
relatively low drive level, and both were given the task of reading or listening
to both high and low transitional sequencing materials, we would predict a

significant interaction between these two variables—the high drive level subjects should be relatively much poorer on comprehension, retention, etc. on the low transitional probability material and relatively better on the high transitional probability material, e.g., the spread of the high drive level group on the two materials should be significantly greater. There are many possible ways to experimentally induce differential drive levels—unpredictable shock might be used, threat of punishment for failure, calling the task 'an important intelligence test,' and even making them extremely hungry, thirsty, or angry. It would also be possible to select two extreme groups on the Taylor Manifest Anxiety Scale, assuming the high scoring subjects to be under generally higher anxiety drive level (this technique has worked well in a number of other situations).

Another study, on perceptual decoding, would be to subject our high D and low D groups to Miles' Kinephantoscope (ambiguous figure capable of multiple interpretations), predicting fewer alternatives and longer 'holding' of the dominant interpretation in the high D group. A variant of the latter design would put verbal homonyms in ambiguous sentences, predicting along similar lines. A project requiring considerable ingenuity would be to present puns to people under high and low D, puns involving usually a shift from the more probable significance of a word to a less probable significance, the prediction being that under high D people will be less likely to 'catch on' and perhaps more annoyed when they do. Is it true that highly anxious people (or angry people, or hungry people, or tired people) are more oblivious to plays on words—as decoders?

(B) *Specific S_D.* Many of the experiments undertaken by Bruner and Postman and their associates on the effects of motivational factors upon perception are interpretable as effects of specific motive states upon decoding. The effects of value systems (religious, theoretical, economic, etc.) upon facilitating perception of co-valuant words presented in the tachistoscope is a case in point (assuming that motivational factors can be disentangled from frequency-of-usage factors— cf., work of Howes and Solomon).[78] So-called 'free' association is another standard experimental situation in which specific motivational factors play a part— witness the use of this technique in 'lie-detection' and in psychotherapy to get at unconscious complexes. An experiment by Foley and Matthews[79] has demonstrated that the associations made to words like *administer* and *binding* vary appropriately with the amount of professional training in either law or medicine. In all of these cases, however, manipulation of motive or interest state is indirect in terms of subject selection—and frequency-of-usage variables therefore probably are confounded. One can speculate on the possibility, however, of creating interest of children in animals vs. routes, for example, and then presenting messages like 'Bear right;' the general design here would be to study the associations or other indices of decoding significance resulting from the presentation of homonyms, under differential motivation. Capitalizing on the difficulties of our young minister above, it should also be possible to study the effects of differential motivation upon misperception of signs, e.g., pairs like *applesauce* and *applause*, under tachistoscopic or other experimental conditions.

[78] *Psychological Review* **57**. 229–34 (1950).
[79] *Journal of Experimental Psychology* **33**. 299–310 (1943).

7.1.2.2. *Encoding operations and motivation.* (A) *Generalized D.* A basic design much like that proposed for decoding can be suggested here. Using the same predetermination of transitional probabilities (nouns to verbs, adjectives to nouns, and so forth—see section 5.4), subjects can first become familiar with lists of these words and then use them as the vocabularies for spontaneously encoding short stories, while under either high or low generalized D. Again it would be predicted that the average transitional probabilities of sequences spontaneously encoding under high D would be higher than when encoding under relatively low D. Another experimental approach to this problem would be to solicit spontaneous messages from high and low D subjects and then give systematically mutilated portions of them (cf., 'Cloze' method, section 5.3.4) to other groups of subjects to be filled in—predicting that the materials of high D subjects would yield higher average fill-in scores than the materials produced by relatively low D subjects.

Another approach would utilize tape recorded interviews obtained from patients undergoing psychotherapy: using judgments of the therapist as a criterion of periods of relatively high and low D (anxiety), excerpts would be mutilated and given to other people for reconstruction—prediction is that the sequences produced under high D should be more susceptible to correct reconstruction. Recordings made of people speaking under high D (anger, fear, and so on) may be compared with recordings by the same people later discussing the same events—using the same mutilation and fill-in technique—and one would make the same prediction as to the transitional predictability of the sequencing. Linguists could analyse any of these experimental and control productions in terms of the diversity of constructions and so forth displayed. Type-token ratios, another measure of language diversity or flexibility, could also be taken.

(B) *Specific S_D.* As pointed out earlier, it is extremely difficult to think up adequate ways of experimentally manipulating specific motive states, such as are presumed to contribute to the selection among alternative semantic and grammatical forms in encoding. Therefore, we may start by indicating in general terms the effects to be expected. In the utterances produced by a speaker in a specific motive state, the *stress* on those units related to (e.g., 'expressing') the motive state should be increased, the *pitch* of those units should be higher, and (as a secondary effect) the *vowel lengths* should be greater. Here we are referring to nonphonemic stress, pitch and vowel length, and in languages where these message characteristics are phonemic these effects should be continuous beyond the purely phonemic elements.[80] All of these affects are attributable to the relation of response amplitude to amount of reaction potential as determined by drive.

Following the relation between reaction potential and latency, it would be expected that those semantic units associated with specific drive should tend to be encoded earlier in an utterance, e.g., motive states should affect the *ordering*

[80] In discussion the question was raised as to how generally, across languages, do the elements of messages invested with greatest interest have the greatest stress, highest pitch, and lengthening of vowels; most of the linguists felt that while not universal, there would be a general trend in this direction.

of units in messages. Where alternative constructions are available in the language this will show up in selection among these alternatives. Interest in the actor enhances initial encoding of this unit, hence an active construction; interest in an object, on the other hand, enhances initial selection of this unit, hence a passive construction (example: 'A very young boy won the diving championship' vs. 'The diving championship was won by a very young boy').[81] Interest in the action itself increases the probability of encoding the verb first, and hence selection of a command or exhortatory construction (e.g., 'Eat your dinner' or 'Run for your life!'). The position of subordinate clauses in utterances should be particularly susceptible to the effects of motivation—interested in the conditional status of the matter, I am likely to say, "If you wish, we can go to the movies" rather than "We can go to the movies, if you wish."

In general, one would expect these differential motive states of speakers to operate within the existing rules of the language, by selecting among alternate constructions and using non-phonemic possibilities for emphasis. However, sufficiently strong motivation combined with insufficient flexibility in the language structure may produce errors—the speaker breaks through the grammatical constraints of the system. Thus, at a picnic one of our linguists heard a man say, 'Garlic I taste!' when startled by a strong flavor. When one looks for them, he finds many such lapses in everyday speech under motivated conditions. Errors of this type are particularly hard to eradicate in the encoding of children—the "Me and Johnny went . . ." is in part a reflection of the youngster's ego-involvment in himself. Also, other things equal, one would expect the effects of specific motive states to show up most clearly in those aspects of the message which are in 'free' variation.[82] It should also be noted that since the effects of specific S_D persist through utterances one would expect motivation to produce redundancies wherever possible—for example, the negation oriented individual who tells the policeman, "I ain't never done nothing to nobody nohow." Finally, one would expect certain types of 'slips of the tongue' to be due to the moving forward in the sequence of items of greater interest, where phonetic similarities facilitate this intrusion—large samples of 'slips' would have to be collected and analysed to test this notion.

But how is one to manipulate the specific motive states of speakers with respect to particular items in potential utterances in such ways as to test these predictions? As suggested earlier, the sequence of events in psychotherapy offers some possibility of independent estimation of speaker states. Carroll, also mentioned above, has tried manipulating the interest of students in a classroom situation in either the actor or the objects acted upon, with predicted results. In another experiment conducted in Carroll's laboratory, two students were separated by a panel, each given a set of objects, pegs and a board, and given a specific schedule of questions to ask—'Is your left hand peg blue?,' 'Give me your orange block' and so forth. The syntactical characteristics of answers to specific questions were studied. This suggests another kind of control over the interest state of the decoder-encoder—the nature of the information requested by another communicator. One could ring changes on this model as a means of investigating

[81] Carroll reports a classroom experiment on this problem with positive results.

[82] Greenberg mentioned an African language, Hausa, which ideally illustrates this matter—complete flexibility in order permits the item of maximal interest to come first in utterances.

the present problem. Within the same general situation, it should also be possible to increase the general drive level—e.g., making it a competitive situation, a 'test of intelligence,' giving certain objects reward or threat value, and so forth.

7.2. Meaning

7.2.1. Meanings of 'Meaning'[83]

There is a vast literature concerning the subject of 'meaning,' with contributions from the fields of philosophy, philology, literary criticism, linguistics, and psychology. For a key concept, however, the variability in meaning of this chameleon-like word is notable. It is not our purpose in this section to review all or even a small part of the applications of the term 'meaning' in this literature. Rather, we intend only to outline the dimensions of a field of denotation within which, we believe, lie most of the important meanings of 'meaning' found in scientific discourse.

Ogden and Richards[84] pointed out the necessity of an adequate theory of signs as a prerequisite for understanding the nature and kinds of meaning. Charles W. Morris took up this task and has laid the foundations for such a theory.[85] He has delineated the three principal aspects in the study of sign function: *semantics* (the relation of signs to things signified), *pragmatics* (the relation of signs to elicited behavior), and *syntactics* (the relation of signs to signs within a system of signs); and he has dealt with the classificatory problems resulting from the phenomena of perceptual constancy and of equivalences, both in signs and denotata. Modern linguistics, largely independent of Morris's work, has developed a highly effective classificatory scheme for dealing with alternatives and equivalences in language signs, but, at least in its American development, it has generally avoided dealing with problems outside of those having to do with the *forms* of language signs, or 'syntactics' in Morris's terms. The success of this method in this area of application, however, has prompted some anthropologists to apply a similar method in the analysis of sign-to-denotatum relationships, i.e., of 'semantics' in Morris's terms.[86] Lastly, recent developments in the formulation of behavior theory by experimental psychologists throw additional light on the nature of sign behavior. In this formulation the contributions of Morris's work and of modern linguistics find added relevance and are seen in their relation to the total problem of sign behavior.

As an approach to the consideration of the possibilities in the meaning of 'meaning,' let us consider the position of the currently dominant trend in American linguistics. Bloomfield[87] defined the *meaning* of a linguistic form as "the situation in which the speaker utters it and the response which it calls forth in

[83] Floyd G. Lounsbury.

[84] C. K. Ogden and I. A. Richards, *The meaning of meaning*[8] (London and New York, 1948).

[85] Charles W. Morris, Foundations of the theory of signs, *International Encyclopedia of Unified Science* 1. 2 (Chicago, 1938); also: *Signs, language and behavior* (New York, 1946).

[86] E.g., see Ward H. Goodenough, *Property, kin, and community on Truk*, Yale University Publications in Anthropology, No. 46, esp. pp. 103–110 (New Haven, 1951).

[87] Leonard Bloomfield, *Language*, chapter 9 (New York, 1933).

the hearer." He continues, "The speaker's situation and the hearer's response are closely co-ordinated, thanks to the circumstance that every one of us learns to act indifferently as a speaker or as a hearer. In the causal sequence—speaker's situation → speech → hearer's response—the speaker's situation, as the earlier term, will usually present a simpler aspect than the hearer's response; therefore we usually discuss and define meanings in terms of a speaker's stimulus." Bloomfield further distinguishes between the multitudinous unique total situations which prompt us to utter any one linguistic form, and the common distinctive semantic features which all of these situations share and which alone have relevance to the linguistic problem. These latter he refers to as 'distinctive meaning.'[88] Having proceeded this far, Bloomfield paints a very discouraging picture of the linguist's possibilities for understanding and handling meaning. To describe adequately the speaker's situations and the hearer's responses would require unattainable knowledge in the natural sciences, sociology, physiology, and psychology. Even if the external situations and the overt responses could be adequately described and classified, the internal states of the speaker's and hearer's bodies would be imponderable variables. In his development of linguistic method, however, Bloomfield points out that for the analysis of linguistic form a knowledge of meaning is largely unnecessary. All that is relevant is to test for differential meaning, i.e., whether two forms mean the same or different. This being the case, and the linguist's business being conceived as the analysis of linguistic form, linguistics could proceed without further concern for theories of meaning. The so-called American school of linguistics, receiving its orientation from Bloomfield, has gone ahead on this basis, developing the procedures and refining the theoretical underpinnings of the analysis of linguistic form, apart from and independent of the analysis of meaning. Its only acknowledged dependence upon meaning was the now classical question of 'same or different.' Even this apparently simple question, however, cannot always be answered satisfactorily. Here, however, instead of depending on a theory of meaning, linguists have largely operated by rule of thumb. There have been attempts to show theoretically at least that even this minimal dependence on meaning is unnecessary. Although not all are agreed on this point, most are satisfied that to try to analyze the two problems of form and meaning simultaneously adds confusion rather than clarification. Some favor the analysis of each of the two systems independently and only then the analysis of the relationships between them. The structures of the two systems are not isomorphic and the relationship between them is not one of simple matching. Others, however, tend to view the two systems as isomorphic and attempt to define the linguistic units in such a way as to preserve this isomorphism. The units of form in such an analysis attain a complexity and irregularity, however, which betray their dual nature. Exponents of this latter

[88] Bloomfield also used the term 'linguistic meaning' for the distinctive semantic features, but we have avoided introducing this label here, and have used his alternative term, for the reason that the phrase 'linguistic meaning' has recently come to be used in a quite different sense as noted below.

position see in the analysis of form the whole problem of linguistics. Analysis of 'meaning' is felt to be unnecessary for linguistics, but when achieved by some other discipline, would be expected to present parallels or correlates to the linguistic analysis. Instead of looking for the meaning of a linguistic form in non-linguistic situations and non-linguistic responses, a 'meaning' is sought rather in the extended contexts of preceding linguistic situations and following linguistic responses. One writer, summarizing this position, puts it thus:

"Could we perhaps do something further with 'meaning' inside linguistics? Yes, but only on condition that we distinguish sharply between the inside and the outside. Let the sociologists keep the outside practical meaning; then we can undertake to describe the pure linguistic meaning. We can do it thus:

"Among permissible combinations of morphemes, some are commoner than others. Thus there are conditional probabilities of occurrence of each morpheme in context with others. . . .

"Now the linguist's 'meaning' of a morpheme (or of a combination thereof, of any complexity up to a complete utterance, which might even be a whole book or poem) is by definition the set of conditional probabilities of its occurrence in context with all other morphemes—of course without inquiry into the outside, practical, or sociologist's meaning of any of them. . . . So far we have done almost nothing with pure linguistic 'meaning' as so defined, for the obvious reason that its mathematics is of the continuous sort, which we are not accustomed to handling. . . . Still a beginning has been made on a structural semantics by one linguist. . . . This work is very recent, and is the most exciting thing that has happened in linguistics for quite a few years. . . ."[89]

Perhaps we can illustrate this approach by means of a simple example. Consider the English suffix -ly. Generally this element is said to have two meanings (or it may be said to be two different morphemes): (1) the 'adverbial meaning' as in he did it poorly, and (2) the 'adjectival meaning' as in it's a likely story or a goodly number. Let us consider only the first of these two, the adverbial suffix. Compare the sentences he did a poor job and he did the job poorly. The determinants of the occurrence of the segment -ly in the second sentence lie entirely with that sentence itself, that is, within the fairly immediate context. Such a segment is often called in contemporary linguistic terminology an 'empty morph,' inasmuch as it is devoid or empty of any non-linguistic situational meaning, and has its occurrence determined entirely by features of the purely linguistic context. Its 'meaning' then, is only of the 'linguistic' sort, as the above-quoted writer uses the term. For no other segment of this sentence, however, can the occurrence be defined purely in terms of determinants lying within the sentence. The approach described in the above quotation, instead of seeking meaning in non-linguistic contextual determinants of occurrence, would seek to pin it down in terms of determinants of occurrence in larger and larger purely linguistic contexts. For the majority of lexical items such a definition of meaning, while theoretically tenable, becomes methodologically useless in the ordinary type of linguistic text analysis. The 'linguistic meaning' of a given word may not be

[89] Martin Joos, Description of language design, *The Journal of the Acoustical Society of America* **22**. 6. 708 (1950).

found in the linguistic context of that word in any given text or even in a very large collection of texts in which that word occurs one or more times. The linguistic contexts which suffice to determine the 'meaning' of a form may be of the order of size comparable to the total of the past language experience of the informant. While such a body of text is both unattainable and unanalyzable, the linguistic meaning of a form may often be uniquely defined in terms of features of a relatively limited amount of specially elicited linguistic context, such as that elicited by the semantic differential (see section 7.2.2.) or by various other psychological or linguistic testing devices.

7.2.1.2. *Situational vs. behavioral meaning.* The dichotomy between situational and behavioral meanings is foreshadowed in Bloomfield's definition of meaning quoted earlier, where he includes "the situation in which the speaker utters [a form] and the response which it calls forth in the hearer." The dichotomy applies as well to linguistic meaning (as described above) as it does to extralinguistic meaning, for the total stimulus situation antecedent to any speech event or fraction thereof may include not only extralinguistic but also linguistic determining factors; and the total behavioral response may include linguistic as well as extralinguistic behavior.

Morris's three-way breakdown of sign relations provided a framework for defining three kinds of meaning. The relationship of sign to things signified Morris called 'designation,' and the study of such relationships he called 'semantics.' The relationship of sign to sign within a system of signs he called 'implication' (signs 'implicate' other signs), and the study of such relationships he called 'syntactics.' The relationship of signs to elicited behavior Morris called 'expression' (signs 'express' interpretants or behavioral responses), and the study of such relationships he called 'pragmatics.' Applying the term meaning in its widest extent, to contexts of all sorts, there may thus be distinguished three kinds of meaning: designative meaning (semantic), implicative meaning (syntactic), and expressive meaning (pragmatic). The choice of labels, however, is not the most felicitous. Rather, we may refer to them as situational meaning, linguistic meaning, and behavioral meaning, respectively.

This presents a trichotomy rather than the 2x2 division which would be expected from the two dichotomies *linguistic vs. extralinguistic* and *situational vs. behavioral*. The trichotomy results from lumping together the entire linguistic portion of any behavior chain, and from disregarding the fact that a stimulus situation may consist of both linguistic and nonlinguistic stimuli and that a total response may contain both linguistic and nonlinguistic responses. Inasmuch as linguistic analysts customarily isolate out only the linguistic portions of a behavior chain for their study, there is a certain practical justification for this. There are problems in the psychology of language, however, where it is relevant to distinguish, in respect to a given form, the antecedent conditions from the following developments within the linguistic stream.

A recent trend in American structural linguistics has been to be concerned only with the so-called linguistic meaning. Lexicography is concerned with designative meaning, i.e., situational meaning. Psychologists are interested principally in behavioral meanings. Anthropological studies are directed to both designative and behavioral meaning.

7.2.1.3. Internal vs. external loci for 'meaning.' In section 2.2.2 of this volume are described the 'empty organism' formulation and the 'mediation' formulation of behavior theory. The inadequacy of such stringent behaviorist formulations as those of the empty-organism type becomes particularly obvious when applied to language behavior. As Bloomfield recognized when he spoke of the speaker's internal states, and as all who have approached meaning from the vantage point of literature and the arts have recognized, intervening internal variables must be allowed for. While not directly observable, they are yet not entirely beyond the reach of psychological techniques of investigation. The justification for a 'mediational' formulation within a still cautious behaviorist methodology has been presented elsewhere. In any case, the internal mediation processes must be referred to in our survey of the definitions of meaning. Some of the diversity in definitions and uses of the term 'meaning' has been on the issue of the locus assigned to 'meaning.' Some behaviorists would refer only to externally observable situations and/or responses, while others are referring to internal states of the organism, or more specifically to states in the mediation process. Therefore this dichotomy must be admitted as another dimension of the 'meaning' field. The dichotomy *internal vs. external* applies to all of the types isolated thus far. Behaviorists, both among psychologists and linguists, who resist the interpolation of mediational phases in their behavior formulations are forced to admit only 'externals' in their definitions of meaning. Some of those who favor the reckoning with mediational phases are quite as emphatic in having the term 'meaning' apply only to mediational responses, even though these are not observable directly and may be inferred only by means of devious testing devices or from clinical data. Many definitions and uses of 'meaning,' on the other hand, are quite unclear in this aspect of their·reference.

7.2.1.4. Particular vs. general; totality vs. distinctive features. A further respect in which definitions of meaning differ is in whether they have the term refer to a single total immediate context, or to the class of many or of all total contexts, or to the common features of all such contexts of the given language sign. Many definitions, of course, are ambiguous on this point and pay no attention to these distinctions. Some, however, do, as in Bloomfield's 'meaning' (total immediate context) and his 'distinctive meaning' (common distinctive features of contexts).

This dimension of difference cuts across all of the other dimensions previously described. Thus, one may speak of a single nonlinguistic or linguistic, external or internal, situation or behavioral response connected with a given sign; or of all such situations or responses; or of the common distinctive features of these. One may be concerned at different stages of his work with all of the three possibilities in this trichotomy. Thus a linguist proceeds from a single linguistic context of a form, to a collection of many linguistic contexts of the form, to the abstraction of the common distinctive features of these contexts. Similarly an anthropologist, in the study of a kinship system for example, proceeds from a collection of kinsmen and kin-types (the 'genealogical method' in anthropological

field work), to kin-classes (the native classification as given by native terminology), to the distinctive semantic features of the kin-classes (the product of
anthropological analysis).

This trichotomy closely parallels Morris's distinctions between 'denotatum,'
'designatum,' and 'significatum.' We need only modify the term 'class of many
or all total contexts' so as to admit of potential as well as actual situations, or
assumed or imagined as well as real situations, or rather to admit of a class as
a 'kind' whether or not there exists a real representative of the class. Morris's
term 'denotatum' refers to real instances, if any. A sign may or may not have
any denotata. (E.g., I may or may not have an 'uncle.' If I do, he, John Doe—if
that be his name—is a denotatum of the language-sign 'my uncle' when I use it.)
The term 'designatum' refers to a recognized kind or class which may or may
not have any real or immediate representatives. (The description of what
'uncles' are or may be is the designatum of the sign. Thus, in our kinship system,
the designatum of 'uncle' is the class consisting of the types father's brother,
mother's brother, father's sister's husband, mother's sister's husband, etc.)
The 'significatum,' on the other hand, consists of the defining features of the
designatum class. (In terms of components in the semantic dimensions which
underlie the structure of our kinship system, the significatum of 'uncle' would
be the distinctive common semantic features of the class, viz., kinsman, male,
first-degree collaterality, and first or higher ascending generation.)

7.2.1.5. *The dimensions of difference in definitions of meaning.* The set of four
dimensions of difference described above serves quite well as a framework within
which to understand many of the definitions and uses of the term 'meaning'
which we have encountered in linguistic, psychological, and philosophical
writings. It is probably not adequate—i.e., probably does not recognize enough
kinds of difference—to serve as a framework for classifying all of these definitions
and uses. There is, furthermore, often the problem of interpreting just what a
given writer was aiming at. Most scientific writers, however, are sufficiently
specific and clear so that this difficulty is at a minimum. In the references to
meaning in literary criticism this problem is of greater magnitude but also of
less importance to us at the moment.

We may represent these dimensions, and the possibilities (components) in
each dimension, as follows:

    I. S:R (stimuli vs. responses, or situational vs. behavioral)

    II. E:I (external vs. internal)

    III. N:L (nonlinguistic vs. linguistic contexts)

    IV. $T:\sum T:D$ (a total context vs. all total contexts vs. distinctive features
          common to all total contexts).

In terms of components from these dimensions we may now represent, by way
of example, a few of the better known conceptions of 'meaning':

Bloomfield's 'meaning': $(S + R) \cdot (E + I) \cdot N \cdot T$

Bloomfield's 'distinctive meaning': $S (E + I) \cdot N \cdot D$ [Bloomfield mentions
only situations (S) in his discussion of 'distinctive meaning,' though he included
both situations and behavior in his definition of 'meaning.' Perhaps $(N + L)$

should be substituted for N in 'distinctive meaning' above, depending on the interpretation of one of Bloomfield's remarks.]

Joos's 'linguistic meaning': $(S + R) \cdot E \cdot L \cdot D$

Morris's 'denotatum': $S \cdot E \cdot N \cdot T$

Morris's 'designatum': $S \cdot E \cdot N \cdot \sum T$

Morris's 'significatum': $S \cdot E \cdot N \cdot D$

Behavioral mediational 'meaning' (Osgood): $R \cdot I \cdot N \cdot D$

Substitution theory 'meaning' (1): $S \cdot E \cdot N \cdot (T, D?)$

Substitution theory 'meaning' (2): $R \cdot E \cdot N \cdot (T, D?)$.

7.2.2. *Measurement of Connotative Meaning*[90]

The use of the semantic differential as a possible measuring instrument is suggested at several places in this report. For this reason, as well as for its intrinsic interest in psycholinguistics, a brief description of this instrument and its possible applications is given here.[91] The aspect of meaning to which this measuring device is assumed to provide an index is the distinctive psychological state of the communicator which occurs whenever a sign is either presented (decoding) or produced (encoding). The semantic differential is a combination of association and scaling procedures. A sample of potential bi-polar associations to a particular concept is provided for the subject, his task being simply to indicate the direction of each association and its intensity on a 7-step scale. In other words, from the myriad of linguistic and non-linguistic behaviors mediated by semantic states, a small but carefully devised sample is selected.

7.2.2.1. *Logic of semantic differentiation.* The label 'semantic differential' points quite accurately to its intended operation—a multivariate differentiation of concept meanings in terms of a limited number of semantic scales of known composition.[92] The logic of the present instrument can be summarized as follows: (1) *The process of description or judgment can be conceived as the allocation of a concept to an experiential continuum defined by a pair of polar terms.* The content of most complex verbal assertions, e.g., 'Black bean soup is quite thick in consistency,' can be reduced to the allocation of a concept to a scale:

BLACK BEAN SOUP thick ___:X:___ : : : ___ thin.

The greater the intensity of strength of association, the more extreme the allocation in one direction or the other. (2) *Many different continua of judgment are essentially equivalent and hence may be represented by a single dimension.* Judgments on a set of scales such as *good-bad, fair-unfair, clean-dirty, kind-cruel, noble-bestial,* and so forth are very highly correlated and can be shown to represent mainly a single, 'evaluative' factor. (3) *A limited number of such continua,*

---

[90] Charles E. Osgood.

[91] The experimental and theoretical background of this method is described in The nature and measurement of meaning, *Psychological Review* **49**. 197–237 (1952), and some applications are described in a subsequent mimeographed report.

[92] The term is not to be confused with the General Semanticist's structural differential which involves logical operations of a quite different sort.

representative of the dimensionality of meaningful judgments, can be used to define a semantic space within which the meaning of any concept can be specified. This indicates some variant of factor analysis as the basic methodology.

7.2.2.2. *Factor analysis of meaning.* A set of 20 familiar concepts (such as LADY, SIN, FATHER, BOULDER, and RUSSIAN) was judged in randomized order against 50 7-step scales defined by frequently used polar opposites by 100 college student subjects. The 50/50 correlational matrix obtained by correlating the judgments on each scale with those on every other scale was factor analysed by Thurstone's centroid method. Four factors were extracted.

The first factor identified itself as *evaluative* by inspection of the scales which have high and pure loadings on it: *good-bad, clean-dirty, tasty-distasteful, valuable-worthless, pleasant-unpleasant,* and so on. The second factor identified itself fairly well as a *potency* variable: *large-small, strong-weak, heavy-light,* and *thick-thin* had high loadings on only this factor. The third factor appeared to be an *activity* variable: high and pure loadings were obtained for *fast-slow, active-passive,* and *hot-cold.* The fourth factor was small in magnitude and indefinite as to nature. Of the total variance in judgments available for apportionment (e.g., reliable variance), the three factors isolated account for about 60 per cent, of which more than half is evaluative. The remaining 40 per cent is presumably attributable to a large number of specific (probably denotative) factors.

7.2.2.3. *Semantic profiles, distances, and structures.* The factor analysis of meaning is not an end in itself. Its purpose is to make possible the selection of a minimum number of specific scales which taken together, will give the maximum coverage of the semantic space. Ideally, we should like to select one specific polar scale to represent each factor, this scale being maximally loaded on this factor and minimally on all other factors. In practice, of course, due to imperfect reliability, lack of 'pure' scales in the language and so forth, a small sample of scales representing each factor is used.

When a group of subjects (1, 2, 3, . . . *n*) rate a set of concepts (A, B, C, . . . *N*) on the system of scales (a, b, c, . . . *n*) which constitutes the semantic differential, a cube of data is generated. Each cell in this cube represents, with a number from 1 to 7, the judgment of a particular concept against a particular scale by a particular subject. A single slice of the cube represents the complete data for a single subject—all of his judgments of a group of concepts on a group of scales. It is also possible to collapse the cube along the subject dimension, producing a single set of numbers (e.g., averages of subjects). The following operations can be applied to either individual or group (mean) data.

(1) *Meaning of a concept.* Table 1 represents a single slice of this cube, i.e., raw data for a single subject. For purposes of illustration, nine scales are shown, arranged in terms of loadings on the three factors already isolated. Low numbers refer to the polar terms to the left, high numbers to polar terms on the right. The *profile* of numbers in each column is one way of describing the meaning of that concept, within the limited coverage of the factors so far isolated. For this subject, WHITE ROSE BUDS are *good, impotent,* and *passive;* HERO is *good, potent,* and *active;* etc. These descriptions are admittedly gross, highlighting the connotative aspects of meaning and failing to catch many denotative aspects. A far more efficient way of representing the meaning of a concept is available, however, deriving from the mathematical logic of factor analysis. Given orthogonality of

TABLE 1

		A QUICKSAND	B WHITE ROSE BUDS	C DEATH	D HERO	E METHODOLOGY	F FATE	G VIRILITY	H GENTLENESS	I SUCCESS	J SLEEP	
I	a good	7	1	7	1	1	5	1	2	1	3	bad
	b beautiful	7	1	7	2	3	5	2	1	2	2	ugly
	c fresh	6	1	7	1	1	6	1	3	1	2	stale
II	d strong	1	7	2	1	3	3	1	7	1	5	weak
	e large	1	7	3	1	6	4	1	4	1	3	small
	f loud	5	7	4	3	5	6	1	7	2	7	soft
III	g active	7	7	7	1	3	7	1	7	1	7	passive
	h tense	6	7	6	5	2	5	2	7	4	7	relaxed
	i hot	7	5	7	1	3	6	1	3	1	5	cold

the factors (here, three in number), *the meaning of any concept can be specified as a point in the n-dimensional space defined by the factors* (in this case, a solid, three-dimensional space), *this point being the intercept of the projections on each of the factors*. Thus, the meaning of WHITE ROSE BUDS can be defined as 1 7 7 (median positions on each of the three factors in order), the meaning of HERO as 1 1 1, FATE as 5 4 6, and SLEEP as 2 5 7. Means for a group of subjects, for each concept against each scale, can be computed and treated in the same way, in which case the 'cultural meaning' of a concept is being specified. This conception of meaning as a point in n-dimensional space (or a volume in the case of group data where the variability is given) has both the advantage of economy in description and of a mathematical rationale.

(2) *Difference in meaning.* In semantic measurement we will often want to indicate the degree of difference (or, conversely stated, similarity) in meaning, between two concepts for the same individual or group, between two people or groups for the same concept, or between two time points of measurement (e.g., change in the meaning of a concept for an individual or group). The following formula is used here: $D = \sqrt{\Sigma d^2}$ where d is the difference between two concepts (or individuals) on a single scale. The relation of this measure to the generalized distance formula in mathematics has the advantage of providing us with a rationale quite compatible with the entire logic our methods have been following: under certain specifiable conditions, D provides a direct index of the distance between two points in the n-dimensional space defined by our factors. The chief conditions are that the factors be orthogonal and that they be equally represented in the set of scales.

(3) *Semantic Structure.* D also has the advantage of extreme computational simplicity. Given a raw score matrix such as that shown as Table 1, one simply sums the squared differences on each scale between each concept and every other concept, extracting the square root of the sum. The complete operation on a small matrix like that shown for one individual can be done with a small desk calculator and table of square roots in a few minutes. This operation generates a D-matrix, such as that shown as Table 2 for these same data. This table gives the 'distances' of every concept from every other concept in equivalent units. Since these distances are all relative to the same dimensions, they have the additional

TABLE 2

	A	B	C	D	E	F	G	H	I	J
A										
B	13.34									
C	2.65	12.77								
D	12.77	12.04	13.27							
E	12.41	8.31	12.12	7.14						
F	4.90	9.38	4.12	11.53	9.17					
G	13.78	13.64	14.11	3.61	7.35	12.57				
H	11.66	4.24	11.36	10.15	8.60	8.00	12.33			
I	13.08	12.61	13.49	1.41	7.14	11.87	2.24	11.18		
J	9.27	5.10	9.43	9.85	8.25	6.32	11.75	3.46	10.54	

advantage of 'plottability' within a space having the same dimensionality as the number of factors. In the present case, restriction to three factors yields a reasonably accurate plot in three dimensions, e.g., a solid model which concisely represents all of these 'distances' and provides an attractive way of demonstrating data. Although such pictorial representations are limited to a three-factor system, the mathematical model is good to any number of dimensions. The smaller any distance in such a matrix, the more similar in meaning the concepts involved, e.g., D (HERO) and I (SUCCESS) above.

The semantic differential is not a specific test form but a procedure. The scales used will differ from problem to problem, but are selected in terms of known factor composition. Whereas in the study of social attitudes scales such as *fair-unfair, valuable-worthless*, and *clean-dirty* may be chosen to represent the evaluative factor, in the study of aesthetic meanings equally evaluative scales such as *pleasant-unpleasant, beautiful-ugly*, and *tasty-distasteful* may be more appropriate. Nor is the method limited to either isolated stimuli or verbal stimuli; complex verbal signs can be studied as well as non-verbal signs (auditory patterns, cartoons, etc.). A number of applications have been made—to the study of attitude change, to changes in meaning during the course of psychotherapy, to the measurement of identification, to the study of dream and political symbolism, and even to some problems in aesthetics—and others are contemplated. Here we are interested in possible applications to psycholinguistic problems.

7.2.2.4. *Application to some psycholinguistic problems*. The problem of meaning is a central one in the area covered by psycholinguistics. To the extent that the semantic differential provides a satisfactory index of even limited aspects of meaning—chiefly connotative aspects at its present level of development—it should be useful in a variety of psycholinguistic problems, some of which have been indicated elsewhere in this report.

(1) *Laws of word mixture*. An interesting problem, for people in linguistics and the humanities as well as for psychologists, concerns how the meanings of combinations of signs relate to the meanings of the components. Are there analogies with the laws of color mixture? One law is that complementary colors (opposites) cancel each other toward neutral grey—will the combination of words of opposed meaning tend toward a meaningless result, for example, the

meaning of A SUBTLE OAF? Another law of color mixture is that the hues of mixtures must always lie between those of primaries (e.g., red and green yield yellow, red and yellow an orange, etc.). Will the point in semantic space representing A CAT-LIKE WRESTLER fall on a line between the points representing WRESTLER and CAT-LIKE? In the color space, any mixture *must* fall on the line connecting the components—will this be true for ordinary word mixtures? Would STRONG POWER, perhaps lie *further* away from the origin than either of the components? From the color mixture analogy it also follows that any mixture must be less saturated than its components. This is probably not true for word mixture—a STURDY TREE would probably be further from the origin than either of the components.

Enough illustrations have been given to indicate the general proposal here. We wish to determine if there are any general laws governing semantic combination. The existence of a mathematical model (e.g., the semantic space about an arbitrary origin defined by a set of factor coordinates in which any meaning is represented as a unique point) facilitates the statement of hypotheses and indicates the nature of the tests to be made. The general procedure would be to have the same subjects, at different times, differentiate various component words and combinations of these components, and then determine if any general statements can be made about the semantic results of combinations. There may be some indirect utility for linguistics here, for example on the problem of semantic units. Whereas the combinations POWERFUL MALE and MASCULINE POWER should fall on the line in semantic space defined by the locations of MALE (MASCULINE) and POWER (POWERFUL), and the combination DOGGY HEAT fall on the line defined by HEAT and DOG, this would not be true for the combination HOT DOG—indicating that this has become a new semantic unit.

(2) *Quantitative study of opposition.* Some 20 or more years ago C. K. Ogden brought out a delightful little book on the nature of opposition. In it he analysed on logical grounds various types of opposites. The semantic differential seems to offer a quantitative way of approaching the same problem. Complete or *logical opposites* should yield perfectly reciprocal profiles, i.e., determine points in the semantic space which are at equal distances on opposite ends of a single straight line through the origin. FRESH (*good*, *active*, and *somewhat strong*) and STALE (*bad*, *passive*, and *somewhat weak*) might be an example. What might be called *psychological opposites* would be polar with respect to one dimension but fall at the same locus on others, i.e., define a line parallel to one factor but displaced from the origin. An example might be GOD (*good*, *strong*, and *active*) and DEVIL (*bad*, *strong*, and *active*). A third type might be called *relational contrasts*, which are not really opposites at all. Examples would be SOLDIER and SAILOR, HAND and FOOT, DOG and CAT—in such cases the points in semantic space are not in opposite directions of the space, in all probability, but rather close together. They display strong *linguistic* contrast, in that they constitute minimal pairs which have nearly identical contextual samplings

(i.e., occur in the same environments). This type of measurement would also permit definition and comparison of *degrees* of opposition among a group of possibilities (as found in standard dictionaries of similars and opposites).

(3) *Onomatopoeia.* Another problem of interest to the linguist as well as the psychologist and student of aesthetics concerns the possible meanings associated with speech sounds. There seems to be almost universal agreement among linguists that sound symbolism is a myth, or better that it is always a function of particular associations with meaningful words in a given language. Thus the common association of /i/ with smallness and thinness is simply a cultural accident. This attitude doesn't jibe with the existing evidence, such as it is— the studies of Sapir, Stanley Newman, Fischer-Jørgensen, and a few others are all positive in trend, although inadequate in controls. The proposed investigation would employ a complex analysis of variance design in which the same phones (initial, medial, and terminal) would be made to occur in various phonetic environments in nonsense syllables for English and some other language, say Spanish. These materials would be tape recorded by a trained phonetician; subjects would use the semantic differential to register the connotative meanings of each sound. Question 1. Do speakers of English show consistent deviations in meaning as a function of a particular phone, regardless of the total sound context (e.g., does /s/ tend to make a nonsense combination *smaller, thinner,* and *more active* regardless of context)? Question 2. Do listeners who speak another language show correlated effects, e.g., are the onomatopoeic effects common cross-linguistically? Question 3. Can these onomatopoeic effects be related to general synesthetic phenomena, e.g., will higher pitch vowels tend to be *smaller* and *brighter* than low pitch vowels?

(4) *Cross-cultural generality of semantic factors.* An underlying theoretical question is the generality of semantic factors cross-culturally and cross-linguistically. If it could be shown that essentially the same factors operate in the meaningful judgments of all people, regardless of culture, race, and language— that they all differentiate concepts in terms of evaluation, potency, activity, and so forth—then many new approaches to cross-cultural communication and understanding would be opened up. One could, for example, do a much better job of explaining his own nation's values, interests and motives if he could choose concepts and qualifiers in the other language which he knew had corresponding significances.

(5) *A functional dictionary of connotative meaning.* Almost daily professional people who deal with communication—teachers, writers, journalists propagandists, advertisers, politicians, and so on—are faced with the problem of selecting words to convey their intentions to others. The ordinary dictionary provides little information on connotations, and Roget's Thesaurus is not only indefinite in this respect but is also prone to projection on the part of the user (e.g., he selects in terms of his private meanings rather than those typical of his audience). The work done so far on the measurement of meanings of adjectives and nouns encourages us to believe that at some later time, when the factor system has been better stabilized, it will be feasible to construct a *functional*

(e.g., representative of word-meanings as they are used by people) and *quantized* (e.g., presented in terms of quantitative units provided by the differential) dictionary of connotative meanings.

The operations of semantic differentiation allow us to indicate the meaning of any verbal concept as a point in an n-dimensional space; this point can also be defined by a series of index numbers representing locations along the set of factors. Using a sample of subjects, carefully drawn to be representative of the population, the point (and the index numbers) would represent the mean location of the sample and another number would indicate the dispersion of the individual points about this mean (i.e., the variability in meaning of this concept). The concepts in this functional dictionary would be arranged in double classification: once in ordinary alphabetical arrangement (e.g., NOBLE: 134xxxx, indicating this word to be extremely favorable, somewhat potent, neither active nor passive, and so on for additional factors) and once according to location in semantic space (e.g., under 134xxxx in a distribution running the gamut from 7777777 to 1111111 one would find NOBLE along with all other words having the same connotative meaning, and in their neighborhood would be found similar meanings).

There are several ways in which such a functional dictionary could be used. For example, one could look up a particular noun, such as WARRIOR, and find a group of adjectives having closely similar connotative meaning, or one could find another group of adjectives similar in all respects except one, say evaluation (e.g., if WARRIOR were 322xxxx, one might look under 722xxxx and find words like *vicious*, *savage*, and *barbaric*). In other words, one could move in any desired direction from a given point in the space and find appropriate words. Wishing to choose an adjective which accurately represents *for other people* one's *own* meaning for a concept, one could quickly differentiate his own meaning for the concept and then look into the functional dictionary under the index thus derived for words having appropriate connotation. An interesting derivative of this work could be study of *semantic isoglosses* (e.g., geographical boundaries across which the meanings of common words shift) in much the same manner that linguists have studied phonemic isoglosses.

7.3. *Information Transmission by Language Messages*

Language is the chief ingredient of the cement which holds societies together over both space and time. One of the prime goals of the student of communication is therefore an understanding of the way in which information (in the colloquial sense) is transmitted from one individual to another via language messages. Measurement of information transfer in this sense may make use of information theory. One may estimate the reduction in uncertainty of the behavior of a human destination as a function of messages received from another human source. The reduction in uncertainty (or increase in predictability) could be expressed as so many 'bits' of information (in the mathematical sense). This approach is most applicable when the codes used by source and destination are the same. When source and destination use different and equally arbitrary codes, however—that is, when we are dealing with information transfer in translation situations—new problems are introduced and information theory conceptions require some extension.

7.3.1. *Information Transmission without Code Translation*[93]

In section 2.3. of this report, one bit of information was defined as the amount of information needed to specify one of two classes of equally probable events. There are at least two possible modifications of this definition which allow us to measure the amount of information transmission in a language message. These modifications are discussed below and their usefulness evaluated.

7.3.1.1. *Information transmitted by language signals.* The first modification of the definition of the unit of information is as follows: *If each of two equiprobable language stimuli unequivocally elicits a different response, then each of the pair of stimuli transmits one bit of information.* From this definition it is easy to proceed to a general equation for measuring information transmission in terms of such units. Let s be any of a set of language stimuli, S, each of which elicits a response r which is one of set of responses, R. Let p(s) and p(r) be the probabilities of any s or r, and let $p_s(r)$ be the appropriate conditional probability. Furthermore, let us assume that these probabilities are unchanged throughout the period of measurement.

This entire set of definitions permits us to treat language message stimuli as a set of input events, the responses to these stimuli as output events, and the receivers of these messages as communication channels. Thus it is possible to use the conventional measurement of information transmission, I_t, which will give the average amount of information transmitted by the set S. Using the symbols introduced above, I_t becomes $I_t = H(R) - H_s(R)$. If responses to the stimuli are independent of the stimuli, then $H(R) = H_s(R)$ so that $I_t = 0$. If only one response is made to each stimulus (i.e., if for every s, only one $p_s(r) = 1$), then $H_s(R) = 0$ and $I_t = H(R) = H(S)$.

An example of the kind of situation to which this sort of information measurement is appropriate is that of military drill in which language stimuli serve as stimuli for a set of immediately executed responses. In such situations, the language stimuli serve as signals in the same manner that traffic lights or the dials on a control panel serve as signals. However, many language messages do not serve as signal stimuli in this sense but rather serve to modify behavior to stimuli *other than* those in the message itself. Another modification of the definition of the unit of information measurement which may be supplied in this kind of situation is given below.

7.3.1.2. *Information transmitted by conventional language messages.* The second modification of the definition of the unit of information measurement is as follows: *If the receivers of a message make two responses randomly to each of two equiprobable stimuli before message reception but make only one of these responses to the stimuli after message reception, then one bit of information has been trans-*

[93] Kellogg Wilson.

mitted by the message. Let S and R be classes of extra-message stimuli and responses and let s and r be any members of these classes. Let p(s) represent the probability of any s and assume that all p(s) remain unchanged by transmission and reception of the message. Let $p_s(r)$ be the pre-message conditional probability of a response r to a stimulus s and let $p_s'(r)$ be the corresponding post-message probability.

Using the entire set of definitions introduced above, our measure of I_t becomes

$$I_t = H_S(R) - H_s'(R) = -\sum_s p(s) \sum_r p_S(r) \log_2 p_S(r) + \sum_s p(s) \sum_r p_s'(r) \log_2 p_{s_1}'(r).$$

If the message has no effect on behavior and $H_s'(R) = H_S(R)$, then $I_t = 0$. If the message eliminates the entropy of behavior so that behavior is completely predictable and $H_s'(R) = 0$, then $I_t = H_S(R)$, the pre-message behavioral entropy. In general, I_t gives the amount of the entropy change produced by the message where the unit of change is the amount of entropy reduction associated with the development of a perfect discrimination from a random discrimination between two equiprobable stimuli.

This measure has two characteristics which should be noted.

(a) I_t is dependent on the characteristics of the receivers and on the situation in which the set of $p_s(r)$'s and $p_s'(r)$'s are estimated.

(b) I_t is dependent on the pre-message behavioral tendencies of the receivers.

Unlike the previous measure of I_t, which considers the probabilities of the elements in the message, this measure treats the message as a sort of unitary *deus ex machina* which somehow modifies response tendencies. This sort of treatment allows us to avoid estimation of the probabilities of the units of the message but at best only permits us to postpone the identification of the message units which produce behavioral change and the means by which this change occurs. Unfortunately, our present knowledge permits us to only speculate concerning these units and the nature of their effects.

7.3.2. *Information Transmission with Code Translation*[94]

Translation is usually regarded as a tool which is improved only by experience and good judgment on the part of translators. The development of information theory techniques and electronic computers has created increasing interest in both theoretical and practical problems of translation, and it may be worthwhile to analyse translation as a psycholinguistic process (see also section 6.2). Information theory provides a general model in which the translator, whether human or machine, is treated as a channel, the foreign or 'from' language (FL) is the input, and the translation or 'to' language (TL) is the output. (For problems of translation as currently viewed by some linguists, see now also International Journal of American Linguistics 20:4 [1954]).

7.3.2.1. *Need for addition to information theory model.* Let us first imagine a machine translator between languages A and B. If whenever a given input

[94] Susan M. Ervin.

state in A occurs (e.g., scanning of the German word *Pferd*) the machine reliably produces a specific output state in B (e.g., prints the English word *house*), conditional entropy would be zero and information transmission would appear to be perfect—except that it could be complete gibberish. What is accomplished here is actually a translation of the FL into some one of a near infinity of *possible* TL's, but not English. We would like our machine translator to produce with equal consistency the output *horse* when *Pferd* occurs—and this is only a minimal requirement. This highlights a fundamental limitation of information theory— it has nothing to say about the *correspondence* between the states of two systems associated in a channel. The measured information transfer would be the same and maximal for a machine which translated *Pferd/house* and so forth at random as for a machine which translated *Pferd/horse* and so forth, as long as *some* specific output state was completely dependent upon each specific input state.

Figure 21 may help to make this situation clear, as well as the kind of extension needed. Some SOURCE, perhaps the writer of a book of perhaps the reporter of certain NON-MESSAGE EVENTS, encodes in MESSAGE SYSTEM A (FL); the role of the translator, human or machine, is to decode these signals and then encode *non-corresponding but equivalent* signals in MESSAGE SYSTEM B (TL); this translated message may then be decoded by some DESTINATION and it may influence his behavior with respect to certain NON-MESSAGE EVENTS. The crux of the problem lies in the phrase, 'non-corresponding but equivalent' above. We must take as given the fact that the message events in two languages cannot be corresponding in any physical sense (except for occasional cognates and the like) *but can be equivalent in the sense that they are associated with corresponding states in source and destination systems.*

The particular physical events which, in the message code, come to represent semantic states or non-message events are completely arbitrary; on the other hand, given the similarity of human organisms and the generality of learning principles, one would expect considerable correspondence in semantic states (e.g., the behaviors of both German and English speakers to the object HORSE may be similar and hence the representational processes associated with *Pferd* in the one case and *horse* in the other could be similar). In other words, *equivalence* of events in FL and TL is defined by *correspondence* of those events in source and destination which are associated with the FL and TL events respectively. Input *Pferd* is equivalent to output *horse* in translation because the semantic intention in the German source encoding *Pferd* corresponds closely to the se-

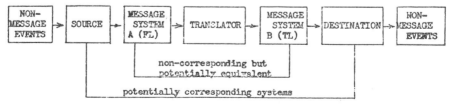

Figure 21

mantic significance in the English receiver decoding *horse*. This analysis admittedly throws the gates wide to the demon 'meaning' (with all its fuzziness and complexity), but to rule it out seems to also rule out by definition the central problem.

The necessary addition to information theory measures can only be suggested here. The following notions[95] may be useful in describing the translation process:

Correspondence between any two systems is the proportion of the states in one that are identical with states of the other.

Stability of a system (e.g., translator) refers to the reliability with which it transforms input states into predictable output states.

$$S = H(O) - H_I(O)$$

This measure is equivalent to that of information transfer in section 7.3.1.1. and indicates the degree to which states in TL are predictable from states in FL, regardless of their translation equivalence.

Translation-equivalent states of two message systems are those associated with corresponding states in sources (using one language) and destinations (using the other language). The rules for specifying such correspondences would, of course, need to be made explicit.

Fidelity of a system (e.g., translator) is the validity with which it transforms input states into equivalent output states.

$$F = \sum_{m,n} p(m, n = m)$$

Where m is any one of the states of the FL and n is any one of the states of the TL. $p(m, n = m)$ is simply the probability of a corresponding state of TL occurring with a given state, m, of FL. This is not an information theory measure and does not yield an estimate of information transfer in bits; rather, it is a simple percentage measure—the proportion of all input events which result in equivalent output events, as these have been defined.

The specification of states of message systems which are correlated with states of encoders and decoders (problem of units), establishing criteria of stability, establishing criteria of fidelity, and the treatment of non-equivalent states are all problems which arise no matter what kind of analysis of the translation process one chooses and no matter whether one deals with human or machine translation. The following discussion attempts to highlight certain of these problems, but does not provide any definite answers to them.

7.3.2.2. *Specification of states of message systems.* (1) *The size of units.* Since the establishment of units of equivalence must be done on the basis of meaning, the choices of units to be used in describing states of the systems cannot be arbitrary. There may be situations in which it would be appropriate to deal with morphemic units, or utterances or sequences of utterances as units. For example, the following two utterances have a correspondence of meaning even though the smaller units do not correspond: 'The barn door is locked' = 'Precautions have been taken.' The size of the unit used in establishing correspondence

---

[95] Terminology and definitions are from Osgood and Wilson, *A general model of the communication process*, unpublished mimeographed paper.

may restrict the kind of operations possible in measuring stability and fidelity; the procedures one would use to establish meaning equivalence for two morphemes might not be the same as those used in measuring equivalence for two utterances.

(2) *Simultaneous states.* As soon as one attempts to establish correspondence between two utterances it becomes clear that there may be complex interrelations between morpheme choice, order, grammatical patterns, stress, and pitch.

For example, in the following sentences changes in English stress and intonation correspond to changes in French intonation and constructions.

a $_2$Is $_3$patriotism a $_1$vir$_3$tue?   a'   Le patriotisme est une vertu?
                                                      a"   Le patriotisme est-ce une vertu?
                                                      a'" Est-ce que le patriotisme est une vertu?
b $_2$Is $_3$patriotism a virtue?   b'   Est-ce le patriotisme qui est une vertu?
c $_2$Is patriotism a $_3$virtue?   c'   Est-ce une vertu que le patriotisme?
d $_3$Is patriotism a vir$_2$tue?   d' $_3$Est-ce que le patriotisme est une vertu?

English sentences *a* and *b* differ only in intonation patterns; in French the difference is one of grammatical construction. The difference between *b* and *c* is chiefly one of stress, but *b'* and *c'* differ again in grammatical construction. On the other hand, the French *a' "* and *d'* differ only in intonation, but the corresponding English *a* and *d* differ both in stress and intonation. It is possible to set up rules for this set of translations, but the description of states must simultaneously include stress (for English), intonation, and grammatical construction pattern if it is to handle the correspondences adequately. Some of the initial work on this general problem has already been done by those studying machine translation.

7.3.2.3. *Establishing criteria of stability.* The stability measure could be applied to the same input at different points in time, or to input as translated by different translators—in other words, it can be used either as a measure of test-retest reliability or as a measure of intercoder reliability.

In either case it is necessary to decide how large a class of events shall be considered the same event for purposes of scoring stability. For example, the same input event may result in the following output events: 'crimson,' 'red,' and 'blue.' These might be considered three different events, two, or perhaps even one. Even in a translation situation in which the alternative possible output events are arbitrarily limited there will be a problem of degrees and kinds of meaning difference between the possible output events. A stability measure which is equally sensitive to trivial and to gross differences may prove to be less useful than one which takes into account semantic relations between output events. Unfortunately, although linguistic analysis may help to classify some differences—for example, in grammatical structure of two utterances—it stops short of the semantic evaluation which is necessary in order to deal with degrees of difference. Some other methods are necessary in dealing with this problem. It would probably be advisable at this point to set up an experiment with limited output alternatives and develop some provisional classifications. It may be found that for this kind of work even a crude method of meaning measurement is adequate.

Among the methods which should be investigated further in this context are the following:

(a) *Rating by speakers.* This is the simplest and possibly the most comprehensive method. It is not known how much agreement can be reached, or what the effects of various kinds of instructions on speakers asked to rate differences in meaning may be.

(b) *The semantic differential.* This method has been applied to words in context and it may prove adaptable to the problems of meaning differences between utterances. Like the word association method, however, it uses a lexical item as the primary stimulus and may not be sufficiently sensitive to grammatical relations, for example.

(c) *Word associations.* One method of establishing a measure would be to have subjects associate to words in a context, giving a series of associations to the same word. These associations could be listed in rank order of frequency, and the lists equated in length by omission of the least frequent items on the longer lists. A measure of likeness in lexical meaning of two items is the proportion of identical associations given to them.

7.3.2.4. *Establishing criteria of fidelity.* The crucial operation in establishing fidelity is actually demarking the equivalent units in input and output systems. Equivalent message events have been defined as those associated with identical (or, at least, highly similar) semantic states in encoder (FL) and decoder (TL). In order to establish such identity, there must be some common system to use for comparison; this might be called the yardstick system. In practice, the two yardstick systems used in translation are external referents and the mediating systems of bilinguals. A third system might consist of non-linguistic responses to the test events by monolinguals who speak the input and output languages.

(a) *The judgment of bilinguals.* Asking a bilingual whether two utterances in different languages have the same meaning is a procedure which presents some of the same problems as the rating of meaning differences by speakers of one language. It is not clear what kind of meaning he is thinking of when he makes the judgment, nor is it known how much likeness of meaning he considers necessary to justify a statement of identity. It may be that one translation conveys the emotional tone of the FL utterance more fully but that another is referentially more exact. Another difficulty is that it is not known how much the judgment of bilinguals regarding meanings may be distorted by the knowledge of two languages (see section 6.2). If, for example, it were shown that bilinguals and monolinguals typically have different semantic differential profiles for the same words, the judgment of bilinguals regarding the connotative subtleties of many words would have to be questioned.

(b) *External definition by referents.* Another method would be establishing common referents through determining the range of objects and situations to which a term or set of terms can refer. This would show quite definitely when a term in one system has only partial referential overlap with one in another system, but there are at least three major drawbacks: It is necessarily laborious in any instance where many terms are involved. Furthermore, the method is most useful for objects and becomes less useful for abstractions and for emotional referents or complex referents. Finally, there are certain kinds of correspondence—such as certain propositional values or feelings about the proposition, which might be conveyed by style—which it would be almost impossible to demonstrate through this method.

(c) *The semantic differential.* If a translatable form of the semantic differential could be obtained, using cross-culturally uniform dimensions, responses to the differential might be used as a test for equivalence of meaning. The differential would have certain advantages here. It could show whether items which are referentially equivalent according to ostensive definition have a shift in meaning in certain contexts. 'Applesauce' or 'baloney' have been given as examples of identifiable substances according to one usage, but in other contexts the terms take on entirely different meanings about synonymous with 'nonsense.' 'Applesauce' according to the second meaning is not 'sauce made of apples' at all; the differential could show when a combination of morphemes gives rise to a meaning not predictable from the component morphs and their rules of combination (see section 7.2.2.4 under 'word mixture'). The differential may also be sensitive to differences in meaning due to differences in the social situations or speakers associated with certain terms, although this fact remains to be demonstrated. For example, it might show that a 'gat' and 'un pistolet' are not equivalent semantically.

(d) *Responses to utterances.* If utterances can be constructed so that some overt response is required to them, preferably non-linguistic, equivalence of response under comparable conditions could be considered a measure of meaning equivalence in the total utterance. This is a method which could be used to show differences in meaning arising from other sources than lack of fidelity in translation of lexical states alone. One of the difficulties in this procedure is that it requires the use of bilinguals so that response differences in the two languages are not due to culture differences. Using sufficiently large matched groups of subjects, one could test which of several versions of the TL produced responses most like those given to the FL utterance.

7.3.2.5. *Treatment of non-equivalent states.* Assuming that one establishes equivalences between lexical elements, intonation, stress, and grammatical constructions there will still be certain non-equivalent states left over. These features of the TL which cannot be predicted from the FL, even when translation procedures have maximum fidelity, are of two kinds: One consists of states required by the rules of the code, such as the gender suffixes on Spanish adjectives. These states do not present a problem, because presumably they are completely predictable from knowledge of the equivalent states in the FL plus the rules of the TL code. Thus, if it is known that 'girl' corresponds to 'muchacha' it can be predicted that other forms bearing a specifiable relation to 'muchacha' will have feminine suffixes when Spanish is the TL. There are other kinds of states required by the code which are not entirely predictable from the rest of the utterance in some contexts. Such, for example, are English tense and number. These forms require some semantic information; they are not redundant, except insofar as one is dealing with agreement. If English is the TL, and one is using as an FL a language which does not specify number, the English code requires information which is not directly dependent on that supplied by the FL. If this information can be obtained from context by explicit rules there is no difficulty. However, it may have to be inserted by sheer guessing on the part of the translator. On the other hand, the FL may codify information which is not normally codified in the TL.

Many instances of loss of information in translation probably arise from apparent stylistic awkwardness arising from an attempt to codify all the information conveyed by the FL. For instance, several Northwest Coast languages require specification of the source of information in making assertions. If this part of the input were translated into English output the result would not only be awkward but it would mean undue emphasis. Codifying of information in the TL which that language rarely codifies itself may be misleading. A translation from Korean which translated social status information fully might give a false impression of the intent or effect of the utterance. Certainly its effect on an English listener would not be the same as the effect of the input utterance on a Korean, which might be an indication in itself of distortion of meaning.

One might consider these as rather precious points, but they are questions of judgment which face any translator and hence suggest studies of factors in making such choices. Such studies might vary the kind of instructions given translators, e.g., the kind of information supplied to them about the intent of the speaker or the purpose of the translation or the target audience. Since variation in the information contained in equivalent states may lead to shifts in treatment of non-equivalent states, the message itself should also be manipulated by the experimenter.

7.3.2.6. *A note on back-translation.* One of the most convenient techniques for pointing up lack of fidelity in a translation is retranslating the material into the FL. Essentially this method repeats the translation process through a *different system*. There is no reason, therefore, to expect that even a translation with maximum fidelity can be retranslated to utterances identical with the initial input. One reason for this change is that the probabilities of certain translations may differ when a given language is input rather than output, due to differences in frequency of usage of partially equivalent terms and differences in the variety of referents for each term.

For example, assume in the following set of French and English terms that 'box' is used for more terms than 'boîte;' for many of the referents of 'box,' the French term would be 'étui.' In this system, the probability of occurrence of the term 'box' is therefore greater than the probability of 'boîte.' Further, the term 'portfolio' has only one corresponding French term, 'serviette,' but 'serviette' has three corresponding English terms. 'Portfolio' would occur less frequently than 'serviette.'

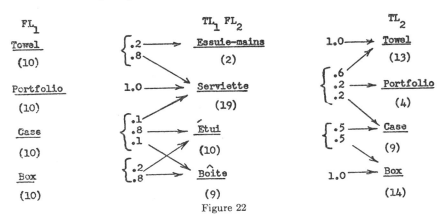

Figure 22

The consequences on the back-translation can be seen from the input-output probabilities in a minimum context arrangement. The highly frequent term 'box' is back-translated as 'box' 90 per cent of the times it occurs in FL_1 and in addition 10 per cent of the FL_1 occurrences of 'case' are back-translated as 'box,' resulting in an increase in frequency of 'box.' The infrequent 'portfolio' fares less well in back-translation and loses 60 per cent of its frequency in FL_1. It appears in TL_2 only 20 per cent of the times it occurred in the FL_1 input, in addition to being back-translated in place of 16 per cent of the occurrences of 'towel' and two per cent of the occurrences of 'case.'

Back-translations may reveal instances of only partial equivalence, but it is necessary to have sufficient frequencies of occurrence to establish the probabilities. In the above example, back-translation shifted the frequencies markedly in three of the four terms, pointing to the possibility of only partial correspondence in referents. Some guesses about the semantic relations between the terms can be gathered by examining the probabilities within the matrices. If there are traditional translation terms, back-translation cannot be used for revealing non-equivalence, because it results in reciprocal biases in the two translation processes. Thus, if 'aimer' were always translated as 'love' in English, and vice versa, the partial equivalence between the two terms would never be revealed in back-translation into French. Experimentation with back-translation using frequency data thus may demonstrate its possibilities and limitations as a tool for revealing partial or complete non-equivalence in translation.

7.4. Language, Cognition, and Culture[96]

The relation of language to culture and cognition is of particular concern because of the determinative influence which language is supposed to exert on the other two variables. The writings of Benjamin Whorf and the others who have followed his example present this view in its clearest form, although the general thesis has a long tradition both on this continent with Franz Boas and Edward Sapir and in Europe from Herder through von Humboldt to Ernst Cassirer, Leo Weisgerber, and Jost Trier. However, research in this area has been complicated by terminological and methodological confusion and failure to state hypotheses in testable form. Recently, this thesis has been studied critically by several groups of interested anthropologists, linguists, and psychologists. The Wenner-Gren Foundation International Symposium on Anthropology[97] and the Conference of Anthropologists and Linguists[98] included the Weltanschauung problem on their agenda, and a special Conference on Ethnolinguistics[99] was held specifically to consider its ramifications and to develop a program of research. The material presented at these meetings can neither be summarized nor adequately evaluated in the space available here, although it certainly influenced the discussions of the seminar.

7.4.1. Terminological Problems

A necessary prerequisite for research in this area is independent definitions of the critical terms. One common confusion, most typical of those who deal with the problem in 'language vs. culture' terms, is failure to distinguish language as a message system external to the particular user from language as states of its users, e.g., as meanings, attitudes and the like. We restrict the term

---

[96] Donald E. Walker, James J. Jenkins, and Thomas A. Sebeok.

[97] A. L. Kroeber, ed. Anthropology today (Chicago, 1953).

[98] C. Levi-Straus, et al., Results of the Conference of Anthropologists and Linguists, Indiana University Publications in Anthropology and Linguistics, Memoir 8 (1953).

[99] Conference on Ethnolinguistics, Chicago, March 23–27, 1953.

'language' to the former (messages) and use the term 'cognition' for the latter (states of its users). Within this restriction of the term 'language' there is still another confusion—between what has come to be called *langue* (the system or codification) and *parole* (the particular manifestations or instances of language behavior). This comes out clearly in statements such as "anything *can* be expressed in any language, but the structure of a given language will favor certain statements and hinder others." For the most part (e.g., in Whorf's work), the question has centered about the relation of systems of codification ('langue') to cognition and culture, and we accordingly restrict our usage of the term 'language' to mean codification. The term 'culture' seems too broad to be dealt with successfully, at least at the research level. For our own purposes, therefore we substitute the term 'behavior,' by which we mean overt activities with respect to social and physical objects which may be to varying degrees shared with other members of a language community.

If language were to be treated as somehow independent of culture, it would be necessary to develop experimental situations which are wholly 'culture-free' in which we could observe behavior. However, the vast literature criticizing these attempts is a demonstration of the pitfalls which await the unwary here. The search for universally familiar or unfamiliar test materials is only a beginning. Culturally conditioned differences in motivation, personality, and so forth immediately interject themselves. The dilemma is made clear by considering the two courses of action available: first, one may make an *a priori* judgment that an experimental situation is culture-free—but the history of such attempts indicates that no two authorities ever agree. Secondly, one may try to demonstrate empirically that a situation *is* culture-free. This involves comparing across a large number of cultures and demonstrating lack of difference in the behavior elicited in this situation—but such experimental situations would be useless from that point on, since the ultimate objective is to study differences between cultures. In other words, it seemed to the seminar that the notion that 'language is independent of culture' is patently untestable.

We may rephrase the general issue here as follows: *we wish to set up experimental situations in which relations between codification, cognition, and behavior can be studied.* By *codification* we will mean all those aspects of speech behavior which are forced upon the individual speaker by the rules of his language, infringment of which results in defective communication. Codification must be thought of as including the phonemic, morphemic, and syntactic structure of a given language, as well as the lexicon. If I am to communicate about colors I must employ the color-terms available in the language, and languages will differ in how their color terminology 'carves up' the physical spectrum: I must also follow the grammatical rules by which lexical items are compounded in the language. By *cognition* we will mean those representational processes in language users whereby certain stimulus patterns (signs) come to stand for other stimulus patterns (significates). Cognitive processes will be functioning in such total activities as perceptual organization, recognition, retention, thinking, concept formation, and problem solving. By *behavior* we will mean nothing more than these total activities—of perceptual organization (e.g., sorting colored yarns into discrete piles), recognition (e.g., pointing to those color patches previously shown amongst a larger number), and so forth. One of the major hypotheses under test, of course, is that these performances will vary as a function of codification of language.

7.4.2. Methodological Problems

The human infant enters this world at some place on its surface and finds himself among adults who have certain stable ways of behaving toward physical objects and in social situations and who use a language which has a certain codification. Gradually he learns how to behave like others do, i.e., learns the culture, and in doing so simultaneously develops elaborate systems of cognitions (ways of perceiving, meanings, associations, attitudes, and so forth), *and* also simultaneously he learns the language, associating auditory stimulus patterns with cognitions (decoding) and cognitions with vocal behaviors (encoding), both according to the rules of the code. Given this complete interweaving of culture, cognition, and language in the course of development, it is not surprising that social scientists later find it difficult to disentangle the threads. The greatest single pitfall in the way of research in this area is thus *circularity of inference.* "People in different cultures have different 'world views' *because* their languages differ (e.g., the Hopi have different time conceptions because their language uses a different tense system). How do we know their 'world views' differ? Why, because they use language differently!" To escape from this tautological trap, the independent and dependent variables, language structure and 'world view,' must be independently measured.

(1) *Independent indices.* It is possible to describe similarities and differences in *codification* of languages almost completely independent of the cognitions and behaviors of their users. This is the special technical job of descriptive linguists, and their only dependence upon the cognition-behavior of informants is solicitation of judgments of same or different in meaning. It is not so easy to distinguish *cognitions* from *behavior.* As a matter of fact, all the psychologist or anthropologist can observe is situations and behaviors—cognitive states are always matters of inference. However, there are reliable rules for making such inferences *and it is possible to experimentally segregate the behavioral indices of cognitions from the behavioral performances that serve as the dependent variables in concrete research situations.* This will be evident in the design of some of the experiments which follow. Of course, in many cases it is not necessary to make a sharp distinction between cognition and behavior; it may be sufficient to demonstrate that behavior-as-dependent-upon-cognition is influenced by codification.

(2) *Fallacy in translation methods.* A method frequently used by Whorf and others to 'prove' that differences in 'world view' stem from differences in codification is to translate some utterance from one language quite literally and in most general, abstract terms into another, usually English. Thus we find what we would call a 'dripping spring' being translated from Apache 'as water, whiteness moves downward,' and implications for 'world view' or ways of perceiving are drawn from the differences *in English.* Lenneberg has criticized this procedure on several grounds.[100] Indeed, if we were to translate the English statement *a/drip(p)/ing/spring* into its most literal and abstract terms, we would come out with something like "An instance of the general class, characterized by liquid falling in small, natural segments, process on-going, eruption of water," and most speakers of Eng-

---

[100] *Language* **29**. 463–71 (1953).

lish would fail to recognize their own 'world view'! Another limitation of the translation method is that it distorts the significance of metaphors, with which languages abound but which have lost their literal significance entirely. What would the Apache ethnolinguist conclude about the English 'world view' from literal translations of 'in the face of,' 'breakfast,' 'beforehand,' and the like?

(3) *Intra-cultural and cross-cultural designs.* The Weltanschauung problem seems to require experimental designs which draw comparisons across cultures, and most of the research—or perhaps better, observation—has been of this sort. But this is not necessarily the case. As will be seen below, many of the specific hypotheses which derive from the general thesis that language affects thought and culture can be as adequately tested within a single language-culture community. If it can be shown that the way a single language codifies continuous sensory experiences affects the behavior of its users with respect to these sensory experiences, this certainly makes more feasible the broader notion that between-culture/between-language differences in codification should affect behavior. And, as a matter of fact, intra-cultural designs usually offer more stringent controls than cross-cultural designs, because of the difficulty in the latter case of disentangling 'cultural' variables from codification per se.

7.4.3. *Restatement of Hypotheses and Concrete Research Designs*

In the most general sense, Whorf assumed that people in different cultures perceive the world differently and drew his data for this assertion chiefly from differences in language. What is asserted beyond this point is hard to come to grips with. Sometimes it seems to be implied that people see the world differently *because* they have different languages and sometimes it appears that people perceive the world differently and this is *merely correlated* with language differences. Available evidence seems to justify the statement of correlation, but the causal direction is by no means clear. Obviously, what one is actually claiming is of the utmost importance in any serious attempt to deal with the Weltanschauung problem experimentally, and the following statements try to formulate an interrelated set of hypotheses in testable form. Illustrative experiments, both available and proposed, are described under each hypothesis.

7.4.3.1. *Cognition and behavior.* Although not directly involved in the Whorf view, since nothing here is said about language per se, an assumption underlying all of this work is that cognitive states are determinants of overt behavior—or, more generally, that ways of perceiving and conceiving the world affect behavior norms toward physical objects and in social situations (culture). The reverse relation must also be stated—that behavior influences cognitions—and this, in the more general form, is the notion that people in different cultures will view the world differently, quite apart from and beyond language factors per se.

Hypothesis I. The cognitive states associated with stimuli influence the responses made to these stimuli. The independent variable here is cognitive state, which must be indexed independently of the measurement of the overt behavior to test situations, which is the dependent variable. The type of cognitive state involved in a given experiment may be 'way of perceiving,' meaning, attitude, or so on, and the behavior observed may be solution of problems, simple bodily movement, or even 'cultural response,' such as normative behavior to an eclipse or lack of rain. At the common-sense level, this hypothesis is trite. Obviously, how a man reacts to a situation—by fighting, by running, by spending his money, by praying—depends upon what the situation means to him; obviously, how a member of any culture responds to a Rorschach test depends upon how he perceives it, upon what significance the shapes have to him. But this hypothesis can have more subtle implications, as the following experiments show.

Cofer and his coworkers have shown that the ability to solve a problem may hinge on the presence of word associations. They experimented with the Maier 'two-string problem' in which two strings are suspended from the ceiling in such a manner that a subject cannot reach both strings at once. The problem is to tie them together. One 'insightful' solution is to tie something on one string, making a pendulum, start it swinging, hold the other string, and catch the pendulum string at the end of its return arc. By the use of word association techniques it was found that people making 'pendulum solutions' had the association 'rope-swing' at fairly high strength. In a second experiment subjects were asked to learn lists of paired words. One group learned 'rope-swing' as a pair in a list. Other groups did not have these words paired, although the individual words were in the lists. At a later time these groups were tested on the two-string problem, and the group which had learned the appropriate word pair made the most pendulum solutions. (None of the subjects knew there was a connection between the memorizing and the problem solving and none of them cited the word association as a reason for giving that particular solution.) In other studies Cofer has shown that it is also possible to inhibit correct solutions by having subjects learn misleading associations.

Sets of semantic relations may also influence problem solving. It has been shown that certain descriptive dimensions are highly interrelated—words like 'up' and 'top' are associated with 'light' (in weight), 'light' (in color), and 'small,' while words like 'down' and 'bottom' are associated with 'heavy,' 'dark,' and 'large.' Thus we may think of a set of covariant dimensions: 'up-down,' 'top-bottom,' 'light-heavy,' 'light-dark,' and 'small-large.' Solley[101] has shown that congruence of these dimensions may facilitate problem solving and incongruence may hinder problem solving. His experimental task was the classic 'pyramid puzzle.' The subject is presented with a board with three pegs in it. On one of the pegs is a pyramid of disks of decreasing size. The problem is to transfer the pyramid to one of the other pegs, moving only one disk at a time and never putting a larger disk on top of a smaller one. If the task starts with an inverted pyramid, the rules are the same except that a smaller disk may not be placed upon a larger one. Varying the color, weight, and size of the disks, Solley found that the most rapid solutions were made in the situation in which all the dimensions were congruent (i.e., the top disk was smallest, lightest in weight and in color, while the bottom disk was largest, heaviest and darkest). The most difficult situation was that in which the concordance of the verbal relations with the problem was least. As each dimension was altered, the problem became more difficult.

These studies are intra-cultural, but the same or similar designs could be used cross-culturally. For example, could it be shown that the various types of solutions of the hanging-strings problem (pendulum, tying an extension on one string, elevating oneself by standing on some object, etc.) have significantly different frequencies for members of different cultures? Assuming that members of different cultures have somewhat different semantic structures (e.g., such that *light-dark* is independent of *up-down*, for example), would their performance on Solley's pyramid problem differ? A number of designs of this sort are feasible.

Hypothesis II. The behavior initially elicited by stimuli influences the cognitive

---

[101] Unpublished research, University of Illinois.

states that come to be associated with signs of these stimuli. This is the converse of Hypothesis I, and it raises the issue as to the origin and development of cognitive processes. A large number of psychologists, despite their haggling over mechanism, would agree that meanings, ways of perceiving, concepts, and the like develop out of the matrix of behavior toward objects and situations. Even at the sub-human level of the rat, many experiments demonstrate that the significance of an originally neutral stimulus, e.g., a buzzer signal, can be modified by association with food, shock, and the like and the total behaviors these stimulus-objects elicit. Similarly, at the intra-cultural human level, we usually attribute the fact that one individual reacts with submissiveness and another with hostility to authority symbols, for example, to differences in the meanings of such symbols to them, these in turn being based on past experiences. At the cross-cultural level, it is often said that some peoples view the world as hostile, some as friendly, some divide it into things and actions, and some view it as all of one piece. The present hypothesis would imply that differences in language structure are not essential, that behavior-cognition relations may be sufficient.

7.4.3.2. *Codification and cognition.* Here we come most directly into the Whorf problem. In the broadest sense, we ask if the structure of a language has an influence upon the 'world view'—perception, thought, memory, and even philosophy—of the people employing it. When the question is pared down to researchable size, the answer clearly seems to be positive. But we must also ask the converse question: Does the 'world view' of a people influence the structure of their language? Whether one concludes 'yes' or 'no' here seems to depend upon what is included in the notion of 'structure,' as we shall see. We do not need to ask about relations between our third variable, behavior, and codification, since it would probably be agreed by everyone that the only way in which the structure of language can influence overt behavior (or 'culture') is via the mediation of cognitive states—and conversely, the only way in which behavior (or 'culture') can influence the structure of language is also via the mediation of cognition.

Hypothesis III. The form of codification of the language used to talk about stimuli influences the cognitions associated with these stimuli. Here the independent variable is codification, as indexed usually by linguistic methods, and the dependent variable is cognitive states, *as indexed by certain criterion behaviors.* These criterion behaviors are usually some standard psychological measure of symbolic activity, such as recognition, recall or reproduction in the case of memory, sorting behaviors in the case of concept formation, scoring of 'stories' or 'protocols' obtained from TAT or Rorschach in the case of 'ways of perceiving,' and so on. The codification variable may be relative availability of labels in the lexicon, presence or absence of certain grammatical characteristics, and so forth.

(1) *Intra-cultural approaches.* A number of studies on the influence of labeling upon *retention* are available in the standard psychological literature. Language may function here as a marker to alter the memory of particular characteristics of a stimulus or to differentially facilitate the remembering of certain aspects of situations. An early study by Lehmann in 1889 showed that subjects could dis-

tinguish more easily between shades of gray if they had heard numbers associated with them. More typical was an experiment by Carmichael, Hogan, and Walter. It was shown that the names given to diagrams affected the reproduction of the diagrams when the subjects were later asked to draw them. For example, for a stimulus figure of two circles connected by a straight line, subjects in one group were told that it might help them to remember the figure if they remembered the word 'spectacles' and another group was given the key word 'dumbbells.' When asked to draw the figures at a later date, the first group tended to distort the figure by making the straight line much like the nosepiece of a pair of spectacles; the second group tended to make the line thicker and the circles into elipses resembling dumbbells.

A more recent, and more directly relevant, experiment has been reported by Lenneberg. First a sample of English speakers was shown a considerable number of color patches comparable in all respects but hue and asked to label them. It was found that while certain patches yielded highly consistent labels (e.g., patches falling close to that part of the spectrum with which the familiar label 'red' is associated), other patches showed little agreement, many compound descriptions (such as 'a sort of yellowish green'), and blocking. Presumably if latencies had been measured they would have shown a corresponding increase. This step constitutes an empirical estimation of the way in which English lexical codification 'carves up' the stimulus dimension of wave-length of light. (We assume—and experimental evidence supports it—that this particular segmentalization of the spectrum is not forced by the human receptor apparatus.) The question, tested in the second step of the study, is this: will the codification of color terminology (here, labelability) affect cognitive processes? The cognitive process studied, with a different group of subjects, was retention as measured by recognition over a short interval. Shown a sample of 20 color patches, say, and then shown, after an interval, 40 patches in which the original 20 are included, will subjects tend to recognize readily labelable colors more correctly than less readily labelable ones? Statistically significant differences were obtained in favor of the hypothesis. This experiment samples only one of many possible stimulus continua and only one of many possible cognitive processes; the method is admirably suited to testing the general hypothesis.

But what is the mechanism here? How does the availability of a culturally standardized label (and associated mediation process) facilitate recall, perceptual isolation, common classification in sorting and so on? An experiment by Lawrence on the enhancement of discrimination of cues by rat subjects is relevant here.[102] He found that forcing rats to 'pay attention' to a given set of cues (e.g., black vs. white walls), by making these the discriminanda in a prior discrimination problem, markedly facilitated transfer to quite different discrimination problems in which the same cues were involved. Rats could even reverse a discrimination to such 'attended' cues better than to others. This seems quite analogous to the role of language labels with humans—stimulus patterns that come to be associated with distinctive labels, and acquire differential meaning on the basis of prior differential

[102] D. G. Lawrence, Acquired distinctiveness of cues; II. Selective association in a constant stimulus situation, *Journal of Experimental Psychology* **40**. 175–88 (1950).

reinforcement, later prove to be more distinctive, whether in retention, in categorizing, in perception, or so forth. But what is the mechanism?

The following type of experiment might get at the answer. A control group is shown a set of gray patches of varying brightness and simply tested for recognition after a delay interval. Various experimental groups would be given the same task, but with modifications in the prior exposure designed to test the following hypotheses: (1) The facilitation may be due to the association of some distinctive additional cue with the gray. A series of non-speech sounds, such as patterns of notes could be used here. (2) The facilitation may be due to a self-produced movement by the subject. Subjects could be instructed to make certain movements to each of the grays (preferably overt, although thinking about movements may also prove to be relevant). (3) The facilitation may be due to the fact that a speech sound is heard and can be reproduced to facilitate recognition. Nonsense syllables could be used for this condition, although in a sense giving a name to the color would make the syllable meaningful. (4) The facilitation may be due to complex discriminatory associations with meaningful sounds. Names do not usually exist in isolation but indicate that the object is not something else. For this variation meaningful words would be used. (5) The facilitation may be due to the secondary reward value of making distinctions marked by language. One could enhance the secondary reward value of the markers in any of the above designs by associating them with differential reinforcement.

Traditional *concept formation tests* involve presentation of stimuli that can be grouped according to various categories or dimensions. Such a design can be illustrated concretely by reference to a well known concept formation testing device, the Vigotsky blocks. Twenty-two blocks differing in height, top surface area (width), shape, and color are to be divided into four classes, the 'correct' solution involving the intersection of two dichotomies: high-low and large-small. These classes are identified in information fed back to the subject by nonsense syllables; thus the high-small blocks are called MUR, the low-small ones CEV, the high-large ones BIK, and the low-large ones LAG. These 'names' are irrelevant to the solution, but some subjects attempt to find clues to the basis of classification in them. Thus MUR has been interpreted as the French word for wall, while BIK and LAG become 'big' and 'large,' respectively. This effect suggests the usefulness of varying the concept markers linguistically and determining the effect upon sorting behavior.

The semantic implications of *grammatical categories* can also be studied. In some languages, for example, gender may be applied to inanimate objects. In French semantic choice is necessary only in a few cases such as adjectives treated as nouns—e.g., *le génévois, la génévoise*. It is clear, however, that whenever a sex distinction is reasonable, certain endings are used with the feminine and others with the masculine. One might expect, then, that in the use of gender affixes with inanimate objects there might be some generalization from the meaning difference associated with gender when there is a semantic difference. Lists of randomly selected masculine and feminine nouns could be analyzed with the semantic differential. If there is any generalization between the various nouns in the same gender category, there should be some differences in the distribution of the profiles for the two groups. This difference should be in the same direction as the difference between masculine and feminine forms of adjectives and the profiles for 'masculine' and 'feminine.'

A considerable amount of observational evidence has been offered in the literature in support of the general thesis that the lexical or structural characteristics of language influence overt behavior directly. Typical is Whorf's analysis of many hundreds of reports of circumstances surrounding the starting of fires. For example, a man reports to his insurance company that a certain gas drum is 'empty' and later tosses a burning cigarette into it, causing an explosion. Whorf argues that this behavior is a result of the meaning of 'empty' in English, leading its users to disregard the explosive vapor. As Lenneberg points out, however, English is quite capable of yielding the sentence 'This empty gas drum is filled with explosive vapor.' It seems much more likely that this is an instance of the influence of cognitive states upon behavior, i.e., the burning cigarette was carelessly thrown into the vapor-filled drum because the man perceived it as containing nothing inflammable. Much of the evidence of this sort, if our argument is valid, really belongs under Hypothesis I above and has nothing directly to do with the relation of codification to behavior.

(2) *Cross-cultural approaches.* Much of the anecdotal evidence on the Weltanschauung problem is cross-cultural in nature, but most of it runs into the methodological complications discussed earlier in this section—particularly circularity of inference and use of translation to prove differences in cognitive states. Most of the techniques discussed under intra-cultural approaches are applicable here, as are a number of additional methods which are briefly described below.

The *design developed by Lenneberg* for studying the effects of color labeling upon perception and retention is readily adaptable to cross-cultural tests. Work with the Zuni is now in progress. The question is to what extent recognition of colors can be shown to be influenced by differences in codification of colors in different languages, with experimental procedures held constant. The chief difficulty, of course, is to hold experimental procedures constant. One usually finds that cultures exert subtle but yet powerful effects upon performance in experimental situations—attitudes toward testing situations, motivation, what is assumed by the subject to be significant, desires to please or not please the investigator, and so forth. A design much like Lenneberg's could be used to get at the possible way in which differences in the codification of the time continuum affect cognitive states. The English language, for example, selects out certain intervals—the 'second,' the 'minute,' the 'hour' and so on—and applies these high frequency labels to them. Could it be shown, first intra-culturally, that English language users are more accurate in estimating intervals that cluster about these labeled segments than in estimating intervals of a relatively unlabelable magnitude? Could it then be shown cross-culturally that accuracy of interval estimates (or other indices of temporal cognitions) is influenced by differences in codification of the time continuum? There are many other dimensions of experience beyond color and time that could be studied in this manner, of course.

The phenomena above are researchable cross-culturally because physical and biological conditions (e.g., of color production and reception) are constant. Many other cultural 'objects' are constant across two or more cultures despite language differences, and these should be equally researchable. The biological relations among individuals, for example (e.g., father, mother, grandfather, cousin, etc. as defined biologically), are constant across cultures, yet the ways kinship codifications assign relationships differ—could differences in perception, attitude, and the like be shown to vary on this basis? Many cultures share the 7-day week system, but the codifications differ.

A different type of cross-cultural investigation would make use of the kind of *communication situation devised by Carroll* and described elsewhere in this section (7.1). Suppose that two individuals who speak the same language are placed at tables separated by a screen and both have before them the same set of objects (such as blocks and pegs of various shapes, sizes, and colors). One individual acts as the encoder; given a certain arrangement of his materials (by the experimenter), he must use his language to communicate this arrangement to the other individual, who acts as the decoder. Questions by the decoder may either be allowed or not. If a suitably varied set of arrangements and materials were devised (involving semantic relations of order, distance, direction, color, size, shape, being under, over, beside, and so forth), it should be possible to study the general question of whether or not certain languages facilitate or hinder the communication of certain types of information. Would the Navajo, for example, have particular difficulty with communicating the order of events? Would the East Indian typically have trouble with relative distances between objects? Or would it be found that all languages can be used equivalently to communicate anything? In view of Lenneberg's findings with respect to color, this last possibility seems unlikely—presumably English speakers would have trouble communicating the selection of blocks or pegs of low color labelability.

Finally, *the bilingual individual* seems to provide an exceptionally favorable ground for testing this hypothesis—cross-culturally and cross-linguistically within the same individual in some cases, cross-linguistically but within the same individual bearing the same culture in other cases. With the compound-type bilingual (cf., section 6.2) we are dealing with two different language systems but (presumably) with a constant set of cognitions; with the coordinate-type bilingual, on the other hand, we are dealing with two different language systems *and* two somewhat different cognitive systems (and cultures). While language-plus-cognition differences in the latter case may be expected to produce differences in behavior in standard test situations, will language differences per se have any effect in the former case? Several experimental procedures can be suggested here.

(1) *Comparative use of the semantic differential.* If the dimensions of the semantic differential can be assumed to be even roughly translatable, a method of comparing responses of bilinguals to those of monolingual speakers could be developed. One would look for shifts in bilinguals toward an intermediate meaning on the scales on which there are differences between monolinguals in the two languages. Under certain conditions—perhaps a certain kind of social setting for the bilingual or translating experience—there may be inhibition of this generalizing process, and bilingual scales may diverge even more sharply than do monolingual scales on the dimensions for which differences are found in the two languages. The types of words used will be important variables as exemplified in the following cases:

(a) Words which are alike in form class and 'phonemic shape' but are of varying degrees of closeness in meaning in the two languages. For the clearly unlike meanings one would expect minimum generalization, about as much as one would find between homonyms in the same language. E.g.: unlike—French and English *sensible*; more alike—French and English *sympathy*.

(b) Words which are alike in form class, and are common translations, but differ in stimulus similarity. One might expect more generalization than for words which include a different form class as a homonym of similar meaning. E.g.: English *sleep* is both noun and verb; French *sommeil* is only a noun.

(c) Words which have the same common translation word in the second language. One might expect such words to show a shift towards greater similarity of profile due to the common translation word. This hypothesis could be tested without the assumption of translatability of the material E.g.: English *dream*; French *songe* and *rêve*.

(2) *Verbal responses to non-verbal stimuli.* If two languages apply labels to delineate classes in a domain differently, one would expect that bilingual boundaries would shift, at least for continuous stimuli. For example, given the spectrum boundaries used by English speakers for *green* and by French speakers for *vert*, one might expect a shift in bilinguals. If the ambiguous areas in one language are fairly great with considerable uncertainty about labeling and if the other language clearly includes a border area under one of the labels, the second language's boundaries might determine the range of physical stimuli encompassed by the terms in each language. However, in a finely discriminated area without much uncertainty in either language, some compromise boundary may result. If English monolinguals divide the area between *yellow* and *green* approximately equally, while the French monolinguals restrict *jaune* more narrowly compared to *vert*, the bilingual might be expected to shift the English boundary toward the yellow end and achieve some sort of compromise for both languages.

If one language makes finer discriminations of a given set of stimuli than the other language does, bilinguals may try to approximate the differentiations of the first language by elaborations in the second. In some cases a direct borrowing of terms may occur. For example, the Zuni have a word which includes both yellow and orange according to English labels. The younger Zuni who are more often bilingual have borrowed the English term *orange* so that they make a differentiation similar to that made by English monolinguals. Alternatively, without borrowing the term they might have tried to approximate it by calling the colors identified as orange in English a combination of yellow and red or some similar circumlocution. With emotions a similar process may take place. In Crow the same term is used for situations where English would use *surprise* and *fear*, and it may be translated as either. However, one might expect bilinguals who are asked to compare emotional situations in Crow to distinguish in some way between the situations because of the fact that English requires it.

(3) *The Thematic Apperception Test* can also be used to explore the effects of language variation upon response to constant stimuli for bilinguals. The latent content of TAT protocols for both languages of the bilingual would be compared with those for matched monolinguals. The data from such a design could be used to check variations in the bilingual's responses from one language to another. Questions: Does the compound-type bilingual show any differences in what is perceived in the pictures as a function of the language he is using? Does the coordinate-type bilingual show such differences? In what ways do the perceptions of bilinguals differ from those of matched monolinguals? Under what conditions does borrowing from one language to the other occur in bilinguals?[103]

Hypothesis IV. The cognitions associated with stimuli influence the form of codification of the language used to talk about these stimuli. This reversal of the usual Weltanschauung notion may strike one as absurd at first glance, but in certain respects, at least, it is obviously valid.

One underlying proposition here is that perceptual processes of human organisms—particularly principles of grouping, figure-ground, continuity, closure and constancy (cf., section 3.1)—determine what segments or patterns in the continuously variable physical environment will typically acquire labels. The detachability of leaves from trees, for example, makes it more probable that languages in general will have separate labels for 'tree' and 'leaf' than for 'trunk' as differentiated from 'branch.' Similarly 'hand' should be distinguished from 'arm' more regularly than upper forearm from lower forearm by separate labels. Separate labels for boys vs. men should be more common than separate labels for men of 30–40 vs. men of 40–50. Research on this proposition would require independent assessment of the 'discriminability' of a wide sample of such physical and social objects and situations (either directly through perception techniques or indirectly through physical measurement on such objects in relation to perception theory) and correlation of this set of facts with cross-cultural frequency of language distinction by labeling.

Another proposition here is that the lexicon of a language should be isomorphic, so to speak, with the pattern of the culture of its users. If one group of people lives mainly by fishing, their language lexicon should be appropriately expansive and discriminative in this area—names for varieties and sub-varieties of fish, names for types of boats and nets and hooks, and names for the many, many

---

[103] Susan Ervin is presently collecting data from bilinguals with this hypothesis in mind.

details of social organization that surround fishing. A group of people that has an elaborate and complicated kinship and marriage system should have an equally elaborate and complicated system of kinship and marriage terms. This proposition seems almost trite, of course. However, it clearly fits the hypothesis stated above. It is absurd to assume that people develop a fishing complex, for example, *because* they happen to have a language with lots of terms relevant to fishing! In this connection, Hoijer has described a correlation between the Navajos' grammatical preoccupation with movement and their nomadic life; again, it would seem absurd to conclude that the Navajos took to a nomadic way of life *because* their language happened to have this grammatical characteristic.

A Survey of Psycholinguistic Research, 1954-1964

by A. RICHARD DIEBOLD, JR., *Harvard University*

The discursive survey which follows is an attempt to give what we might call an "intellectual history" of psycholinguistics, with special emphasis on developments in the field during the past ten years. It is not easy to define the term "psycholinguistics," which represents a miscellany of theoretical and experimental approaches to certain aspects of human language and verbal behavior. As we shall see, the reasons are rather tenuous for claiming that there actually is a science of psycholinguistics separable from the established disciplines from which it has evolved. Nevertheless, there does exist a range of research activities (and publications deriving from them) which linguists and other behavioral scientists agree in labelling "psycholinguistic," indicating that there is a special niche in psychology for linguistically-oriented research, and conversely in linguistics for psychologically-oriented research on language and verbal behavior.

Before proceeding to a more concerted attempt to characterize the field, I will offer as a broad working definition the one given by Osgood and Sebeok on page 4 of the present volume, viz., that psycholinguistics "is concerned in the broadest sense with relations between messages and the characteristics of human individuals who select and interpret them." The intellectual history in which Osgood and Sebeok's monograph has played a central role is an especially interesting one for linguistics, since it reflects a minor revolution within the history of linguistic theory as a whole. The need for such a revoluton was early argued by Sapir:

It is peculiarly important that linguists, who are often accused, and accused justly, of failure to look beyond the patterns of their subject matter, should become aware of what their science may mean for the interpretation of human conduct in general. Whether they like it or not, they must become increasingly concerned with the many anthropological, sociological, and psychological problems which invade the field of linguistics (Sapir, 1929:214).

It is an easy task to document just such an "invasion" of linguistics as Sapir envisioned, by reviewing some of the problems proposed by behavioral scientists, engineers, philosophers, educators, and others. There has been no lack of interest in essentially linguistic problems on the part of scholars and laymen outside the ranks of linguists. Unfortunately, many of the problems posed have involved aspects of language and verbal behavior which linguists were poorly equipped to handle, or which they regarded with considerable disinterest. Much of the research ancestral to contemporary psycholinguistics thus evinces a striking lack of contact with linguistics, and the want of linguistic sophistication which is sometimes betrayed is no doubt partly a response of despair or estrangement on the part of outsiders who sought linguists' views. This is certainly the situation which has obtained in the United States, where the activity we would now call psycholinguistic grew up on the periphery of linguistics.

Why is there a field known as psycholinguistics? The best answer to this question is that linguists traditionally have been remarkably narrow in their purview of language. Some of the many topics which linguists have disdained as "irrelevant" or "uninteresting," and which they have relegated to the margins of their discipline, have developed into separate fields of inquiry. The reason for this is not far to seek. Especially if we focus our attention on descriptive linguistics and linguistic theory, it is clear that linguists have been primarily concerned with *langue*, in the sense that de Saussure used this term to refer to the abstract linguistic system underlying verbal behavior. Thus, within the broad definition of psycholinguistics offered above, linguists have been concerned at most with the descriptive characterization of the "messages" and with constructing abstract models which can be devised to account for their structure.

Traditionally, linguistics has not concerned itself as much with *parole*, that which de Saussure regarded as the overt, actualized aspect of verbal behavior, let alone with the relation of particular messages to each other, or to "the characteristics of human individuals who select and interpret them," or to the social and cultural matrix in which they are produced. Yet it is precisely the relations between messages and the characteristics of their users which have been of primary concern to the psychologist, and the relation of these to the social and cultural matrix are of concern not only to the psychologist but to the anthropologist and sociologist as well. Thus an argument could be advanced that linguistic theory has been almost exclusively involved with the formal accounting of *langue*, and has been vigorously anti-reductionist. Support for this argument could be mustered by examining the curiously marginal status accorded phonetics and semantics in much of linguistic theory, especially before widespread psycholinguistic activity began.

A proper appreciation of these basic differences in focus will explain some of the communication gaps which still separate linguistics from other behavioral sciences interested in verbal behavior. It is only strange that these differences in emphasis have been missed by psychologists, "who have long realized that a description of what an organism does and a description of what it knows can be very different things" (Chomsky, 1963:326). The full explanation for this misunderstanding must be sought in the history of psychological theory, a venture which will not be undertaken in this review, save by occasional oblique reference to the impact of behaviorism on psycholinguistic research. The contemporary deemphasis of extreme behaviorism in psychology is correlated with rapid developments in the investigation of the cognitive and neurophysiological aspects of language and verbal behavior; this is no more an accident,

I believe, than the prior association of Bloomfieldian linguistics (with its mechanistic concern for discovery procedures) and a general behavioristic approach in psychology, emphasizing readily observed and controlled stimulus-input and response-output sequences.

The events which have freed the psychologist to become interested in *langue* deserve recounting. Parts of this history have already been written (e.g., Alkon, 1959), but a non-partisan overview remains the most pressing epistemological need in psycholinguistics. The current results of this reorientation—which psychologists and linguists of a former generation would have concurred in calling "mentalistic"—will be a major theme in the present survey. It is interesting, and indicative of the positive impact of psycholinguistics on the theory of linguistic structure, that the most recent theoretical writings now evince a concern for the congruence of linguistic with psychological models. Linguists and psychologists, in a quest for corroboration of their theories, often reduce from linguistic to psychological findings, and vice versa. I will return to give many examples of this trend.

By the 1940s it was apparent in the United States that the attention of linguists was being attracted to certain developments in other behavioral sciences. Lévi-Strauss, writing in 1945 on the developing liaison between anthropology and linguistics, even spoke of the *noblesse oblige* enjoining linguistics to monitor work in adjoining fields where others were attempting to apply their methods and results (Lévi-Strauss, 1945).

Although "psycholinguistics" has been talked about since 1950 (the term itself appeared somewhat earlier, in the 1940s), it is evident that the jelling of the field has come about only recently. Its earlier internal diversity is reflected in the journals in which its practitioners published, according to their affiliations as psychologists, communications engineers, acousticians, or whatever. Unlike linguistics proper, with its many long-established journals and serial publications, psycholinguistics has had to publish its writings through such disparate organs as the *Journal of Abnormal and Social Psychology*, and the *Journal of the Acoustical Society of America*, to mention only two. More recently, to be sure, the British journal, *Language and Speech*, and several rarely perused German and Russian periodicals have supplied a more specialized outlet. Moreover, several American serial publications (most notably the *Annual Review of Psychology* and *The Psychological Bulletin*[2] have long provided some coverage of ongoing psycholinguistic research, although not always under that name. With the advent of the new *Journal of Verbal Learning and Verbal Behavior*, we can hope for a gathering together of some of the far-flung results of earlier effort (in spite of the monopoly, in the first issues of this journal, of papers relating to operant conditioning of verbal behavior). It is the jelling of diverse earlier efforts which is the focal point of this intellectual history.

Many histories have their particular turning points, often marked by monuments which thereafter become charters for future developments. Psycholinguistics is no exception. In the early 1950s, the Social Science Research Council formed a Committee on Linguistics and Psychology. In the summer of 1953, after earlier occasional meetings of the Committee, the Council sponsored the Summer Seminar on Psycholinguistics, which brought many of the Committee members together at Indiana University. The exact purposes and membership of that gathering have been stated in the foreword and preface of this volume. The monograph[3] reprinted herein, *Psycholinguistics: A Survey of Theory and Reseach Problems* (1954), resulted from this seminar. Within a year or two of its appearance, this monograph became the charter for psycholinguistics, firmly establishing the discipline's name. It so successfully piqued the interest of linguists and other behavioral scientists that the volume itself was soon out of print, and also became notoriously difficult to obtain second-hand, or even in libraries. For these reasons alone, the decision of the Indiana University Press to reprint the monograph was a happy one.

Perhaps as an outgrowth of the interest aroused by the 1953 seminar and the 1954 survey, several other psycholinguistic projects were subsequently sponsored by the Social Science Research Council. Among the most notable of these is the Southwest Project in Comparative Psycholinguistics. The activities of this research project have been discussed in various preliminary reports by Casagrande (1956, 1960). Carroll has prepared a bibliography, complete as of February 1962, which lists 26 publications resulting directly from this research (Carroll, 1962).

Another extremely important development was the appearance in 1961 of a long-awaited reader, *Psycholinguistics: A Book of Readings,* edited by Sol Saporta. The Saporta reader reflects an awareness that the field of psycholinguistics now engages many personnel and possesses an extensive literature; it is especially welcome when one considers the scattered nature of the relevant writings. It is also a testament to the fact that there is an ever-growing number of university courses variously titled "psychology of language," "psycholinguistics," "linguistic psychology," etc.

In my survey of recent research in the field of psycholinguistics, I will use as a framework the categories and the contents of Saporta's reader. Although the categorization is somewhat arbitrary, these categories represent the various topical subfields implicitly recognized as constituting the subject matter of psycholinguistics. My goal will be to examine the readings contained in Saporta's book as exemplars of the types of research and thinking that have been done in each of these subfields. The topical sections used by Saporta are as follows:

1. The nature and function of language.
2. Approaches to the study of language.
3. Speech perception.
4. The sequential organization of linguistic events.
5. The semantic aspects of linguistic events.

6. Language acquisition, bilingualism, and language change.
7. Pathologies of linguistic behavior.
8. Linguistic relativity and the relation of linguistic processes to perception and cognition.

Cursory perusal of the sections will suggest some areas of omission, "areas" here being taken to mean subfields within psycholinguistics which are at least distinguished by having their own associated bodies of literature. In Section 9, three such areas are discussed (a) mass communication, (b) non-verbal communication, and (c) "zoosemiotics," the term recently proposed for "the discipline, within which the science of signs intersects with ethology, devoted to the scientific study of signalling behavior across animal species" (Sebeok, 1963:465).

Too strict an adherence to these topical categories would make it difficult to discuss developmental trends which are affecting psycholinguistics as a whole. Thus, whenever it has seemed important to examine such a trend, I have done so at the expense of continuity. This is one respect in which the present survey departs from my earlier study (1964b) on which it is based. Another departure is the decreased concern with the pedagogical value of the particular selections contained in Saporta's reader. In evaluating the selections, I have used instead, as a basic criterion, the extent to which a particular paper offers a truly representative sampling of the research activities associated with that subtopic. Finally, my earlier review concentrated on studies which were available to Saporta when his reader was in its final stages of compilation (i.e., up to 1960). The present survey covers many more recent materials which have appeared since the publication of the Saporta reader.

In the course of thus characterizing the field by surveying the activities being conducted within it, I have also consulted other survey studies[4] which have either attempted to delimit the field of psycholinguistics as a whole or which have surveyed particular subareas.

1. *The Nature and Function of Language*

This first part of Saporta's reader contains two papers, J. Lotz's "Linguistics: symbols make man" (1956) and F. W. Householder's "On linguistic terms," based on his "On linguistic primes" (1959). Both authors deal with what language "is" is terms of what the linguist is principally interested in. The Householder paper, a most useful inclusion, acquaints the novice with various live issues in descriptive linguistics and linguistic theory. It is explicit about differences in approach, yet it treats this variation within one framework. In this respect, it compares favorably with a parallel paper written a decade ago by Haugen (1951).

What emerges immediately from these papers is that descriptive linguistic analysis has traditionally approached a language (usually a small sample of it) as a closed system, one in which it is always possible to segment the physical continua which constitute *speech* samples into the "primes" and "mapping units" discussed by Householder. As will become apparent in Parts 3 and 4, the perception of primes by speakers of the language and the mechanics of their combination pose key problems for psycholinguistics.

But what should have been made apparent at the beginning, either by editorial comment or by a representative paper, are some of the basic problems posed by the primes themselves. I will mention three such problems here, the first and second are related. (1) Are these primes true universals of language? (2) And, if so, what sort of psychological reality have they for the speakers of a particular language? Householder addresses the first of these questions, assuring his readers that the "phoneme" and the "morpheme" (actually the "word") are true universals, and so too is the structure (the "mapping units"), in the sense that there are always stateable constraints on the random occurrence of the primes. By careful reading of the Lotz and Householder papers together, the newcomer may infer from various remarks that these primes have some sort of reality outside the mind and methods of the analyst. They do not provide a sufficient introduction to either language universals or to psychological reality, two crucial topics in contemporary research on language and verbal behavior.

Questions about language universals and language typology have been paired in recent decades, especially now that new trends and interests in the study of language (such as psycholinguistics) have revived a flagging concern with typology. It is significant that the Committee on Linguistics and Psychology of the Social Science Research Council (SSRC) recently organized a Conference on Language Universals, the proceedings of which have just been published (see Greenberg, 1963).

Furthermore, revisions in our views of grammatical theory incorporate a concern with universals as a major factor in the justification of grammatical models (e.g., Katz and Postal, 1964, esp. 159 ff.). The last few years have also seen the rise to prominence of a descriptive methodology which offers as yet unevaluated but pedagogically highly promising results; this is the so-called "contrastive grammar," which typically compares the structural similarities and differences between a target and source language. For theoretical purposes, continued pursuit of contrastive analyses will greatly increase our knowledge of language universals and typology, and the efforts in this direction by the Center for Applied Linguistics (which has been responsible for much activity in this area) should be encouraged.

The introductory papers in Saporta's reader seem to overlook the fact that it is not primarily the universality of a prime, like the phoneme, that is of interest, but rather the implicative universals relating to its perception, its feature composition, its sequential constraints, and other factors. Jakobson and Halle's paper, covered in Part 6, provides some examples of what is needed for an introduction to the study of universals. Many of these "near-universals" involve structural relationships which co-occur in diverse natural languages with more than chance frequency, and which therefore demand explanation and consideration by an adequate theory of language. The fact that many of these typological correlations must be statistically determined leads to another general problem for "the nature and function of language":

(3) The third basic problem posed by the existence of linguistic primes relates to their quantification and their incorporation into structural models. The most salient characteristic of linguistic primes themselves, in contrast to the physical continua which contain them, is their discreteness, their discontinuity. It is in this sense that linguistic units lend themselves so well to qualification (e.g., by statistical frequency) and to model-building, since they invite substitution into quantum mathematics. Moreover, it is obviously their quantitative attributes which distinguish linguistic primes from the species units of other behavioral sciences: e.g., the "culture trait" of anthropology, or the "response" of behaviorist psychology. This may explain why these other behavioral sciences have come to be very impressed with the *operational procedures* for analysis and with the techniques of descriptive taxonomy practiced by linguists. The "segmentability" and the quantum mechanics available to linguists strikes these other practitioners as very rigorous, and unattainable with the species units in their own fields.

The 1954 survey, especially in the sections on information theory written by Wilson and on entropy measures by Wilson and Carroll, presaged an important future role for mathematics in psycholinguistic research. Now, a decade later, with the appearance of such studies as those by Chomsky and Miller in the recent *Handbook of Mathematical Psychology* (Luce, Bush, and Galanter, 1963), it is obvious that the student seriously interested in psycholinguistics will have to master statistics and finite mathematics.

Such knowledge will be necessary in order to properly grasp the import of many relevant studies in which statistics is a basic tool for investigation and means for presentation. Applied statistics has supplied us with much raw data, some of which is still being analyzed; the Thorndike-Lorge frequency list (1927) is but one example. Zipf's investigations with rank-frequency distributions (1932, 1949) and Mandelbrot's (1954, 1961) papers interpreting Zipf are frequently cited examples of "linguistic statistics." Herdan's *Type-token Mathematics* (1960) is a good introductory guide to the application of statistical procedures to linguistic problems, and contains a useful annotated glossary of statistical terminology. Particular applications of statistics to psycholinguistic problems are found in Miller and Chomsky, 1963.

A knowledge of finite mathematics will help avoid a danger well posed by Plath: "One of the greatest dangers involved in the construction of mathematical models of language, particularly quantitative ones, is that indiscriminate introduction of mathematical apparatus inevitably leads to the generation of meaningless and misleading results" (1961:22,23). While the danger of obtaining misleading results is certainly a real one, there is also a growing body of meaningful and heuristic results which are so couched in mathematical proofs and symbolic logic, that ever more mathematical competence is demanded of the student who would understand them. For a full appreciation of this warning, let the mathematically unsophisticated reader attempt to follow the arguments contained in several of Chomsky's important papers (most notably those of 1956 and 1963) ; without some knowledge of mathematics, the task is insuperable.

Perhaps the major shortcoming of this introductory section of the psycholinguistics reader, like the 1954 survey, is its failure to clarify the distinction that must be made between a model which deals with linguistic *competence* alone and one which deals with various behavioral manifestations of that competence, such as language acquisition, speech perception, and speech production. In fairness to the collaborators of the 1954 survey, it must be stressed that their efforts occurred before the distinction had been dramatically clarified in linguistics by the emergence of a theory of language structure called "generative grammar." This is one of the revolutionary developments which separates the intellectual climate of psycholinguistics today from that of 1954.

This difference in focus is one which psychologists might clarify by distinguishing between *linguistic competence* and *linguistic performance,* and linguists through the Saussurean dichotomy between *langue* and *parole,* referred to earlier. There can be little doubt that losing sight of this distinction has brought about a myopia which has contributed to communication gaps, not only between linguists and psychologists, but also between internal divisions within their respective ranks. Consider the possibilities for misunderstanding between strict behaviorists (in both linguistics and psychology), chiefly interested in linguistic performance, and their colleagues who are more concerned with the unobservable cognitive structures which constitute linguistic competence. There are unfortunately few discussions of the nonequivalence of linguistic competence and performance; Katz and Postal (1964) and especially Postal (1964a) contain interesting statements, as do Chomsky and Miller (1963) and Chomsky (1963).

2. *Approaches to the Study of Language*

Reading through the important papers in this second part of Saporta's reader, it is easier to appreciate the diversity of thought within linguistics than to perceive any common denominator. The section includes: L. Bloomfield, "A set of postulates for the science of language" (1926) ; two chapters from N. Chomsky, *Syntactic Structures* (1957) ; C. F. Hockett's review of C. L. Shannon and W. Weaver, *The Mathematical Theory of Communication* (1953) ; B. F. Skinner's introductory chapter to his

Verbal Behavior (1957) ; and L. Krasner, "Studies of the conditioning of verbal behavior" (1958).

We might ask why Bloomfield's article was included, or, why it was included without editorial comment. In the first part of this paper, Bloomfield is very terse about the exclusion of psychology from any of the postulates which follow. Present-day students not better acquainted with Bloomfield's writings will seize this as confirmation of the overly mechanistic approach to language which it is now fashionable to attribute to him. To be sure, Bloomfield was interested in developing rigorous discovery procedures and historical techniques, at a time when too few existed. And connections do exist between these endeavors of Bloomfield and some latter-day traditions of descriptive analysis which have been legitimately criticized as "taxonomic" and "data-cataloguing" (see, for example, Lees, 1957, 1960).

What is improper, considering the intellectual legacy from Bloomfield, is to overstate his mechanistic view. It is too easy to equate mechanism with anti-psychology. Fries (1961) has supplied a strong counter-argument to the charge of Bloomfield's anti-psychology. He has admirably restressed what many knew already, viz., that Bloomfield was interested in avoiding the teleological reasoning about language which older mentalistic psychology had facilitated. Nowhere in Bloomfield's writings is there a denial of the role of psychological factors. For example, he writes : "Needless to state that sound-change and analogy are not, as far as we know, subject to our needs or expression, but are respectively, psychophysiologic and psychologic processes that occur involuntarily and cannot be directed by our needs and desires" (Fries, 1961:200). There *is,* however, a denial of the possibility of interpreting linguistic phenomena in terms of psychology, and the most widely read statement of it is in the Bloomfield paper chosen for inclusion in Saporta's reader. It is not claimed by this extended observation that Bloomfield has been portrayed out of context in Saporta's reader. The point is rather that some sort of context should have been supplied to permit a greater appreciation of his role in the history of linguistics.

Several chapters from Chomsky's *Syntactic Structures* are found sprinkled throughout Saporta's reader. The two included in this part of the reader are Chapter 2, "The Independence of Grammar," and Chapter 6, "On the Goals of Linguistic Theory." These chapters are so well conceived that they lose none of their original persuasiveness when standing alone.

The "Independence of Grammar" contains a discussion of grammaticality which will clue the interested student into future problems awaiting psycholinguistic research. But there is a behaviorist objection to the notion of grammaticality which Chomsky's chapters will not dispel. This objection has nowhere been more bluntly formulated than in Olmsted's admonition concerning "one of the more persistent errors committed by linguists who are not at home among the techniques of psychology; viz., inventing judgments which 'the native speaker' is said to make, in the absence of adequate evidence, and sometimes without any evidence whatsoever, other than the investigator's own overtrained bias" (1955:47).

Even if *Syntactic Structures* does not come to grips with the problem of determining how grammaticality is to be tested, several studies influenced by Chomsky can nevertheless be cited which obviate Olmsted's reservations concerning the intuitive quality of the concept. One is Maclay and Sleator's (1960) carefully controlled study of native speakers' responses to differentially grammatical tokens in their language. The paper provides an insightful discussion of the "same or different" criterion employed in procedural analysis, and then reports an experiment in which respondents reported their judgments on the (1) "grammaticality," (2) "meaningful"-ness, and (3) "ordinariness" of a set of sentences. Hill (1961) also deals with notions of grammaticality, although not experimentally. Insightful discussions of the linguistic informant's judgments during field work are contained in Gudschinsky (1958), Hoijer (1958), and Waterhouse (1961).

Chomsky's chapters in the reader examine and reject some of the vague operational approaches traditionally relied upon to specify grammaticality (e.g., semantics, statistical approximation). They stress the need to construct a recursive generator which will produce "all of the grammatical sequences of L and none of the ungrammatical ones." The fact that "all the grammatical sequences of L" is envisioned as an infinite set of sentences, has disturbed many psychologists (and linguists) who are well aware of the finite capacity of the speaker, "finite" at least in terms of storage capacity and inductive faculties. Yet that the set of sentences with which the speaker copes is for all practical purposes infinite, has probably never been doubted. It is very easy to demonstrate that, both in production and in recognition, the organism is coping with an overwhelming proportion of tokens which are for him novel combinations. As we shall see, an argument from the study of language acquisition offers striking support of this.

One of the major contributions of generative grammar has been the demonstration that "knowledge by a finite organism of an infinite set of linguistic facts is neither paradox nor contradiction, but results from the fact that there are kinds of finite entities which specify infinite sets of objects" (Postal, 1964a:247). The specification of these particular "kinds of finite entities" has, of course, been the seminal contribution of generative grammar theory: "Either we can try to develop an operational test of some sort that will distinguish between sentences and nonsentences or we can attempt to construct a recursive procedure for enumerating the infinite list of sentences" (Chomsky and Miller, 1963:283). Most psychologists have despaired of the former approach (despite the interest in

Sprachgefühl mentioned above with respect to the notion "grammatical"), but the differences in conceptualization between generative grammar and earlier approaches have been quite missed by some linguists (e.g., Bolinger 1960; Hill, 1961).

The specification of this recursive procedure itself could never have been developed without the mathematical prowess, mentioned in Part 1, which the theoreticians responsible for formulating generative grammar have brought to bear on the problem. This has certainly played a role in the conceptualization of two crucial properties of the generative grammar: its recursive character and the incorporation of a particular type of rule termed "transformational." The former property permits generation of an infinite set of sentences; the latter in part accounts for numerous aspects of linguistic competence (such as the relations "felt" between certain syntactic derivations) which have hitherto been left outside the province of linguistic theory. Basic pedagogical treatments of generative grammar include Bach (1964) and Katz and Postal (1964). The gap between generative grammar and earlier theories of linguistic structure, in their relative ability to explicate linguistic competence, is tellingly documented in Postal (1964b). With regard to the so-called "projection problem"—the formulation of "rules which project the finite set of sentences which he [the speaker] has fortuitously encountered to the infinite set of sentences of the language" (Katz and Fodor, 1963:171) —the difference between the two types of theory is no longer relative, but revolutionary.

At the same time it now appears that grammatical transformations, more than any other notion of the generative concept of grammar, have contributed to a recent reblurring of the distinction between the formal linguistic account of a language and the production of actual sentences in that language. "Transformations are often erroneously conceived to be direct descriptions of processes that a speaker follows in constructing sentences (the same statement holds for generative theories as a whole)" (Bach, 1964:64). An example of this blurring is found in Osgood (1963c). The status of Miller's work with the cognitive transformations inferred as mirroring grammatical transformations (Miller, 1962a; Miller, Ojemann, and Slobin, 1962) remains to be fully appraised (see below).

Chomsky, far more than most linguists, has been concerned with the problem of justification of grammars, and with the relationship of grammatical models to (hopefully corresponding) psychological models of perception, cognition and acquisition:

In part, these questions belong to theoretical psychology. But purely linguistic research can play a fundamental role in adding substance to these speculations. A perceptual model that does not incorporate a descriptively adequate generative grammar cannot be taken very seriously. Similarly, the construction of a model of acquisition (whether a model of learning, or a linguistic procedure for discovery of grammars) cannot be seriously undertaken without a clear understanding of the nature of the descriptively adequate grammars that it must provide as output, on the basis of primary linguistic data (Chomsky, 1962a:556).

It is evident from current research that some of the psycholinguistic questions touched upon in *Syntactic Structures* are receiving attention. The timing of Saporta's reader did not permit inclusion of some particularly interesting studies which have been stimulated by Chomsky's work. Miller, for example, has articles and manuscript materials which treat various psycholinguistic problems in the context of generative grammar theory. His recent papers describe experiments in perception (testing apprehension of the relationships between certain syntactically related but physically dissimilar utterances) which argue strongly for the "psychological reality" of grammatical transformations (Miller, Ojemann, and Slobin, 1962; Miller, 1962a).

Shannon's "The mathematical theory of communication" and Weaver's "Recent contributions to the mathematical theory of communication" (Shannon and Weaver, 1949) have exerted a tremendous influence on the development of psycholinguistics, at least to judge from the frequency of references to it since its appearance. Shannon's paper presented an analysis of information transmission, based on probability theory, providing a means for quantifying the probability of occurrence, both between paradigmatic alternatives and among syntagmatic combinations. The basic probability concept, "entropy," and its quantum, the "bit," are now a part of the metalanguage of linguistics. Highly formulaic and embedded in mathematical proofs, the Shannon paper must have resisted full comprehension by many of its readers. The truth of the matter is that most of us read Weaver's exposition and understood some of Shannon's by virtue of Weaver's less mathematical approach.

Some were even more enlightened in 1953 and 1954 by reading one of three papers which appeared in those years. The first is George Miller's "What is information measurement?" (1953), which provides an elementary and very clear answer to the question raised in its own title. It is doubly valuable in its attempts to show the relevance of information theory for psychology.

The second paper is Kellogg Wilson's "The information theory approach," a section of the 1954 survey, which offers perhaps the most useful of all of the introductions to the technical mathematical aspects. Wilson concludes with a consideration of the applicability of information measurement, and generalizes that the measures will be most heuristic for psycholinguistics in their investigation of "how much effect the pattern of antecedent events has on the occurrence of subsequent events, and hence the degree to which sequences of such events are structured (i.e., non-random)."

The third paper is Hockett's (1953) lengthy review of Shannon and

Weaver's book. Not nearly as concise as the Miller or Wilson paper, Hockett's review is of far greater importance to the development of psycholinguistics, since it goes to its great length in attempting to show the relevance of information theory to linguistic problems. Indeed, the bulk of the review (after a several page reexposition of the theory itself) is devoted to considering various linguistic applications, such as to phonemicizing. The review singles out problems which have only recently gained attention, e.g., the role of paralinguistic phenomena such as voice modifications in conveying information in the channel, and several questions are raised about the continuity of segments whose implications still remain undeveloped. This is a key paper for psycholinguistics.

The article by Skinner which follows in the reader is the first chapter of his book *Verbal Behavior* (1957). An important point made in this paper is that other disciplines, notably linguistics, have approached verbal behavior without consideration of the speaker, and that the only domain in which the speaker can receive proper treatment is in psychology. As Lounsbury has so well generalized, the linguist traditionally has been only rarely "concerned with the stimulus conditions under which a verbal response is produced or with the nature of the stimulus-response connection and its establishment in the individual" (1963:552-3). But as regards his "causal or functional" analysis, I am at a loss to see how Skinner's approach is an appreciable improvement over "the doctrine of the expression of ideas" which he attacks; perhaps it is an improvement in that it avoids introspection as a research technique. Both the functional analysis of verbal behavior and the antique psychology of ideas, however, are alike in assigning much of the speech act to the unobservable internal make-up of the speaker.

Since it is obvious that the present writer suffers from a tendency to malign operant models, it would be fair to first describe the instrumental approach used by Skinner and his followers, or at least to define the term "operant." "Operant" is one of those psychological terms (together with "latency" and "mediational") which recur frequently in psycholinguistics, but which defy precise definition or, depending on the whims of their immediate employer, exhibit a polysemy of frightening flexibility. Most commentators on Skinner's work agree in calling the approach "instrumental learning" and in treating it within a typology of learning theories. Lambert (1962), Mowrer (1960), and Osgood (1963a, 1963c), offering extensive discussions of the role of learning theory in psycholinguistics, all agree on a basic distinction within the typology which separates "instrumental learning" from the other varieties which in the main are modern descendants of classical Pavlovian learning theory.

Skinner himself has called the classical approach the study of "respondent" behavior, or behavior which is elicited by (i.e., in response to) receipt of specific stimuli. In contrast to respondent behavior, Skinner sees higher animals (and humans using verbal behavior in particular) as emitting behavior which is not directly elicited and whose recurrence depends upon its reinforcement. [When reinforcement is rewarding such that the originally spontaneous response becomes instrumentally conditioned to a rewarding reinforcing stimulus, the established sequence is called an operant.] To measure the probability or strength of emission of the desired operant is to measure its frequency. Since Skinner believes that verbal behavior is exemplary operant behavior, the way to account for it is "to look for the conditions under which various stimuli can come to control or influence the probability of emission of particular verbal responses" (Osgood, 1963a :250), and it is precisely on this quest that *Verbal Behavior* takes off.

In contrast to instrumental learning, there are several models which ultimately derive from classical Pavlovian learning theory. Lambert's and Osgood's approaches are closely related and are classified as the same type by those writers. Lambert calls these models of learning "classical," whereas Osgood calls them "two-stage mediational models." They agree that this model differs in certain fundamental respects from Skinner's. In the original classical conditioning situation there is always a pairing of an arbitrary stimulus with a "natural" stimulus, the natural stimulus having an established elicitative bond with a specific response in the organism. Learning is said to occur as the arbitrary ("conditioned") stimulus comes to elicit the response originally appropriate only to the natural ("unconditioned") stimulus. The basic mechanics of this learning process are attested by a wealth of empirical information drawn from experimentation with many species of animals.

Learning theory has been used as a means for analyzing two basic psycholinguistic problems: the first is "how words are used in communication, either as units or as elements in larger response sequences" and the second is the "symbol-referent problem." It is the second which has attracted most of Osgood's attention and, although discussion of his work in semantics will be reserved for Part 5, there are several important concepts that should be mentioned at this point. Both Lambert and Osgood admit that their model is weak in its assignation of much of the speech process to unobservable states within the speaker; both speak of the difficulty in explaining how (especially in verbal behavior) the transfer of evocative capacity is effected, the more so since one has to posit natural (unconditioned) response sequences as a basis for the conditioned transfer to the verbal symbols.

Osgood (1963c), however, has been more bold in offering a hypothesis to account for this transfer, and it is in this context that it is important to understand the meaning of "mediational." According to Osgood, the transfer occurs when the symbols learned "come to evoke some miniature replica of the actual responses made to the referent, and these responses, referred to as 'representational mediational responses,' constitute the meanings of the symbol. They *represent* or stand for the full pattern of responses made to the referent, they *mediate* or link the responses made to the referent with those made to the symbol, and they are some form of nervous system *response*" (Lambert, 1962:5,6). The diagram below (*Figure 1*) illustrates Osgood's conceptualization of the process underlying the two-stage stimulus-response nexus; the instance here diagrammed is

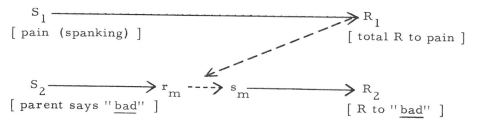

Figure 1. (Adapted from Cofer, 1961, p. 93.)

the child's learning of the sign stimulus "*bad*" (S_2) through associative conditioning with spanking (S_1). The sequence ($r_m \longrightarrow s_m$) represents, for Osgood, the meaning of "bad." Osgood now has more elaborate "three-stage" models which purportedly obviate some of the objections (to be discussed in Part 5) which have been levelled at the two-stage model (Osgood, 1963a, 1963c).

Many problems are involved in any evaluation of these different approaches. There are issues here, involving past and current trends in psychology, which will escape the notice of many linguists. Not the least is the superficial resemblance of Osgood's concept of "representational mediational responses" to the now discredited views of Watson, the founder of behaviorism, concerning subvocal somatic correlates to speech which he viewed as the basis for thinking and cognition (e.g., see Watson, 1920). Thorson's research (1925) disproved Watson's propositions, but their influence has persisted up through contemporary work on language acquisition (see Part 6).

Clearly what is needed in any psycholinguistics reader is some sort of introduction to the psychological theory and methods which psychologists have applied to verbal behavior. If I had my choice of two additional papers to suggest for inclusion in Saporta's reader, I would without hesitation have selected Chomsky's review (1959) of Skinner's *Verbal Behavior* as one. It is of interest to note parenthetically that several Soviet psychologists, working particularly with language acquisition, were amazed and amused by *Verbal Behavior*, in spite of a demonstrably behaviorist orientation. Suffice it to note here that Tikhomirov's review (1959), arguing on different premises, arrives at much the same conclusions as Chomsky did in his. In this country *Verbal Behavior* also received straw-man treatment in reviews by Osgood (1958) and Morris (1958).

The other paper I would have selected would have been a psychologist's account of the differences between various learning models available for psycholinguistic theory, and would have included some sort of caution about the reduction of linguistic to psychological phenomena. I think it accurate to say that there was only one paper with these qualifications available at the time when the contents of Saporta's reader were drawn up; this is Jenkins' section in the 1954 survey entitled "The learning theory approach." Apart from the clear distinctions which he draws between particular approaches, Jenkins has presented a discussion of the general nature of psychological theories which, considering its condensed scope, is as informative as many book-length treatises.

It might be wondered why I choose to discuss at this point the neurophysiological bases of language. The answer is that the operant conditioning approach in psycholinguistics has consciously and successfully striven to avoid this topic. Because Skinner seems to reject considerations of theory, it is difficult to gather from his writings just how far the operant conditioning approach has neglected the internal organization of the speaker and therefore also consideration of the various "intervening variables" which others, even strict behaviorists, have on occasion imposed between the stimulus input and the response output. It is peculiar that so much of the work carried on in operant conditioning does so without reference to the findings of other specialties such as descriptive linguistics and, of immediate concern now, neurophysiology.

Many psycholinguists are becoming increasingly concerned with the neurophysiological matrix of speech. The development is of course related to and reinforced by the growth of neurophysiological psychology, which is an important contemporary trend in American psychology. There is even a label available for the designation of the linguistic phase of this interest, namely, "neurolinguistics," recently proposed by Edith Trager (1961).

Neurophysiology has of course an older association with the study of speech disorders, dating from the writings of Head and others at the beginning of this century and back to Broca in the last. Recently this association has been renewed by the appearance of an important study by Penfield and Roberts (1959) and the equally important review of it by Lenneberg (1960a). But the context in which I especially want to mention neurophysiology is the recurrence of references to it in current theorizing about the acquisition and functioning of the speaker's linguistic competence. Consider the following remarks taken from recent comments by Chomsky:

The fact that all normal children acquire essentially comparable grammars of great complexity with remarkable rapidity suggests that human beings are somehow specially designed to do this, with data-handling or "hypothesis-formulating" ability of unknown character and complexity (1959:57); and with reference to perception, that "it is possible that ability to select out of the complex auditory input those features that are phonologically relevant may develop largely independent of reinforcement, through genetically determined maturation. To the extent that this is true, an account of the development and causation of behavior that fails to consider the structure of the organism will provide no understanding of the real processes involved" (1959:44).

Compelling statements proposing the neurophysiological basis of speech are found in Lenneberg's recent paper, "Language, evolution and purposive behavior" (1960b). The thesis of this study is that man "may be equipped with highly specialized innate propensities that favor, and, indeed, shape the development of speech in the child and that the roots of language may be deeply grounded in our biological constitution, as for instance our predisposition to use our hands" (1960b:869). One of the major problems here is phylogenetic: we are still quite ignorant about the inferred origins of language in a non- or pre-human communication system and are thus denied the insights that a "linguistic paleontology" might provide. Rather we must rely essentially on comparative anatomy, and on comparative neurophysiology in particular, and also on comparative studies of primate communication systems (see Part 9). As neurologists and ethologists fill in the gaps, these arguments become ones of logic, as they must be. There is no independent witness to the evolution of language; e.g., there is no corroboratory evidence in the form of an archaeological record such as we have for cultural evolution, nor of a fossil record such as we have for biological evolution.

The implications of my comments so far might appear to be that learning theory as an approach to verbal behavior is not amenable to integration with neurophysiology. Fortunately, however, this is not the case. Many of the possibilities which both Chomsky and Lenneberg envision with regard to a neurophysiological approach to language were anticipated or subsequently experimented with in work by Hebb and his associates at McGill University (e.g., Hebb, 1949, 1958). Lambert describes Hebb's aim as extending "the significance of psychological concepts, especially those concerned with complex cognitive processes, by relating them to what is known about the neurology of the central nervous system" (Lambert, 1962:13). From Hebb's work, significant evidence has accumulated to say that there is verbal input storage, retainable over long periods of time, which can be released without the environmental stimulation conceived as necessary by instrumental learning theory; this is a crucial finding for psycholinguistics.

The great number of papers surveyed in Krasner's "Studies of the conditioning of verbal behavior" (1958) still does not convey the true extent of the enoromus literature concerning word association and other verbal conditioning experiments. No attempt will be made here to survey all the relevant literature, for this is a research area in which there has been considerable repetition. There has been much time for studies of verbal conditioning to accumulate; they were first made famous by Jung shortly after the turn of the century, and go back at least as far as Ebbinghaus' endeavors in the late 19th century. Indeed, Cofer sees the whole field as a single tradition, stemming from Ebbinghaus, and relentlessly concerned with "the learning and retention of lists of discrete items in an effort to describe and to explain basic associative processes and the conditions of which they are a function" (1961:1).

This reviewer perceives the mainstream of the movement as being isolated from other psycholinguistic research activities and quite encysted in experimentation with numerous variables (many relatively minor) which have been observed or suggested to exert differential effects on rote learning. It is therefore not surprising to discover that this is an area of little interdisciplinary communication, and relative to the amount of research effort expended, one from which linguistic and psycholinguistic theory have profited the least. The communication gap cuts both ways, for there is frequently manifest within the field a baleful ignorance of relevant and heuristic developments in linguistics.

There are some gaps in Krasner's coverage of both older and more recent research in the area of verbal conditioning. Some earlier omissions can be culled from Miller (1951a, 1951b), from more up-to-date surveys by Adams (1957), Dulany (1961), and Salzinger (1959), who survey this specific topic, and by Osgood (1963a). Much ongoing research is reported in articles appearing in the *Journal of Verbal Learning and Verbal Behavior* and the *Journal of Abnormal and Social Psychology*, and to a lesser extent in the *Journal of Experimental Psychology*. General methodological critiques are available; Marshall and Cofer (1963) and Postman (1962) are very useful. More specific methodological problems, such as the analysis of recognition as a measure of retention (e.g., Murdock, 1963), have received concerted attention at several recent symposia devoted to verbal learning and associational processes. These symposia include three from which the proceedings have been published in readily accessible form, namely, Cofer (1961), Cofer and Musgrave (1963), and Jenkins (1959).

Developmental trends in this area chiefly involve experimentation with the host of variables which have been proposed as effecting differences in the acquisition, transfer, and retention of rote-learned verbal materials. Out of these have no doubt emerged some important results. Certainly one of the more inescapable is the realization of the importance, in verbal conditioning, of the context in which the verbal units occur. Context factors such as sequential expectancies are now viewed as a major source of variance in verbal conditioning experiments. Some of the pertinent research, in view of its relevance to the study of transitional dependencies, will be discussed in Parts 3, 4, and 5 below.

One real value of the Krasner paper lies in its discussion of areas *other* than learning theory in which the results of verbal conditioning experiments might contribute substantial insights and applications. The potential contribution which most impressed Krasner was in the techniques of psychotherapy, which he views as "directive in nature" and "teach-able." "The therapist uses cues, often without his own awareness, to modify, guide, or manipulate the patient's verbal behavior." Equally important applications to teaching are discerned by Lambert, who sees the value of operant conditioning for language teachers (or language machines) "who can be either effective or ineffective as social reinforcers of their students' attempts to develop appropriate verbal habits" (1962:11).

Krasner leaves undeveloped a consideration which he raises about the design of many verbal conditioning experiments, the subjects' occasional perception of the relationship between the experimenter's induced stimulus and associate. Typically such subjects are then excluded from further participation, thus imposing prevalent but as yet unanalyzed variable factors. A few experimenters have actually turned their attention to this problem; it is mentioned in Adams (1957), and is the primary focus in Spielberger (1962), Spielberger and Levin (1962), and Levin (1962). A study by Fuhrer and Eriksen (1960) examined the implications of the subjects' "unconscious perception" of the conditioning relationship, and an earlier study (Eriksen and Kuethe, 1956) reports successful avoidance conditioning achieved without the subjects' awareness. The dependence of verbal conditioning on the performer's awareness is obviously one of the more important queries to be answered in this field.

The interest in the "directive" aspects of verbal learning in such social interactions as psychotherapy, manifested in Krasner's paper as well as in the studies of Fuhrer and Eriksen (1960) and Eriksen and Kuethe (1956), suggests hitherto unappreciated possibilities for using verbal conditioning not only in psychiatry, but in experimental clinical and social psychology as well (see also Ullmann, Krasner, and Collins, 1961). The diagnostic value (of perturbations in expected associations) for various types of anxiety, hypertension, and motivational problems, has been discussed by Brody (1964), Buss and Gerjuoy (1958), Korchin and Levine (1957), Sarason (1957), and Taylor (1958). "Other-directedness" is apparently manifest in verbal as well as other social behavior, as shown in recent studies of verbal conditioning as related to various sorts of social approval, ranging from small groups (e.g., Crowne and Strickland, 1961) to audience-speaker interaction (e.g., Levin, Baldwin, and Gall-wey, 1960). The experimenter-bias effects of certain types of verbal cuing is discussed by Hildum and Brown (1956) and Sandler (1962). (The directive role of non-verbal cues is discussed in Part 9.)

3. Speech Perception

Part III of Saporta's reader contains: J. D. O'Connor, "Recent work in English phonetics" (1957) ; E. Fischer-Jørgensen, "What can the new techniques of acoustic phonetics contribute to linguistics?" (1958) ; A. M. Liberman, "Some results of research on speech perception" (1957) ; and

G. A. Miller and P. E. Nicely, "An analysis of perceptual confusions among some English consonants" (1955).

Interest in speech perception, at first concentrating mainly on the auditory recognition of speech sounds, has enjoyed great currency since the beginning of the 1950's. This can be regarded as a core area of psycholinguistics, the result of the coming together of acoustic phonetics and communications engineering, and those psychologists who found in the contact of these fields a novel and fertile area in which to investigate perception. G. A. Miller's book, *Language and Communication* (1951b), was an early and influential response, and his chapter on the "Perception of speech" was an important early synthesis.

Fischer-Jørgensen makes the point in her paper that the communications engineer· (unlike the acoustic physicist) has interests in speech which closely parallel those of the linguists, viz., that he "is directly interested in the functional aspect of speech sounds; he wants to find those sound features which are relevant for communication; he will also, like the linguist, be interested in relating the acoustic phenomena to the activity of the speaker and to the perception of the hearer." Since it was engineers who were designing all the attractive new gear for acoustic analysis, interdisciplinary contact was inevitable. Moreover, the contact proved to be a fruitful one for all parties, as amply demonstrated in Miller's book and in work which proceeded to emerge from various projects of the Haskins Laboratories, from the Bell Telephone Laboratories, and from the M.I.T. Acoustics Laboratory.

The weighty *Handbook of Experimental Psychology* (Stevens, 1951), containing important papers by Miller, Licklider, and von Békésy, had the desirable effect of calling the attention of psychologists to the linguistic aspects of communication and perception. *The Journal of the Acoustical Society of America* (particularly during a peak period of activity in the mid-1950's) was soon laden with articles on speech perception and became a more familiar periodical to many American linguists than the older phonetics journals. Typical of the activity at that time, in 1952 the Acoustical Society of America sponsored "A conference on speech analysis," bringing together linguists, psychologists, and communications engineers, and producing an important group of papers published in the society's journal; these included Fischer-Jørgensen (1952), Pike (1952), and Licklider (1952).

It would be to wander too far afield to mention available introductions to acoustics and acoustic phonetics in this survey. Good bibliographic coverage through the year 1956 is provided in Fischer-Jørgensen (1958), and in Fant (1960), who carries the coverage into 1960. A disarmingly simple and sound introduction is available in a new study by Denes and Pinson (1963), while Fant (1960) remains the standard major reference text.

The O'Connor paper, principally a review of results, makes a distinction among the personnel interested in perception, between "linguistic phoneticians" and "linguistic experimentalists." Most of the psycholinguistic work in perception has been experimental. And the development of the "new techniques" discussed by Fischer-Jørgensen has made for the possibility of very carefully controlled experimentation indeed. Unfortunately, many of these new techniques (and the instruments which they use) are highly complex and it might reasonably be argued that papers descriptive of the techniques and methods themselves might have been included in Saporta's reader. For example, Miller's paper, "The perception of speech" (1956), offers a far clearer discussion of the notion of psychological similarity of stimuli (and of the "analysis of confusion" designed as a technique for measuring similarity) than is available in his and Nicely's applied study in the reader.

The analysis of confusion practiced by Miller and his colleagues is not the only experimental approach to the recognition of speech sounds. A more dramatic approach involves the use of speech synthesizers. An informative discussion of this approach is offered in the Liberman paper, which reviews some results of the Haskins Laboratories' various quests for "the acoustic cues on which . . . perception depends." Using spectrograms and instruments such as their Pattern Playback, they proceed to "make controlled changes in various aspects of the acoustic pattern, and then to evaluate the effects of those changes on the sound as heard." Some of their results will be mentioned below.

There is yet a third experimental approach to the recognition of speech sounds, which is not represented in the reader. This is experimentation with tape-splicing, which is more easily and less expensively carried out when synthesizing, and hence more in range for student projects and budgets. I missed either Schatz's (1954) or Malécot's (1960) interesting papers in the reader.

Liberman brings up the issue of "auditory feedback," and his comments, together with Fischer-Jørgensen's, outline some of the possible explanations to account for tie-ins between the articulatory, acoustic, and auditory phases of speech sounds. Chiefly on the basis of experiments with English consonants, Liberman argues that "speech is perceived by reference to articulation—that is, that the articulatory movements and their sensory effects mediate between the acoustic stimulus and the event we call perception," and that "the mediating articulation not only produces distinctive proprioceptive stimuli, but also external sounds which can be matched against the sounds being perceived." The present viewpoint of the Haskins investigators, expressed recently by Abramson, is that the psychological invariance underlying perception must reside in the neural codings of the articulatory movements:

A link between the perception of speech sounds and feedback from the articulatory movements that the hearer would use in producing these sounds, leads to categorical perception when the phonemic distinctions involve no intermediate articulations; in phonemic distinctions which rest on articulatory continua, perception will be less categorical, and differential discrimination ought then to be fairly constant throughout the range of variation (1961).

The fact that some sort of neurological servosystem does monitor coding cannot be doubted; numerous experiments have suggested this, although the exact motor processes have all been inferred (e.g., Fairbanks, 1954). But it is equally obvious from recent investigation of language acquisition and speech disorders, that receptive perception, i.e., the decoding of messages by the hearer, cannot depend on such a servosystem as described, the obvious countercase being where speech is understood by the hearer who is congenitally defective for speech production (see Part 6). The outstanding problem in this area may well turn out to be our relative ignorance of the receptive apparatus itself and its neurophysiological functionings. Recent investigations by Mol, von Békésy, and others may fill in some of the gaps in the future.

The selection of readings contained in this section of Saporta's reader is a good one, but is of course restricted to the perception of phonological units. Many other experiments have focused rather on the perception of larger, meaningful units (usually the "word"). Most of these experiments have been concerned with the role of redundancy in recognition and learning tasks, and one of the major psycholinguistic generalizations which we are able to offer derives from them, viz., that recognition and learning performance increase directly with the experimental increase in redundancy. These experiments will receive extensive discussion in Part 4 below.

Accumulating evidence from numerous experiments in perception during the past decade suggests that the "distinctive auditory cue" is a complex stimulus, rarely simply correlated to the phoneme segment which purportedly includes it. Oversimplified models of perception have produced simple-minded notions about the process of decoding. H. Mol has been active in combatting some of these inadequate models, and his comments about one prevalent view of perception are very timely: "The mechanism of recognizing spoken words and sentences is no doubt voice-operated but it may not be regarded as the acoustic counterpart of an electrical teleprinter which prints letters that are unambiguously labelled by the electric signals it receives from a transmission line" (1963:50). The papers included in the reader all herald this conclusion, although it actually is not very clearly formulated in these readings.

Phonemic theory has long held that there is a constancy or invariance in the production of phonemes, and that contrast is implemented by the distinctive common denominator which all allophones of a particular phoneme share. The various non-distinctive attributes of the allophones were correctly viewed as the conditioned features dependent on the larger (usually immediately including) phonemic context, such that one could speak of this intersegmental dependency as a form of redundancy. The contemporary challenge to the concept of the phoneme as a psycholinguistic prime derives from the fact that its perception is not a direct function of phonetic substance; it is an indirect function, in which as much information for discriminatory perception is derived from the context. And it is extremely important to appreciate that the concept of "context" itself has become much more catholic during the course of the past decade. An asemantic immediate environment (defined in terms of adjacent phonological units) has been found inadequate, and it has been well argued that the much larger grammatical context is part of the cue-producing environment.

The view that perceptual invariance cannot be simply contained in the signal input is gaining ever wider acceptance. It has been most compellingly argued by Chomsky (1962a), Halle (1959), and Lees (1962), but it is not entirely novel to their writings. Pike (1959), for instance, conceded some alternatives to the view of language involving the phonological principles of invariance and linearity.

Psycholinguistic evidence for the new view derives from a number of experiments. That hearers can correctly identify vowel phonemes in a restricted context such as a CVC-syllable was early thrown open to question by Peterson and Barney's study (1952). Brown and Hildum (1956) have shown that perceptual discrimination, particularly the identification of given phonemes, is related to the probabilities of occurrence which those phonemes have in the specific larger context in which they were presented. Mol and Uhlenbeck (1959) have summarized experiments which indicate that contextual clues yield information useful for perception, and that their suppression greatly decrease the hearer's correct decodings of chosen tokens. The reviewer concurs again with Mol's evaluation, viz., "the lesson of all those investigations is that the phonic data the ear extracts from the sound waves do not form the only source on which the listener bases his identifications" (1963:52). Again fuller discussion is deferred until the following section.

Much of the work carried out in perception and speech has involved correlations of auditory with acoustic and articulatory units. Some investigations have been concerned, however, with the auxiliary role of visual clues in speech perception. Rubenstein and Aborn (1960) report on experiments by Sumby and Pollack (1954) and O'Neill (1954); the former demonstrate the increased importance of visual clues under conditions of interference with the speech signal, and the latter show that visual clues contribute more to accurate perception of consonants than of vowels, more for vowels than words, and more for words than phrases. The importance of visual clues was subtly involved in Householder's (1956) experiments with hearers' perception of English final unreleased p, t, k.

One interesting alley off the thoroughfare of perception studies involves the variable which we might classify as the hearer's "personal attention." I refer now to channel noise over which the hearer has some voluntary control, and not to the experimentally produced channel distortions which occur in many perception studies. This attention variable would include conscious attempts to block out or distort the impinging message. It would also include the hearer's effort to single out one message from a channel choked with several, e.g., as in the co-occurrence of messages from radio stations transmitting at the same point on the band. Broadbent (1957, 1958, 1962), who has done some work with the individual hearer's perception of several simultaneous messages, has found that if the hearer is exposed to a channel with two voice messages, he usually understands only one. Broadbent's work in this area leads him to conclude that there is a selective mechanism in the central nervous system (an "attention mechanism") which permits differential perception.

A problem wide open for psycholinguistic experimentation is the validation of "distinctive-feature analysis," the basic conceptualization of which is presented in Halle (1957, 1959, 1962), and further discussed in Chomsky (1962a) and Chomsky and Miller (1963). Particularly important for a full understanding of the speech recognition process would be experimentation with "feature opposition"; it would not seem too difficult, for instance, to determine whether or not oppositions are inherently binary. The Miller and Nicely study (1955) offers one research design through which such experimentation could be implemented. The conclusion of their study, as a matter of fact, indicates that several oppositions within the distinctive feature roster have discriminatory value of great power, although these were more effective in distinguishing one class of phonemes from another, than in distinguishing between members of a given class (such as "voiceless stops"). Also relevant here is the continuing experimentation with speech synthesizers (e.g., Liberman, Harris, Eimas, Lisker, and Bastian, 1961; Fry, Abramson, Eimas, and Liberman 1962). Most of this research indicates that perceptual distinctiveness is a very direct function of articulatory contrasts. Related are first, the vaguer issue of the "psychological reality" of phonological units (for which Sapir's 1933 classic still provides rewarding reading) and, second, the more important issue of the incorporation of perception into a general theory of language. Some models proposed for speech recognition are discussed by Miller and Chomsky (1963), including an important paper by Halle and Stevens (1962). The further pitfalls of confusing a model of linguistic structure with a model of speech performance (here recognition models) is touched upon in Katz and Postal (1964) (esp. pp. 166 ff) and in Postal (1964a).

4. *The Sequential Organization of Linguistic Events*

Part IV of Saporta's reader contains another chunk from N. Chomsky's *Syntactic Structures,* his Chapter 3, "An elementary linguistic theory"

(1957) ; K. S. Lashley, "The problem of serial order in behavior" (1951) ; G. A. Miller and J. A. Selfridge, "Verbal context and the recall of meaningful material" (1950) [the paper is incorrectly dated 1953 in the reader] ; G. A. Miller, "Free recall of redundant strings of letters" (1958) ; and D. Howes and C. E. Osgood, "On the combination of associative probabilities in linguistic contexts" (1954).

In spite of the relatively early dates of some of these studies, they excellently represent the work in this area. The problems relating to sequential organization are among the knottiest of all those awaiting resolution. Moreover, they constitute an area which behaviorist psychology in this country has avoided altogether. There is no better evidence for this than Lashley's study, which is widely quoted in psychology (and now in linguistics as well) as a declaration of interest in the overlooked internal make-up of the organism responsible for its integrated sequential behavior. Since the time of its appearance, interest has focused more and more on the intervening hook-ups between easily observed stimulus input and response output sequences.

During the same time, advances in neurophysiological psychology have conferred an earlier lacking legitimacy to dissecting the "black box." Numerous associated endeavors could be cited. It is revealing to observe the florescence of studies in cognition which these developments encouraged, a trend which will receive only this nodding recognition here. It is linguistically interesting to observe the neologisms and euphemisms which have evolved to break away from the mechanistic behaviorist terminology of earlier decades: "perceptual organization," "cognitive schemata," etc., which finally permitted the reappearance of "mind." For example, "I now believe that mind is something more than a four-letter Anglo-Saxon word—human minds exist and it is our job as psychologists to study them" (Miller, 1962a:761). But a more important observation is that, in the past decade, verbal behavior has become a frontier area for psychologists concerned with studying the integration of behavior: "Moreover, I believe that one of the best ways to study a human mind is by studying the verbal system that it uses" (Miller, 1962a:761). This sentiment was anticipated by Lashley in the paper included in the reader: "Certainly language presents in a most striking form the integrative functions that are characteristic of the cerebral cortex and that reach their highest development in human thought process."

Lashley sets the stage for psycholinguistic investigation in this area: "This is the essential problem of serial order: the existence of generalized schemata of action which determine the sequence of specific acts, acts which in themselves or in their associations seem to have no temporal valence." The relevant experimentation with these schemata has to date been far removed from any examination of their possible neurophysiological bases. (The consequent importance of the study of speech disorders will receive comment in Part 7.) Much is known about the specific afferent paths leading from the receptors to the cortex and similarly about the efferents leading to the motor areas used in speech. Much has also been discovered about the localization of specific functions in the cerebral cortex (through the work of Penfield and others). Very little is known, however, about the precise processes of decoding and encoding, let alone the problems of storage and linkage between the sensory projection and motor areas. Hebb and Osgood have been much concerned with working out the central nervous system's substructure for speech and the above mentioned problems of storage and linkage. I would characterize their efforts as partially complementary, and more crudely by the image of Hebb working from the inside (from the neurophysiological bases) outward, and Osgood from the outside (from the behavioral manifestations of speech) inward. A promising point of contact between Osgood's model of speech and Hebb's is that the "cell assemblies" (reverberatory circuits) postulated by the latter may be the somatic counterpart to Osgood's "mediational response" processes. A too brief and therefore tantalizing glimpse into this train of thought is available in Osgood's discussion of his own "three-stage" model of speech (1963a, 1963c) ; another brief and enthusiastic glimpse is afforded by Lambert's recent review (1962). The psycholinguistic contributions toward an understanding of behavioral organization, as we shall see, have all been inferential; but this in no way reduces their importance for a theory of language.

An important point about the development of psycholinguistic theory is not mentioned in the papers included in this section of Saporta's reader. Just when grammatical theory and studies of perception were becoming productively involved in the sequential aspects of speech, information theory (largely through the impact of Shannon and Weaver and their interpreters, such as Hockett) offered an attractive approach to its quantification which obscured the psychological insights offered by Hebb and Lashley. It obscured their insights because it sharpened focus on only one narrow aspect of sequential behavior, viz., its stochastic properties. The result of this restriction was a great emphasis on "transitional dependencies," which were investigated with a variety of techniques concentrating solely on the effect of antecedent contexts of the message on the occurrence of subsequent units. These transitions were measured in terms of their probabilities, and the whole frame of reference permitted a model of speech characterized by associative probabilities.

Linguistic method . . . identifies sets of discrete alternative units at each level of analysis. Learning theory models involve the central notion of associative hierarchies. At each level of behavioral organization, we must assume that particular antecedents are associated with sets of alternative subsequent events (divergent competitive hierarchies) and that particular subsequents are associated differentially with sets of antecedent events (convergent facilitative hierarchies). A major point of articulation is that between these associative hierarchies of learning theory and the substitution classes of linguistics, and information theory provides a highly generalizable method of describing the structure or degree of organization of these associative systems which result in linguistic responses. The convergent effects of antecedent context upon modifying the probabilities of alternative responses, raising the probabilities of some and lowering others, corresponds to the reduction of conditional uncertainty or entropy in information measurement (Osgood, 1963a:270).

The cognate model for speech acquisition, using associative probabilities, is a primitive learning theory model in which entropy profiles are transposed into "response probabilities" and "associative hierarchies." The learner is purported to acquire these response patterns (let us temporarily call them "types") inductively through exposure to numerous well-formed "tokens" which he hears uttered in his community. One is reluctant, however, to push this model beyond the sorts of simple phrase-structure sequences involved in most psycholinguistic experiments. In many experiments, typically, positional "types" are equated with the form-classes (and their simple linear orderings) yielded by immediate constituent analysis. One of the difficulties inheres in immediate constituent analysis itself, since that model treats as unrelated events many sequence types which are intuitively perceived as closely related by the native speakers (e.g., the relationship of an active sentence to its passive transform).

The fact that a simple stochastic model poses an insuperable obstacle to the child's actual learning of his language has been demonstrated by Miller in his chapter on language acquisition in *Plans and the Structure of Behavior* (Miller, Galanter, and Pribram, 1960). More general comments on the limitations of the stochastic model, both as a model for acquisition and as a model for production, is contained in Galanter and Miller (1960), and a more recent analysis of its employment in psycholinguistics is given in Miller and Chomsky (1963).

All these immediate context models have recent support, however, from communications engineering and a decade's worth of psycholinguistic endeavor involving experimentation with the role of sequence constraints as contextual clues. It was early discovered in perception experiments dealing with "distinctive" speech sounds, that if contextual clues are eliminated or suppressed, perceptual constancy is correspondingly reduced (see Part 3). So, too, with various identification and recall tasks involving words and phrases presented with and without their grammatical contexts. Earlier studies, such as that of Miller, Heise, and Lichtern (1951), embody the stochastic model directly from information theory: the greater intelligibility of words in context is attributed to the reduction of possible alternates because of the sequence constraints on certain form-classes. Entropy rises as the antecedent contexts are eliminated; i.e., the hearer's uncertainty increases as sequential predictability is disturbed.

This pattern can be seen in the design of the Miller and Selfridge (1950) paper: "By verbal context, as opposed to total context, we mean only the extent to which the prior occurrence of certain verbal elements influences the talker's present choice." These authors construct a clever learning

task involving strings with sequences of varying degrees of approximation to permitted English word order. Their results suggest that sequential dependencies, rather than meaning, enhance correct recall: "If the
nonsense [of remoter approximations] preserves the short range associations of the English language that are so familiar to us, the nonsense
is easy to learn."

Saporta's organization of the readings in this section of his reader is
superb. Miller's article on "Free recall of redundant strings of letters"
(1958) follows on the heels of the Miller and Selfridge paper in the reader.
This pairing very clearly offers an example of the cumulative effects of
research in this area, since the second builds on the first, spelling out very
clearly how its results have been incorporated into other experiments and
theory-building. The paper itself reports on a very well-controlled investigation of recall of structured (therefore redundant) strings of letters
as opposed to random strings. The results show predictably that the redundant strings are learned faster, but that with the increase in redundancy comes a decrease in information conveyed. Equally important,
Miller integrates his findings in this experiment with the 1958 Chomsky
and Miller paper concerning finite state models.

With apologies to the authors because of their tremendous investment
in time, I find the Howes and Osgood (1954) paper very difficult to read.
Moreover, in spite of (or perhaps because of) the formulae which bristle
on every page, the relevance is of the variables being tested is not clear.
The authors describe a word association experiment designed to test the
effects of a varied compound 'stimulus on an expected associate; the experiment shows that the effects of their variables ("interposition," "density," and "frequency") are statistically significant.

The selections in this part of Saporta's reader are not rich biblio-
graphically. The reader can gain an appreciation of the range of research
problems in this area that were awaiting investigation a decade ago, by
reference to Section 5 ("Sequential psycholinguistics") of the 1954
Psycholinguistics monograph reprinted in the present volume. Good reviews of subsequent developments may be found in Rubenstein and
Aborn's survey (1960), especially in their section "Probability of language segments," and in Osgood's more recent survey (1963a).

Structural context as it relates to auditory perception is discussed in
Pollack and Picket (1964), with reference to experiments on the intelligibility of speech segments excerpted from larger discourses. An excellent paper by O'Neill (1957) shows that more words are recognized in
noisy channels when included in larger redundant contexts than when
produced alone. Bruce (1958) reports on the variable accuracy in perception of sentences, depending on the context-induced set of the hearer
—in this case, merely whether or not the subject was apprised of the topic
of a possible (but not presented) larger surrounding discourse. More
general issues relating to contextual constraints upon learning (as well

as upon perception) are discussed in a number of interesting papers, including Aborn, Rubenstein, and Sperling (1959) ; Cofer (1960) ; Howes (1957) ; and Rubenstein and Pollack (1963). The specific role of the grammatical form class receives attention in Deese (1962b) ; Ervin (1963) ; McNeill (1963) ; and Miller (1962b).

The problem of isolating the psycholinguistically distinctive units of sequential encoding has elicited some interesting experiments with pausal phenomena, which are investigated not only as possible boundary indicators but also as measures of latency of transitional dependencies. Goldman-Eisler has written several papers on this topic (1955, 1961), although her primary interest is in the study of prosodic features as indicators of certain types of personality disorders (see Part 9). An especially interesting paper in this vein is Maclay and Osgood's (1959) study of hesitation phenomena in English, which suggests that pauses are a function of increased entropy at certain stateable sequential positions. The constraints imposed by syntactic rules are discussed in several papers by Epstein (1961, 1962, 1963), in Miller (1962a), and in Mehler (1963), and the constraints of semantic rules are dealt with in Marks and Miller (1964) and also in Miller (1962a).

Another fascinating tack for the interested student is to explore the implications for sequential decoding and encoding (and storage) contained in Miller's work with immediate memory span; his "magical number" paper (1956) has already had some impact on grammatical theory. Apart from the fact that a model for speech production must represent the speaker with a finite memory, there are interesting suggestions that certain grammatical constructions (e.g., some relative and passive transformations in English) are devices which reduce overloading of the storage capacity of the speaker.

Yngve has discussed storage capacity in various syntactic structures (chiefly in English) and has concluded that many constructions function so as to minimize "grammatical depth" and to prevent overload. He has argued this convincingly in several papers (1960, 1961, 1962) in which the focus, to be sure, is rather on the temporary memory spans of computers being programmed for sentence construction tasks. Brief discussion of Yngve's suggestions is available in a recent paper by Chomsky (1961b), and in another by Plath (1961), and more extensive treatment is available in Miller and Chomsky (1963).

Of the many insights offered by the several Chomsky chapters, none is more relevant here than the conclusion of his Chapter 3, "An elementary linguistic theory," which forms part of this section of the reader: "It seems quite clear that no theory of linguistic structure based exclusively on Markov process models and the like, will be able to explain or account for the ability of a speaker of English to produce and understand new utterances, while he rejects other new sequences as not belonging to the language." This and Chomsky's Chapter 2 (included in Part II of the reader) are too succinctly presented to paraphrase or explicate here. His demonstration of the independence of grammar from some of the various approaches to its formulation (through semantics and statistical orders of approximation), and the demonstration of the inadequacy of the finite state model, have become widely known. The student who reads Chomsky's Chapter 3 must wonder, in the face of such forceful argumentation, whether the articles which follow it in this part of Saporta's reader (Lashley's excepted) really point the way to fruitful psycholinguistic research for the future, since all are involved with limited left-to-right structures.

Some confusion will be avoided if the student appreciates the fact that Chomsky is not immediately concerned with constructing a model of the language user (see Part 2). This fact has been more sharply enunciated by Chomsky since the publication of his *Syntactic Structures;* e.g., "The attempt to develop a reasonable account of the speaker has, I believe, been hampered by the prevalent and utterly mistaken view that a generative grammar in itself provides or is related in some obvious way to a model for the speaker" (1961b:14). The question of ultimate goals for linguistic theory has also received more expanded exploration by Chomsky in his more recent articles, and the student should apprise himself of the content of several of these later studies (e.g., 1961a, 1961b, 1962a, 1962b, and 1963).

It is especially exciting that the work of Miller and others is beginning to offer corroboratory support for the "psychological reality" of many of the abstract characterizations of the user's linguistic competence which are contained in a formalized generative grammar (see Part 2) ; a case could be made for Chomsky's being overly cautious in his appraisal of the explanatory power of generative grammar theory.

5. *The Semantic Aspects of Linguistic Events*

Part V of the reader contains: B. F. Skinner, "The problem of reference," (part of Chapter 5 of his *Verbal Behavior, 1957*) ; L. Bloomfield, "Meaning," (Chapter 9 of his *Language, 1933*) ; W. V. Quine, "The problem of meaning in linguistics," (Chapter 3 of his *From a Logical Point of View, 1953*) ; N. Chomsky, "Syntax and semantics," (Chapter 9 of his *Syntactic Structures, 1957*) ; R. Wells, "Meaning and use" (1954) ; C. E. Osgood, G. Suci, and P. Tannenbaum, "The logic of semantic differentiation" (most of Chapter 1 of their *The Measurment of Meaning, 1957*) ; and I. Pool, "Trends in content analysis today: a summary" (the final chapter of *Trends in Content Analysis, 1959*, which Pool edited).

This assortment represents a tremendous tour de force on a topic which traditionally has supported as many approaches as there were investigators willing to approach it. It is interesting to notice that these readings, with the exception of Wells's, are parts of much larger pronouncements on verbal behavior and/or linguistics, all of which have been obliged to cope with "the reference problem," i.e., with "meaning." Considering the diversity of thought represented by these readings, one might conclude correctly that this has been an avenue of inquiry characterized by much individual and little concerted effort. This aspect of the climate of semantics has been aptly characterized by Katz and Fodor in their recent proposal for a semantic theory. These writers point out that "semantics suffers not from a dearth of facts about meanings and meaning relations in natural languages, but rather from the lack of an adequate theory to organize, systematize, and generalize these facts" (1963:170). Weinreich similarly maintains that there is little theory available for a consideration of semantic universals, and that even such undirected particularistic studies of meaning as are available suffer from being "on the whole preoccupied with the one semiotic process of naming, i.e., with the use of designators in theoretical isolation; they pay relatively little attention to the combinatory semiotics of connected discourse" (1963:115), let alone undertaking to carry out extensive cross-language comparisons.

There are a number of rather basic differences between the linguist's approach to the analysis of expression (which has been the main concern of descriptive linguists, at least in this country) and his initial probings into the analysis of meaning or content. I will not consider here the many pronouncements in American writings asserting that the analysis of expression is the only legitimate concern of descriptive linguists, nor the logical gymnastics performed by many analysts in attempting to avoid problems of meaning in their actual analyses; for a discussion of this topic, see Wells (1951). The less extreme view in American descriptive linguistics merely claims that the expression plane of a language can be descriptively analyzed more or less independently of the content plane which is in some way correlated with it. The proviso "more or less independently" allows for the fact that expression is only rarely analyzed in total abstraction from content, since the operational procedures employed in isolating linguistic primes involve the criterion of "same or different."

"Same or different" is the basis for a game played between analyst and informant that most behavioral scientists would regard as a primitive controlled experiment in which, by manipulation of units in the expression, the linguist contrives to effect or avoid a correlated change in content. The resemblance of "substitution" and "commutation" procedures in linguistic analysis has been explicitly recognized by Haugen (1951). Further discussion of this interesting parallel is available in Fischer-Jørgensen (1956) for phonology, and in Diderichsen (1958) for phonology and morphology.

How have linguists attempted to describe the structure of content? Let us first restrict our attention to a consideration of discovery and segmentation procedures. Although there have been several general approaches to·devising an operational procedure which will consistently yield a semantic prime, the prime itself has been very reluctant to emerge. Wells has argued that if content is subjected to analysis in total abstraction from expression, the linearity which permits segmentation of expression does not obtain: "since the C-plane has no proper counterpart to temporal order, it cannot have analogues to those E-facts [viz., phonemes and morphs] that depend essentially on temporal order" (1958:659).

Related problems revolve about the factor of continuity, which one is obliged to take into account in semantic analysis. Traditionally, the procedures used to isolate linguistic units of expression have been based on the discovery of discrete discontinuous attributes (see Part 1). Linguists have been frustrated in their attempts to carry over these discovery procedures into semantic data which subvert the quantum mathematics. Nevertheless, there are prevalent one-to-one correspondences between the planes of content and expression, as manifest in the much-studied relationships of words to their referent-objects. Analysis of these correspondences has led several workers, including Jakobson (1948) and Ebeling (1962), to delimit as a semantic prime those recurrent distinctive features of meaning which Ebeling calls "semantic minimums," viz., "the ultimate semantic constituents which are separately interchangeable in the positions where they occur. . . . In this sense, the semantic minimums are on a par with the distinctive features in phonemics" (1962:92).

A commutation-like procedure is employed by Ebeling to yield these features. Their recurrences and discreteness are established by proportional equations (e.g., *stallion:mare = ram:ewe*), which Ebeling claims are amenable to precise psycholinguistic experimentation with untutored speaker-subjects. Ebeling's method is considerably more refined than this review will be able to demonstrate. What is important to add is that his method assumes as co-occurrent the discovery of significant units between content and expression. Moreover, recognition of semantic resemblances has some priority since this "furnishes the directives for the decomposition of the chain into morphemes" (1962:113) : "A relevant morphemic feature presents itself to the investigator as a correspondence between one or more phonemes on the one hand and one or more semantic minimums on the other" (1962:114).

Several problems are associated with postulating a semantic prime, and some have immediate psycholinguistic relevance. Operational procedures for morphological analysis early ran afoul of so-called "submerged" semantic components, a variety of semantic minimum never discretely associated with a given unit of expression (e.g., with a morph). Such submerged or covert features are often especially evident in inflectional paradigms wherein several obvious semantic dimensions (e.g., number, aspect) are operating, but where the words cannot be segmented into morphs that are discretely associated with any one component of meaning.

Many pseudosolutions such as the postulation of "portmanteau" segments were proposed, but the only development of any immediate fruitfulness was that which we now loosely call "componential analysis." Componential analysis will receive further and more detailed attention in Part 8, especially with reference to its psycholinguistic implications. Here it will suffice to mention some of the earlier influential studies in componential analysis and to indicate some of the implications this approach might have for broader problems in semantic analysis. One early influential demonstration of componential analysis was Harris (1948). An insightful exploration of the applicability of componential analysis to meaning is contained in Lounsbury (1956), and an extended application to lexicography is contained in Malkiel (1959).

Componential analysis has forced its practitioners to be much more explicit about their semantic theories and methods for semantic analysis than has hitherto been customary. Since componential analysis yields (often covert), paradigmatic structure within semantic domains, investigators have become much more aware of the contrastive and hierarchical structuring of content and, in particular, of the distinction which many European linguists make between "form" and "substance" within content. This is suggested by the terminology that is now appearing in anthropological literature devoted to ethnoscience. Here appear terms such as "segregate," "contrast set," "(criterial) attributes," and others, which reveal their backgrounds chiefly in cognition psychology but also in lexicography. Definitions of these terms are given in Frake (1962) and in Conklin (1962), among others. The relationship of componential analysis and ethnoscience to cognition psychology becomes especially evident upon comparing these papers with Brown's "Language and categories," an appendix to Bruner, Goodnow, and Austin (1957), and with perception theory in Kilpatrick (1955).

Although I am not certain that the parallel will be accepted, to me these terms seem to reflect an indigenous American attempt to devise a set of discovery procedures for the descriptive analysis of the "form of content," applying to "form" and "substance" the basic dichotomy which glossematics makes in both expression and content. I use "glossematics" here to refer to an approach. The approach itself is penetratingly discussed in Wells (1951) and Fischer-Jørgensen (1949). A general introduction to the methods and theory of glossematics is available in Hjelmslev and Uldall (1957), and applications of the approach to the analysis of content can be found in *Recherches structurales 1949*, particularly in the papers by Diderichsen (1949) and Lotz (1949).

Some of the features of the glossematic theory which find possible relevance here include the manner in which the relationship between expression and content is envisioned. Analysis of the form of expression and content can be carried out in abstraction from the descriptive characterization of their substances, and it is this study of formal properties which is of most interest linguistically. The antithesis between form (the abstract relational properties of a system) and substance (the specification of the physique of individual units in the system, as in the phonetic description of a particular allophone) in part finds expression in the American systems of hierarchical analysis. Thus a "higher level" is in some ways a formal statement of a lower level which, relative to the upper, specifies substance. For example, as above, a phonemic analysis is in part a formal statement based on the substantive facts of the underlying phonetics of the language. The distinction, not always easy to apply, is not only a logical nicety; it is crucial for much of psycholinguistic research.

The whole concept of a psychological equivalence category devolves on a distinction between form and substance. Linguists, unlike some social scientists, have available highly efficient techniques for deciding when two events are the same, i.e., in some way linguistic equivalents of each other. This is not a matter of crude physical measurement; rather, it is a way of measuring psychological equivalence, and the psychological equivalence of two entities often obtains in spite of physically measurable differences in substance between them.

Let the student beware, however, that while these discovery procedures have been remarkably well worked out for the analysis of expression, this has not been the case for the analysis of content, notwithstanding the promising advances of componential analysis. This will become abundantly clear from the selections contained in this section of Saporta's reader. What will also become clear is that the selections have precious little to say about two central topics: a general theory of semantics, and the different "kinds" of meaning which might be distinguished.

It is most difficult at this stage of our knowledge to outline the relevance of a general semantic theory to psycholinguistics, or to predict in what ways psycholinguists might be helpful in the construction of such a theory. As an example of the sort of contributions which psycholinguistic research might offer, one can cite the exciting experiments concerning semantically determined combinatory rules which have been reported by Miller and Isard (1963). In these experiments the respondents' auditory perception of test sentences differed according to whether these were grammatical, anomalous (i.e., semantically devious or non-meaningful, although grammatical), or ungrammatical. The report is especially interesting for its discussion of semantic rules and the role of these rules in the perception of speech. More recent experiments with "semantic rules" are reported in Marks and Miller (1964).

Of the proposals for a semantic theory surveyed by the reviewer, only one adequately spells out the general form that such a theory must take and the sort of linguistic competence to be accounted for by that theory. This is the study by Katz and Fodor (1963) referred to above. Katz and Fodor deal with the "speaker's ability to interpret sentences." They set as the practical goals of a semantic theory the description and explanation of this "interpretative ability of speakers by accounting for their performance in determining the number and content of the readings of a sentence, by detecting semantic anomalies, by deciding on paraphrase relations between sentences, and by marking every other semantic property or relation that plays a role in this ability" (1963:176). Their paper offers considerable clarification of the issue of the separation of grammar and semantics.

This issue has several facets. One that has been raised by Chomsky in his *Syntactic Structures* (1957) is that the property of grammaticality cannot be equated with the meaningfulness of the utterance being tested for that property. The independence of grammaticality from semantics has been questioned by Putnam (1961), who finds that the putative sharp demarcation between ungrammatical and semantically devious is difficult to discern.

Another facet of the problem is raised by Chomsky in "Syntax and semantics," Chapter 9 of his selection from *Syntactic Structures,* appearing in this section of Saporta's reader. This is the question of whether discovery procedures in linguistic analysis and the linguistic primes which they yield can be defined independently of meaning. Chomsky again builds a strong case for the autonomy of grammar from semantics, and again Putnam (1961) offers reservations, in this case independently echoed in two critical reviews of Chomsky's work, by Haas (1958) and by Matthews (1961).

But it is interesting to notice that a semantic component is now viewed as the second of two important interpretive elements in the generative grammar, the other interpretive component being phonological. Katz and Postal's recent *An Integrated Theory of Linguistic Descriptions* is to a large extent an attempt to "provide an adequate means of incorporating the grammatical and the semantic descriptions of a language into one integrated description" (1964:x). For the limits of the semantic competence specified by their model, see Postal (1964a) and Katz and Fodor (1963).

It is unfortunate that no paper is included which discusses more clearly the relationship of content and expression, or which attempts to describe the possible varieties of meaning. The Bloomfield "Meaning" paper (1933) fails as a candidate on both fronts. The welter of linguistic, stylistic, and paralinguistic phenomena which are paraded in this paper adds support to Bloomfield's contention that a scientific semantic analysis is beyond the means of linguistic methodology. But the case for this view is surely overstated. It is true that Bloomfield's position strongly influenced subsequent developments in American linguistics, which has neglected semantic analysis, but this does not emerge from the paper itself, and should have been supplied by editorial comment. The student-reader may already hold to the widespread fallacy that Bloomfield opted to ignore meaning altogether. Although a careful reading of his 1933 paper will dissuade him from this belief, the possibility for confusion might have been lessened by inclusion of one of Bloomfield's later papers (e.g., 1939) wherein the whole topic of meaning receives a more precise and coherent treatment.

Within the reader, Wells's paper, "Meaning and use," is very interesting in its own right. Moreover, it puts Bloomfield's approach to meaning into a broader framework by examining its position in an intellectual history of recent philosophical treatments of meaning, chiefly those of Russell and Wittgenstein. Quine's paper, "The problem of meaning in linguistics," offers an extensive discussion of synonymy and its position in the conceptualization and analysis of meaning.

A still not outdated work by Charles W. Morris might have provided the framework we seek. This is his famous "Foundations of the theory of signs" (1939), a classic paper which might have considerably enhanced Saporta's reader. In it, Morris sets out to carefully distinguish between different kinds of meaning: "The confusion regarding the meaning of 'meaning' lies in part in the failure to distinguish with sufficient clarity the dimension of semiosis which is under consideration" (1939:121). For reasons that we shall discern shortly, American psychologists and linguists are most familiar with the imperfect dichotomy between "denotative" and "connotative" meaning. This dichotomy can be related only in a haphazard manner to the different kinds of meaning which are so clearly described in Morris' paper. A strict usage of "denotative" in Morris' sense would restrict us to examining "the relations of signs to the objects to which the signs are applicable" (1939:84), the area of inquiry he calls "semantics" proper. But surely most linguists would want to include the study of meanings implicated by the relations of signs one to another, what Morris calls the "syntactic dimension of semiosis." (It is the confluence of the semantical and syntactical dimensions of semiosis which underlies the distinction, often difficult to effect, between linguistic and grammatical meaning.) "Connotative meaning" relates largely to what Morris called the "pragmatical dimension of semiosis," i.e., the study of the "relation of signs to interpreters."

One of the best programmatic accounts of meaning is Carroll's recent study (1964), in which he discusses, among other topics, the relationship of semantics to the categorization of experience and concept formation. The paper also contains one of the clearest expositions of the distinction between denotative and connotative meaning.

The relevance of meaning for verbal learning has received considerable recent attention. Some recent work is surveyed in Bousfield (1961). Recent papers include Deese (1962a); Goss (1961); Noble (1952); and Staats (1961), in which there is concern for the role of conditioning in concept formation. A number of different dimensions are being investigated, including the process called semantic satiation; see, for example, Lambert and Jakobovits (1960) and Miller (1963).

It is evident that what energy linguists have invested in semantic analysis has been devoted to studying the denotative relationships between words and their referents. Among psychologists interested in semantics, many have similarly concerned themselves with this phase of semiosis. This interest is apparent, for instance, in discussions of language acquisition wherein the establishment of the contracts between signs and referents is of central concern. One theoretical approach for studying the assignation of denotative meanings is presented in Skinner's "The problem of reference," included in this part of the reader; the approach itself has been discussed earlier in Part 2.

On the other hand, psychologists have also been very much concerned with the relationship between linguistic signs and their users, the relationship which Morris calls the "interpretant" and which he treats as a central problem of pragmatic analysis. Morris' definition of "interpretant" involves assuming dispositional tendencies in the interpreter: "The interpretant is the habit of the organism to respond, because of the sign vehicle, to absent objects which are relevant to a present problematic situation as if they were present" (1939:109). It is easy to see here the influence which Morris exerted on both Osgood's and Skinner's views on semantics. However divergent the approach and focus of the latter two men are from each other and from Morris, both represent attempts to construct a theory of dispositions based on reinforcement.

The psychologist's interest in the interpretant is best seen in Osgood's development of the "semantic differential," a technique for pragmatic analysis designed "to assess certain symbolic processes assumed to occur in people when signs are received and produced" (Osgood, 1959:192). The semantic differential, derived ultimately from investigations with synesthesia, is a technique using multiple factor analysis which discloses dimensional structure within "semantic space." Various concepts are subjected to semantic differentiation along certain adjectival scales which express connotative, affective values by which the speaker-subject judges the concept.

The technique was discussed at length in a book which has become well known to psychologists and which has become an object of controversy among linguists. It is not surprising, considering its sweeping title, that Osgood, Suci, and Tannenbaum's The Measurement of Meaning (1957) confused many linguist readers. What was expected, evidently, was a new approach to the lexicographic problems viewed as the central concern of semantic analysis. But instead of a technique for analyzing the denotative meaning of lexical items, the reader encountered "a kind of dimensional analysis of their affective and evaluative meanings" (Lounsbury 1959:196).

Unfortunately, the distinctions between denotative meanings, which are linguistically relevant, and connotative meanings, which are psychological, are not clearly developed by the authors of The Measurement of Meaning. But the lack of clarity had one very fruitful result: a series of analytic (and in one instance, critical) reviews appeared by linguists who sought to distinguish sharply between the different types of meaning and to explicate the mechanics of the factor-analysis procedures used in the semantic differential. In order of appearance, these reviews include Wells (1957), Weinreich (1958a), and Carroll (1959). It is interesting that this distinction was again blurred by Osgood in a recent paper (1963b), reporting on the quantification of meaning.

It is important that Saporta's reader introduces the student to the semantic differential, since this technique has gained wide use in psychology. Moss (1960) reviews some of the current research. Not only is the original Osgood, Suci, and Tannenbaum book in wide currency, but so also are several derivative sources, including a "semantic atlas" of a lexicon of 360 items and a study of the distances between the concepts involved (Jenkins, Russell, and Suci, 1958, 1959). Within a relatively short period of time, the semantic differential has been adapted for use in an impressive array of investigations, including its applications "to the study of attitude change, to changes in meaning during psychotherapy, to the generality of semantic factors across language and culture, and to a variety of communication problems in aesthetics, advertising, and mass media effects" (Osgood, 1963a: 272).

Particularly interesting for the reviewer were the applications of this technique to the measurement of bilingual dominance (Lambert, Havelka, and Crosby, 1958) and to clinical investigations (Osgood and Luria 1954, Luria, 1959), and its tentative application as a tool for measuring cross-cultural differences in connotative meanings. This last category includes a large group of papers: Kumata and Schramm (1956); Maclay and Ware (1961); Prothro and Keehn (1957); Suci (1960); Tanaka, Oyama, and Osgood (1963); and Triandis and Osgood (1958). The reviewer concurs with its users that the semantic differential, however inappropriately named, offers promising results.

Another aspect of psychologists' research with the nature of the interpretant is manifest in "content analysis," which has been recently characterized as a method for "using events in messages as a means of either drawing inferences about their sources or making predictions about effects on their receivers" (Osgood, 1963a:301). The ongoing research, its methods, problems, and findings, are ably sketched in Pool's paper, "Trends in content analysis today: a summary" (1959), the final selection in this part of Saporta's reader.

6. *Language Acquisition, Bilingualism, and Language Change*

Part VI of Saporta's reader offers an interesting and valuable assortment of readings: J. B. Carroll, "Language development in children" (1960); R. Jakobson and M. Halle, "Phonemic patterning" (1956); W. F. Leopold, "Patterning in children's language" (1953/54); J. Berko, "The child's learning of English morphology" (1958); U. Weinreich, "Languages in contact" (1953) ; U. Weinreich, "Mechanisms and structural causes of interference" (1953) ; E. Haugen, "The bilingual individual" (1956) ; and W. E. Lambert, J. Havelka, and C. Crosby, "The influence of language-acquisition contexts on bilingualism" (1958).

Scanning these titles might prompt one to ask what they all have to do with one another, and more particularly, what bearing any has on linguistic change. The thematic unity perhaps will become apparent below, but the answer in part must be that the topics in this section were taken over wholesale from Chapter 6 ("Diachronic psycholinguistics") of the 1954 *Psycholinguistics* monograph, which had the same organization. More important to register is the observation that many of the suggestions for research made during the 1953 Social Science Research Council conference were subsequently carried out in the articles included in the reader. This is clearly an area where psycholinguistics has much to offer for a general theory of language, and where the stimulus of the 1953 conference has already produced some of the most noteworthy gains.

It is remarkable how little attention linguists have given to the acquisition of speech in children, to the loss of speech through age or pathology, and to the consideration of those abnormal situations wherein speech is not acquired at all. It would be interesting if future chroniclers of linguistics in this country were able to show that a strict ahistorical bent in descriptive linguistic theory had successfully postponed the linguist's involvement with linguistic ontogeny until this late date.

"Language acquisition," further unspecified, can clearly refer to two rather separate developments: (1) the learning of the primary language, normally a joint enterprise of the child's maturation and socialization, and (2) the learning of a secondary language (without restriction as to the age of the speaker). All available evidence, Berlitz notwithstanding, indicates that these are qualitatively distinct developments except in those cases when a child at an early age becomes a coordinate bilingual in a secondary language. Particularly if we inquire into the later acquisition of a secondary language (and the practical and pedagogical implications which are involved in foreign language teaching), these are best viewed as related but quite separate topics.

"Linguistic ontogeny" is a more happy cover term than "learning" for the aspect of language acquisition which concerns primary language development. Moreover, it has the virtue of indicating one very important tie-in between psycholinguistics and linguistic problems that are usually considered "historical" in nature. That is, linguistic ontogeny can be understood as either concerning the child's acquisition of his language, or as concerning the impact which the children of a speech community effect on its *langue*, with their own innovations. Inquiry into the innovating role of the child and his contribution to linguistic change is a fascinating topic, one which has been little studied and which is unfortunately more amenable to speculation than observation. Hockett's (1950) excellent article on this aspect of ontogeny has not elicited the interest it deserved, and hopefully it will be selected for inclusion in some future reader.

The child's acquisition of language, however, has a long history of investigation, and today many of the psychologists interested in language are concerned with this subject in particular. Perusal of the contents of recent linguistics journals reveals that this interest is no longer exclusive to the psychologists.

It is noteworthy that longitudinal studies of children's development of verbal behavior have generally examined the acquisition of either the reference system (content) or of the linguistic system (expression); only rarely has the total integrated task been investigated. This is abundantly clear when we examine those studies centrally concerned with the child's acquisition of a reference system and his exploitation of that system in perceptual and cognitive development, as manifest in the child's evolving conceptualization of his world. Relevant here are the studies of Piaget and his colleagues and students in Switzerland, of Ljublinskaja and others in Russia, and of Bruner and his associates in the United States. Piaget's work is rapidly growing; much of his earlier work is reevaluated in Piaget (1955) and Inhelder and Piaget (1958). Flavell (1963) offers a recent comprehensive introduction to this school. Luria and Yudovich (1959) is an exemplar of a large body of recent Russian literature on concept formation; additional earlier references are contained in Luria (1959a).

Bruner, Goodnow, and Austin's *A Study of Thinking* (1957) exemplifies the heavily experimental bent of some of the current research on concept formation in the United States. Some earlier general considerations on concept formation are contained in Heidbreder (1945, 1948); Levit (1953); and Vinacke (1951, 1954). Carroll (1964) has supplied the most readable and insightful of recent articles on concept formation; both this and his 1963 paper are discussed below. Church's *Language and the Discovery of Reality* (1961) has an informative discussion of the development of thought concerning concept formation, and Hunt has written a recent monograph on the topic, entitled *Concept Learning: An Information Processing Problem* (1962). (Some contributions of verbal learning experiments to concept formation are discussed in Part 5.)

The accusation that much of the European work on concept formation is alinguistic in approach seems justified. To be sure, the child's acquisition of a new concept (e.g., measurement of space) is inferred from the child's new verbalizations, but Piaget, Heidbreder, and others, are interested in this event as a manifestation of the child's maturing intellect, and not in the linguistic correlates. As Berko and Brown have commented, "Piaget is inclined to see through words as though they were not there and to imagine that he directly studies the child mind" (1960: 536).

More serious criticism is offered by Carroll, who objects also to the[o] term "concept formation" itself, claiming that the concepts involved were often formed at an earlier age. He suggests that "most problem-solving situations involve concept evocation rather than the formation of new concepts" (Carroll, 1958c:196). Osgood has different reservations; he points out that there have actually been very few studies of concept formation, and that, moreover, what is involved "is essentially the problem of learning meanings" (Osgood 1963a:228).

Carroll has concluded a recent article with a summary justification for this alinguistic approach:

> It has been necessary . . . to point out that concepts are essentially nonlinguistic (or perhaps better, alinguistic) because they are classes of experience which the individual comes to recognize as such, whether or not he is prompted or directed by symbolic language phenomena. Because the experiences of individuals tend to be in many respects similar, their concepts are also similar, and through various processes of learning and socialization, these concepts come to be associated with words (Carroll 1964:201,2).

Dramatic support for Carroll's and similar assertions concerning the independence of concept formation from productive linguistic skills comes from the investigations of concept formation in the absence of language, as in deaf children. Pertinent here are the carefully executed and thoughtfully presented experiments by Furth (1961). In passing, one must note the exclusion of any study of "concept formation" in the Piaget vein from this section of Saporta's reader; nor did the topic receive anything but brief mention in the 1953 SSRC conference.

More linguistically oriented expositions of the child's acquisition of reference are discussed in several of the papers in this part of the reader. Brown's chapter, "The original word game" (1958), is very instructive. Its purview of the total task facing the child acquiring language is more comprehensive than either the Carroll (1960) or Leopold (1953/54) selections in the reader, which touch only fleetingly upon the acquisition of reference.

Linguistically oriented studies specifically devoted to the problem of the acquisition of the reference system are few. Berko and Brown's (1960) study contains a section on the methodological problems involved, and offers some possible testing procedures for assessment of the child's acquisition of general rules of reference. Riess's (1946) investigation of the associative generalizations of conditioned responses to homonyms and synonyms is interesting, although it is Berko and Brown's evaluation of the findings which are important. Commenting of Riess's discovery that older children generalized responses to synonyms, in contrast to the younger children who generalized most readily to homonyms, they conclude: "Here is evidence that responses trained to one word will be extended to others linked with it through the reference system" (Berko and Brown 1960:539).

Werner and Kaplan's "The acquisition of word meanings: a developmental study" (1950) was one of the earlier examples of a series of experiments in which, typically, referential acquisition is examined by having subjects factor out or accrete meanings to nonsense words (which are usually imbedded in larger meaningful contexts). Another example of this type of study is that of Spiker, "Experiments with children on the hypothesis of acquired distinctiveness and equivalence of cues" (1956).

A paper by Lenneberg (1957) carries these experiments further and attempts to construct a labelling experiment for adults, using color classification learning tasks which would be an analogue to the child's. This study prompted Rubenstein and Aborn to conclude that

> . . . the task faced by the child in learning a language is considerably different from the usual adult language-learning task, where the classification of referents may require only a shift in labelling, or acquisition of classification schemes that are parallel to already conceptualized schemes. To the child, language learning involves the acquisition of classification schemes where dissimilar stimuli are sometimes given the same name and where similar stimuli are sometimes given different names (1960:307).

An interesting developmental study of children's reference is reported on by Ervin and Foster (1960).

The most elaborate psychological discussion of the acquisition of meaning is found in the writings of Osgood and his commentators, where it forms a necessary foundation to his behavioristic semantic theory. More extended discussion of Osgood's theory is contained in Parts 2 and 5 of this survey, but a recent observation by Lambert is relevant here since it points up a major gap and block to the study of the acquisition of meaning:

> For Osgood, the meaning of a sign or symbol *is* the mental or neurological counterpart, in attenuated form, of the actual emotional and behavioral responses which have habitually been made to the referent for which the symbol stands. That is, linguistic symbols are originally learned in a context where they are repeatedly paired with their appropriate referents (Lambert, 1962:5).

The obvious problem is that work in this area has either proceeded without reference to concurrent linguistic development (e.g., Piaget), or has had to rely on purportedly analogous experimental conditions involving subjects, often adult, who have already acquired their primary language (e.g., Lenneberg's study mentioned above). The sad fact remains that little experimental psycholinguistic work has been directed to that key integrative development in the child which Lounsbury succinctly characterized as "a very extensive naming vocabulary based on recognition of both static and dynamic qualities of things in the environment, with the vocabulary in part already morphologically differentiated" (1963:556). As we can see, most acquisition studies have concentrated "on mastery of the code for referential function" (Hymes, 1962:39).

When can the child be said to have acquired his language? There is clearly a difference to be drawn between the continued learning of new vocabulary, derivational patterns, and peripheral optional syntactic structures that will occupy the individual throughout his life-span, on the one hand, and the acquisition of phonology and the basic grammatical apparatus (and its functionings) which are the key issues in the child's acquisition, on the other. The articles included in Saporta's reader do not discuss these qualitative differences between early learning and later accretions to the basic schemata (or later learning of secondary languages).

Menyuk, in two papers (1963a, 1963b), is concerned with adapting Chomsky's partial generative grammar of English (1957, 1962b) so that it can account for some of the closed-system competence of young children's speech as well as developmental processes in later continuing acquisition. Her recent investigations have led her to conclude that "the data obtained seem to indicate that the children in this population, at age 3, have incorporated most of the basic generative rules of grammar that we have thus far been able to describe and are using these rules to understand and produce sentences" (1963b:438).

More recent research has yielded additional conclusions about developmental trends in child language learning. Brown and Fraser (1963) and Brown and Bellugi (1964) provide many insights about the developmental aspects of sentence formation (see below). Brown and Berko (1960), Ervin (1961), and Entwisle, Forsyth, and Muuss (1964) all offer mutually corroborative data suggesting that children's word associations are markedly different from those of adults. Ervin (1961) concluded that this difference involves a simple shift from the child's syntactically contiguous associations to the adult's predominant use of paradigmatic replacement associations. Apparently association performances are marked by age differences in much later life as well (see Korchin and Basowitz, 1957).

Nor is the question of developmental stages, and earlier as opposed to later learning, of purely psychological import. Several writers have suggested that many of the processes of historical change in language can be understood only in terms of a psychologically determined structural stability. One clear case is the several times offered hypothesis that the differential persistence of "peripheral" as opposed to "core" elements in language structure is directly related to early learning. This hypothesis is offered in both of the larger studies from which the Weinreich (1954) and Haugen (1956) papers were taken, and found earlier expression by Tesnière (1939) and Whitney (1881), among others. The notion that the hierarchical structure of language is differentially susceptible to the pressures which produce linguistic change is too important psycholinguistically to be left dangling.

If the studies available have not come to grips with these basic ques-

tions, they have at least made great progress in the descriptive characterization of what is involved in early learning. It is with the tasks posed
by this characterization that the Carroll (1960), Jakobson and Halle
(1956), Leopold (1953/54), and Berko (1958) papers in the reader are
concerned.

Carroll's paper contains a good bibliography, which includes references
to a number of excellent survey and bibliographic studies. Especially to
be noted are W. F. Leopold, *Bibliography of Child Language* (1952) ;
M. M. Lewis, *Infant Speech: A Study of the Beginnings of Language*
(1951) ; and D. McCarthy, "Language development in children" (1954).
It touches upon various problems in research methodology and discusses
work directed toward the description of various pre-language stages of
development, such as the constitutionally determined "cooing" and "babbling" states. Unfortunately there is little said (except by way of acknowl-
edging that it exists) about the process of differential reinforcement
which fixes the child's language-learning propensities onto the code of
the particular language spoken in his community.

The Jakobson and Halle paper, well known in its original larger context, *The Fundamentals of Language* (1956), offers an interesting but as
yet untested hypothesis for the sequential development of phonology in
the child, which purportedly obtains (at least in certain fundamental
developments in feature contrasts) in all languages. Although certain
general propositions of this hypothesis can be accepted, the more detailed
developmental sequence, which is also assumed to be universal, has never
been attested empirically, nor do the authors offer any suggestions for
carrying out the necessary experimentation. The Leopold paper in Saporta's reader is in some respects repetitious of Carroll's, and one of his
other papers (e.g., 1939-47, 1948, 1952) would have been a more valuable
inclusion in the reader.

With respect to the child's acquisition of grammar, most earlier studies
agreed that children tend to generalize on the basis of the most productive
morphophonemic, inflectional, and derivational rules, to the extent that
they "over-generalize." Berko and Brown summarize these findings to
say "that small children produce new forms by analogy with words they
already know, and the direction of the new forms is toward eliminating
the irregularities and inconsistencies of the language . . . the equivalent
of saying *I ringed* and *two mouses*" (Berko and Brown, 1960:542).

To Brown and his associates goes much of the credit for devising tests
of the child's processes of acquisition. The language-acquiring child being
somewhat less than an ideal experimental subject, some of these tests have
been rather ingenious. This section of Saporta's reader might have been
enhanced by a paper discussing the research problems involved in studying child language, since the problems are many. For example, is the "ob-
tained/not obtained" criterion in children's speech an accurate analogue
of "grammatical/nongrammatical" in the adult's? How does one decide

when a novel combination occurs, and more important, whether it is the result of imitation or the extension by analogy of some already acquired implicit rule? Berko and Brown's (1960) study of research methods would have been the ideal inclusion. However, Berko's 1958 paper, "The child's learning of English morphology," is typical of the experimental approach advocated, and it is very gratifying to find it included. Irwin's study (1960), appearing in the same volume as the Berko and Brown paper (Mussen, 1960), offers complementary information on experimental work, and is useful in addition for its references on childhood language disorders.

It is surprising to find that there are few corresponding studies concerned with the child's acquisition of phonology. The Albrights' (1956) study "The phonology of a two-year old child" would have made an interesting complement to Berko's paper, and so also Irwin and Chen's (1946) study of the appearance of phoneme (contrasts) in child speech, if accompanied with needed editorial cautions. Evidence is accumulating (and this does not emerge from either the Albrights' or the Irwin and Chen study) that the acquisition of phonology is inextricably bound up with the learning not of the important paradigmatic contrasts and their detailed environmental expressions, but rather of psychologically larger units, words and phrases. Thus it appears "that discrimination of critical phonemic cues are developed 'incidentally' in the course of learning to behave differentially to meaningful speech units" (Osgood, 1963a:279).

Evidence is also accumulating that the child achieves a receptive prowess which is often significantly ahead of his productive control. The fact that receptive control can exist *even without* production has been recognized, as in the case of such abnormal conditions as anarthria, in which the child (because of congenitally conferred motor defects) never acquires a speaking ability in his language. Lenneberg (1962b) has reported in detail on one such case, typical of many others, in which a patient without productive skills nevertheless had acquired language in the sense that he possessed the grammatical schemata necessary for decoding, i.e., for understanding. This study in particular strikes deep at those motor theories of language acquisition which attach primary importance to the roles of imitation and the developing motor speech skills, and it lends support to the view that decoding as well as encoding skills are "dependent upon the *acquisition of a single set of organizing principles*" (Lenneberg, 1962b:424).

Brown and his associates have been very active in further pursuing the child's acquisition of language and in experimenting with many of the variables such as "imitation," so-called "telegraphic speech," etc., which have traditionally posed problems to its investigation. It is interesting to note that Brown and Fraser (1963) and Brown and Bellugi (1964) are currently entertaining the hypothesis that child speech is a systematic reduction of adult speech, in which the telegraphic style of the child is just one part of "an interation cycle between the mother and child that amounts to a pair of reciprocal transformations: the child reduces its mother's speech and the mother expands the child's" (Brown, 1962:4). They have been busy experimenting with tests to control "imitation" as opposed to "production" (as an encoding event). Not the least of the questions involved is whether or not the child can engage in accurate repetitions of sentences without first having gained receptive mastery over the syntactic structurings involved (Fraser, Bellugi, and Brown, 1963).

The surveyor would like to recommend some topics for consideration in future investigations in this area of the child's developing linguistic competence. One possibility would be to examine the extensive descriptive information which is already available documenting "baby talk" in various languages. The problem with much of this descriptive material, however, is that it does not describe actual conversational interaction between the adult and child, although evidence from work with retarded children suggests that there are hitherto unappreciated regularities in the adult speaker's conversational reductions (e.g., see Spradlin and Rosenberg, 1964). A related matter is the as yet unanalyzed conversational interactions between children. Again, evidence from the study of retarded children suggests that there is much still to be learned about the structure of such dialogue (e.g., see Rosenberg, Spradlin, and Sanford, 1961). In view of the fact that little is known about the characteristics of adult conversational speech, this lacuna is less surprising. The investigation of child-adult nonverbal interaction has hardly begun, although the role of experimenter-bias (using both verbal and gestural cues) in children's word associations has been briefly examined by Rowley and Keller (1962).

It is apparently true that children go through a developmental sequence characterized by certain universally occurring maturational sequences, and in the process of socialization, begin to speak the language of the community wherein they live, sometimes on the basis of relatively brief exposure to it. This has the ring of a truism. Nevertheless, we are forced to say "apparently" because we lack good cross-cultural data on children's acquisition of language, although Lenneberg and others have recently addressed their attention to this question. But such evidence as can be presently mustered strongly suggests several hypotheses which are crucial to a comprehensive theory of language and verbal behavior.

The first hypothesis is that there is a critical age for language acquisition, a conclusion drawn from the study of various speech disorders, from the study of interrupted acquisition, and from the study of second language learning. (An irrefutable case for the existence of a critical age for language acquisition will be embodied in Lenneberg's forthcoming book, *The Biological Foundation of Language*.) A second hypothesis comes from appreciating that the child, with a finite memory and within a very brief time-span, acquires the sorts of linguistic competence which enable him (as either hearer or speaker) to cope with an *infinitude* of utterances in his language, to either understand them or to produce them in the appropriate contexts. The realization follows that language competence develops without the reinforcing contingencies which Skinner and others would have us believe are crucial. This is because language acquisition now appears to be more critically bound to constitutionally determined maturation and to mere exposure to the language, than to a learning situation characterized by impossibly large numbers of grammatical tokens and corrections by adults. Some of the consequences of this realization for a theory of language have already been discussed in Part 4. The study of language acquisition is an area within psycholinguistics from which we can expect many exciting developments.

There are many interests affiliated with the study of language contact and bilingualism. The full range of these interests is better caught by Weinreich and Haugen in their respective reports delivered at the Eighth International Congress of Linguists (Weinreich, 1958b; Haugen, 1958) than in the papers of theirs which are included in Saporta's reader. The main fields of interest have been, first and foremost, the linguistic analysis of the results of bilingualism (i.e., linguistic borrowings) and only secondly, the sociological setting in which language contact and bilingual behavior occur. Neither of these areas are immediately relevant here.

There are, however, a number of problems involved in bilingual behavior which are of crucial concern for psycholinguistics. And as a general introduction to bilingualism, Saporta could not have assembled a better group of papers for his reader. Weinreich's *Languages in Contact* (1954), the book from which his two papers in the reader are taken, and Haugen's *Bilingualism in the Americas* (1956), from which the Haugen selection is taken, regardless of their increasing outdatedness, are the two most authoritative surveys of bibliography and research problems available. Vildomec's new book, *Multilingualism* (1963), offers insightful theoretical discussion of the topic and includes a bibliography useful for its up-to-dateness. A recent study of linguistic borrowing of note is that of Deroy (1956). Numerous recent papers dealing with the sociological aspects of bilingualism are enumerated in several of the survey studies mentioned in footnote 4, especially Bright (1963) and Lounsbury (1961), and older references are included in Weinreich (1954) and Haugen (1956).

Lambert's is among the most authoritative work currently being conducted on psycholinguistically interesting problems in bilingualism. The Lambert, Havelka, and Crosby (1958) paper in Saporta's reader is only one of several very competent studies which have been undertaken by Lambert. Some of the other research which he has conducted or participated in is indicated in the brief bibliography appended to the 1958 paper. A far better review of Lambert's work, however, is contained in his own recent survey (Lambert, 1962). In this survey Lambert suggests that, as a central frame of reference, "it is of psychological interest to understand how bilinguals can learn two symbols for each referent and yet manage to use each language system with a minimum of inter-lingual interference" (p. 27). This paper is primarily devoted to turning up psycholinguistic insights for second language teaching. But actually, the two sections of relevance here ("A psychology of bilingualism" and "A social-psychology of second language learning") are anything but pedagogical in their orientation, although the implications for education are certainly present. For example, in discussing the age of learning of a second language, and having mentioned the traditional fears of deleterious effects of the process on personality and on intelligence, Lambert makes the startling disclosure that the bilingual subjects in his experiments "are *far superior* to monolinguals on both verbal and nonverbal tests of intelligence" (p. 30) ; this is attributed to a possibly greater "cognitive flexibility." An important dimension in successful second language learning is "an appropriate attitudinal orientation toward the other language" (p. 37).

These and many other observations provide a wealth of new insights into second language learning in both its applied and theoretical aspects. Further and more detailed results of the Montreal research with second language learning are contained in Lambert, Gardner, Barik, and Turnstall (1963) and in the important report by Peal and Lambert (1962). This group has also done several studies on attitudinal dimensions of second language learning (e.g., Anisfeld, Bogo, and Lambert, 1962).

Ervin and Osgood's distinction between "coordinate" and "compound" bilingualism, which they proposed in the 1954 survey, has been widely used in experimental work dealing with bilingual behavior. This distinction is based on variation in the mediation model of acquisition, viz., whether referents are separate or merged. Osgood indicates elsewhere (Osgood, 1963a :285 f) that he believes the psycholinguistically important issues in bilingualism relate to the determination of the "degree" and "type" of bilingualism in the individual, "type" to be expressed in the coordinate/compound dichotomy. Attempts to measure language dominance in multilingual persons have encountered some difficulties for the experimenters ; see, for example, Lambert, Havelka, and Gardner (1959) and Diebold (1963). More information on dominance is provided by recent experiments with interlingual word associations (Kolers, 1963) and with bilinguals' projective content (Ervin, 1964).

We can thus see that the central concern is how the bilingual speaker becomes "inputted" for two language codes and then how the codes are used differentially. "How the codes are kept separate" loads the question, for empirical evidence suggests that two (or more) codes are rarely employed by the individual without interferences of various sorts from one to the other. Overt manifestation of interference is relative, of course, ranging from hardly perceptible (e.g., in the case of the coordinate bilingual who is "code-switching") to very obvious (e.g., in the strong "foreign accent" and grammatical errors of the subordinately bilingual speaker in his secondary language). But Lambert, Ervin, and others, have been less interested in the linguistic quantification of interlingual interference than in dominance, associative interferences, recall, and biculturalism. A case in point is the Lambert, Havelka, and Crosby paper, in which associative interference is found to be a function of the social learning situation, in either "separated" or "fused" social contexts.

The omission of the role of psycholinguistics in second language teaching from Saporta's reader can be defended on the grounds that there is just too immense and specialized a literature on foreign language teaching. But no thoroughgoing coverage of psycholinguistics should fail to mention its potential contribution to those applied ventures. Foreign language teaching has already experienced various palace revolts and Copernican revolutions. But there still remain key issues in language teaching which are more than matters of efficacy of teaching methods and which depend on the skills of the psycholinguist for their ultimate resolution. Although the alert reader will be able to conjure up many more, let me mention here only one issue with which psycholinguists have become involved: the student's aptitude for second language learning. John Carroll has been especially active in this area, having devised a language aptitude test of great promise. The psycholinguistic import can be grasped immediately from some of the factors involved, such as associative memory, inductive language-learning capacity, etc. (see Carroll, 1958a, 1962a).

"Linguistic change" is related to "bilingualism," if the latter is viewed as one possible mechanism responsible for the former. There are no papers in the reader specifically devoted to linguistic change. The important contributions of psycholinguistics to the study of linguistic change probably lie ahead and perhaps outside the area of bilingualism. Any theory of linguistic change will have to account for the other principle types of change involved, particularly sound changes and the various types of analogic change. And almost certainly, such a theory will have to consider sociolinguistic factors which are beyond the scope of this discussion.

There are several important diachronic processes which the linguist relies upon in historical work, the etiology of which will ultimately demand a psycholinguistic explanation. Here I am thinking of the observations (embodied as some sort of ill-defined premises or rules-of-thumb in historical linguistics): (1) that sound change is structurally regular, and (2) that the hierarchical structure of language is differentially susceptible to change. The comparative method operates on just these assumptions. A proposal for the relatability of two languages have been traditionally based on the discovery of systematic sound correspondences between certain of their forms which can be regarded as "core" elements (such as basic vocabulary and basic inflectional apparatus), relatively resistant to replacement by borrowings. Such sound correspondences are usually the result of systematic divergent descent from a common ancestral unit.

One property of sound change has discouraged attempts to explain its workings: that is its "unconscious" quality, the fact that the changes operate systematically in a language "without exception" and beyond the awareness and control of the speakers. The "sound laws" proposed during the last century were, of course, particularistic statements descriptive of phonological change in the language under study. They were universal only in the sense of their systematic operation within one language. These "laws" were thus never deduced from a general theory of linguistic change. Rather they involved a primitive induction by which the linguist merely indicated the necessary and sufficient conditions for the emergence of the particular sound change.

Attempts to deal with the causes of sound change and its regularity have met with little encouragement. Sapir, in his book *Language* (1921), proposed that linguistic change exhibited a predictable directional tendency, a vaguely stated notion of structurally predetermined change which he called "drift." Sapir's concept of drift has been widely misunderstood, especially by anthropologists who interpreted it as invoking mystical evolutionary doctrines. As late as 1953, Bidney could admonish that "no one insisted more strongly than he [Sapir] upon the individual nature of 'genuine' culture. Yet, in essential agreement with the prevalent climate of opinion, he maintained that language manifested a 'drift,' or long-range historical trend, which transcended the conscious efforts of the individuals who utilized a given language. . . ." (1953:93). Recently much interest has come to be focused on drift, especially in regard to phonological change. Martinet's important paper of 1952 has developed into a theory of sound change. This paper, and Martinet's book *Économie des changements phonétiques* (1955) which in part resulted from it, have exerted much influence in certain circles.

The immediate relevance of analogic change for psycholinguistics needs no comment. Nor is the interest recent. The philologist Albert Thumb, in several papers and finally in a co-authored volume with the psychologist Marbe (Thumb and Marbe, 1901), was very concerned with analogic changes and their expression as lapses in language acquisition and in word and idiom formation. And Hermann Paul (1960) before Thumb offered a very coherent picture of the workings of *Analogiebildung* and its important role as a mechanism of linguistic change.

In Chapter 6 of the *Psycholinguistics* monograph, there is an excellent section on "Language change" by Greenberg, Osgood, and Saporta. The subsection on "Formal change" contains a good discussion of the principal types of linguistic change, which makes it a valuable introductory paper on the topic. The discussions of "entropy balance" and numerous other matters with tantalizing applicability to historical problems, make the present republication of the monograph all the more appreciated.

7. *Pathologies of Linguistic Behavior*

Part VII of Saporta's reader is modest in scope but includes five recent and useful papers: B. Flanagan, I. Goldiamond, and N. Azrin, "Operant stuttering: the control of stuttering through response-contingent consequences" (1958); R. Jakobson, "Aphasia as a linguistic problem" (1955); H. Schuell and J. J. Jenkins, "The nature of language deficit in aphasia" (1959); H. Goodglass and J. Hunt, "Grammatical complexity and aphasic speech" (1958); and W. E. Lambert and S. Fillenbaum, "A pilot study of aphasia among bilinguals" (1959).

In 1960 Rubenstein and Aborn reported, after their survey of the studies known to them, that "the research in the area of language disturbances has been quite unsatisfying from a psycholinguistic point of view.... The fact remains that we have little by way of systematic knowledge of disturbed language and that very little more has accrued during the past five years" (1960:308). I hope to show that these authors' conclusions were not entirely valid, and certainly the advances since their time of writing have been appreciable. At any rate, the papers included in this section of the reader reveal the progress in linguists' thinking about language disorders even before 1960.

One of the traps in dealing with a topic like "language disturbance" is its rather uncertain bounds. Rubenstein and Aborn, for instance, evince very catholic criteria, treating within this one category those aspects of stylistic variation which have been discussed elsewhere as "paralanguage" as well as physiologically-based disorders such as aphasia. Thus, a well-known functionally-oriented study by Lorenz and Cobb (1954) is discussed within the same framework as a well-known organically-oriented study by Luria (1958), concerned with the correlations between the site of lesions in the cortex and the recognized "types" of aphasic disorders.

The Flanagan, Goldiamond, and Azrin (1958) paper, the only one in this section that does not deal with aphasia, discusses the relationship of stuttering to the patient's anxiety. It reports on an experiment in which stuttering was experimentally conditioned to adversive stimuli. The suppression of the stuttering response was observed when the onset of the unpleasant stimulus was made contingent upon the stuttering response itself. A more general introduction to this class of disorders can be found in Johnson and Leutenegger's treatise on stuttering (1956). Current bibliographic information appears in the *Journal of Speech and Hearing Disorders*, and a wide range of material is discussed in Travis (1957).

Among the most dramatic effects of brain injury are the various adventitious language disorders collectively called aphasia. Two world wars have left us with an incredible number of brain lesions, representing a gamut of injuries and attendant impairments of behavior. Some of these conditions could never occur naturally in a population, and most of them for ethical reasons could never be experimentally induced. In spite of the prevalence of these language pathologies in our population and in spite of the availability of subjects so afflicted, the very fact that the traumata have not been experimentally induced has limited what we have been able to learn about the nature of the putative correlations between localization of the lesion and the extent of the damage.

Nevertheless, comparative descriptive studies are still yielding important information. The work of Luria (e.g., 1958, 1959b) and his collaborators, for instance, promises an early comprehensive picture of the physiological correlates of various aphasias. Complementary data have come from the study of localization of various functions in the cortex by direct experimental stimulation. Relevant here is the earlier-mentioned research of Penfield and his collaborators (e.g., Penfield and Roberts, 1959). Cursory comparison of Brain's (1961) or Russell's (1961) contemporary surveys with Goldstein's (1948) of a decade past will convince the reader that, at least as it concerns the physiological factors underlying aphasia, Rubenstein and Aborn's evaluation of research in this field is indeed questionable.

Moreover, the past decade has seen some felicitous rethinking about the typologizing of aphasia and about the linguistic importance of aphasia for a general theory of language. There have been some advances in the descriptive characterization of aphasia, as in Fillenbaum and Jones' (1962) use of the "cloze technique." Characteristically, Saporta's reader has avoided any strongly physiologically-oriented papers, although the introduction to Schuell and Jenkins (1959) contains a valuable thumbnail history of the neurological theorizing from de Broca through the work of Hughlings Jackson and Henry Head, down through contemporary research.

Jakobson has been responsible for much of the rethinking about aphasia on the part of linguists. The paper included in the reader is only one of several from this author's hand. The papers he has written during the past decade all derive from ideas first made known in his *Kindersprache, Aphasie und allgemeine Lautgesetze* (1941). His interest is principally in deriving laws of implication for a general theory of language, through examining the process and states of aphasic disintegration.

Jakobson claims that the phonological disintegration characteristic of the aphasic's linguistic regressions is a mirror-image of the child's acquisition of its sound-pattern. The theoretical import of this observation has been spelled out in more detail in a better-known study by Jakobson and Halle (1956), which has attracted some adverse comment (Joos, 1957a).

A second observation reported by Jakobson is that there are two fundamental types of aphasic disturbance, representing respective impairment of the two basic linguistic processes implied in speech: selection and combination. Impairment of the selection process is reflected in so-called "similarity disorders" while impairment of the combinatory process produces "contiguity disorders." Jakobson considers this basic dichotomy between similarity and contiguity disorders to override the older distinctions between "motor-productive" and "sensory-receptive" types.

That impairment in the sensory modality is rarely independent of corresponding damage to the motor modality (and vice versa) has been demonstrated clinically, and it is the purpose of the Schuell and Jenkins (1959) paper to show an even more striking unity underlying all aphasic disorders. Their study is valuable for its introductory sketch of available theories of language deficit. The running commentary on these theories is often critical, as when Schuell and Jenkins reject Jakobson's model of aphasia on the grounds of its failure to utilize careful longitudinal studies. The main conclusion of the paper is that there is "a single dimension of language deficit rather than the multiple dimensions or typologies suggested in the past." This unidimensionality is adduced through a carefully executed Guttman Scale analysis.

Goodglass and Hunt (1958), in the next paper in Saporta's reader, focus on the differential impairment of grammatical performance, attempting to elucidate the significance of the older distinction between "agrammatism" and "paragrammatism," the former viewed as an important variety of Jakobson's contiguity disorder. A simple test involving control of English morphophonemics suggests to the authors conclusions markedly divergent from those offered by Schuell and Jenkins: "Our limited sample gives no support to the hypothesis that a common factor explains disturbances both in grammatical expression and in auditory discrimination of grammatical forms."

Lambert and Fillenbaum's paper (1959) reports on a survey which tenuously confirms Weinreich's theoretical distinction between coordinate and compound bilingualism. The distinction is based on the functional independence (in coordinate bilingualism), as opposed to functional dependence (in compound bilingualism), between the speaker's two or more languages. If functional independence is regarded as determined by the social contexts in which the languages are acquired (and of such additional factors as the speaker's age, the affective values attached to the languages, and the speaker's overall competence in his secondary language), it might be expected that coordinate bilinguals would have their languages differentially affected by aphasia-producing damage while the compound would have his languages equally affected. The cases examined by Lambert and Fillenbaum, where information is provided about the extent of deficit and/or about recovery after aphasic insult, confirm the expectation deduced from Weinreich's typology of bilinguals.

An interesting recent discussion of aphasia not included in the reader (nor mentioned in the bibliographies of those that are included) is Roger Brown's observations on the opposition "abstract-concrete" as it is customarily used to characterize aphasic speech. Chapter 8 of his *Words and Things* (1958) includes a very insightful discussion of the opposition in terms of superordinate and subordinate categories within lexical hierarchies. So considered, the opposition becomes a very meaningful one for describing the various deficits such as "categorical rigidity" and other referential difficulties with polysemy to which aphasics are usually subject.

The "pathologies of linguistic behavior" certainly do not stop with stuttering and aphasia. Some indication of the total range of phenomena which fall into this category is available in the previously mentioned works by Brain (1961), Russell (1961), and Travis (1957). Another available source is a recent synopsis by Lenneberg (1964) of language disorders clinically observed in children. Although phrased in terms of symptomatology and prognosis, this study is especially important because of its reliance on carefully controlled longitudinal studies. Lenneberg's forthcoming *The Biological Foundation of Language* will contain much additional material of relevance.

It is noteworthy that this is the one topical category represented in the Saporta reader which was not given consideration at the 1953 Summer Seminar on Psycholinguistics. The most likely reason was that the conference was held at a time before widespread familiarity with Jakobson's and Luria's writings had attracted linguists' attention to the importance which speech pathologies might hold for a general theory of language. Before this acquaintanceship developed, in spite of the interest in aphasia which Bloomfield revealed in the second chapter of his influential *Language*, the study of speech pathology was no doubt also avoided by linguists because it was regarded as an applied discipline.

It is my impression that speech therapists and other specialists in speech pathology unknowingly have much to offer for psycholinguistics and for the theory of verbal behavior in general. Both Goldstein (1948) and Jakobson (1956) stress this point, and this opinion is certain to be supported by Lenneberg's forthcoming book. In the meantime, one notes with satisfaction that the study of speech pathologies is attracting ever more attention by linguists and psychologists, who are discovering—even in the therapist's rules for treatment—hitherto overlooked insights into the nature of language. Nor is this looking afield one-sided; see in this connection a recent article written for linguists by a therapist (Taylor, 1964).

8. *Linguistic Relativity and the Relation of Linguistic Processes to Perception and Cognition*

Part VIII of Saporta's reader offers an interesting assortment: B. L. Whorf, "Science and linguistics" (1940) ; J. H. Greenberg, "Concerning inferences from linguistic to nonlinguistic data" (1954), a paper from the symposium proceedings entitled *Language and Culture* (Hoijer, 1954) ; R. W. Brown and E. H. Lenneberg, "A study in language and cognition" (1954) ; E. H. Lenneberg and J. M. Roberts, "The language of experience" (1956), part of the original of the same title; R. W. Brown, "Linguistic determinism and the part of speech" (1957) ; L. S. Vygotsky, "Thought and speech" (1939), Chapter Seven of his *Thought and Language*, and D. T. Herman, R. H. Lawless, and R. W. Marshall, "Variables in the effect of language on the reproduction of visually perceived forms" (1957).

C. W. Morris' different dimensions of semiosis ("the process in which something functions as a sign," 1939:81) were mentioned in Part 5 of this survey. One of the dimensions distinguished was the "pragmatic," the relations of the sign system to its interpreters. It is this pragmatic dimension, with all the diverse sociological and psychological phenomena associated with it, which offers a target area for the papers included in this final section of Saporta's reader. The topic itself has eluded consistent labelling. "Ethnolinguistics" enjoyed wider currency than its coinage and amorphous reference deserved, and now seems less prevalent, although there have been numerous attempts to revitalize the term (e.g., Fernández Guizzetti, 1960, 1960/61, 1961). A paper by Olmsted (1950) gave the term its early currency; the term's curiously disjunctive reference is shown in Hoijer's (1953) review of this subfield. "Language and Culture" is a frequent title for American university courses designed to concentrate on this topic, and it is regarded by American anthropologists as a core area of "anthropological linguistics." Several reviews indicate the prominence accorded this area in American anthropology and linguistics (e.g., Goodenough, 1956; Hoijer, 1961; Lévi-Strauss, Jakobson, Voegelin, and Sebeok, 1950; and Voegelin and Harris, 1947). It is interesting to note in passing that anthropological linguistics now boasts a formidable book of readings of its own, edited by Hymes (1964).

While not as neat as "ethnolinguistics" or "language and culture," Saporta's descriptive chapter-heading has the merit of leaving less doubt about the purview of its contents. The central problem dealt with in this section is the simple and historically old proposition—constantly resurrected and reformulated—that language and thought are interdependent, and that the structural particulars of one are necessarily replicated in the other. It is significant that in recent times the proposition has been reiterated overwhelmingly in one direction, namely, that the mental functions of a group are in some way dependent upon the structure and content of the language they speak. We can subsume such propositions under a heading called "theories of linguistic relativity" in accordance with usage now familiar. But it must be stressed again that linguistic relativity implies a one-way directionality in the relationship between language and thought, which has never been conclusively demonstrated to exist. Many studies in concept formation imply such a directionality (see Lenneberg, 1962c, and Parts 5 and 6 of the present survey).

Of the published critiques of linguistic relativity, however, only one (Fearing, 1954) is at all explicit about the unexplored reverse possibility. It seems likely that the most important interdependencies will soon be shown to be in the reverse direction: that the striking universals in language structure, which are only now being fully appreciated, are dependent on cognitive schemata which are part of the human constitution. If this is true, a theory of cognitive determinism will displace further inquiry concerning linguistic relativity. We will then return to a view of the relationship between language and thought not unlike that entertained by the Greek philosophers, who saw a basic unity in human cognitive faculties such as logic and reason. It is evident that all branches of psycholinguistics are deeply involved in the resolution of this problem. Particularly important for its resolution are continued advances by psychologists in the fields of cognition and neurophysiology; the continued development of the linguist's interest in semantic theory, linguistic typology, and language universals; and the collection by anthropologists of an adequate range of cross-cultural data bearing on the relationship between "language and culture."

John Carroll, who edited a collection of Whorf's papers, poses the question as to the reasons behind the perennial interest which linguistic relativity holds. His answer is interesting: "Perhaps it is the suggestion that all one's life one has been tricked, all unaware, by the structure of language into a certain way of perceiving reality, with the implication that awareness of this trickery will enable one to see the world with fresh insight" (Carroll, 1956:7). To judge from the selections in Saporta's reader, and from the emphasis which American linguists and other social scientists place on Whorf's ideas, one could believe that this interest stemmed from his and Sapir's writing alone and was, in effect, a peculiarly New World development. This is certainly not the case.

To realize how hoary a tradition linguistic relativity really boasts, one has only to turn to any number of recent German publications devoted to that subject (e.g., Gipper, 1959; Jost, 1960) or to more accessible commentaries on the movement which Basilius (1952) has aptly termed "Neo-Humboldtian ethnolinguistics" (e.g., Fernández Guizzetti, 1961; Öhman, 1953; Shetter, 1962; and Trager, 1959). These studies show clearly how Weisgerber, Porzig, Jost, Ipsen, and others, have built various superficially similar theories of semantics and linguistic relativity on a common foundation propounded by Wilhelm von Humboldt during the mid-nineteenth century.

A proper setting would have to mention the successive modifications of von Humboldt's position and the successive contributions of these scholars, not merely in order to spell out a nice intellectual history, but to point out how this European approach has attempted to solve the theoretical and analytical problems common to all theories of linguistic relativity. Contemporary concern with semantic theory and componential analysis should include, for instance, an examination of the development of the concept of "semantic field," originally proposed by Ipsen and subsequently expanded and modified first by Trier and then by Porzig. While the psychological underpinnings of the European studies are weak, the problems encountered by the Neo-Humboldtians are very much the same as those encountered in the American examinations of Whorf's ideas and as those currently being discovered in ethnoscience. In this respect European criticism of Neo-Humboldtian research is as important to review as the research itself. This criticism is quite abundant, see, for example, Betz (1954) ; Kainz (1956-62) ; and Konradt-Hicking (1956).

The provincialism of American ventures in linguistic relativity is the more remarkable because of the expression of the Neo-Humboldtian position in the writings of Ernst Cassirer, who has been widely read by philosophers and anthropologists in this country. It is significant, although not widely appreciated, that Cassirer changed his views on linguistic relativity, and in his later writings played down the notion that the substance of a particular language exerted specific constraints on its speakers' cognition. Cassirer actually published a self-reinterpretation (1945), and it is interesting to compare this with his earlier summary statements (see, for example, Cassirer, 1933). Lenneberg (1955) has published a penetrating analysis of this change in Cassirer's philosophy in which he compares Cassirer's well-known *Die Philosophie der symbolischen Formen* (1923-9) with a later essay (1944). The American provincialism is surprising also because Whorf is well-known and quoted in Germany and because one American study, a paper by Waterman (1957), offered a comparison between Whorf's idea and semantic field theory.

Whorf's writings (especially his 1949 book) had an immediate effect in this country, especially in anthropological circles, even before his writings were widely distributed. Their reception in anthropology was perhaps encouraged by independently conceived research on linguistic relativity by Dorothy Lee (e.g., 1938, 1944). A decade after the publication of the paper included in Saporta's reader, Whorf's ideas were collectively (and loosely) referred to as his "hypothesis" and the topic of linguistic relativity itself was briefly known as "metalinguistics" (Trager, 1949). There followed at least one program conceived to systematically examine the Whorfian hypothesis, the Conference on the Interrelations of Language and Other Aspects of Culture; Greenberg's paper in the reader is from the published results of this Conference (Hoijer, 1954). This was followed by the publication of a collection of Whorf's papers (Carroll, 1956).

The most recent phase of research activity in linguistic relativity began (partly as a result of the Conference and partly as individual efforts) with serious attempts to formalize the Whorfian hypothesis. Noteworthy attempts include those of Carroll (1958b, 1963), Feuer (1953), Fishman (1960), Gastil (1959), Lenneberg (1953), and the Lenneberg and Roberts paper (1956) contained in Saporta's reader. Fortunately, these attempts at formalization were coordinated with attempts to subject the hypothesis to experimental verification. In addition to the Brown and Lenneberg (1954), Lenneberg and Roberts (1956), and Brown (1957) papers contained in the reader, experimentally-oriented papers include Carroll and Casagrande (1958) and Flavell (1958). This most recent spate of experimental activity includes the Social Science Research Council's Southwest Project in Comparative Psycholinguistics.

Carroll offers a null hypothesis for linguistic relativity, namely, its converse—a theory of "linguistic neutrality which would assert that mental operations and other behaviors are independent of the language in which they are carried out" (1963:2). This carries with it important implications about translatability between languages. The papers in this reader are not concerned with experimentation involving the null hypothesis, nor have there been any serious attempts in the literature to maintain such a position. This is because, on one very low level, languages do differ widely in their hierarchical lexical groupings, specifically in the ways in which superordinate categories are composed. Carroll has aptly described these differenes with reference to second language learning:

> *Convergent* phenomena occur when the referents of two or more symbols in the native language are represented by a smaller number of symbols in the second language. *Divergent* phenomena occur . . . when the second language contains a larger number of symbols and corresponding semantic distinctions than the first language (Carroll, 1963:2).

Similarly, examining the classificatory principles underlying such groupings, Lounsbury uses the "term 'first-line distinctions' to designate distinctions of reference which are made, in usage, by the naming vocabulary of a language; and the term 'first-line ambiguities' to refer to the ambiguities of reference which are present in that same usage" (1963:569). The existence of such category differences, and the attendant problems created for translation, render the null hypothesis void.

But, as most of the papers in the reader point out, this is the weakest of the claims made by Whorf. As his paper "Science and linguistics" indicates, he adduces not only lexical evidence of this sort but also structural-typological differences in grammar to support his claim that it is because of such linguistic differences that "we cut nature up, organize it into concepts, and ascribe significances as we do, largely because we are parties to an agreement to organize it in this way."

Even on this lexical level, Whorf has been subjected to criticism for his naïve use of translation and the implicit assumption he makes that such convergent-divergent differences are somehow replicated by cognitive differences in the speakers. Lenneberg has been particularly critical of the translation issue, in both of the reader papers on which he collaborated and elsewhere (e.g., 1953). Fishman graphically describes the research on this level of the problem as "anecdotal" and resulting merely in "an enchanting catalog of codifiability differences" (1960:327). Beyond this very trivial level (which Fishman calls "Linguistic codifiability and cultural reflections"), there are the "behavioral concomitants" to codifiability; and beyond this lexical level, the cultural and behavioral concomitants to linguistic (grammatical) structure.

Greenberg's study in the reader offers a programmatic statement of the possibilities for making inferences from linguistic to nonlinguistic behavior. It is made unwieldy, however, by incorporation of a cumbersome typology of semantic units, and it does not really come to grips with formalizing the Whorfian hypothesis itself in such a way that it could be tested. Several papers which appeared subsequently, by Carroll (1958b, 1963) and by Fishman (1960), pose the hypothesis better.

The paper by Brown and Lenneberg (1954) represents the first carefully controlled experimental attempt to verify the Whorfian hypothesis, on its lexical level. In this study, color recognition is shown to be dependent on codability factors. The paper is particularly interesting for its ingenious operationalizing of the concepts of category codability and availability. It is interesting that a later experiment by another investigator appeared to completely contradict this finding, but Lenneberg (1961) has recently demonstrated that the original correlation is still valid. The complete Lenneberg and Roberts paper (1956) adds cross-cultural and cross-language perspective to the investigation of color codability, showing the same interdependency among Zuñi speakers. The section included in the Saporta reader gives a very clear theoretical introduction to the problem of experimental verification of linguistic relativity. Brown's paper describes children's allocation of nonsense words to English parts-of-speech categories, as manifest in correct morphophonemic mastery. Thereafter, the children "take the part-of-speech membership of a new word as a clue to the meaning of the word."

A much diluted version of the Whorfian hypothesis has now been offered by Carroll: "Insofar as languages differ in the ways they encode objective experience, language users tend to sort out and distinguish experiences differently according to the categories provided by their respective languages. These cognitions will tend to have certain effects on behavior" (1963:12). And here the matter still rests.

None of the papers in the reader treat a related topic which is of widespread philosophical and anthropological interest. It was customary, in the days before sophistication in language universals permitted otherwise, for social scientists to take firm stands on the issue of whether the languages of preliterate speakers were in any specifiable way "primitive" as compared with the languages spoken by so-called civilized peoples. Majority opinion at the turn of the century was that a very real difference did indeed exist, and this difference was said to lie in the poorly developed capacity for abstraction which was thought to characterize primitive languages and their speakers' intellect; such is the argument, for example, proposed by Lévy-Bruhl (1922).

Brown (1958) has offered an original analysis of the opposition "concrete-abstract" which is assumed to differentiate primitive from civilized languages. If his account does not conclusively settle the question, he at least succeeds in giving precise definitions to the concepts involved, and this will no doubt have a beneficial effect on future discussions. Since the "concrete-abstract" opposition is usually viewed as an evolutionary progression from dominance of the former mode to the latter, the evolutionary question arises. Are there languages which in some way can be said to be more "highly evolved" than others? The only recent non-sentimental attempt to weigh the issue is an unfortunately little-read paper by Hymes (1961c).

The Vygotsky paper on "Thought and speech" is one of the most fortunate inclusions in Saporta's reader. This chapter, selected from his *Thought and Language* (1934), gives some indication not only by Vygotsky's control over continental literature on psychology and linguistics, but also over the contemporary ventures with language and thought in the United States. Vygotsky's non-provincialism is reflected in his anxiety about a compartmentalized approach to a theory of language, in which semantics, grammar, phonetics, etc., would each become encysted disciplines—a fear which was certainly realized in subsequent developments in Amerian linguistics. In his introduction to a 1962 M.I.T. translation of Vygotsky's book (1962), Bruner argues quite convincingly that "Vygotsky is an original" whose approach and interpretations are difficult to place within a history of psychological thought. The advent of his 1934 *Thought and Language* in complete translation into English will no doubt exert appreciable effect on current thought on concept formation and other developmental approaches to cognition, and on ethnoscience.

The first chapter of *Thought and Language* (not included in the reader), in effortless prose, proposes many of the ideas about cognitive processes which are today pretentiously presented as conceptual innovations.

The most important role the paper plays in the reader, in contrast to the other papers contained in Part VIII, is to confront the student with the proposition that speech and thought are independent, at least ontogenetically, having "different genetic roots." The essence of his developmental theory is that

... in the speech development of the child, we can with certainty establish a preintellectual stage, and in his thought development, a prelinguistic stage. ... Up to a certain point in time, the two follow different lines, independently of each other. ... At a certain point these lines meet, whereupon thought becomes verbal and speech rational (Vygotsky, 1962:44).

Vygotsky's interest is focused mainly on those developmental phases in children during which speech and thought are, according to his scheme, independent. In this respect, his interests and experimental approaches closely parallel Piaget's, whose earlier work Vygotsky was well acquainted with. Their differences are somewhat less than Vygotsky avers, as a recent commentary by Piaget (1962) confirms. However, Vygotsky is more linguistically oriented, and my surmise is that he has been more impressed than Piaget with the later (adult) correspondences between particular language structures and the cognitive schemata of the speakers. The putative difference is easily caught in Vygotsky's words:

Piaget believes that egocentric speech stems from the insufficient socialization of speech and that its only development is decrease and eventual death. Its culmination lies in the past. Inner speech is something new brought in from the outside along with socialization. We [Vygotsky] believe that egocentric speech stems from the insufficient individualization of primary social speech. Its culmination lies in the future. It develops into inner speech (Vygotsky, 1962:135,6).

The "Thought and word" chapter of the book contains a wealth of ideas about research designs for testing various aspects of egocentric speech and concept formation, which deserve following up. The book as a whole has much to recommend it, including Vygotsky's insightful criticism of associational theory, and his sophisticated distinction between substance (analysis into "elements") and form (analysis into "distinctive units").

The paper by Herman, Lawless, and Marshall, as its descriptive title suggests, describes an experiment in which language-influenced reproductions of visual forms were elicited under various control situations involving the subjects' awareness of the impending task of reproducing the visual forms, and the exposure time for the stimulus figures. Like a number of similar studies, the experiment revolves around the subjects' tendency to reproduce amorphous or ambiguous visual forms as more similar to the referent experimentally associated with them than the original unlabelled forms actually were.

This is the place to register the absence of an old psycholinguistic chestnut: there is no paper devoted to sound symbolism or to other sound-based synesthesias like "color-hearing," which have long been observed to have communicative value. Brown has an excellent chapter in his *Words and Things* (1958) devoted to a review of the topic with extensive references to earlier work. Subsequent research includes papers by Brown and Nuttall (1959), Miron (1961), and Taylor (1963); visual-verbal synesthesia is discussed by Osgood (1960). The topic is lent additional appeal by Bloomfield's discussion of sound symbolism in the chapter (from his book *Language*) included in Part V of Saporta's reader. Since the time of Bloomfield's writing (1933), linguists have tended to ignore the problem as uninteresting, but it is obvious that recent interest in language universals will oblige them to reexamine the data, since evidence suggests that at least one type of sound symbolism is universal. Moreover, the relevance of sound symbolism to the descriptive analysis of at least one language (English) has been amply demonstrated; see, for example: Marchand (1959) ; Markel and Hamp (1960) ; and Wells and Keyser (1961).

The Saporta reader does not document one very sensible development which has resulted from a revived interest in "language and culture"— the collection of more linguistic and cultural materials for testing some of the premature Whorfian hypotheses. This task seems to have fallen to social anthropologists, who have accepted the duties with surprising fervor. As a matter of fact, collective concern with ethnoscience, with its assemblage of concepts and techniques derived from linguistics, represents one of the most productive fads in American anthropology. This review will not attempt to survey the pertinent research in ethnoscience since it is not (in its present still very descriptive state) of immediate concern to the psycholinguist with his more experimental bent; moreover, a number of surveys are available.[5]

The anthropologists' output in this area will be of significance for psycholinguistics, although it involves several difficulties. One of these is that, without concern for the universal comparative aspects of ethnoscience, research in this area will become bogged down in particularistic interpretations of individual cases, just when the trend in psycholinguistics (and linguistics in general) is swinging toward concern for language universals and a general theory of language. The need for concerted effort is caught in recent remarks by Casagrande:

... [psycholinguistics] most characteristically deals with the *generic* function in shaping cognitive processes, while [ethnolinguistics] is typically concerned with the *comparative* problem of how structural differences among languages, in both their lexical and grammatical aspects, systematically relate to differences in the cognitive processes or other behavior of their speakers. The two approaches are complementary (1963: 231).

Another problem is that much of semantic field analysis has dealt with semantic domains where the associated lexical sets have yielded easily to componential analysis. We need think here only of the many studies of kinship terminology and native biotic taxonomies to realize how loaded these fields are in favor of rigorous structural analysis. The control situation is almost ideal: the referents, as objects named, are physically discrete and can be relatively easily manipulated, linguistically if not physically. It will be interesting to see if componential analysis can be successfully extended outside of the highly structured lexical domains wherein it has been so effective.

The key problem revealed by ethnoscience and componential analysis has been neatly described by Frake as that of "demonstrating the cognitive saliency of componential solutions . . . and of relating terminological attributes to actual perceptual discriminations" (1962:83). This poses much the same problems concerning psychological reality (here cognitive) that the existence of linguistic primes does (there perceptual). One solution is to give a strictly formal account of the componential analysis without regard to its behavioral correlates. But this clearly removes the analysis in question from the realm of pragmatics, placing it rather into semantics. Better known examples of such semantic analyses include Haugen (1957), Lotz (1949), and Wonderly (1952). These studies may be contrasted with the formal analyses contained in Brown and Ford (1961), Brown and Gilman (1960), Burling (1963), De Soto and Bosley (1962), Frake (1961), and Lounsbury (1956), in which there is appreciably more concern with the psychological and sociological correlates of the terminological systems under analysis.

The attempt to elucidate the native speaker's cognitive awareness of the classifying principles underlying his folk taxonomy will involve the anthropologist with some knotty problems in cognition psychology. Not the least will be his behaviorist heritage, which will tempt him to apply simple learning theory concepts to induce the cognitive structure underlying the classification. Barring this regression, it will be necessary for him to understand the rapidly developing trends in cognitive theory, and it is in this respect that research in ethnoscience will become increasingly dependent upon psycholinguistics.

9. *Other Topics*

Many of the references cited in Footnotes 2 and 3 will convey the impression that there are hardly any bounds which can be effectively placed on the field of focus for psycholinguistics, as long as one's investigation somehow treats language with reference to the speaker. George Miller's "The psycholinguists'" (1964), an evaluation of the ideas which prompt the increasing flock of psycholinguists to their seemingly disparate endeavors, is perhaps the most thoughtful. (This article is reprinted as an appendix to the present volume.)

In defense of the discipline's progress, we can take his view that semantic "accepting and interpreting is just now coming into scientific focus" (p. 31)—by which he refers to much of the research discussed in Part 5 of this survey—and let this prognosis be compared with that set forth by Bloomfield in 1933. In spite of his optimism, however, Miller views many topics and interests, which logically *deserve* psycholinguistic attention, as being still too much terra incognita to be explored with our present theoretical stance and available experimental and analytic techniques. He insists, for instance, that "pragmatic questions involving belief systems are presently so vague as to be hardly worth asking" (p. 31).

Similarly, there are several other topics which, no matter how early recognized, must still wait for another generation of behavioral scientists. An example is the interrelationships of social and cultural contexts to the linguistic events which occur within them, of so much concern to the anthropologist Malinowski with his interest in language as a "mode of action" (see Malinowski, 1923, and Firth, 1957). It would be an easy task to extend this list of topics which are still beyond the pale of psycholinguistics. The reader who has carefully digested the sections of the 1954 Psycholinguistics monograph reprinted herein may even come to wonder if such a list can have an end. Like those motivated to make a personal investment in any developing behavioral science, the psycholinguist is at once both embarrassed and excited by the many unanswered questions which lie ahead.

Leaving the matter of future developments, we shall now mention a few topical areas, omitted from the preceding survey, which already possess associated research and bodies of literature. The first topic, which was not included either in the Saporta reader or in the 1954 Psycholinguistics monograph, is the area of "public opinion and mass communication." This is surely of interest to many sociologists and social psychologists. But although this area logically belongs within a general pycholinguistics, its omission from the above-mentioned treatises is a defensible one. For unlike most of the other subfields included in our topical purviews, this area boasts a developed body of literature, complete with several books of readings of its own, not to mention several research organizations (such as the University of Illinois Institute of Communications Research) devoted to its nurture. Some glimpses of the developments in this area are provided in Brown (1958) and Pool (1959), but the topic will not receive further attention here.

In contrast, the two remaining topics boast only a very scattered literature. In the remarks which follow, it will be my purpose not only to sponsor their admission to psycholinguistics (where they now belong only by default, if at all), but also to offer a very brief survey of some of the available literature of note. Earlier publications will receive more extended treatment here than in other sections above, because of the isolated nature of the relevant research activity.

In my introductory section, I called these topics "non-verbal communication" and "zoosemiotics." As we shall see, these terms were chosen because they happen to label dominant interests *within* the more inclusive areas of inquiry under discussion here. As might be expected, clarity of reference is sacrificed by naming a superordinate category after one of its constituent subordinates.

The surveyor feels justified in making this digression on several grounds: (i) The most important reason is that the new psycholinguistics could provide the integrative force which would reduce to order the diversity manifest in the research to be mentioned below. (ii) It would be most parochial to continue to examine human communication only in the light of that aspect of it (language) which linguists have deemed worthy of investigation. (iii) Many of the questions from these marginal areas, which earlier encouraged speculation (through want of adequate empirical data), can now be answered on the basis of new discoveries. (iv) The 1954 Psycholinguistics monograph mentions frontier areas (those below being some principal examples), and it would be useful to establish the foresight demonstrated at the 1953 Summer Seminar by documenting some of the developmental trends which its participants foresaw.

One way to approach the area of inquiry which includes non-verbal behavior is to first state that the persons most active in its investigation have been anthropologists and psychiatrists. Many commentators have been quick to auger an increasingly important role within linguistics for the study of paralanguage, of gestural systems, various speech surrogates, and the like. But there is always a limbo-like air surrounding the mention of such research. Rubenstein and Aborn (1960), for instance, mention slow development in this area, but they discuss most of the paralinguistic studies they mention within a general category of "language disturbances." Their observations are independently echoed by Hymes (1961a), who recounts how the individual or quantitatively varying attributes in speech (of central interest in paralinguistics) were pruned off by descriptive linguistic procedures as unnecessary and complicating, indeed forbidden, factors in the formal analysis of the language. Nevertheless, an awareness of such quantitative variations has occasionally forced itself to the fore in descriptive analysis.

An interesting attempt to distinguish between these and other distinctive prosodic features is found in Stockwell, Bowen, and Silva-Fuenzalida (1956). Following the reprinted version of their study in *Readings in Linguistics* (Joos, 1957b), an editorial comment by Joos predicts that the study of "vocalizations" constituted the (then) next frontier area for descriptive linguistics. Jakobson and Halle (1956) make a distinction between "expressive" and other (linguistic) distinctive features but fail to extend further attention to the former units.

Why is it that paralanguage has for so long escaped scrutiny? One reason may be that we tend to speak through the paralinguistic system in a manner which correctly suggests that we are much less conscious about the paralinguistic than about the linguistic channel. But as a matter of fact, it appears that whereas the messages conveyed by the two channels are in some as yet unstudied way highly corroboratory and complementary, the two must be regarded as functionally independent, and that on occasion (and according to the dictates of our particular cultural conditioning) we can use the two systems simultaneously to deliver two quite different messages.

There are many examples of the speaker's paralinguistic competence which clearly argue for its functional independence and psychological reality: the child's ability to interpret adult vocalizations before he is able to recognize or himself produce the linguistic units involved is one such instance; the proficient actor's ability to convey emotions by somehow mimicking the distinctive aspects of paralanguage which are associated with various emotional states in off-stage life; the psychiatrist's ability to identify certain emotional states or attitudes from his patient's "manner of speaking"; all of these examples of paralinguistic competence and performance highlight the communicative relevance of non-verbal vocalizations which co-occur with verbal behavior. It is important to note that the distinction between the two channels used to be phrased as "verbal" (linguistic) and "vocal" (paralinguistic).

Paralanguage has nevertheless been of long-standing interest to individual investigators. Sapir's article, "Speech as a personality trait" (1927), was a pioneer study on which much later work has been based, particularly the work of Newman (1944) and Herzog (1949). Henry (1936) and Sanford (1942a, 1942b) also contributed valuable early papers. Hymes' review (1961a) lists and discusses several of these early studies.

In the mid-1950s there were again numerous individual studies of paralanguage. At first, a number of papers appeared from the psychiatrists' camp. Goldman-Eisler (e.g., 1956) offered interesting insights into the relationship between the rate of speech and the respiration cycle, and the correlation of these to factors of tension in neurotic patients. Like many other workers who became interested in non-verbal communication problems at this point, Goldman-Eisler has continued to conduct research in this area; many of her earlier papers are listed and discussed in a more recent study (1961). Matarazzo, Saslow, and Matarazzo (1956) investigated the duration of periods of silence and of speech in patient interviews, suggesting a technique for measuring the duration (by the "interaction chronograph") and offering proposals to account for some of the observed correlations. Kasl and Mahl (1956) suggested their own measures for verbal interaction. Mahl reported on experiments which demonstrated that certain types of "speech disturbances and silence seem to be expressive attributes that are useful as anxiety indices" (1956). The interest of psychiatrists in speech silences during patients' discourses was further manifest in Starkweather's important study (1956b), which demonstrated the agreement of a group of psychiatrists on the subtle speech modifications and silences which in prior practice they had intuitively associated with hypertension. More articles in this vein from this period are mentioned in Rubenstein and Aborn (1960).

It is unfortunate that the important contributions from the linguists' camp did not appear until after this first flurry of psychiatric articles. Pittenger and Smith's (1957) and McQuown's (1957) articles in the journal *Psychiatry* could have greatly enhanced the value of the abovementioned psychiatrists' reports through contribution of more precise descriptive techniques. (Subsequent psychiatrists' reports on non-verbal communication have shown considerable more linguistic sophistication; see below.)

There early emerged three basic problems in connection with the study of paralanguage which required cooperation by linguists (these problems apply to the study of the gestural communication channel as well) : (i) the analytic problems of how to segment the behavior observed into recurring units, to devise a notation for these, and to isolate their distinctive components; (ii) the development of a meaningful taxonomy; and (iii) the determination of the constitutional limits on variability-in the behavior manifest in these channels, as evidenced by cross-cultural differences in such behavior.

Pittenger and Smith (1957) and McQuown (1957) laid important groundwork for the resolution of the first and second problems, and a recent study (Pittenger, Hockett, and Danehy, 1960) has developed and applied this groundwork to a detailed descriptive specification of the non-verbal (as well as linguistic) phenomena in a psychiatric interview. Trager (1958) outlines a taxonomic system based on this same tradition, and has since published papers (1960, 1961) showing the application of this descriptive scheme to the Taos language and culture. In consonance with many linguists' views, Trager regards paralanguage as an independent communication system. Its exclusion from a "theory of lanuage in the strict sense" is further suggested by Joos in a recent prognosis of trends in linguistics (1961).

While considerable progress has thus been made toward the resolution of the first two of the basic problems posed above, the third question about constitutional determinants of paralinguistic (and gestural) behavior still awaits comparable groundwork. The groundwork will involve asking many basic questions. Are some of the vocal contours (and part of the gestural repertoire) a part of human biology, basically alike for all humans and permitting only limited culturally imposed variation? Much cross-cultural work needs to be undertaken to determine this constitutional element, and along with that, much comparative primatology. But the climate is again favorable for this sort of investigation, as recent papers on the evolution of language indicate.

It might be argued that some of the published results of paralinguistic investigations are too recent and weakly inductive to appraise, and just such criticism is accumulating. For example, Hymes has asserted: "At present the focus of this work is chiefly on identifying and describing the relevant features. How these features occur relative to each other, how their distribution of occurrences interrelates with such things as situation, role, personality . . . most of this is yet to be determined" (1961a: 322). Lenneberg evinces similar disappointment when, in his review of Pittenger, Hockett, and Danehy (1960), he complains about missing "a discussion of at least the theoretical possibility of discovering a range of cues" (1962:73).

Nevertheless, when one collates the investigations carried out to date (and there have been many more than this review has room to mention), it does seem that there are distinctive affective features which are susceptible of componential analysis. This fact emerges very clearly from the many studies in which judges are given some diagnostic task to be based on listening to recorded texts. Starkweather (1964) has recently reviewed a large number of these studies and concludes:

> The studies of speech without meaningful content clearly indicate that information about the speaker is carried in the voice and is not dependent on an understanding of the verbal content. Judges of this material show considerable agreement when they are asked to have opinions about the emotion being expressed, either to identify it or to indicate the strength of the particular feeling. We have the clear impression that judgments are related to significant changes in pitch, rate and volume among other physical characteristics of the voice, but untrained judges are unable to describe these characteristics consistently.

The recency and taxonomic character of non-verbal communication and the terminological difficulties are not sufficient reasons for its neglect. Fortunately, relevant research seems to be gathering momentum, as evidenced by the recent Indiana University Conference on Paralinguistics and Kinesics, from which a number of papers are now available (see Sebeok, Hayes and Bateson, 1964). The distinctive role of paralanguage has been investigated with reference to spontaneous discourse (Maclay and Osgood, 1959) and dialogue (Livant, 1963). Several very sophisticated discussions about the experimental control of linguistic and paralinguistic variables are available, of which one of the outstanding is that of Kramer (1964). Paralinguistic phenomena have entered into many conditioning experiments involving experimenter bias (see Page 2).

Related interest in kinesics has been in evidence for a decade. Better-known earlier studies include La Barre (1947) and Birdwhistell (1952). Despite the severe limitations of negligible progress in this area, a number of interesting experiments have been reported in which gesture and body position have been used as the crucial variable in studies of experimenter bias (e.g., Reece and Whitman, 1962; Ekman, 1964).

Terminological differences, not unexpectedly, plague this area. "Paralinguistics" and "kinesics" have both experienced attempts at precise definition and delineation, but there remain overlappings of conceptual categories, and the terms themselves are still not widely used. Particularly in the earlier writings of the 1950s, there existed a welter of terms for phenomena which linguists could only agree to call extra- and non-linguistic.

"Content-free speech" is only one example of such terms. To the psychiatrists who coined it, "content-free speech" referred to the second of two co-occurrent communication channels inherent in speech production. The first is what linguists study as "expression," or rather the part of expression which is the meat of descriptive linguistics, viz., the phono-logical and grammatical primes and their syntactic structure. Stark-weather (e.g., 1956a, 1956b, 1964), Davitz (e.g., Davitz and Davitz, 1959) and others see this channel as conducting semantic information, that is, the content of speech, as linguists use the term "content." Simultaneous with content-speech is the second content-free channel which conducts "affec-tive" as opposed to "semantic" information, by "voice quality." A sample passage from a 1956 article by Starkweather is enough to boggle the unprepared linguist-reader: "The voice quality is also thought to be under less conscious control than the content and to contain information that may be at variance with the content of the message" (1956a:121). "Con-tent-free speech" has also come to refer to recorded bodies of speech which have been run through low-pass filters such that features conveying af-fective qualities are retained while linguistic intelligibility is suppressed.

By the late 1950s, one begins to encounter "nonverbal communication" as a technical term for content-free speech, as well as a cover-term for what is involved in the combined purview of paralinguistics and kinesics. The encounter could only bring dismay to the communications engineer, social psychologist, and ethologist, in whose fields that term is employed with quite different references. Investigators such as E. T. Hall (1959) have given the term wide currency in their contrastive cultural studies, in approximately the same meaning as used by Starkweather, Trager, Bird-whistell, and others.

This discussion was not intended to cover other forms of (human) non-verbal communication, such as various speech surrogate systems (written languages, so-called drum and whistle languages, and other cultural in-ventions), however fertile investigations of these phenomena might be for psycholinguistic theory. The relevance of such surrogate systems for the analysis of psychological reality, or what the engineer calls the "fidelity criterion," is obvious. The reader is directed to Cherry (1957) for some general considerations and to Stern (1957) for an insightful discus-sion of several types of speech surrogates.

Those with a psychiatric bent may be disappointed to discover that functionally-based speech "disorders" will receive only this nodding recognition. The Lorenz and Cobb (1954) study cited in Part 7 is one of only a very few references dealing with this topic that will be found in the bibliography which follows. There is a large literature dealing with such subjects as the content analysis of "schizophrenic speech," to mention only one example, and there is a pressing need for someone conversant with this literature to review it and comment on its relevance for psycholin-guistics.

The third and last topic of omission, to be discussed only briefly, is that referred to earlier as "zoosemiotics" (Sebeok, 1962). Again, as with non-verbal behavior, this labels only one dominant interest within a much larger category of pursuits ("semiotics") which logically includes it. Perhaps this topic can be best introduced by enumerating the key questions which research in this area is expected to answer for psycholinguists: (1) What is the general nature of animal communication systems?; and (2) What are the (evolutionary) origins of human language?

Those who have contributed most to the literature in this field are anthropologists, zoologists, and psychologists. Many substantive contributions of significance have emanated particularly from specialists within these fields who are best qualified to address these problems, namely, ethologists, primatologists, physical anthropologists, and those psycholinguists concerned with the biological bases of language.

It is surprising to discover, just at the time when significant substantive insights are being achieved by these specialists, that theoreticians among anthropologists tend to be adopting the same speculative stance which, before the turn of the century, enjoined the intellectual obloquy of such questions as the origin of language (see Diebold, 1964a). The major difficulty lies in the tradition in anthropological theory which (first assuming that language is the sine qua non of culture) argues on purely logico-typological grounds for various purportedly crucial differences between human and non-human communicative behavior.

This tradition has produced several widely read studies which have become as legitimately influential as they are incisive, including those of White (1949) and of Hockett (1960). The specialist can take little exception to the general arguments embodied in these papers, although there are certainly more comprehensive and psychologically palatable overviews, such as that of Sebeok (1962). Extensive bibliographic coverage of many of the more psycholinguistically relevant studies is provided in Hockett and Ascher (1964), Kainz (1961), Marler (1959, 1961), and Sebeok (1962, 1963).

The problems involving speculation arise when these typological discussions are augmented by considerations of the origin of language and its phylogenetic links with other primate communication systems. The surveyor chooses to leave prosecution of these charges to detailed, authoritative studies, such as those of Kainz (1961) and Lenneberg (forthcoming).

NOTES

1. This survey is based on an earlier study, my review of Sol Saporta, ed., 1961, *Psycholinguistics: A Book of Readings*, New York (see Diebold, 1964b). While many passages remain unchanged, the original study has been considerably revised and expanded, and contains a separate and enlarged bibliography. My earlier survey of psycholinguistics contained fairly extensive bibliographic coverage and a discursive (and, at times, too personal) commentary on developmental trends. A preprint version of that review was widely circulated, and I was gratified by the many critical responses elicited from the recipients. Many of their suggested changes have been incorporated

into the present survey, including bibliographic addenda and corrigenda, and for these I wish to express my appreciation.

With no offense to many others too numerous to mention, I want to acknowledge particular indebtedness to Robert B. Lees, Eric H. Lenneberg, and Thomas A. Sebeok for their comments and help; to Lois A. Levin for her research activities on my behalf; and to Bernard B. Perry, Director of the Indiana University Press, for his enthusiastic encouragement. Special thanks are hereby extended Glenn H. Matthews, of Prentice-Hall Inc., and John W. Parker, of Holt, Rinehart and Winston, Inc., for generous purveyance of their firms' produce.

Some of the research undertaken in connection with this paper was supported in part by a grant from the National Institutes of Health (MH 07124–01), and by funds from the William F. Milton Fund, both at Harvard University where the author is Assistant Professor of Social Anthropology and Linguistics, in the Department of Social Relations.

2. In its earlier volumes, *The Psychological Bulletin* contains a number of surveys which are now mainly of historical interest. These include Mead (1904), Esper (1921), Adams and Powers (1929), and McGranahan (1936). The only other American journal which regularly surveys psycholinguistic activity is the *International Journal of American Linguistics*, which in its recently instituted Abstracts section, has printed collections of abstracts prepared by Susan M. Ervin. See *I.J.A.L.* 28. 205–9 (1962) and 30. 184–93 (1964).

3. In the pages that follow, this monograph appears cited in various ways. Sometimes the usual form for bibliographic citations is followed, *viz.*, "Osgood and Sebeok, 1954." Often, however, this work is referred to simply as "the 1954 survey" or "the 1954 monograph." Reference to the "1953 conference" will be taken to mean the (1953) Summer Seminar on Psycholinguistics, sponsored by the Social Science Research Council. "SSRC," according to prevalent convention, will be used as an abbreviation for the latter organization. Another departure from standard bibliographic citation occurs in the case of Sol Saporta, ed., 1961, *Psycholinguistics: A Book of Readings*, New York, which is usually referred to as "Saporta's reader."

4. In preparing this review, the following sources (alphabetically arranged) were found to be particularly useful for their own coverage of psycholinguistic publications and research, or for their insightful commentaries on psycholinguistics and its various subfields: Berko and Brown (1960); Bright (1963); Brown (1958); Carroll (1955, 1958c); Cherry (1957); Chomsky (1959); Cofer (1961); Cofer and Musgrave (1963); Delacroix (1933); Greenberg (1963); Hall (1951, 1952); Henle (1958); Hamp (1961); Hymes (1961a, 1962); Irwin (1960); Kainz (1946, 1956-62); Lambert (1962); Lounsbury (1959, 1962, 1963); Miller (1951a, 1951b, 1954, 1962a, 1964); Miller and Chomsky (1963); Mowrer (1954, 1960); Olmsted (1955); Olmsted and Moore (1952); Osgood (1963a, 1963b, 1963c); Osgood and Sebeok (1954); Pronko (1946); Rubenstein and Aborn (1960); Saporta (1961); and Sebeok (1962). The reviewer was privileged to peruse preliminary chapters of Lenneberg's forthcoming book, *The Biological Foundation of Language*, and found it to be extremely useful.

Some earlier European research (which we would now call "psycholinguistic") is cited in Carroll, 1955, Delacroix, 1933, and Kainz, 1946. The present survey, however, concentrates on North American research activities. With certain noteworthy exceptions, this *is* the region where the most intensive psycholinguistic research has evolved and is being currently pursued. European efforts have been most outstanding in the domains of concept formation, physiological psycholinguistics, and general semantics. Relevant European contributions are mentioned in this survey at appropriate points.

5. Discussion of this anthropologically-based research is available in Brown (1958), Carroll (1955), Conklin (1962), Frake (1962), French (1963), Hymes (1961a, 1961c), Lounsbury (1959, 1962, 1963), and Sturtevant (1963). Exemplary applications include Frake (1961) and Wallace and Atkins (1960).

BIBLIOGRAPHY

Abbreviations:

I.J.A.L.	*International Journal of Amerian Linguistics*
J.A.S.A.	*Journal of the Acoustical Society of America*
J.A.S.P.	*Journal of Abnormal and Social Psychology*
J.V.L.V.B.	*Journal of Verbal Learning and Verbal Behavior*

Aborn, M., H. Rubenstein, and T. D. Sterling, 1959, "Sources of contextual constraint upon words in sentences," *J. Exper. Psych.* 57. 171–80.

Abramson, A. S., 1961, Identification and discrimination of phonemic tones, Mimeo, New York.

Adams, J., 1957, "Laboratory studies of behavior without awareness," *Psych. Bull.* 54. 383–405.

Adams, S., and F. F. Powers, 1929, "The psychology of language," *Psych. Bull.* 26. 241–60.

Albright, R. W., and J. B. Albright, 1956, "The phonology of a two-year old child," *Word* 12. 382–90.

Alkon, P. L., 1959, "Behaviourism and linguistics: an historical note," *Language and Speech* 2. 37–51.

Anisfeld, M., N. Bogo, and W. E. Lambert, 1962, "Evaluational reactions to accented English speech," *J.A.S.P.* 65. 223–31.

Bach, E., 1964, *An Introduction to Transformational Grammars*, New York.

Basilius, H., 1952, "Neo-Humboldtian ethnolinguistics," *Word* 8. 95–105.

Berko, J., 1958, "The child's learning of English morphology," *Word* 14. 150–77.

Berko, J., and R. Brown, 1960, "Psycholinguistic research methods," *The Handbook of Research Methods in Child Psychology*, P. H. Mussen, ed., New York, 517–57.

Betz, W., 1954, "Zur Ueberprüfung des Feldbegriffs," *Zeitschrift für vergleichende Sprachforschung* 71. 189–98.

Bidney, D., 1953, *Theoretical Anthropology*, New York.

Birdwhistell, R. L., 1952, *Introduction to Kinesics*, Louisville.

Bloomfield, L., 1926, "A set of postulates for the science of language," *Language* 2. 153–64.

Bloomfield, L., 1933, *Language*, New York.

Bloomfield, L., 1939, "Linguistic aspects of science," *International Encyclopedia of Unified Science*, O. Neurath, R. Carnap, and C. Morris, eds., Chicago, 1. 215–76.

Bolinger, D., 1960, "Linguistic science and linguistic engineering," *Word* 16. 374–91.

Bousfield, W. A., 1961, "The problem of meaning in verbal behavior," in *Verbal Learning and Verbal Behavior*, C. N. Cofer, ed., 81–109.

Brain, R., 1961, *Speech Disorders*, Washington.

Bright, W., 1963, "Language," *Biennial Review of Anthropology 1963*, B. J. Spiegel, ed., Stanford, 1–29.

Broadbent, D. E., 1957, "A mechanical model for human attention and immediate memory," *Psych. Review* 64. 205–15.

Broadbent, D. E., 1958, *Perception and Communication*, New York.

Broadbent, D. E., 1962, "Attention and the perception of speech," *Scientific American*, 205.

Brody, N., 1964, "Anxiety and the variability of word associates," *J.A.S.P.* 68. 331–4.

Brown, R., 1957, "Linguistic determinism and the part of speech," *J.A.S.P.* 55. 1–5.

Brown, R., 1958, *Words and Things*, Glencoe.

Brown, R., 1962, The acquisition of language, Mimeo, Cambridge, Mass.

Brown, R., and U. Bellugi, 1964, "Three processes in the child's acquisition of syntax," *Harvard Educational Review* **34**. 133–51.

Brown, R., and M. Ford, 1961, "Address in American English," *J.A.S.P.* **62**. 375–85.

Brown, R., and C. Fraser, 1963, "The acquisition of syntax," in *Verbal Behavior and Learning*, Cofer and Musgrave, eds., 158–209.

Brown, R., and A. Gilman, 1960, "The pronouns of power and solidarity," *Style in Language*, T. A. Sebeok, ed., New York, 253–76.

Brown, R., and D. C. Hildum, 1956, "Expectancy and perception of syllables," *Language* **32**. 411–9.

Brown, R., and E. H. Lenneberg, 1954, "A study in language and cognition," *J.A.S.P.* **49**. 454–62.

Brown, R., and R. Nuttall, 1959, "Method in phonetic symbolism experiments," *J.A.S.P.* **59**. 441–5.

Bruce, D. J., 1958, "The effect of listeners' anticipations on the intelligibility of heard speech," *Language and Speech* **1**. 79–97.

Bruner, J. S., J. J. Goodnow, and G. A. Austin, 1957, *A Study of Thinking*, New York.

Burling, R., 1963, "Garo kinship terms and the analysis of meaning," *Ethnology* **2**. 70–85.

Buss, A. H., and I. R. Gerjouy, 1958, "Verbal conditioning and anxiety," *J.A.S.P.* **57**. 249–50.

Carroll, J. B., 1955, *The Study of Language*, Cambridge, Mass.

Carroll, J. B., ed., 1956, *Language, Thought, and Reality: Selected Writings of Benjamin Lee Whorf*, New York.

Carroll, J. B., 1958a, "A factor analysis of two foreign language aptitude batteries," *J. Gen. Psych.* **59**. 3–19.

Carroll, J. B., 1958b, "Some psychological effects of language structure," in *Psychopathology of Communication*, P. H. Hoch and J. Zubin, eds., New York, 28–36.

Carroll, J. B., 1958c, "Process and content in psycholinguistics," in *Current Trends in the Description and Analysis of Behavior*, R. Glaser et al., eds., Pittsburgh, 175–200.

Carroll, J. B., 1959, Review of *The Measurement of Meaning*, C. E. Osgood, G. Suci, and P. Tannebaum, in *Language* **35**. 58–77.

Carroll, J. B., 1960, "Language development in children," *Encyclopedia of Educational Research*, New York.

Carroll, J. B., 1962a, "The prediction of success in intensive foreign language training," *Training Research and Education*, Pittsburgh, 87–136.

Carroll, J. B., 1962b, Publications resulting from, or based in part on materials collected with the aid of the Southwest Project, Mimeo, Cambridge, Mass.

Carroll, J. B., 1963, "Linguistic relativity, contrastive linguistics, and language learning," *International Review of Applied Linguistics in Language Teaching* **1**. 1–20.

Carroll, J. B., 1964, "Words, meanings, and concepts," *Harvard Educational Review* **34**. 178–202.

Carroll, J. B., and J. B. Casagrande, 1958, "The function of language classifications in behavior," *Readings in Social Psychology*, E. E. Maccoby, T. M. Newcomb, and E. L. Hartley, eds., New York, 18–31.

Casagrande, J. B., 1956, "The Southwest Project in Comparative Psycholinguistics: a progress report," *Social Science Research Council Items* **10**. 41–5.

Casagrande, J. B., 1960, "The Southwest Project in Comparative Psycholinguistics: a preliminary report," *Selected Papers of the Fifth International Congress of Anthropological and Ethnological Sciences*, A. F. C. Wallace, ed., Philadelphia, 777–82.

Casagrande, J. B., 1963, "Language universals in anthropological perspective," in *Universals of Language*, J. H. Greenberg, ed., 220–35.

Cassirer, E., 1923–9, *Die Philosophie der symbolischen Formen, I–III*, Berlin.

Cassirer, E., 1933, "La lanage et la construction de monde des objets," *J. Psychologie Normale et Pathologique* **30**. 18–44.

Cassirer, E., 1944, *An Essay on Man*, New Haven.

Cassirer, E., 1945, "Structuralism in modern linguistics," *Word* 1. 99–120.

Cherry, C., 1957, *On Human Communication: A Review, a Survey, and a Criticism*, New York.

Chomsky, N., 1956, "Three models for the description of language," *I.R.E. Trans. on Info. Theory* 2. 113–24.

Chomsky, N., 1957, *Syntactic Structures*, The Hague.

Chomsky, N., 1959, Review of *Verbal Behavior*, B. F. Skinner, in *Language* 35. 26–58.

Chomsky, N., 1961a, "Some methodological remarks on generative grammar," *Word* 17. 219–39.

Chomsky, N., 1961b, "On the notion 'rule of grammar,' " *Proceedings of Symposia in Applied Mathematics*, Providence, 12. 6–24.

Chomsky, N., 1962a, "The logical basis of linguistic theory," *Preprints of Papers for the Ninth International Congress of Linguists*, M. Halle, ed., Cambridge, 509–74.

Chomsky, N., 1962b, "Explanatory models in linguistics," in *Logic, Methodology and Philosophy of Science*, E. Nagel, P. Suppes, and A. Tarski, eds., Stanford, 528–50.

Chomsky, N., 1963, "Formal properties of grammars," in *Handbook of Mathematical Psychology*, D. R. Luce, R. R. Bush, and E. Galanter, eds., New York, 2. 323–418.

Chomsky, N., and G. A. Miller, 1958, "Finite state languages," *Information Control* 1. 91–112.

Chomsky, N., and G. A. Miller, 1963, "Introduction to the formal analysis of natural languages," *Handbook of Mathematical Psychology*, D. R. Luce, R. R. Bush, and E. Galanter, eds., New York, 2. 269–321.

Church, J., 1961, *Language and the Discovery of Reality*, New York.

Cofer, C. N., 1960, "An experimental analysis of the role of context in verbal behavior," *Trans. New York Academy of Sciences* 22. 341–7.

Cofer, C. N., ed., 1961, *Verbal Learning and Verbal Behavior*, New York.

Cofer, C. N., and B. S. Musgrave, eds., 1963, *Verbal Behavior and Learning: Problems and Processes*, New York.

Conklin, H. C., 1962, "Lexicographical treatment of folk taxonomies," in *Problems in Lexicography*, F. W. Householder and S. Saporta, eds. (Indiana University Research Center in Anthropology, Folklore and Linguistics, Pub. 21), Bloomington, 119–41.

Crowne, D. P., and B. R. Strickland, 1961, "The conditioning of verbal behavior as a function of the need for social approval," *J.A.S.P.* 63. 395–401.

Davitz, J. R., and L. J. Davitz, 1959, "The communication of feelings by content-free speech," *J. Communication* 9. 6–13.

Deese, J., 1960, "Frequency of usage and number of words in free recall: the role of association," *Psych. Rep.* 7. 337–44.

Deese, J., 1961, "From the isolated verbal unit to connected discourse," in *Verbal Learning and Verbal Behavior*, C. N. Cofer, ed., 11–41.

Deese, J., 1962a, "On the structure of association meaning," *Psych. Review* 69. 161–75.

Deese, J., 1962b, "Form class and the determinants of association," *J.V.L.V.B.* 1. 79–84.

Delacroix, H., 1933, "Linguistique et psychologie," *J. de psychologie* 30. 798–825.

Denes, P. B., and E. N. Pinson, 1963, *The Speech Chain: The Physics and Biology of Spoken Language*, Baltimore.

Deroy, L., 1956, *L'emprunt linguistique*, Liège.

DeSoto, C. B., and J. J. Bosley, 1962, "The cognitive structure of a social structure," *J.A.S.P.* 64. 303–7.

Diderichsen, P., 1949, "Morpheme categories in modern Danish," *Recherches structurales 1949*, 134–55.

Diderichsen, P., 1958, "The importance of distributional versus other criteria in linguistic analysis," *Proceedings of the Eighth International Congress of Linguists*, Oslo, 156–82.

Diebold, A. R., Jr., 1963, "Code-switching in Greek-English bilingual speech," *Report*

A SURVEY OF PSYCHOLINGUISTIC RESEARCH, 1954-1964 279

of the Thirteenth Annual Round Table Meeting on Linguistics and Language Studies (Monograph Series on Languages and Linguistics, No. 15), Washington, D.C., 53–62.

Diebold, A. R., Jr., 1964a, Comment on Hockett and Ascher's "The Human Revolution," Current Anthropology 5. 158.

Diebold, A. R., Jr., 1964b, Review of Psycholinguistics: A Book of Readings, S. Saporta, ed., in Language 40. 197–260.

Dittmann, A. T., and L. C. Wynne, 1961, "Linguistic techniques and the analysis of emotionality in interviews," J.A.S.P. 63. 201–4.

Dulany, D. E., 1961, "Hypotheses and habits in verbals 'operant conditioning,'" J.A.S.P. 63. 251–63.

Ebeling, C. L., 1962, Linguistic Units, The Hague.

Ekman, P., 1964, "Body position, facial expression, and verbal behavior during interviews," J.A.S.P. 68. 295–301.

Entwisle, D. R., D. L. Forsyth, and R. Muuss, 1964, "The syntactic-paradigmatic shift in children's word associations," J.V.L.V.B. 3. 19–29.

Epstein, W., 1961, "The influence of syntactical structure on learning," Amer. J. Psych. 74. 80–5.

Epstein, W., 1962, "A further study of the influence of syntactical structure on learning," Amer. J. Psych. 75. 121–6.

Epstein, W., 1963, "Temporal schemata in syntactically structured material," J. Gen. Psych. 68. 157–64.

Eriksen, C. W., and J. L. Kuethe, 1956, "Avoidance conditioning of verbal behavior without awareness: a paradigm of repression," J.A.S.P. 53. 203–9.

Ervin, S. M., 1961, "Changes with age on the verbal determinants of word association," Amer. J. Psych. 74. 361–72.

Ervin, S. M., 1963, "Correlates of associative frequency," J.V.L.V.B. 1. 422–31.

Ervin, S. M., 1964, "Language and TAT content in bilinguals," J.A.S.P. 68. 500–7.

Ervin, S., and G. Foster, 1960, "The development of meaning in children's descriptive terms," J.A.S.P. 61. 271–5.

Esper, E. A., 1921, "The psychology of language," Psych. Bull. 18. 490–6.

Fairbanks, G., 1954, "A theory of the speech organism as a servosystem," J. Speech and Hearing Disorders 19. 133–9.

Fant, G., 1960, Acoustic Theory of Speech Production, The Hague.

Fearing, F., 1954, "An examination of the conceptions of Benjamin Whorf in the light of theories of perception and cognition," Language in Culture, H. Hoijer, ed., Chicago, 47–81.

Fernández, Guizzetti, G., 1960, "Guillermo de Humboldt, padre de la etnolingüística," Cuadernos del Instituto Nacional de Investigaciones Folklóricas (Buenos Aires) 1. 229–45.

Fernández, Guizzetti, G., 1960/61, "Proyecciones filosóficas de algunas teorías etnolingüistas contemporaneas, I & II," Revista de antropología (São Paulo) 8. 43–62; 9. 51–60.

Fernández, Guizzetti, G., 1961, "Nuevos aportes a la etnolingüística," Anales de arqueología y etnología (Mendoza) 16. 11–33.

Feuer, L. S., 1953, "Sociological aspects of the relation between language and philosophy," Philosophy of Science 20. 85–100.

Fillenbaum, S., and L. V. Jones, 1962, "An application of 'cloze' technique to the study of aphasic speech," J.A.S.P. 65. 183–9.

Firth, J. R., 1957, "Ethnographic analysis and language with reference to Malinowski's views," in Man and Culture: An Evaluation of the Work of Bronislaw Malinowski, R. Firth, ed., London, 93–118.

Fischer-Jørgensen, E., 1949, "Danish linguistic activity," Lingua 2. 95–109.

Fischer-Jørgensen, E., 1952, "The phonetic basis for identification of phonemic entities," J.A.S.A. 24. 611–17.

Fischer-Jørgensen, E., 1956, "The commutation test and its application to phonemic analysis," *For Roman Jakobson: Essays on Occasion of his Sixtieth Birthday*, M. Halle, et al., eds., The Hague, 140–51.

Fischer-Jørgensen, E., 1958, "What can the new techniques of acoustic phonetics contribute to linguistics" *Proceedings of the Eighth International Congress of Linguists*, Oslo, 433–78.

Fishman, J. A., 1960, "A systematization of the Whorfian hypothesis," *Behavioral Science* 4. 323–39.

Flanagan, B., I. Goldiamond, and N. Azrin, 1958, "Operant stuttering: the control of stuttering behavior through response-contingent consequences," *J. Experimental Analysis of Behavior* 1. 173–7.

Flavell, J. H., 1958, "A test of the Whorfian hypothesis," *Psych. Rep.* 4. 455–62.

Flavell, J. H., 1963, *The Developmental Psychology of Jean Piaget*, Princeton.

Frake, C. O., 1961, "The diagnosis of disease among the Subanun of Mindanao," *Amer. Anthro.* 63. 113–32.

Frake, C. O., 1962, "The ethnographic study of cognitive systems," in *Anthropology and Human Behavior*, T. Gladwin and W. C. Sturtevant, eds., Washington, 72–93.

Fraser, C. R., U. Bellugi, and R. Brown, 1963, "Control of grammar in imitation, comprehension, and production," *J.V.L.V.B.* 2. 121–35.

French, D., 1963, "The relationship of anthropology to studies in perception and cognition," *Psychology: A Study of a Science*, S. Koch, ed., New York, Vol. 6, Study 2. 388–428.

Fries, C. C., 1961, "The Bloomfield 'school,' " in *Trends in European and American Linguistics: 1930-1960*, C. Mohrmann, A. Sommerfelt, and J. Whatmough, eds., Utrecht, 196–224.

Fry, D. B., A. S. Abramson, P. D. Eimas, and A. M. Liberman, 1962, "The identification and discrimination of synthetic vowels," *Language and Speech* 5. 171–89.

Fuhrer, M. J., and C. W. Eriksen, 1960, "The unconscious perception of the meaning of verbal stimuli," *J.A.S.P.* 61. 432–9.

Furth, H. G., 1961, "The influence of language on the development of concept formation in deaf children," *J.A.S.P.* 63. 386–9.

Galanter, E., and G. A. Miller, 1960, "Some comments on stochastic models and psychological theories," in *Mathematical Methods in the Social Sciences*, K. J. Arrow, S. Karlin, and P. Suppes, eds., Stanford, 277–97.

Ganzer, V. J., and I. G. Sarason, 1964, "Interrelationships among hostility, experimental conditions, and verbal behavior," *J.A.S.P.* 68. 79–84.

Gastil, R. B., 1959, "Relative linguistic determinism," *Anthropological Linguistics* 1: 9. 24–38.

Gipper, H., ed., 1959, *Sprache, Schlüssel zur Welt: Festschrift für Leo Weisgerber*, Düsseldorf.

Goldman-Eisler, F., 1955, "Speech-breathing activity—a measure of tension and affect," *British J. Psych.* 46. 53–63.

Goldman-Eisler, F., 1961, "Continuity of speech utterance, its determinants and its significance," *Language and Speech* 4. 220–31.

Goldstein, K., 1948, *Language and Language Disturbances: Aphasic Symptom Complexes and Their Significance for Medicine and Theory of Language*, New York.

Goodenough, W. H., 1956, "Cultural anthropology and linguistics," *Bull. Philadelphia Anthropological Society* 9: 3. 3–7.

Goodglass, H., and J. Hunt, 1958, "Grammatical complexity and aphasic speech," *Word* 14. 197–207.

Goss, A. E., 1961, "Verbal mediating responses and concept formation," *Psych. Review* 68. 248–74.

Greenberg, J. H., 1956, "Concerning inferences from linguistic to nonlinguistic data," in *Language in Culture*, H. Hoijer, ed., Chicago, 3–19.

Greenberg, J. H., ed., 1963, *Universals of Language*, Cambridge, Mass.

Gudschinsky, C. S., 1958, "Native reactions to tones and words in Mazatec," *Word* 14. 338–45.

Haas, W., 1958, Review of *Syntactic Structures* by N. Chomsky, in *Archivum Linguisticum* 13. 196–209.

Hall, E. T., 1959, *The Silent Language*, New York.

Hall, R. A., Jr., 1951, "American linguistics: 1925–1950," *Archivum Linguisticum* 3. 101–25.

Hall, R. A., Jr., 1952, "American linguistics: 1925–1950," *Archivum Linguisticum* 4. 1–16.

Halle, M., 1957, "In defense of the number two," *Studies Presented to Joshua Whatmough on his Sixtieth Birthday*, E. Pulgram, ed., 65–72.

Halle, M., 1959, *The Sound Pattern of Russian: A Linguistic and Acoustical Investigation*, The Hague.

Halle, M., 1962, "Phonology in generative grammar," *Word* 18. 54–72.

Halle, M., and K. N. Stevens, 1962, "Speech recognition: a model and a program for research," *I.R.E. Trans. on Info. Theory* 8. 155–9.

Hamp, E. P., 1961, "General linguistics: The United States in the Fifties," in *Trends in European and American Linguistics 1930–1960*, C. Mohrmann, A. Sommerfelt, and J. Whatmough, eds., Utrecht, 165–95.

Harris, Z. S., 1948, "Componential analysis of a Hebrew paradigm," *Language* 24. 87–91.

Haugen, E., 1951, "Directions in modern linguistics," *Language* 27. 211–22.

Haugen, E., 1956, *Bilingualism in the Americas* (Publications of the American Dialect Society, No. 26), University of Alabama.

Haugen, E., 1957, "The semantics of Icelandic orientation," *Word* 13. 447–59.

Haugen, E., 1958, "Language contact," *Proceedings of the Eighth International Congress of Linguists*, Oslo, 772–85.

Hebb, D. O., 1949, *Organization of Behavior: A Neuropsychological Theory*, New York.

Hebb, D. O., 1958, *A Textbook of Psychology*, Philadelphia.

Heidbreder, E., 1945, "Toward a dynamic psychology of cognition," *Psych. Review* 51. 1–22.

Heidbreder, E., 1948, "Studying human thinking," in *Methods of Psychology*, T. G. Andrews, ed., New York, 96–123.

Henle, P., ed., 1958, *Language, Thought, and Culture*, Ann Arbor.

Henry, J., 1936, "The linguistic expression of emotion," *Amer. Anthro.* 38. 250–6.

Herdan, G., 1960, *Type-token Mathematics: A Textbook of Mathematical Linguistics*, The Hague.

Herman, D. T., R. H. Lawless, and R. W. Marshall, 1957, "Variables in the effect of language on the reproduction of visually perceived forms," *Perceptual and Motor Skills* 7. 171–86.

Herzog, G., 1949, "Linguistic approaches to personality," in *Culture and Personality*, S. S. Sargent and M. W. Smith, eds., New York, 93–102.

Hildum, D. C., and R. Brown, 1956, "Verbal reinforcement and interviewer bias," *J.A.S.P.* 53. 108–11.

Hill, A. A., 1961, "Grammaticality," *Word* 17. 1–10.

Hjelmslev, L., and H. J. Udall, 1957, *Outline of Glossematics* (Travaux du Cercle Linguistique de Copenhagen, Vol. 10), Copenhagen.

Hockett, C. F., 1950, "Age-grading and linguistic continuity," *Language* 26. 449–57.

Hockett, C. F., 1953, Review of *The Mathematical Theory of Communication*, C. E. Shannon and W. Weaver, in *Language* 29. 69–93.

Hockett, C. F., 1960, "Logical considerations in the study of animal communication," in *Animal Sounds and Communication*, W. E. Lanyon and T. N. Tavolga, eds., Washington, 392–430.

Hockett, C. F., and R. Ascher, 1964, "The human revolution," *Current Anthropology* 5. 135–68.

Hoijer, H., 1953, "The relation of language to culture," *Anthropology Today*, A. L. Kroeber, ed., 554–73.

Hoijer, H., ed., 1954, *Language in Culture*, Chicago.

Hoijer, H., 1958, "Native reaction as a criterion in linguistic analysis," *Proceedings of the Eighth International Congress of Linguistics*, Oslo, 573–91.

Hoijer, H., 1961, "Anthropological linguistics," in *Trends in European and American Linguistics 1930–1960*, C. Mohrmann, A. Sommerfelt, and J. Whatmough, eds., Utrecht, 110–27.

Householder, F. W., 1956, "Unreleased *p*, *t*, *k* in American English," in *For Roman Jakobson: Essays on the Occasion of his Sixtieth Birthday*, M. Halle et al., eds., The Hague, 235–44.

Householder, F. W., 1959, "On linguistic primes," *Word* 15. 231–44.

Howes, D., 1957, "On the relation between the probability of a word as an association and in general linguistic usage," *J.A.S.P.* 54. 75–85.

Howes, D., and C. E. Osgood, 1954, "On the combination of associative probabilities in linguistic contexts," *Amer. J. Psych.* 67. 241–58.

Hunt, E. B., 1962, *Concept Learning: An Information Processing Problem*, New York.

Hymes, D. H., 1961a, "Linguistic aspects of cross-cultural personality study," *Studying Personality Cross-culturally*, B. Kaplan, ed., Evanston, Ill., and Elmsford, N.Y., 313–59.

Hymes, D. H., 1961b, "On typology of cognitive styles in language," *Anthropological Linguistics* 3: 1. 22–54.

Hymes, D. H., 1961c, "Functions of speech: an evolutionary approach," in *Anthropology and Education*, F. C. Gruber, ed., Philadelphia, 55–83.

Hymes, D. H., 1962, "The ethnography of speaking," in *Anthropology and Human Behavior*, T. Gladwin and W. C. Sturtevant, eds., Washington, D.C., 13–53.

Hymes, D. H., ed., 1964, *Language in Culture and Society: A Reader in Linguistics and Anthropology*, New York.

Inhelder, B., and J. Paiget, 1958, *The Growth of Logical Thinking*, New York.

Irwin, O. C., 1960, "Language and communication," in *Handbook of Research Methods in Child Development*, P. H. Mussen, ed., New York, 487–516.

Irwin, O. C., and H. P. Chen, 1946, "Development of speech during infancy: curve of phoneme types," *J. Exper. Psych.* 36. 431–6.

Jakobson, R., 1941, *Kindersprache, Aphasie und allgemeine Lautgesetze*, Uppsala.

Jakobson, R., 1948, "The phonemic and grammatical aspects of language in their interrelations," *Actes du Sixième Congrès des Linguistes*, Paris, 4–18.

Jakobson, R., 1955, "Aphasia as a linguistic problem," in *On Expressive Language*, H. Werner, ed., Worcester, 69–81.

Jakobson, R., and M. Halle, 1956, *Fundamentals of Language*, The Hague.

Jenkins, J. J., ed., 1959, *Associative Processes in Verbal Behavior*, Minneapolis.

Jenkins, J. J., W. A. Russell, and G. J. Suci, 1958, "An atlas of semantic profiles for 360 words," *Amer. J. Psych.* 71. 688–99.

Jenkins, J. J., W. A. Russell, and G. J. Suci, 1959, "A table of distances for the semantic atlas," *Amer. J. Psych.* 72. 623–5.

Johnson, W. J., and R. R. Leutenegger, 1956, *Stuttering in Children and Adults*, Minneapolis.

Joos, M., 1957a, Review of *Fundamentals of Language*, R. Jakobson and M. Halle, in *Language* 33. 408–15.

Joos, M., ed., 1957b, *Readings in Linguistics*, Washington, D.C.

Joos, M., 1961, "Linguistic prospects in the United States," in *Trends in European and American Linguistics 1930–1960*, C. Mohrmann, A. Sommerfelt, and J. Whatmough, eds., Utrecht, 11–20.

Jost, L., 1960, *Sprache als Werk und wirkende Kraft*, Berne.

Kainz, F., 1946, *Einführung in die Sprachpsychologie*, Vienna.

Kainz, F., 1956–62, *Psychologie der Sprache*, *I–V*, Stuttgart.

Kainz, F., 1961, *Die Sprache der Tiere*, Stuttgart.

Kanfer, F. H., 1959, "Verbal rate, content and adjustment ratings in experimentally structured interviews," *J.A.S.P.* **58.** 305–11.

Kasl, S. V., and G. F. Mahl, 1956, "A simple device for obtaining certain verbal activity measures during interviews," *J.A.S.P.* **53.** 388–90.

Katz, J. J., and J. A. Fodor, 1963, "The structure of a semantic theory," *Language* **39.** 170–210.

Katz, J. J., and P. M. Postal, 1964, *An Integrated Theory of Linguistic Descriptions*, Cambridge, Mass.

Kilpatrick, F. P., 1955, "Perception theory and general semantics," *ETC.* **12.** 257–64.

Kluckhohn, C., 1961, "Notes on some anthropological aspects of communication," *Amer. Anthro.* **63.** 895–912.

Kolers, P. A., 1963, "Interlingual word associations," *J.V.L.V.B.* **2.** 291–300.

Konradt-Hicking, M., 1956, "Wortfeld oder Bedeutungsfeld (Sinnfeld)?" *Zeitschrift für vergleichende Sprachforschung* **73.** 222–34.

Korchin, S. J., and H. Basowitz, 1957, "Age differences in verbal learning," *J.A.S.P.* **54.** 64–9.

Korchin, S. J., and S. Levine, 1957, "Anxiety and verbal learning," *J.A.S.P.* **54.** 166–71.

Kramer, E., 1964, "Elimination of verbal cues in judgment of emotion from voice," *J.A.S.P.* **68.** 390–6.

Krasner, L., 1958, "Studies of the conditioning of verbal behavior," *Psych. Bull.* **55.** 148–70.

Kumata, H., and W. Schramm, 1956, "A pilot study of cross-cultural methodology," *Public Opinion Quarterly* **20.** 229–38.

LaBarre, W., 1947, "The cultural basis of emotion and gestures," *J. Personality* **16.** 49–68.

Lambert, W. E., 1962, Psychological approaches to the study of language, Mimeo, Montreal.

Lambert, W. E., and S. Fillenbaum, 1959, "A pilot study of aphasia among bilinguals," *Canadian J. Psych.* **13.** 28–34.

Lambert, W. E., R. C. Gardner, H. C. Barik, and K. Turnstall, 1963, "Attitudinal and cognitive aspects of intensive study of a second language," *J.A.S.P.* **66.** 358–68.

Lambert, W. E., J. Havelka, and C. Crosby, 1958, "The influence of language-acquisition contexts on bilingualism," *J.A.S.P.* **56.** 239–44.

Lambert, W. E., J. Havelka, and R. C. Gardner, 1959, "Linguistic manifestations of bilingualism," *Amer. J. Psych.* **72.** 77–82.

Lambert, W. E., and L. A. Jakobovits, 1960, "Verbal satiation and changes in the intensity of meaning," *J. Exper. Psych.* **60.** 688–99.

Lashley, K. S., 1951, "The problem of serial order in behavior," in *Central Mechanisms in Behavior*, L. A. Jeffress, ed., New York, 112–36.

Lee, D., 1938, "Conceptual implications of an Indian language," *Philosophy of Science* **5.** 89–102.

Lee, D., 1944, "Categories of the generic and particular in Wintu," *Amer. Anthro.* **46.** 362–9.

Lees, R. B., 1957, Review of *Syntactic Structures*, N. Chomsky, in *Language* **33.** 375–408.

Lees, R. B., 1960, "A multiply ambiguous adjectival construction in English," *Language* **36.** 207–21.

Lees, R. B., 1962, What does phonemics clarify? Mimeo, Urbana, Ill.

Lenneberg, E. H., 1953, "Cognition in ethnolinguistics," *Language* **29.** 463–71.

Lenneberg, E. H., 1955, "A note on Cassirer's philosophy of language," *Philosophy and Phenomenological Research* **15**. 512–22.

Lenneberg, E. H., 1957, "A probabilistic approach to language learning," *Behavioral Science* **2**. 1–12.

Lenneberg, E. H., 1960a, Review of *Speech and Brain Mechanisms*, W. Penfield and L. Roberts, in *Language* **36**. 97–112.

Lenneberg, E. H., 1960b, "Language, evolution, and purposive behavior," in *Culture in History: Essays in Honor of Paul Radin*, S. Diamond, ed., New York, 869–93.

Lenneberg, E. H., 1961, "Color naming, color recognition, color discrimination: a reappraisal," *Perceptual and Motor Skills* **12**. 375–82.

Lenneberg, E. H., 1962a, Review of *The First Five Minutes*, R. E. Pittenger, C. F. Hockett, and J. J. Danehy, in *Language* **38**. 69–73.

Lenneberg, E. H., 1962b, "Understanding language without ability to speak: a case report," *J.A.S.P.* **65**. 419–25.

Lenneberg, E. H., 1962c, "The relationship of language to the formation of concepts," *Syntheses* **14**. 103–9.

Lenneberg, E. H., 1964, "Language disorders in children," *Harvard Educational Review* **34**. 152–77.

Lenneberg, E. H., forthcoming, *The Biological Foundation of Language*.

Lenneberg, E. H., and J. M. Roberts, 1956, *The Language of Experience* (Indiana University Publications in Anthropology and Linguistics, Mem. 13), Baltimore.

Leopold, W. F., 1939–47, *Speech Development of a Bilingual Child: A Linguist's Record*, 4 vols, Evanston.

Leopold, W. F., 1948, "The study of child language and infant bilingualism," *Word* **4**. 1–17.

Leopold, W. F., 1952, *Bibliography of Child Language*, Evanston.

Leopold, W. F., 1953/54, "Patterning in children's language learning," *Language Learning* **5**. 1–14.

Levin, H., A. L. Baldwin, and M. Gallwey, 1960, "Audience stress, personality, and speech," *J.A.S.P.* **61**. 469–73.

Levin, S. M., 1961, "The effects of awareness on verbal conditioning," *J. Exper. Psych.* **61**. 67–75.

Lévi-Strauss, C., 1954, "L'analyse structurale en linguistique et en anthropologie," *Word* **1**. 33–53.

Lévi-Strauss, C. R. Jakobson, C. F. Voegelin, and T. A. Sebeok, 1950, *Results of the Conference of Anthropologists and Linguists* (Indiana University Publications in Anthropology and Linguistics, Mem. 8), Baltimore.

Levit, M., 1953, "On the psychology and philosophy of concept formation," *Education Theory* **3**. 193–207.

Lévy-Bruhl, L., 1922, *La mentalité primitive*, Paris.

Lewis, N. M., 1951, *Infant Speech: A Study of the Beginnings of Language*, New York.

Liberman, A. M., 1957, "Some results of research on speech perception," *J.A.S.A.* **29**. 117–23.

Liberman, A., K. S. Harris, P. Eimas, L. Lisker, and J. Bastian, 1961, "An effect of learning on speech perception: the discrimation of durations of silence with and without phonemic significance," *Language and Speech* **4**. 175–95.

Licklider, J. C. R., 1952, "On the process of speech perception," *J.A.S.A.* **24**. 590–4.

Livant, W. P., 1963, "Antagonistic functions of verbal pauses and the solution of additions," *Language and Speech* **6**. 1–4.

Lorenz, M., and S. Cobb, 1954, "Language patterns in psychotic and psychoneurotic subjects," *Archives of Neurology and Psychiatry* **72**. 665–73.

Lotz, J., 1949, "The semantic analysis of the nominal bases in Hungarian," *Recherches structurales 1949*, 185–97.

Lotz, J., 1956, "Linguistics: symbols make man," in *Frontiers of Knowledge*, L. White, Jr., ed., New York, 207–31.

Lounsbury, F. G., 1956, "A semantic analysis of the Pawnee kinship usage," *Language* 32. 158–94.

Lounsbury, F. G., 1959, "Language," in *Biennial Review of Anthropology 1959*, B. J. Siegel, ed., Stanford, 185–209.

Lounsbury, F. G., 1962, "Language," in *Biennial Review of Anthropology 1961*, B. J. Siegel, ed., Stanford, 279–322.

Lounsbury, F. G., 1963, "Linguistics and psychology," in *Psychology: A Study of a Science*, S. Koch, ed., New York, Vol. 6, Study 2, 552–82.

Luce, R. D., R. R. Bush, and E. Galanter, eds., 1963, *Handbook of Mathematical Psychology*, 2 vols., New York.

Luria, A. R., 1958, "Brain disorders and language analysis," *Language and Speech* 1. 14–34.

Luria, A. R., 1959a, "The directive function of speech, I: its development in early childhood," *Word* 15. 341–52.

Luria, A. R., 1959b, "The directive function of speech, II: its dissolution in pathological states of the brain," *Word* 15. 453–65.

Luria, A. R., and F. I. Yudovich, 1959, *Speech and the Development of Mental Processes in the Child*, London.

Luria, Z., 1959, "A semantic analysis of a normal and a neurotic therapy group," *J.A.S.P.* 58. 216–20.

Maclay, H., and C. E. Osgood, 1959, "Hesitation phenomena in spontaneous English speech," *Word* 15. 19–44.

Maclay, H., and M. D. Sleator, 1960, "Responses to language: judgments of grammaticalness," *I.J.A.L.* 26. 275–82.

Maclay, H., and E. E. Ware, 1961, "Cross-cultural use of the semantic differential," *Behavioral Science* 6. 185–90.

Mahl, G. F., 1956, "Disturbances and silences in the patient's speech in psychotherapy," *J.A.S.P.* 53. 1–15.

Malécot, A., 1960, "Vowel nasality as a distinctive feature in American English," *Language* 36. 222–29.

Malinowski, B., 1923, "The problem of meaning in primitive languages," in *The Meaning of Meaning*, C. K. Ogden and I. A. Richards, London, 451–510.

Malkiel, Y., 1959, "Distinctive features in lexicography," *Romance Philology* 12. 366–99; 13. 111–55.

Mandelbrot, B., 1954, "Structure formelle des textes et communication," *Word* 10. 1–27.

Mandelbrot, B., 1961, "On the theory of word frequencies and on related markovian models of discourse," *Proceedings of Symposia in Applied Mathematics*, Providence, 12. 190–219.

Marchand, H., 1959, "Phonetic symbolism in English word-formation," *Indogermanische Forschungen* 64. 146–68.

Markel, N. N., and E. P. Hamp, 1960, "Connotative meanings of certain phoneme sequences," *Studies in Linguistics* 15. 47–61.

Marks, L. E., and G. A. Miller, 1964, "The role of semantic and syntactic constraints in the memorization of English sentences," *J.V.L.V.B.* 3. 1–5.

Marler, P., 1959, "Developments in the study of animal communication," in *Darwin's Biological Work: Some Aspects Reconsidered*, P. R. Bell, ed., Cambridge (England), 150–206.

Marler, P., 1961, "The logical analysis of animal communication," *J. Theoretical Biology* 1. 295–317.

Marshall, G. R., and C. N. Cofer, 1963, "Associative indices as measures of word relatedness: a summary and comparison of ten methods," *J.V.L.V.B.* 1. 408–21.

Martinet, A., 1952, "Function, structure, and sound change," *Word* 8. 1–32.

Martinet, A., 1955, *Économie des changements phonétiques*, Berne.

Matarazzo, J. D., G. S. Saslow, and R. G. Matarazzo, 1956, "The interaction chrono-graph as an instrument for objective measurement of the interaction patterns during interviews," *J. Psych.* 41. 347–67.

Matthews, P. H., 1961, "Transformational grammar," *Archivum Linguisticum* 13. 196–209.

McCarthy, D., 1954, "Language development in children," in *Manual of Child Psychology*, L. Carmichael, ed., New York, 492–630.

McGranahan, D. V., 1936, "The psychology of language," *Psych. Bull.* 33. 178–216.

McNeill, D., 1963, "The origin of associations within the same grammatical class," *J.V.L.V.B.* 2. 250–62.

McQuown, N. A., 1957, "Linguistic transcription and specification of psychiatric interview materials," *Psychiatry* 20. 79–86.

Mead, G. H., 1904, "The relation of psychology and philology," *Psych. Bull.* 1. 375–91.

Mehler, J., 1963, "Some effects of grammatical transformations on the recall of English sentences," *J.V.L.V.B.* 2. 346–51.

Menyuk, P., 1963a, "Syntactic structures in the language of children," *Child Development* 34. 407–22.

Menyuk, P., 1963b, "A preliminary evaluation of grammatical capacity in children," *J.V.L.V.B.* 2. 429–39.

Miller, A., 1963, "Verbal satiation and the role of concurrent activity," *J.A.S.P.* 66. 206–11.

Miller, G. A., 1951a, "Speech and language," in *Handbook of Experimental Psychology*, S. S. Stevens, ed., New York, 789–810.

Miller, G. A., 1951b, *Language and Communication*, New York.

Miller, G. A., 1953, "What is information measurement?" *Amer. Psych.* 8. 3–11.

Miller, G. A., 1954, "Psycholinguistics," in *Handbook of Social Psychology*, 2, G. Lindzey, ed., Cambridge, Mass., 693–708.

Miller, G. A., 1956a, "The magical number seven, plus or minus two: some limits on our capacity for processing information," *Psych. Review* 63. 81–97.

Miller, G. A., 1956b, "The perception of speech," in *For Roman Jakobson: Essays on the Occasion of His Sixtieth Birthday*, M. Halle et al, eds., The Hague, 353–59.

Miller, G. A., 1958, "Free recall of redundant strings of letters," *J. Exper. Psych.* 56. 484–91.

Miller, G. A., 1962a, "Some psychological studies of grammar," *Amer. Psych.* 17. 748–62.

Miller, G. A., 1962b, "Decision units in the perception of speech," *I.R.E. Trans. on Info. Theory* 8. 81–83.

Miller, G. A., 1964, "The psycholinguists: on the new scientists of language," *Encounter* 23. 29–37.

Miller, G. A., and N. Chomsky, 1963, "Finitary models of language users," in *Handbook of Mathematical Psychology*, D. R. Luce, R. R. Bush, and E. Galenter, eds., New York, 2. 419–91.

Miller, G. A., E. Galanter, and K. H. Pribram, 1960, *Plans and the Structure of Behavior*, New York.

Miller, G. A., G. A. Heise, and W. Lichten, 1951, "The intelligibility of speech as a function of the context of the test materials," *J. Exper. Psych.* 41. 329–35.

Miller, G. A., and S. Isard, 1963, "Some perceptual consequences of linguistic rules," *J.V.L.V.B.* 2. 217–28.

Miller, G. A., K. E. Ojemann, and D. Slobin, 1962, A psychological method for investigating grammatical transformations, Mimeo, Cambridge, Mass.

Miller, G. A., and P. E. Nicely, 1955, "An analysis of perceptual confusions among some English consonants," *J.A.S.A.* 27. 338–52.

Miller, G. A., and J. A. Selfridge, 1950, "Verbal context and the recall of meaningful material," *Amer. J. Psych.* **63**. 176–85.

Miron, M. S., 1961, "A cross-linguistic investigation of phonetic symbolism," *J.A.S.P.* **62**. 623–30.

Mohrmann, C., A. Sommerfelt, and J. Whatmough, eds., 1961, *Trends in European and American Linguistics 1930–1960*, Utrecht.

Mol, H. 1963, *Fundamentals of Phonetics*, The Hague.

Mol, H., and M. Uhlenback, 1959, "Hearing and the concept of the phoneme," *Lingua* **8**. 161–85.

Morris, C. W., 1939, "Foundations of the theory of signs," in *International Encyclopedia of Unified Science*, O. Neurath, R. Carnap, and C. Morris, eds., Chicago, 1: 1. 77–137.

Morris, C., 1958, "Words without meaning: a review of B. F. Skinner's *Verbal Behavior*," in *Contemporary Psych.* **3**. 212–14.

Moss, C. S., 1960, "Current and projected status of semantic differential research," *Psych. Review* **10**. 47–54.

Mowrer, O. H., 1954, "The psychologist looks at language," *Amer. Psych.* **9**. 660–92.

Mowrer, O. H., 1960, *Learning Theory and the Symbolic Processes*, New York.

Murdock, B. B., Jr., 1963, "An analysis of the recognition process," in *Verbal Behavior and Learning*, Cofer and Musgrave, eds., 10–32.

Mussen, P. H., ed., 1960, *Handbook of Research Methods in Child Development*, New York.

Newman, S. S., 1944, "Cultural and psychological features in English intonation," *Transactions of the N.Y. Academy of Science* **7**. 45–54.

Noble, C. E., 1952, "The role of meaningfulness (m) in serial verbal learning," *J. Exper. Psych.* **43**. 437–46.

O'Connor, J. D., 1957, "Recent work in English phonetics," *Phonetica* **1**. 96–117.

Öhman, S., 1953, "Theories of the 'linguistic field,'" *Word* **9**. 123–34.

Olmsted, D. L., 1950, "Ethnolinguistics so far," *Studies in Linguistics, Occasional Papers, No. 2*, Norman.

Olmsted, D. L., 1955, Review of *Psycholinguistics: a survey of theory and research problems*, C. E. Osgood and T. A. Sebeok, eds., *Language* **31**. 46–59.

Olmsted, D. L., and O. K. Moore, 1952, "Language, psychology and linguistics," *Psych. Review* **59**. 414–20.

O'Neill, J. J., 1954, "Contributions of the visual components of oral symbols to speech comprehension," *J. Speech and Hearing Disorders* **19**. 429–39.

O'Neill, J. J., 1957, "Recognition of the intelligibility of test materials in context and isolation," *J. Speech and Hearing Disorders* **22**. 87–90.

Osgood, C. E., 1958, "A question of sufficiency: a review of B. F. Skinner's *Verbal Behavior*," in *Contemporary Psych.* **3**. 209–12.

Osgood, C. E., 1959, "Semantic space revisited," *Word* **15**. 192–201.

Osgood, C. E., 1960, "The cross-cultural generality of visual-verbal synesthetic tendencies," *Behavioral Science* **5**. 146–69.

Osgood, C. E., 1963a, "Psycholinguistics," *Psychology: a study of a science*, S. Koch, ed., New York, Vol. 6, Study 2. 244–316.

Osgood, C. E., 1963b, "Language universals and psycholinguistics," in *Universals of Language*, J. H. Greenberg, ed., Cambridge, Mass., 236–54.

Osgood, C. E., 1963c, "On understanding and creating sentences," *Amer. Psych.* **18**. 735–51.

Osgood, C. E., and Z. Luria, 1954, "A blind analysis of a case of multiple personality using the semantic differential," *J.A.S.P.* **49**. 579–91.

Osgood, C. E., and T. A. Sebeok, eds., 1954, *Psycholinguistics: A Survey of Theory and Research Problems* (Indiana University Publications in Anthropology and Linguistics, Mem. 10), Baltimore.

Osgood, C. E., G. Suci, and P. Tannenbaum, 1957, *The Measurement of Meaning*, Urbana, Ill.

Paul, H., 1960, *Prinzipien der Sprachgeschichte* (Reprinted), Tübingen.

Peal, E., and W. E. Lambert, 1962, *The Relation of Bilingualism to Intelligence* (Psychological Monographs: General and Applied, 76, no. 546).

Penfield, W., and L. Roberts, 1959, *Speech and Brain Mechanisms*, Princeton.

Peterson, G. E., and H. L. Barney, 1962, "Control methods used in a study of the vowels," *J.A.S.A.* 24. 175–84.

Piaget, J., 1955, *The Language and Thought of the Child*, New York.

Piaget, J., 1962, "Comments on Vygotsky's critical remarks concerning *The Language and Thought of the Child*, and *Judgment and Reasoning in the Child*," issued as a separate appendix to Vygotsky, *Thought and Language*, 1962.

Pike, K. L., 1952, "Operational phonemics in reference to linguistic relativity," *J.A.S.A.* 24. 618–25.

Pike, K. L., 1959, "Language as particle, wave and field," *The Texas Quarterly* 2:2. 37–54.

Pittenger, R. E., C. F. Hockett, ahd J. J. Danehy, 1960, *The First Five Minutes: A Sample of Microscopic Interview Analysis*, Ithaca, N.Y.

Pittenger, R. E., and H. L. Smith, Jr., 1957, "A basis for some contributions of linguistics to psychiatry," *Psychiatry* 20. 61–78.

Plath, W., 1961, "Mathematical linguistics," in *Trends in European and American Linguistics 1930–1960*, C. Mohrmann, A. Sommerfelt, and J. Whatmough, eds., Utrecht, 21–57.

Pollack, I., and J. M. Pickett, 1964, "Intelligibility of excerpts from fluent speech: auditory vs. structural context," *J.V.L.V.B.* 3. 79–84.

Pool, I., ed., 1959, *Trends in Content Analysis*, Urbana, Ill.

Postal, P. M., 1964a, "Underlying and superficial linguistic structure," *Harvard Educational Review* 34. 246–66.

Postal, P. M., 1964b, *Constituent Structure: A Study of Contemporary Models of Syntactic Structure* (Indiana University Research Center in Anthropology, Folklore, and Linguistics, Pub. 30), Bloomington.

Postman, L., 1962, "The effects of language habits on the acquisition and retention of verbal associations," *J. Exper. Psych.* 64. 7–19.

Pronko, N. H., 1946, "Language and psycholinguistics," *Psych. Bull.* 43. 189–239.

Prothro, E. T., and J. D. Keehn, 1957, "Stereotypes and semantic space," *J. Social Psychology* 45. 197–209.

Putnam, H., 1961, "Some issues in the theory of grammar," *Proceedings of Symposia in Applied Mathematics*, Providence, 12. 25–42.

Quine, W. V., 1953, *From a Logical Point of View*, Cambridge.

Recherches Structurales 1949, 1949, (Travaux du Cercle Linguistique de Copenhague, Vol. 5), Copenhagen.

Reece, M. M., and R. N. Whitman, 1962, "Expressive movements, warmth, and verbal reinforcement," *J.A.S.P.* 64. 234–36.

Riess, B. F., 1946, "Genetic changes in semantic conditioning," *J. Exper. Psych.* 36. 143–52.

Rosenberg, S., J. Spradlin, and M. Sanford, 1961, "Interaction among retarded children as a function of their relative language skills," *J.A.S.P.* 63. 402–10.

Rowley, V., and E. D. Keller, 1962, "Changes in children's verbal behavior as a function of social approval and manifest anxiety," *J.A.S.P.* 65. 53–57.

Rubenstein, H., and M. Aborn, 1960, "Psycholinguistics," *Annual Review of Psychology* 11. 291–322.

Rubenstein, H., and I. Pollack, 1963, "Word predictability and intelligibility," *J.V.L.V.B.* 2. 147–58.

Russell, W. R., 1961, *Traumatic Aphasia*, London.

Salzinger, K., 1959, "Experimental manipulation of verbal behavior," *J. Gen. Psych.* **61**. 65–94.

Sandler, J., 1962, "The effect of negative verbal cues on verbal behavior," *J.A.S.P.* **64**. 312–16.

Sanford, F. H., 1942a, "Speech and personality," *Psych. Bull.* **39**. 811–45.

Sanford, F. H., 1942b, "Speech and personality: a comparative case study," *Character and Personality* **10**. 169–98.

Sapir, E., 1921, *Language*, New York.

Sapir, E., 1927, "Speech as a personality trait," *Amer. J. Sociology* **32**. 892–905.

Sapir, E., 1929, "The status of linguistics as a science," *Language* **5**. 207–14.

Sapir, E., 1933, "La réalité psychologique des phonèmes," *J. de psychologie normale et pathologique* **30**. 247–65, now available in D. G. Mandelbaum, ed., *The Selected Writings of Edward Sapir*, 1949, as "The psychological reality of phonemes," Berkeley and Los Angeles, 46–60.

Saporta, S., ed., 1961, *Psycholinguistics: A Book of Readings*, New York.

Sarason, I. G., 1957, "Effect of anxiety and two kinds of motivating instructions on verbal learning," *J.A.S.P.* **54**. 166–71.

Schatz, C. D., 1954, "The role of context in the perception of stops," *Language* **30**. 47–56.

Schuell, H., and J. J. Jenkins, 1959, "The nature of language deficit in aphasia," *Psych. Review* **66**. 45–67.

Sebeok, T. A., 1962, "Coding in the evolution of signalling behavior," *Behavioral Science* **7**. 430–42.

Sebeok, T. A., 1963, Review of M. Lindauer's *Communication among Social Bees*, W. N. Kellogg's *Porpoises and Sonar*, and J. C. Lilly's *Man and Dolphin*, in *Language* **39**. 448–66.

Sebeok, T. A., A. S. Hayes, and M. C. Bateson, 1964, *Approaches to Semiotics*, The Hague.

Shannon, C. E., and W. Weaver, 1949, *The Mathematical Theory of Communication*, Urbana.

Sharp, H. C., 1958, "Effects of contextual constraint upon recall of verbal passages," *Amer. J. Psych.* **21**. 568–72.

Shetter, W. Z., 1962, Review of *Sprache, Schlüssel zur Welt*. H. Gipper, ed., in *Language* **38**. 318–24.

Skinner, B. F., 1957, *Verbal Behavior*, New York.

Spielberger, C. D., 1962, "The role of awareness in verbal conditioning," *J. Personality* **30**. 73–101.

Spielberger, C. D., and S. M. Levin, 1962, "What is learned in verbal conditioning?" *J.V.L.V.B.* **1**. 125–32.

Spiker, C. C., 1956, "Experiments with children on the hypothesis of acquired distinctiveness and equivalence of cues," *Child Development* **27**. 253–63.

Spradlin, J. E., and S. Rosenberg, 1964, "Complexity of adult verbal behavior in a dyadic situation with retarded children," *J.A.S.P.* **68**. 694–98.

Staats, A. W., 1961, "Verbal habit-families, concepts, and the operant conditioning of word classes," *Psych. Review*. **68**. 190–204.

Starkweather, J. A., 1956a, "The communication-value of content-free speech," *Amer. J. Psych.* **69**. 121–23.

Starkweather, J. A., 1956b, "Content-free speech as a source of information about the speaker," *J.A.S.P.* **52**. 394–402.

Starkweather, J. A., 1964, "Variations in vocal behavior," in *Disorders in Communication*, D. M. Rioch, ed., Baltimore.

Stern, T., 1957, "Drum and whistle 'languages': an analysis of speech surrogates," *Amer. Anthro.* **59**. 487–506.

Stevens, S. S., ed., 1951, *Handbook of Experimental Psychology*, New York.

Stockwell, R. P., J. D. Bowen, and I. Silva-Fuenzalida, 1956, "Spanish juncture and intonation," *Language* 32. 641–65.

Sturtevant, W. C., 1963, Studies in ethnoscience, Mimeo, Washington, D.C.

Suci, G. J., 1960, "A comparison of semantic structures in American Southwest culture groups," *J.A.S.P.* 61. 25–30.

Sumby, W. H., and I. Pollack, 1954, "Visual contribution to speech intelligibility," *J.A.S.A.* 26. 212–15.

Tanaka, Y., T. Oyama, and C. E. Osgood, 1963, "A cross-cultural and cross-concept study of the generality of semantic spaces," *J.V.L.V.B.* 2. 392–405.

Taylor, I. K., 1963, "Phonetic symbolism reexamined," *Psych. Bull.* 60. 200–9.

Taylor, J. A., 1958, "The effects of anxiety level and psychological stress on verbal learning," *J.A.S.P.* 57. 55–60.

Taylor, M. L., 1964, "Linguistic considerations of the verbal behavior of the brain damaged adult," *The Linguistic Reporter* 6: 3. 1,2.

Tesnière, L., 1939, "Phonologie et mélange de langues," *Travaux du Cercle Linguistique de Prague* 8. 83–93.

Thorndike, E. L., and I. Lorge, 1927, *The Teacher's Word Book of 30,000 Words*, New York.

Thorson, A. M., 1925, "The relation of tongue movements to internal speech," *J. Exper. Psych.* 8. 1–32.

Thumb, A., and K. Marb, 1901, *Experimentelle Untersuchungen über die psychologischen Grundlagen der sprachlichen Analogiebildung*, Leipzig.

Tikhomirov, O. K., 1959, Review of *Verbal Behavior* by B. F. Skinner, in *Word* 15. 363–67.

Trager, E. C., 1961, "The field of neurolinguistics," *Studies in Linguistics* 15. 70, 71.

Trager, G. L., 1949, "The field of linguistics," *Studies in Linguistics, Occasional Papers, No. 1*, Norman.

Trager, G. L., 1958, "Paralanguage: a first approximation," *Studies in Linguistics* 13. 1–12.

Trager, G. L., 1959, "The systematization of the Whorf hypothesis," *Anthropological Linguistics* 1:1. 31–6.

Trager, G. L., 1960, "Taos III: paralanguage," *Anthropological Linguistics* 2:2. 24–30.

Trager, G. L., 1961, "The typology of paralanguage," *Anthropological Linguistics* 3:1. 17–21.

Travis, L. E., ed., 1957, *Handbook of Speech Pathology*, New York.

Triandis, H. C., and C. E. Osgood, 1958, "A comparative factorial analysis of semantic structures in monolingual Greek and American college students," *J.A.S.P.* 57. 187–96.

Ullmann, L. P., L. Krasner, and B. J. Collins, 1961, "Modification of behavior through verbal conditioning: effects in group therapy," *J.A.S.P.* 62. 128–32.

Vildomec, V., 1963, *Multilingualism*, Leyden.

Vinacke, E., 1951, "The investigation of concept formation," *Psych. Bull.* 48. 1–31.

Vinacke, E., 1954, "Concept formation in children of school ages," *Education* 74. 527–34.

Voegelin, C. F., and Z. S. Harris, 1947, "The scope of linguistics," *Amer. Anthro.* 49. 588–600.

Vygotsky, L. S., 1939, "Thought and Speech," *Psychiatry* 2. 29–54.

Vygotsky, L. S., 1962 (1934), *Thought and Language*, Translated by E. Hanfmann and G. Vakar; Introduction by J. S. Bruner, Cambridge and New York.

Wallace, A. F. C., 1962, "Culture and cognition," *Science* 135. 351–57.

Wallace, A. F. C., and J. Atkins, 1960, "The meaning of kinship terms," *Amer. Anthro.* 62. 58–80.

Waterhouse, V., 1961, "The psychological reality of linguistic structure," in *A William Cameron Townsend*, M. Gamio and R. Noriega, eds., Mexico, D.F., 687–92.

Waterman, J. T., 1957, "Benjamin Lee Whorf and linguistic field theory," *Southwestern J. Anthropology* **13.** 201–11.

Watson, J. B., 1920, "Is thinking merely the action of language mechanisms?" *British J. Psychology* **11.** 87–104.

Weinreich, U., 1954, *Languages in Contact* (Publications of the Linguistic Circle of New York, No. 1), New York.

Weinreich, U., 1958a, "Travels through semantic space," *Word* **14.** 346–66.

Weinreich, U., 1958b, "Research frontiers in bilingualism studies," *Proceedings of the Eighth International Congress of Linguists*, Oslo, 786–97.

Weinreich, U., 1963, "On the semantic structure of language," in *Universals of Language*, J. H. Greenberg, ed., Cambridge, Mass., 114–71.

Wells, R., 1951, Review of *Recherches Structurales 1949*, in *Language* **27.** 554–70.

Wells, R., 1954, "Meaning and use," *Word* **10.** 235–50.

Wells, R., 1957, "A mathematical approach to meaning," *Cahiers Ferdinand de Saussure* **15.** 117–36.

Wells, R., 1958, "Is a structural treatment of meaning possible?" *Proceedings of the Eighth International Congress of Linguists*, Oslo, 654–66.

Wells, R., and J. Keyser, 1961, *The Common Feature Method*, New Haven.

Werner, H., and E. Kaplan, 1950, *Monographs on Social Research on Child Development* **15: 1.**

White, L. A., 1949, "The symbol: the origin and basis of human behavior," in *The Science of Culture: A Study of Man and Civilization*, New York.

Whitney, W. D., 1881, "On mixture in language," *Transactions of the American Philological Association* **12.** 1–26.

Whorf, B. L., 1940, "Science and linguistics," *The Technology Review* **42.** 229–31; 247,8.

Whorf, B. L., 1949, *Four Articles on Metalinguistics*, Washington, D.C.

Wonderly, W. L., 1952, "Semantic components in Kechua person morphemes," *Language* **28.** 366–76.

Yngve, V. H., 1960, *A model and a hypothesis for language structure* (MIT Research Laboratory of Electronics, Technical Report 369), Cambridge, Mass.

Yngve, V. H., 1961, "The depth hypothesis," *Proceedings on Symposia in Applied Mathematics*, Providence, **12.** 130–38.

Yngve, V. H., 1962, "Computer programs for translation," *Scientific American* **206.** 6.68-76.

Zipf, G. K., 1932, *Selected Studies of the Principle of Relative Frequency in Language*, Cambridge, Mass.

Zipf, G. K., 1949, *Human Behavior and the Principle of Least Effort*, Cambridge, Mass.

Appendix

THE PSYCHOLINGUISTS
On the New Scientists of Language
by GEORGE A. MILLER

Psychologists have long recognised that human minds feed on linguistic symbols. Linguists have always admitted that some kind of psycho-social motor must move the machinery of grammar and lexicon. Sooner or later they were certain to examine their intersection self-consciously. Perhaps it was also inevitable that the result would be called "psycholinguistics."

In fact, although the enterprise itself has slowly been gathering strength at least since the invention of the telephone, the name, in its unhyphenated form, is only about ten years old. Few seem pleased with the term, but the field has grown so rapidly and stirred so much interest in recent years that some way of referring to it is urgently needed. *Psycholinguistics* is as descriptive a term as any, and shorter than most.

Among psychologists it was principally the behaviourists who wished to take a closer look at language. Behaviourists generally try to replace anything subjective by its most tangible, physical manifestation, so they have had a long tradition of confusing thought with speech—or with "verbal behaviour," as many prefer to call it. Among linguists it was principally those with an anthropological sideline who were most willing to collaborate, perhaps because as anthropologists they were sensitive to all those social and psychological processes that support our linguistic practices. By working together they managed to call attention to an important field of scientific research and to integrate it, or at least to acquaint its various parts with one another, under this new rubric.[1]

Interest in psycholinguistics, however, is not confined to psychologists and linguists. Many people have been stirred by splendid visions of its practical possibilities. One thinks of medical applications to the diagnosis and treatment of a heterogeneous variety of language disorders ranging from simple stammering to the overwhelming complexities of aphasia.[2] One thinks too of pedagogical applications, of potential improvements in our methods for teaching reading and writing, or for teaching second languages. If psycholinguistic principles were made sufficiently explicit, they could be imparted to those technological miracles of the twentieth century, the computing machines, which would bring into view a whole spectrum of cybernetic possibilities.[3] We could exploit our electrical channels for voice communications more efficiently. We might improve and automate our dictionaries, using them for mechanical translation from one language to another. Perhaps computers could print what we say, or even say what we print, thus making speech visible for the deaf and printing audible for the blind. We might, in short, learn to adapt computers to

Reprinted with permission from *Encounter*, Vol. 23 (1964), No. 1, pp. 29–37.

dozens of our human purposes if only they could interpret our languages. Little wonder that assorted physicians, educators, philosophers, logicians, and engineers have been intrigued by this new adventure.

Of course, the realisation of practical benefits must await the success of the scientific effort; there is some danger that enthusiasm may colour our estimate of what can be accomplished. Not a few sceptics remain unconvinced; some can even be found who argue that success is impossible in principle. "Science," they say, "can go only so far. . . ."

The integration of psycholinguistic studies has occurred so recently that there is still some confusion concerning its scope and purpose; efforts to clarify it necessarily have something of the character of personal opinion.[4] In my own version, the central task of this new science is to describe the psychological processes that go on when people use sentences. The real crux of the psycholinguistic problem does not appear until one tries to deal with sentences, for only then does the importance of productivity become completely obvious. It is true that productivity can also appear with individual words, but there it is not overwhelming. With sentences, productivity is literally unlimited.

Before considering this somewhat technical problem, however, it might be well to illustrate the variety of processes that psycholinguists hope to explain. This can best be done if we ask what a listener can do about a spoken utterance, and consider his alternatives in order from the superficial to the inscrutable.

The simplest thing one can do in the presence of a spoken utterance is to listen. Even if the language is incomprehensible, one can still *hear* an utterance as an auditory stimulus and respond to it in terms of some discriminative set: how loud, how fast, how long, from which direction, etc.

Given that an utterance is heard, the next level involves *matching* it as a phonemic pattern in terms of phonological skills acquired as a user of the language. The ability to match an input can be tested in psychological experiments by asking listeners to echo what they hear; a wide variety of experimental situations—experiments on the perception of speech and on the note memorisation of verbal materials—can be summarised as tests of a person's ability to repeat the speech he hears under various conditions of audibility or delay.

If a listener can hear and match an utterance, the next question to ask is whether he will *accept* it as a sentence in terms of his knowledge of grammar. At this level we encounter processes difficult to study experimentally, and one is forced to rely most heavily on linguistic analyses of the structure of sentences. Some experiments are possible, however, for we can measure how much a listener's ability to accept the utterance as a sentence facilitates his ability to hear and match it; grammatical sentences are much easier to hear, utter or remember than are ungrammatical strings of words, and even nonsense (*pirot, karol, elat,* etc.) is easier to deal with if it looks grammatical (*pirots karolise elatically*, etc.).[5] Needless to say, the grammatical knowledge we wish to study does not concern those explicit rules drilled into us by teachers of traditional grammar, but rather the implicit generative knowledge that we all must acquire in order to use a language appropriately.

Beyond grammatical acceptance comes semantic interpretation: we can ask how listeners *interpret* an utterance as meaningful in terms of their semantic system. Interpretation is not merely a matter of assigning meanings to individual words; we must also consider how these component meanings combine in grammatical sentences. Compare the sentences: *Healthy young babies sleep soundly* and *Colourless green ideas sleep furiously*. Although they are syntactically similar, the second is far harder to perceive and remember correctly—because it cannot be interpreted by the usual semantic rules for combining the senses of adjacent English words.[6] The interpretation of each word is affected by the company it keeps; a central problem is to systematise the interactions of words and phrases with their linguistic contexts. The lexicographer makes his major contribution at this point, but psychological studies of our ability to paraphrase an utterance also have their place.

At the next level it seems essential to make some distinction between interpreting an utterance and understanding it, for understanding frequently goes well beyond the linguistic context provided by the utterance itself. A husband greeted at the door by "I bought some electric light bulbs to-day" must do more than interpret its literal reference; he must understand that he should go to the kitchen and replace that burned-out lamp. Such contextual information lies well outside any grammar or lexicon. The listener can *understand* the function of an utterance in terms of contextual knowledge of the most diverse sort.

Finally, at a level now almost invisible through the clouds, a listener may *believe* that an utterance is valid in terms of its relevance to his own conduct. The child who says "I saw five lions in the garden" may be heard, matched, accepted, interpreted, and understood, but in few parts of the world will he be believed.

The boundaries between successive levels are not sharp and distinct. One shades off gradually into the next. Still the hierarchy is real enough and important to keep in mind. Simpler types of psycholinguistic processes can be studied rather intensively; already we know much about hearing and matching. Accepting and interpreting are just now coming into scientific focus. Understanding is still over the horizon, and pragmatic questions involving belief systems are presently so vague as to be hardly worth asking. But the whole range of processes must be included in any adequate definition of psycholinguistics.

I phrased the description of these various psycholinguistic processes in terms of a listener; the question inevitably arises as to whether a different hierarchy is required to describe the speaker. One problem a psycholinguist faces is to decide whether speaking and listening are two separate abilities, co-ordinate but distinct, or whether they are merely different manifestations of a single linguistic faculty.

The mouth and ear are different organs; at the simplest levels we must distinguish hearing and matching from vocalising and speaking. At more complex levels it is less easy to decide whether the two abilities are distinct. At some point they must converge, if only to explain why it is so difficult to speak and listen simultaneously. The question is where.

It is easy to demonstrate how important to a speaker is the sound of his own voice. If his speech is delayed a fifth of a second, amplified, and fed back into his own ears, the voice-ear asynchrony can be devastating to the motor skills of articulate speech. It is more difficult, however, to demonstrate that the same linguistic competence required for speaking is also involved in processing the speech of others.

Recently Morris Halle and Kenneth Stevens of the Massachusetts Institute of Technology revived a suggestion made by Wilhelm von Humboldt over a century ago.[7] Suppose we accept the notion that a listener recognises what he hears by comparing it with some internal representation. To the extent that a match can be obtained, the input is accepted and interpreted. One trouble with this hypothesis, however, is that a listener must be ready to recognise any one of an enormous number of different sentences. It is inconceivable that a separate internal representation for each of them could be stored in his memory in advance. Halle and Stevens suggest that these internal representations must be generated as they are needed by following the same generative rules that are normally used in producing speech. In this way the rules of the language are incorporated into the theory only once, in a generative form; they need not be learned once by the ear and again by the tongue. This is a theory of a language-user, not of a speaker or a listener alone.

The listener begins with a guess about the input. On that basis he generates an internal matching signal. The first attempt will probably be in error; if so, the mismatch is reported and used as a basis for a next guess, which should be closer. This cycle repeats (unconsciously, almost certainly) until a satisfactory (not necessarily a correct) match is obtained, at which point the next segment of speech is scanned and matched, etc. The output is not a transformed version of the input; it is the programme that was followed to generate the matching representation.

The perceptual categories available to such a system are defined by the generative rules at its disposal. It is also reasonably obvious that its efficiency is critically dependent on the quality of the initial guess. If this guess is close, an iterative process can converge rapidly; if not, the listener will be unable to keep pace with the rapid flow of conversational speech.

A listener's first guess probably derives in part from syntactic markers in the form of intonation, inflection, suffixes, etc., and in part from his general knowledge of the semantic and situational context. Syntactic cues indicate how the input is to be grouped and which words function together; semantic and contextual contributions are more difficult to characterise, but must somehow enable him to limit the range of possible words that he can expect to hear.

How he is able to do this is an utter mystery, but the fact that he can do it is easily demonstrated.

The English psychologist David Bruce recorded a set of ordinary sentences and played them in the presence of noise so intense that the voice was just audible, but not intelligible.[8] He told his listeners that these were sentences on some general topic—sports, say—and asked them to repeat what they heard. He then told them they would hear more sentences on a different topic, which they were also to repeat. This was done several times. Each time the listeners repeated sentences appropriate to the topic announced in advance. When at the end of the experiment Bruce told them they had heard the same recording every time—all he had changed was the topic they were given—most listeners were unable to believe it.

With an advance hypothesis about what the message will be we can tune our perceptual system to favour certain interpretations and reject others. This fact is not proof of a generative process in speech perception, but it does emhasise the important role of context. For most theories of speech perception the facilitation provided by context is merely a fortunate though rather complicated fact. For a generative theory it is essential.

Note that generative theories do not assume that a listener must be able to articulate the sounds he recognises, but merely that he be able to generate some internal representation to match the input. In this respect a generative theory differs from a motor theory (such as that of Sir Richard Paget) which assumes that we can identify only those utterances we are capable of producing ourselves. There is some rather compelling evidence against a motor theory. The American psychologist Eric Lenneberg has described the case of an eight-year-old boy with congenital anarthria; despite his complete inability to speak, the boy acquired an excellent ability to understand language.[9] Moreover, it is a common observation that utterances can be understood by young children before they are able to produce them. A motor theory of speech-perception draws too close a parallel between our two capacities as users of language. Even so, the two are more closely integrated than most people realise.

I have already offered the opinion that productivity sets the central problem for the psycholinguist and have even referred to it indirectly by arguing that we can produce too many different sentences to store them all in memory. The issue can be postponed no longer.

To make the problem plain, consider an example on the level of individual words. For several days I carried in my pocket a small white card on which was typed UNDERSTANDER. On suitable occasions I would hand it to someone. "How do you pronounce this?" I asked.

He pronounced it.

"Is it an English word?"

He hesitated. "I haven't seen it used very much. I'm not sure."

"Do you know what it means?"

"I suppose it means "one who understands.' "

I thanked him and changed the subject.

Of course, understander *is* an English word, but to find it you must look in a large dictionary where you will probably read that it is "now rare." Rare enough, I think, for none of my respondents to have seen it before. Nevertheless, they all answered in the same way. Nobody seemed surprised. Nobody wondered how he could understand and pronounce a word without knowing whether it was a word. Everybody put the main stress on the third syllable and constructed a meaning from the verb "to understand" and the agentive suffix "*er*." Familiar morphological rules of English were applied as a matter of course, even though the combination was completely novel.

Probably no one but a psycholinguist captured by the ingenuous behaviouristic theory that words are vocal responses conditioned to occur in the presence of appropriate stimuli would find anything exceptional in this. Since none of my friends had seen the word before, and so could not have been "conditioned" to give the responses they did, how would this theory account for their "verbal behaviour"? Advocates of a conditioning theory of meaning—and there are several distinguished scientists among them—would probably explain linguistic productivity in terms of "conditioned generalisations."[10] They could argue that my respondents had been conditioned to the word understand and to the suffix—*er*; responses to their union could conceivably be counted as instances of stimulus generalisation. In this way, novel responses could occur without special training.

Although a surprising amount of psychological ingenuity has been invested in this kind of argument, it is difficult to estimate its value. No one has carried the theory through for all the related combinations that must be explained simultaneously. One can speculate, however, that there would have to be many different kinds of generalisation, each with a carefully defined range of applicability. For example, it would be necessary to explain why "understander" is acceptable, whereas "erunderstand" is not. Worked out in detail, such a theory would become a sort of Pavlovian paraphrase of a linguistic description. Of course, if one believes there is some essential difference between behaviour governed by conditioned habits and behaviour governed by rules, the paraphrase could never be more than a vast intellectual pun.

Original combinations of elements are the life blood of language. It is our ability to produce and comprehend such novelties that makes language so ubiquitously useful. As psychologists have become more seriously interested in the cognitive processes that language entails, they have been forced to recognise that the fundamental puzzle is not our ability to associate vocal noises with perceptual objects, but rather our combinatorial productivity—our ability to understand an unlimited diversity of utterances never heard before and to produce an equal variety of utterances similarly intelligible to other members of our speech community. Faced with this problem, concepts borrowed from conditioning theory seem not so much invalid as totally inadequate.

Some idea of the relative magnitudes of what we might call the productive as opposed to the reproductive components of any psycholinguistic theory is provided by statistical studies of language. A few numbers can reinforce the point. If you interrupt a speaker at some randomly chosen instant, there will be, on the average, about ten words that form grammatical and meaningful continuations. Often only one word is admissible and sometimes there are thousands, but on the average it works out to about ten. (If you think this estimate too low, I will not object; larger estimates strengthen the argument.) A simple English sentence can easily run to a length of twenty words, so elementary arithmetic tells us that there must be at least 10^{20} such sentences that a person who knows English must know how to deal with. Compare this productive potential with the 10^4 or 10^5 individual words we know—the reproductive component of our theory—and the discrepancy is dramatically illustrated. Putting it differently, it would take 100,000,000,000 centuries (one thousand times the estimated age of the earth) to utter all the admissible twenty-word sentences of English. Thus, the probability that you might have heard any particular twenty-word sentence before is negligible. Unless it is a cliché, every sentence must come to you as a novel combination of morphemes. Yet you can interpret it at once if you know the English language.

With these facts in mind it is impossible to argue that we learn to understand sentences from teachers who have pronounced each one and explained what it meant. What we have learned are not particular strings of words, but *rules* for generating admissible strings of words.

Consider what it means to follow a rule; this consideration shifts the discussion of psycholinguistics into very difficult territory. The nature of rules has been a central concern of modern philosophy and perhaps no analysis has been more influential than Ludwig Wittgenstein's. Wittgenstein remarked that the most characteristic thing we can say about "rule-governed behaviour" is that the person who knows the rules knows whether he is proceeding correctly or incorrectly. Although he may not be able to formulate the rules explicitly, he knows what it is to make a mistake. If this remark is accepted, we must ask ourselves whether an animal that has been conditioned is privy to any such knowledge about the correctness of what he is doing. Perhaps such a degree of insight could be achieved by the great apes, but surely not by all the various species that can acquire conditioned reflexes. On this basis alone it would seem necessary to preserve a distinction between conditioning and learning rules.

As psychologists have learned to appreciate the complexities of language, the prospect of reducing it to the laws of behaviour so carefully studied in lower animals has grown increasingly remote. We have been forced more and more into a position that non-psychologists probably take for granted, namely, that language is rule-governed behaviour characterised by enormous flexibility and freedom of choice.

Obvious as this conclusion may seem, it has important implications for any scientific theory of language. If rules involve the concepts of right and wrong, they introduce a normative aspect that has always been avoided in the natural sciences. One hears repeatedly that the scientist's ability to suppress normative judgments about his subject-matter enables him to see the world objectively, as it really is. To admit that language follows rules seems to put it outside the range of phenomena accessible to scientific investigation.

At this point a psycholinguist who wishes to preserve his standing as a natural scientist faces an old but always difficult decision. Should he withdraw and leave the study of language to others? Or should he give up all pretence of being a "natural scientist," searching for causal explanations, and embrace a more phenomenological approach? Or should he push blindly ahead with his empirical methods, hoping to find a causal basis for normative practices, but running the risk that all his efforts will be wasted because rule-governed behaviour in principle lies beyond the scope of natural science?

To withdraw means to abandon hope of understanding scientifically all those human mental processes that involve language in any important degree. To persevere means to face the enormously difficult, if not actually impossible task of finding a place for normative rules in a descriptive science.

Difficult, yes. Still one wonders whether these alternatives are really as mutually exclusive as they seem.

The first thing we notice when we survey the languages of the world is how few we can understand and how diverse they all seem. Not until one looks for some time does an even more significant observation emerge concerning the pervasive similarities in the midst of all this diversity.

Every human group that anthropologists have studied have spoken a language. The language always has a lexicon and a grammar. The lexicon is not a haphazard collection of vocalisations, but is highly organised; it always has pronouns, means for dealing with time, space, and number, words to represent true and false, the basic concepts necessary for propositional logic. The grammar has distinguishable levels of structure, some phonological, some syntactic. The phonology always contains both vowels and consonants, and the phonemes can always be described in terms of distinctive features drawn from a limited set of possibilities. The syntax always specifies rules for grouping elements sequentially into phrases and sentences, rules governing normal intonation, rules for transforming some types of sentences into other types.

The nature and importance of these common properties, called "linguistic universals," are only beginning to emerge as our knowledge of the world's languages grows more systematic.[11] These universals appear even in languages that developed with a minimum of interaction. One is forced to assume, therefore, either that (a) no other kind of linguistic practices are conceivable, or that (b) something in the biological makeup of human beings favours languages having these similarities. Only a moment's reflection is needed to reject (a). When one considers the variety of artificial languages developed in mathematics, in the communication sciences, in the use of computers, in symbolic logic, and elsewhere, it soon becomes apparent that the universal features of natural languages are not the only ones possible. Natural languages are, in fact, rather special and often seem unnecessarily complicated.

A popular belief regards human language as a more or less free creation of the human intellect, as if its elements were chosen arbitrarily and could be combined into meaningful utterances by any rules that strike our collective fancy. The assumption is implicit, for example, in Wittgenstein's well-known conception of "the language game." This metaphor, which casts valuable light on many aspects of language, can, if followed blindly, lead one to think that all linguistic rules are just as arbitrary as, say, the rules of chess or football. As Lenneberg has pointed out, however, it makes a great deal of sense to inquire into the biological basis for language, but very little to ask about the biological foundations of card games.[12]

Man is the only animal to have a combinatorially productive language. In the jargon of biology, language is "a species-specific form of behaviour." Other animals have signalling systems of various kinds and for various purposes—but only man has evolved this particular and highly improbable form of communication. Those who think of language as a free and spontaneous intellectual invention are also likely to believe that any animal with a brain sufficiently large to support a high level of intelligence can acquire a language. This assumption is demonstrably false. The human brain is not just an ape brain enlarged; its extra size is less important than its different structure. Moreover, Lenneberg has pointed out that nanocephalic dwarfs, with brains half the normal size but grown on the human blueprint, can use language reasonably well, and even mongoloids, not intelligent enough to perform the simplest functions for themselves, can acquire the rudiments.[13] Talking and understanding language do not depend on being intelligent or having a large brain. They depend on "being human."

Serious attempts have been made to teach animals to speak. If words were conditioned responses, animals as intelligent as chimpanzees or porpoises should be able to learn them. These attempts have uniformly failed in the past and, if the argument here is correct, they will always fail in the future—for just the same reason that attempts to teach fish to walk or dogs to fly would fail. Such efforts misconstrue the basis for our linguistic competence: they fly in the face of biological facts.[14]

Human language must be such that a child can acquire it. He acquires it, moreover, from parents who have no idea how to explain it to him. No careful schedule of rewards for correct or punishments for incorrect utterances is necessary. It is sufficient that the child be allowed to grow up naturally in an environment where language is used.

The child's achievement seems all the more remarkable when we recall the speed with which he accomplishes it and the limitations of his intelligence in other respects. It is difficult to avoid an impression that infants are little machines specially designed by nature to perform this particular learning task.

I believe this analogy with machines is worth pursuing. If we could imagine what a language-learning automaton would have to do, it would dramatise—and perhaps even clarify—what a child can do. The linguist and logician Noam Chomsky has argued that the description of such an automation would comprise our hypothesis about the child's innate ability to learn languages or (to borrow a term from Ferdinand de Saussure) his innate *faculté de language*.[15]

Consider what information a language-learning automaton would be given to work with. Inputs to the machine would include a finite set of sentences, a finite set of non-sentences accompanied by some signal that they were incorrect, some way to indicate that one item is a repetition or elaboration or transformation of another, and some access to a universe of perceptual objects and events associated with the sentences. Inside the machine there would be a computer so programmed as to extract from these inputs the nature of the language, *i.e.*, the particular syntactic rules by which sentences are generated, and the rules that associate with each syntactic structure a particular phonetic representation and semantic interpretation. The important question, of course, is what programme of instructions would have to be given to the computer.

We could instruct the computer to discover any imaginable set of rules that might, in some formal sense of the term, constitute a grammar. This approach—the natural one if we believe that human languages can be infinitely diverse and various—is doomed from the start. The computer would have to evaluate an infinitude of possible grammars; with only a finite corpus of evidence it would be impossible, even if sufficient time were available for computation, to arrive at any unique solution.

A language-earning automaton could not possibly discover a suitable grammar unless some strong *a priori* assumptions were built into it from the start. These assumptions would limit the alternatives that the automaton considered—limit them presumably to the range defined by linguistic universals. The automaton would test various grammars of the appropriate form to see if they would generate all of the sentences and none of the non-sentences. Certain aspects would be tested before others; those found acceptable would be preserved for further evaluation. If we wished the automaton to replicate a child's performance, the order in which these aspects would be evaluated could only be decided after careful analysis of the successive stages of language aquisition in human children.

The actual construction of such an automaton is, of course, far beyond our reach at the present time. That is not the point. The lesson to learn from such speculations is that the whole project would be impossible unless the automaton—and so, presumably, a child—knew in advance to look for particular kinds of regularities and correspondences, to discover rules of a rather special kind uniquely characteristic of human language in general.

The features that human infants are prepared to notice sharply limit the structure of any human language. Even if one imagines creating by decree a Newspeak in which this generalisation were false, within one generation it would have become true again.

Psycholinguistics does not deal with social practices determined arbitrarily either by caprice or intelligent design, but with practices that grow organically out of the biological nature of man and the linguistic capacities of human infants. To that extent, at least, it is possible to define an area of empirical fact well within the reach of our scientific methods.

Another line of scientific investigation is opened up by the observation that we do not always follow our own rules. If this were not so, of course, we would not speak of rules, but of the laws of language. The fact that we make mistakes, and that we can know we made mistakes, is central to the psycholinguistic problem. Before we can see the empirical issue this entails, however, we should first draw a crucial distinction between theories of language and theories of the users of language.

There is nothing in the linguistic description of a language to indicate what mistakes will occur. Mistakes result from the psychological limitations of people who use the language, not from the language itself. It would be meaningless to state rules for making mistakes.

A formal characterisation of a natural language in terms of a set of elements and rules for combining those elements must inevitably generate an infinitude of possible sentences that will never occur in actual use. Most of these sentences are too complicated for us. There is nothing mysterious about this. It is very similar to the situation in arithmetic where a student may understand perfectly the rules for multiplication, yet find that some multiplication problems are too difficult for him to do "in his head," *i.e.*, without extending his memory capacity by the use of pencil and paper.

There is no longest grammatical sentence. There is no limit to the number of different grammatical sentences. Moreover, since the number of elements and rules is finite, there must be some rules and elements that can recur any number of times in a grammatical sentence. Chomsky has even managed to pinpoint a kind of recursive operation in language that, in principle, lies beyond the power of any finite device to perform indefinitely often. Compare these sentences:

(R) *Remarkable is the rapidity of the motion of the wing of the hummingbird.*

(L) *The hummingbird's wing's motion's rapidity is remarkable.*

(E) *The rapidity that the motion that the wing that the hummingbird has has has is remarkable.*

When you parse these sentences you find that the phrase structure of (R) dangles off to the right; each prepositional phrase hangs to the noun in the prepositional phrase preceding it. In (R), therefore, we see a type of recurring construction that has been called right-branching. Sentence (L), on the other hand, is left-branching; each possessive modifies the possessive immediately following. Finally, (E) is an onion; it grows by embedding sentences within sentences. Inside "The rapidity is remarkable" we first insert "the motion is rapid" by a syntactic transformation that permits us to construct relative clauses, and so we obtain "The rapidity that the motion has is remarkable." Then we repeat the transformation, this time inserting "the wing has motion" to obtain "The rapidity that the motion that the wing has is remarkable." Repeating the transformation once more gives (E).

It is intuitively obvious that, of these three types of recursive operations, self-embedding (E) is psychologically the most difficult. Although they seem grammatical by any reasonable standard of grammar, such sentences never occur in ordinary usage because they exceed our cognitive capacities. Chomsky's achievement was to prove rigorously that any language that does *not* restrict this kind of recursive embedding contains sentences that cannot be spoken or understood by devices, human or mechanical, with finite memories. Any device that uses these rules must remember each left portion until it can be related to its corresponding right portion; if the memory of the user is limited, but the number of admissible left portions is not, it is inevitable that some admissible sentences will exceed the capacity of the user to process them correctly.[16]

It is necessary, therefore, to distinguish between a description of the language in terms of the rules that a person *knows* and uses and a description of that person's *performance* as a user of the rules. The distinction is sometimes criticised as "psycholatry" by strict adherents of behaviourism; "knowing" is considered too mentalistic and subjective, therefore unscientific. The objection cannot be taken seriously. Our conception of the rules that a language-user knows is indeed a hypothetical construct, not something observed directly in his behaviour. But if such hypotheses were to be forbidden, science in general would become an empty pursuit.

Given a reasonable hypothesis about the rules that a language-user knows, the exploration of his limitations in following those rules is proper work for an experimental psychologist. "Psychology should assist us," a great linguist once said, "in understanding what is going on in the mind of speakers, and more particularly how they are led to deviate from previously existing rules in consequence of conflicting tendencies." Otto Jespersen made this request of psychology in 1924; now at least the work is beginning.[17]

One example. Stephen Isard and I asked Harvard undergraduates to memorise several sentences that differed in degree of self-embedding. For instance, the twenty-two words in the right-branching sentence, "We cheered the football squad that played the team that brought the mascot that chased the girls that were in the park," can be re-arranged to give one, two, three, or four self-embeddings; with four it becomes, "The girls (that the mascot (that the team (that the football squad (that we cheered) played) brought) chased) were in the park." One self-embedding caused no difficulty; it was almost as easy to memorise as the sentence with none. Three or four embeddings were most difficult. When the sentence had two self-embeddings—"The team (that the football squad (that we cheered) played) brought the mascot that chased the girls that were in the park"—some subjects found it as easy to memorise as sentences with zero or one embedding, others found it as difficult as sentences with three or four. That is to say, everybody can manage one embedding, some people can manage two, but everybody has trouble with three or more.

Records of eye movements while people are reading such sentences show that the trouble begins with the long string of verbs, "cheered played brought," at which point all grasp of the sentence structure crumbles and they are left with a random list of verbs. This is just what would be expected from a computer executing a programme that did not make provision for a sub-routine to refer to itself, i.e., that was not recursive. If our ability to handle this type of self-embedded recursion is really as limited as the experiment indicates, it places a strong limitation on the kinds of theories we can propose to explain our human capacities for processing information.

On the simpler levels of our psycholinguistic hierarchy the pessimists are wrong; much remains there to be explored and systematised by scientific methods. How far these methods can carry us remains an open question. Although syntax seems well within our grasp and techniques for studying semantic systems are now beginning to emerge, understanding and belief raise problems well beyond the scope of linguistics. Perhaps it is there that scientific progress will be forced to halt.

No psychological process is more important or difficult to understand than understanding, and nowhere has scientific psychology proved more disappointing to those who have turned to it for help. The complaint is as old as scientific psychology itself. It was probably first seen clearly by Wilhelm Dilthey, who called for a new kind of psychology—a kind to which Karl Jaspers later gave the name *"verstehende Pschologie"*—and in one form or another the division has plagued psychologists ever since. Obviously a tremendous gulf separates the interpretation of a sentence from the understanding of a personality, a society, a historical epoch. But the gap is narrowing. Indeed, one can even pretend to see certain similarities between the generative theory of speech perception discussed above and the reconstructive intellectual processes that have been labelled *verstehende*. The analogy may some day prove helpful, but how optimistic one dares feel at the present time is not easily decided.

Meanwhile, the psycholinguists will undoubtedly continue to advance as far as they can. It should prove interesting to see how far that will be.

NOTES

1. A representative sample of research papers in this field can be found in *Psycholinguistics, a Book of Readings*, edited by S. Saporta (Holt, Rinehart & Winston, New York, 1962). R. Brown provides a readable survey from a psychologist's point of view in *Words and Things* (Free Press, Glencoe, Illinois, 1957).

2. The CIBA Foundation Symposium, *Disorders of Language* (J. & A. Churchill, London, 1964) provides an excellent sample of the current status of medical psycholinguistics.

3. *Natural Language and the Computer*, edited by P. L. Garvin (McGraw-Hill, New York, 1963).

4. My own opinions have been strongly influenced by Noam Chomsky. A rather technical exposition of this work can be found in Chapters 11–13 of the second volume of the *Handbook of Mathematical Psychology*, edited by R. D. Luce, R. R. Bush, and E. Galanter (Wiley, New York, 1963), from which many of the ideas discussed here have been drawn.

5. W. Epstein, "The Influence of Syntactical Structure on Learning," *American Journal of Psychology* (1961), vol. 74, pp. 80–85.

6. G. A. Miller and S. Isard, "Some Perceptual Consequences of Linguistic Rules," *Journal of Verbal Learning and Verbal Behaviour* (1963), vol. 2, pp. 217–228. J. J. Katz and J. A. Fodor have recently contributed a thoughtful discussion of "The Structure of Semantic Theory," *Language* (1963), vol. 39, pp. 170–210.

7. M. Halle and K. N. Stevens, "Speech Recognition: A Model and a Program for Research," *IRE Transactions on Information Theory* (1962), vol. IT-8, pp. 155–159.

8. "Effects of Context upon the Intelligibility of Heard Speech," in *Information Theory*, edited by Colin Cherry (Butterworths, London, 1956, pp. 245–252).

9. "Understanding Language without Ability to Speak: A Case Report," *Journal of Abnormal and Social Psychology* (1962), vol. 65, pp. 419–425.

10. A dog conditioned to salivate at the sound of a tone will also salivate, though less copiously, at the sound of similar tones, the magnitude declining as the new tones become less similar to the original. This phenomenon is called "stimulus generalisation."

11. *Universals of Language*, edited by J. Greenberg (M.I.T. Technology Press, Cambridge, Mass., 1963).

12. E. Lenneberg, "Language, Evolution, and Purposive Behavior," in *Culture in History: Essays in Honor of Paul Radin* (Columbia University Press, New York, 1960).

13. E. Lenneberg, I. A. Nichols, and E. R. Rosenberger, "Primitive Stages of Language Development in Mongolism," in the *Proceedings* of the 42nd. Annual Meeting (1962) of the *Association for Research in Nervous and Mental Diseases.*

14. The belief that animals have, or could have, languages is as old as man's interest in the evolution of his special talent, but the truth of the matter has long been known. Listen, for example, to Max Müller (*Three Lectures on the Science of Language*) in 1889: "It is easy enough to show that animals communicate, but this is a fact which has never been doubted. Dogs who growl and bark leave no doubt in the minds of other dogs or cats, or even of man, of what they mean; but growling and barking are not language, nor do they even contain the elements of language."

Unfortunately, Müller's authority, great as it was, did not suffice, and in 1890 we hear Samuel Butler ("Thought and Language," in his *Collected Essays*) reply that although "growling and barking cannot be called very highly specialised language," still there is "a sayer, a sayee, and a covenanted symbol designedly applied. Our own speech is vertebrated and articulated by means of nouns, verbs, and the rules of grammar. A dog's speech is invertebrate, but I do not see how it is possible to deny that it possesses all the essential elements of language."

Müller and Butler did not argue about the facts of animal behaviour which Darwin had described. Their disagreement arose more directly from differences of opinion about the correct definition of the term "language." To-day our definitions of human language are more precise, so we can say with correspondingly more precision why Butler was wrong.

15. N. Chomsky, "Explanatory Models in Linguistics," in *Logic, Methodology, and Philosophy of Science*, edited by E. Wagel, P. Suppes, and A. Tarski (Stanford Univ. Press, Stanford, 1962, pp. 528–550).

16. N. Chomsky, *Syntactic Structures* (Mouton, The Hague, 1957).

17. *The Philosophy of Grammar* (Allen and Unwin, London, 1924, p. 344).